Understanding Ukrainian Politics

Understanding Ukrainian Politics

Power, Politics, and Institutional Design

Paul D'Anieri

M.E.Sharpe
Armonk, New York
London, England

Library of Congress Cataloging-in-Publication Data

D'Anieri, Paul J., 1965–
Understanding Ukrainian politics : power, politics, and institutional design /
by Paul D'Anieri.
p. cm.
Includes index.
ISBN-13: 978-0-7656-1811-5 (cloth: alk. paper); ISBN-13: 978-0-7656-1812-2 (pbk.: alk. paper)
ISBN-10: 0-7656-1811-7 (cloth: alk. paper); ISBN-10: 0-7656-1812-5 (pbk.: alk. paper)
1. Ukraine—Politics and government—1991– 2. Power (Social sciences)—Ukraine.
I. Title.

JN6635.D365 2006
320.9477—dc22 2006016004

Printed in the United States of America

The paper used in this publication meets the minimum requirements of
American National Standard for Information Sciences
Permanence of Paper for Printed Library Materials,
ANSI Z 39.48-1984.

∞

BM (c) 10 9 8 7 6 5 4 3 2 1
BM (p) 10 9 8 7 6 5 4 3 2 1

Contents

Ukraine: Borders and Administrative Divisions

List of Tables, Figure, Appendices, and Maps

Tables

Figure

Appendices

Maps

Acknowledgments

A great number of friends and colleagues in several countries provided useful commentary on various parts of the manuscript, in their earlier incarnations as conference papers. Taras Kuzio, who knows more about day-to-day goings on in Ukraine than anyone, has provided feedback on most of the arguments in this book. Our good-natured disagreements about Ukrainian politics have sharpened my thinking considerably. Sarah Whitmore's expertise on the Ukrainian parliament was especially helpful in developing Chapters 7 and 8. Conversations with Lucan Way have helped me refine my theoretical arguments significantly.

Orest Subtelny invited me to participate in a series of workshops in Toronto and in Kyiv, which provided extensive opportunities to develop my ideas in conversations with Ukrainian officials and scholars. I owe a special debt to my host on several trips to Kyiv, Georgiy Khomenko of the Diplomatic Academy of Ukraine, and to Bohdan Myndiuk, who helped organize the trips. A great number of colleagues in Kyiv have shared their time generously, to help me gather data and to help me interpret it. Hrihoriy Perepelytsya has been especially helpful. I have also benefited immensely from my long collaboration with colleagues at Lviv National University, including Anatoliy Romaniuk and Yuriy Shweda. Ivan Vakarchuk, rector of Lviv National University, along with Volodymyr Kyrylych, vice-rector for International Relations, and Viktor Krevs have steadfastly supported wide-ranging cooperation between their institution and the University of Kansas.

The ideas in this book have also benefited from presentations at the Harvard University Ukrainian Research Institute; the University of Toronto Munk Centre for International Studies; the George Washington University Institute for European, Russian, and Eurasian Studies; and the chair of Ukrainian Studies at the University of Ottawa.

At the University of Kansas, I have benefited from the support of the Center for Russian, East European, and Eurasian Studies, and from its past and current directors, Maria Carlson and Erik Herron. The university and its administrators have provided considerable support to Ukrainian studies over the past fifteen years, making it a very supportive place to carry on my research. I received very helpful research assistance from Kara Smith, Sabra Wormington, and Ken Zucher.

This book is dedicated to my wife, Laura. She has patiently supported my research, and has indeed made it possible by bravely parenting our five children whenever I was away working on this project. She did not flinch when I left on a research trip when our daughter was two weeks old, or when a pair of my Ukrainian houseguests split a bottle of Jack Daniel's over dinner and then moved on to champagne. She has taken my research seriously, but has helped me to avoid taking it too seriously. For this and much more, I am grateful to her.

I, of course, am responsible for any inconsistencies, factual errors, or questionable interpretations that remain in the book.

Understanding Ukrainian Politics

1

Introduction

In November 2004 the eyes of the world focused on Ukraine, as the brightly colored banners of the Orange Revolution were unfurled in snowy Kyiv. The sight of hundreds of thousands of young Ukrainians braving freezing weather to overturn the results of a rigged election was inspiring. Equally inspiring was the courage of opposition leader Viktor Yushchenko, who survived a poisoning attempt that ravaged his skin, and continued on to lead the democratic reform movement. The Orange Revolution promised a fundamentally new era of democracy in a country that had never really experienced it. It was seen as finally bringing Ukraine into Europe after centuries of externally enforced separation.

Yet, within a few short months after the Orange Revolution, disillusionment set in, as many of the expected reforms failed to materialize. Corruption prosecutions against the previous leaders were delayed. The review of illegally privatized companies bogged down. Trade legislation needed for Ukraine to join the World Trade Organization was defeated. Several of Yushchenko's cabinet ministers did not give up their seats in parliament, as required by law. Yushchenko's own twenty-year-old son was seen driving about Kyiv in a BMW worth over $100,000. And Yushchenko split bitterly with his partner in revolution, the charismatic Yulia Tymoshenko. A sense that little had changed, or that not enough had changed, quickly emerged. In March 2006, Viktor Yanukovych's Party of Regions, apparently doomed after its effort to steal the 2004 election, won a large plurality in a free and fair parliamentary election. Finally, in August 2006, Viktor Yushchenko agreed to nominate Viktor Yanukovych for prime minister. In the eyes of many observers, the Orange Revolution was undone.[1]

How did the Orange Revolution run into difficulties so quickly? Has the pace of reform merely been slowed, or is there a more fundamental problem? What factors in Ukrainian politics continue to hamper the construction of liberal democracy? The optimism of 2004 appears to have been unwarranted, but it is not clear that the despair of 2006 is based on firmer analytical ground.

This book seeks to answer these questions through a careful analysis of Ukraine's political system. By examining Ukrainian politics prior to the Orange Revolution, we can see the extent of the obstacles to reform. The misjudgment made by many within and outside Ukraine was that Leonid Kuchma, Ukraine's president since 1994, was the heart of the problem, and that replacing him would be a large part of the solution. This book shows that reform in Ukraine is hindered by deep problems in both its political institutions and in the concentration of political power. Kuchma certainly took advantage of these characteristics, but he did not, by himself, create them, and they endure after him.

There are no insurmountable barriers to Ukraine becoming a vibrant democracy, integrated with Europe, and thriving economically. However, for its political problems to be solved, they must be clearly understood.

The Puzzle: Authoritarianism in Ukraine

The faltering of the Orange Revolution surprised most observers, but it is not the first time that Ukraine surged toward consolidated democracy, only to get bogged down. By the end of 1994, Ukraine had established itself as among the most democratic of the post-Soviet countries. In parliamentary and presidential elections earlier that year, incumbent legislators fared poorly, and the incumbent president, Leonid Kravchuk, was defeated. A peaceful transfer of power was never in doubt. Competitive elections and a relatively open contest for power were taken for granted by all participants. This peaceful transition contrasted starkly with events in Russia, where in October 1993, President Yeltsin disbanded the parliament and ordered a military assault on it. When Ukraine held another round of parliamentary elections in 1998, many observers concluded that the country had indeed established itself as a "consolidated" democracy. Political scientist Samuel Huntington has defined a consolidated democracy as one that has had two successful transfers of power.[2]

By 1999, however, Ukrainian democracy was showing signs of strain. In presidential elections that year, the administration of President Leonid Kuchma used a variety of means to foil serious competition. By 2001, when Kuchma was implicated in the murder of an opposition journalist, one could no longer speak of Ukraine as a "democracy" without adding substantial qualification. Terms such as "delegative democracy"[3] and "competitive authoritarianism"[4] were used to characterize Ukraine.

The optimism engendered by the Orange Revolution should have been tempered by the knowledge that a similar optimism had prevailed a decade earlier, but was followed by the steady erosion of democracy under Leonid Kuchma. With the resurgence of Viktor Yanukovych, despair has replaced optimism, but it is not clear whether that despair is warranted, for Yanukovych's return to power represented the playing out of a largely democratic and legal process.[5] The key question in Ukraine's next phase is whether its future will be dominated by the kind of politics that characterized Yanukovych's rise under Leonid Kuchma, or by the kind that characterized his return under free and fair elections. If Ukraine is to consolidate the advances of the Orange Revolution, it is necessary to understand why democracy was not consolidated in the 1990s. Leonid Kuchma was only part of the problem.

Ukraine's Democratic Shortcomings

While Ukraine had many of the attributes of a democracy after 1994, it did not fit the standard definitions used in political science. Adam Przeworski defines a democracy simply as a polity in which parties can lose elections.[6] By this he means that parties have confidence that, if they lose one election, they will still be able to compete in the next one. In Ukraine's 2004 elections, both the ruling group and the opposition feared that if they lost the election they would lose all. Naturally, in such "all or nothing" circumstances, actors have strong incentives to do whatever it takes to prevail.

Robert Dahl argues that democratic institutions are intended above all to provide for political competition that is constrained by rules. The importance of political competition explains why civil liberties such as freedom of the press and freedom of speech are so important.[7] Much of Ukrainian politics after 1999 was occupied with efforts to limit political competition (or to predetermine its outcomes) through a variety of measures. These included interference with civil liberties, harassment of the opposition, and control of the media. The goal of many of Kuchma's policies was to ensure that there was no serious competition for power. He succeeded in large measure, but not completely.

Samuel Huntington states that "elections, open, free and fair, are the essence of democracy, the inescapable *sine qua non.*"[8] Ukraine has had elections, but until 2006 they were not open, free, or fair. Guillermo O'Donnell takes it for granted that democratic institutions "preclude the use or threat of force and the outcomes that this would generate."[9] Force and the threat of it have been a central part of politics in Ukraine. The implicit threat of force was a key part of Kuchma's governing strategy, and the explicit threat of force by thousands of protestors was crucial in ejecting Kuchma's designated successor from power. In these ways, Ukraine before the Orange Revolution did not meet the basic definition of "democracy." While Ukraine after the Orange Revolution does appear to be a democracy, we should probably withhold a definitive judgment.

Explaining the Erosion of Ukrainian Democracy

In order to understand the challenges in building democracy in Ukraine today, we need to understand what undermined it from 1994 to 2004. Authoritarianism emerged in spite of contextual and institutional factors that should have promoted democratization after 1994. Two contextual factors were present. The economy was improving, and the Western countries were actively supporting Kuchma's announced reform programs. Moreover, Ukraine appeared to have established the institutional basis for democracy: It had a constitution modeled on Western examples, a parliament characterized by vibrant debate, and a plurality of political parties.

Despite these favorable factors, democracy eroded rapidly. This weakening of democracy, despite a favorable climate and appropriate institutions, is a central puzzle motivating this book. Solving that puzzle will be essential to assessing Ukraine's chances for consolidating democracy in the coming years. Again since the Orange Revolution, Ukraine faces similarly favorable circumstances, but formidable challenges as well, and again the outcome is not predetermined.

What were the factors that undermined Ukraine's democracy, despite the favorable environment and the apparently appropriate institutions? Do these forces continue to exist after the Orange Revolution? Answering these questions is the central goal of this book. Therefore, the book examines the major institutions and processes of Ukrainian politics, both before and after the revolution. It also seeks to provide an understanding of a broader problem in postcommunist politics, the advent of systems that have regular elections, but are not democratic.

This book will attempt to show how politics in Ukraine actually "works." It also, however, provides an explanation of *why* Ukrainian politics works this way. Why, prior to 2004, were almost all serious political disputes resolved in favor of the president? Why has the Ukrainian parliament been so weak, despite concerted efforts to strengthen its role? Why are political parties so ineffectual and transient, despite electoral laws that were intended to promote consolidation? To what extent will the political and constitutional changes of 2004 put these problems to rest?

Institutional Design Versus Power Politics

It seems that Ukraine has had reasonably designed institutions, but that somehow they have not led to liberal democracy. In many cases, the institutions have seemed inadequate to constrain the behavior of key actors (especially the president). Yet the situation is not one of anarchy. This is crucial, for a polity with imperfect enforcement of rules is very different from one with no enforceable rules at all. Most of the time, Ukraine's formal institutions *do* matter. Unless institutional performance improves, the Orange Revolution will likely be short-lived. Therefore a central question is: why do Ukraine's institutions seem to constrain behavior in some situations and not others?

The requirements and prohibitions of Ukraine's constitution, for example, are inconsistently enforced. And while it is easy to attribute these violations to the vague cause of the "absence of rule of law," such an explanation does not tell us why, in fact, most of the time, the constitution and laws do indeed constrain behavior. In the 2004 election dispute, legal procedures governed the process; in a referendum to amend the constitution in 2000, existing constitutional processes were largely ignored. We cannot say that the rules, laws, and institutions are uniformly irrelevant. Rather they seem to have more "grip" in some situations than others. If we are to understand the nature of politics in Ukraine, and the chances of successfully building democracy there, we must account for this variation.

Answering these questions is not an academic exercise. In the wake of the Orange Revolution, there is a "window of opportunity" for political reform to regain momentum, and for Ukraine to begin moving again in the direction of liberal democracy. Both government and opposition, as well as those who would advise them, need to understand why Ukraine has not achieved liberal democracy, and what the obstacles are. Only then can they make intelligent choices as they recast political institutions and political practices in the country.

Despite the importance of these questions, they have received much less attention than they deserve. Both Ukrainians and Western observers have focused on near-term issues, primarily the 2004 election. The conventional wisdom was that the coming to power of Viktor Yushchenko would automatically solve Ukraine's problems, and that the Orange Revolution was therefore over by the end of December 2004.

While there is no reason to doubt that Ukraine will be better off under Yushchenko than Kuchma, the focus on individual politicians is dangerous, for it deflects attention from underlying problems that will remain in place regardless of who is president. If Yushchenko is to build a liberal democracy in Ukraine, serious change will be needed. Two institutional changes already adopted—the reduction of the president's powers and the adoption of a fully proportional election law—will do more to alter the long-term prospects for Ukraine than the election of a president who will last two terms at most. If positive changes introduced by Yushchenko are to endure after he leaves office, both the rules of the game and the balance of power in Ukrainian politics will need to fundamentally change.

Specific Empirical Questions

In order to answer the broad explanatory questions elaborated above, we need to address a series of specific empirical questions about the working of Ukrainian politics. These questions will structure the book, with each of the empirical chapters focusing primarily on one of the key questions. It is imperative that we search for the underlying as well as the immediate causes of political behavior in Ukraine. For example, in examining how Leonid Kuchma was able to win reelection in 1999 despite his low popularity, one clear answer is that the opposing candidates were badly hampered by an inability to reach the public through the media. While this is true, and well documented, we need to take the next step and ask how the media were so easily controlled, and why opposition parties were unable to do anything about it despite their common interest in changing these practices.

To provide a second example, if we ask why the parliament has been so ineffective, we can answer that it has been ineffective because it has fragmented into many small and amorphous factions. But this answer prompts two further lines of inquiry. First, there are numerous countries, such as Israel, where numerous small parties routinely coalesce to form governing majorities. Why does the opposite seem to happen in Ukraine? Second, to the extent that Ukraine's parliamentary party system is fragmented, is it because public opinion is fragmented, and therefore elects a fragmented parliament? Or is it because there are particular institutional incentives against forming more durable coalitions?

Key Questions to Be Addressed

1. How did the *process* of Ukraine's transition from Soviet rule, which was negotiated rather than revolutionary, constrain subsequent political change? (Chapter Four)
2. How do Ukraine's societal cleavages make democratic rule more difficult? (Chapter Five)
3. Does Ukraine's constitution provide a sound institutional basis for liberal democracy? (Chapter Six)
4. To what extent has Ukraine's electoral law been responsible for parliamentary fragmentation? Will changes that took effect in 2006 improve the situation? (Chapter Seven)
5. To what extent do the parliament's internal rules and procedures inhibit its effective function? (Chapter Eight)
6. How and why was Kuchma able to use "power politics" to shape institutions and to use the formal rules as a political weapon? What are the prospects for "power politics" in post-Orange Ukraine? (Chapter Nine)

7. How does Ukraine compare to other postcommunist and post-authoritarian democracies that have democratic institutions but authoritarian politics? (Chapter Ten)
8. What are the likely effects of the changes that accompanied the Orange Revolution? What further changes are required to prevent another reversion to authoritarianism? (Chapter Eleven)

Broad Themes

We can point to three broad themes that cut across these questions, and will therefore be examined in more than one chapter of the book. A first central theme is to explain the *fragmentation and ineffectiveness of the parliament.* Under Kuchma, parliament was ineffectual because it failed to produce legislation on the key issues facing the country, and also because it allowed much of its prerogative to be taken over by the president. From the Orange Revolution to the 2006 parliamentary elections, parliament was more independent from the executive, but remained badly fragmented. Following the 2006 parliamentary elections, an extended period of bargaining was needed to form a governing coalition. The long-term prospects for the functioning of parliament remain unclear. The inefficacy of the parliament is central to Ukrainian political life, and it would appear to be a crucial obstacle in the establishment of a more liberal democracy.[10] It is hard to imagine how an effective democratic government can govern in a large society without an effective legislature. In fact, there is no example of a successful democracy anywhere in the world that does not have a functioning legislature. Legislative dysfunction is seen as a major cause of the breakdown of new democracies.

The ability of a parliament to function, and the related issue of the functioning of the political party system are generally accounted for in terms of two factors: the preferences of the public (public opinion and "political culture") and the way that votes are translated into the distribution of parliamentary seats (voting rules and institutional design).

In Chapter Five, we examine the argument that societal fragmentation undermines the functioning of parliament. In this view, an ineffective parliament is seen simply as the logical extension of a divided society. If this is true, two momentous conclusions would follow. First, it would appear that, until such societal divisions are overcome, "normal" parliamentary democracy will be impossible. This implies both that some degree of authoritarianism might be a necessary evil in the short term, and that efforts must be undertaken to promote a consolidation of public attitudes. Both of these arguments have been made in the case of Ukraine, but we shall see good reasons to doubt them.[11]

In 2004, the constitution and electoral laws were altered. A change to the election law replaced a mixed system (half the seats elected proportionally, and half in majoritarian districts) with a fully proportional system. Changes to the constitution substantially shifted Ukraine from a presidential to a parliamentary-presidential form of government. It remains to be seen how these changes will play out in practice. Therefore the relative weight of these two sources of parliamentary fragmentation is an important issue.

This brings us to a second broad theme: *institutional design.* Those who focus on political institutions contend that institutional rules can create incentives for coalition and compromise even in very diverse societies. From this perspective, if the parliament is fragmented, it is because political actors have little incentive to coalesce. Students of institutional design point out that various factors, either in the constitutional arrangements (e.g., the choice of a parliamentary or presidential form of government) or in the voting rules (majoritarian versus proportional election laws), have substantial and predictable effects on politicians' and parties' incentives to coalesce. In this view, if there is insufficient consolidation in parliament, the remedy is simply to alter either the role of the constitution or the electoral law, or both. Chapter Six considers the constitution and executive-legislative relations. Chapter Seven examines the electoral law.

Once we have addressed the effects of institutions and possible changes, a question looms that is crucial for any real discussion of change in Ukraine, or any deep understanding of politics in Ukraine. The question is, what accounts for the institutional design that we see? If formal institutional analysis can demonstrate certain potential improvements, why are such changes not adopted?

The answer is that the goal of many actors is not, first and foremost, good government in the abstract, but rather the increase of their own power and prerogatives. At first glance this might strike some as a rather cynical statement, but if one reads the *Federalist Papers*, for example, one sees that it is the understanding underpinning much of the design of the U.S. Constitution. We will explore several cases in which President Kuchma promoted institutional provisions intended to bolster his power. In writing the 1996 constitution, Ukraine's prodemocratic forces supported a strong presidency, because it was a way to reduce the power of the left, which at that time controlled the parliament.

While a rational choice–based institutional analysis can deduce the effects of a given set of formal rules, it cannot explain where those rules come from. To account for the origins of institutions, which at some point must be created either ex nihilo or within a framework that is only partially institutionalized, a historical analysis of the politics behind those arrangements is necessary. This point is emphasized by some of the foremost practitioners of rational choice analysis, such as William Riker, Gary Cox, and George Tsebelis.[12] Tsebelis explains that there can be no rational choice analysis of institutional choice, because rational choice analysis presumes an institutional setup. It cannot therefore, explain that setup.[13] Similarly, Riker contends that "institutions are no more than rules, and rules are themselves the product of social decisions."[14]

To understand which institutions are chosen and why, we examine a third central issue: *power politics*. This refers to the ability of actors to pursue their goals by going outside the established rules. In Ukraine, such power is heavily concentrated in the executive branch. It includes selective law enforcement, regulation of the economy, influence over the media, and other measures.

While societal fragmentation and institutional design might explain the inefficacy of the parliament, they do not directly explain why so much power accrued to the president, or why the institutions have been designed the way they are. In 2001, the parliament repeatedly sought to change the electoral law that would be used in the 2002 parliamentary elections, only to see proposed changes repeatedly vetoed by President Kuchma. Clearly, Kuchma felt that he benefited from the fragmentation of parliament, and sought to prevent it from being strengthened. This argument applies equally to the adoption of the 1995 "Law on Power" and the 1996 constitution, both of which will be examined in detail.

To the extent that the effects of different institutions are clear, politicians will seek to design institutions to suit their objectives. We have seen this phenomenon over and over again in Ukraine, as political elites, envisioning partisan benefits in certain institutional formats, have sought above all to design institutions that favor themselves. If the resources in this game were evenly distributed, this might lead to a balanced political system. But if one group begins the process with extensive control of key political resources, that group can then use institutional design to solidify its hold on power. For this reason, Adam Przeworski has emphasized that systems of checks and balances are most likely to emerge when there is uncertainty about who will benefit from which future arrangements. In situations of uncertainty, actors hedge their bets by ensuring that no single institution will dominate.[15]

Since political actors pursue their self-interest in addition to the public good (or identify the public good with their self-interest), it is necessary to ask what determines who wins these battles. This is where politics gets truly interesting, especially in Ukraine. What resources constitute assets that can be used to win political battles, either about specific policy issues, or about the rules of the game itself? In a Western democracy such as the United

States or the United Kingdom, we think we have a good idea: votes are the main assets, and are translated into political power in readily predictable ways. From votes, and the power they convey, almost all further aspects of power are distributed, including such things as judicial appointments and public spending. However, considerable research as well as casual observation shows that money is a key asset in gaining votes in these societies. Therefore money creates political power in Western democracies, which is why so much effort is spent to raise more money and to limit its influence.

What assets create political power in Ukraine? As in the West, votes are the direct source of political office, and money is crucial to gaining them. But there is a variety of other sources of political influence in Ukraine, such as patronage, law enforcement, and the state role in the economy, which also convey political power in multiple ways. These sources of power are disproportionately controlled by the executive branch of the government. This finding leads to the most significant argument advanced in this study: *The fundamental imbalance in raw political power has been the underlying source of the more immediate problems in Ukrainian government, such as weak parties, selective law enforcement, and a fragmented parliament.* The ways in which Kuchma used this power are the focus of Chapter Nine. This imbalance of de facto power will need to be overcome if the Orange Revolution is to succeed in the long run.

This notion of the "distribution of power" seems more at home in the study of international politics than in the study of domestic democratization. However, the distribution of power domestically has been found to be an important factor in some studies of democratization.[16] This factor is especially important in Ukraine because of the weakness of institutional rules as a constraint on the exercise of power. It is often observed that the rule of law is weak in Ukraine, but we must move beyond that observation to ask how and why it is imperfect.

The problem in Ukraine is not just that it lacks rule *of* law, but that it has rule *by* law, in which the law is a weapon to be selectively applied against one's adversaries. A situation in which bureaucratic and judicial decisions are subject to political interference can have very different implications, depending on whether two opposing forces are equally capable of influencing those decisions, or whether one dominant force can use the law to extend and reinforce its power. Such conditions played a major role in the rise of authoritarianism in Ukraine, and must be overcome if Ukraine is to become truly democratic. Power politics helps to explain the weakness of the rule of law in Ukraine. A situation with poor rule of law in which decisions are arbitrary and capricious is entirely different from one in which decisions are not at all arbitrary, but are controlled by a group with a private agenda.

The "absence of the rule of law" is not simply something that just exists, like bad weather. Rather, it is something that results from the accumulated efforts of interested actors to ensure that decisions support their political interests. Where there is a relatively balanced struggle over implementation of laws and regulations, one might expect that the outcomes, even if highly politicized, will be more or less balanced. But when the levers of influence are held in the hands of one faction, the "rule of law" will favor that faction. Thus, the difference between Ukraine and the United States or the United Kingdom is not simply that there is less political pressure on bureaucrats and judges in the latter two states, but that it is more balanced.

Roots of the Problem: The Institutional Legacy of the Soviet Union

So far we have argued that the key to understanding politics in post-Soviet Ukraine is the concentration of power in the hands of the executive. This begs the question: How did so much power accrue to the executive branch? The answer lies in a fourth theme that is dealt with later in this chapter and in Chapter Four: the *political and institutional legacy of the Soviet Union*. This includes the institutions of the Soviet Union, the process by which it collapsed, and the arrangements that it left behind.

The Soviet Union was characterized by two factors that have had enormous impact on the ability to create liberal democracy in its aftermath. First, the Communist Party held a monopoly on power. Soviet bureaucracies and legislatures (such as the Ukrainian *Verkhovna Rada*) were built upon that monopoly. While the Soviet government had the familiar tripartite division into executive, legislative, and judicial branches, there was no separation of powers in the Soviet system, either in theory or in fact. All three branches were expected to hold to a single line, defined by the executive branch and the Communist Party.

Second, the state controlled nearly the entire economy, even after Gorbachev's reforms. State control of the economy led to a vicious cycle of powerful incentives for corruption. Political authority was a necessary and sufficient condition for acquiring economic power and wealth, sometimes on a fantastic scale. Simultaneously, economic power was necessary and nearly sufficient to obtain political power. This potent combination of political and economic power came to rest among a narrow set of elites closely connected with the state apparatus. This was equally true in Russia and in the other post-Soviet states. To put it simply, political power is highly concentrated in Ukraine because it started out that way, and because the system tends to reinforce that concentration rather than to disperse it.

If Ukraine had undergone a political revolution in 1991, the Soviet system of centralized power might have had less influence on post-Soviet Ukraine. Because Ukraine focused on national independence rather than political revolution, it built its new institutions very much *within* the institutional framework constructed by the Soviets (and with almost all of the same personnel). Independent Ukraine's institutions were not designed starting from a "blank slate." Unlike in Poland, there were no "roundtable talks" at which a new framework for constituting political authority was negotiated between the communists and their opponents. Nor was there any process to broadly distribute state property.

To say that authoritarianism was inevitable would be to go too far, especially because the system did not immediately move in that direction. It would be more accurate to say that the system was very vulnerable to a chief executive who sought to use the state apparatus to control both the economic and political spheres in the country. Leonid Kravchuk did not seem to be such an executive. Nor initially did Leonid Kuchma, but by 1999 he was using every lever available to use the state–economy combination to eliminate meaningful competition. One interesting question that we cannot answer, due to a lack of real data, is whether Kuchma came to power in 1994 intending to accumulate uncontested power, or whether his authoritarianism emerged later.

Alternative Explanations

In order to properly evaluate the main argument of this book, that Ukraine's slide to authoritarianism was a result of a fundamental imbalance in the distribution of political power, it is necessary to clarify the main competing explanations. Only in comparison with these hypotheses can the utility of the argument presented here be weighed meaningfully.

Two alternative explanations predominate. One derives from the "institutional design" school of comparative politics research. In this perspective, the main problem is to get the formal rules—the constitutional arrangements, electoral laws, and related arrangements—properly designed. Doing so, presumably, will best align the interests of political officeholders with those of citizens. My argument does not contradict this one, but rather finds it to be very incomplete, and hence of limited utility.

Formal institutional arrangements cannot be viewed as neutral or as a "fundamental" factor. Rather, they themselves are the products of the power and interests of the actors that design them. In that sense, the explanation is incomplete in viewing institutional design only as an independent variable and not as a dependent one. This incompleteness leads to an important distortion: viewing the problem as one of institutional design creates the impression, sometimes stated sometimes not, that the problem is a technical or intellectual one. The only challenge, in this view, is the intellectual one of how best to design the institutions to fit the conditions and the goal. The goal is assumed to be identical for everyone: a well-functioning democracy. In reality, producing democracy is not alone on most actors' agendas, or even at the top. An interest/power-based approach sees the problem as fundamentally political—concerning who gets what—as well as technical.

The question for most parties involved in framing institutions is not only how to produce democracy, but how to protect or expand one's power and wealth. Therefore, a discussion of what would be the technically "best" or even adequate institutional design is irrelevant if this design is not in the interest of powerful actors. Thus, an important aspect of the Orange Revolution is the fact that a wide range of elites coalesced around the amendment of the constitution to weaken the powers of the presidency. Had Yushchenko won an overwhelming victory, it would have been much harder to persuade him to accept these changes.

The second major competing explanation emerges from the literature on Ukraine. Many students of Ukrainian politics and society have argued that the fundamental problem obstructing the construction of democracy in Ukraine is that of societal divisions. Some refer to regional, ethnic, and linguistic cleavages, while others focus on the weakness of Ukrainian national identity.[17] As with the institutional design argument, this one is not wrong, but rather is incomplete. The following chapters will offer evidence to show how divisions, especially between left and right, make it much easier for an authoritarian centrist to take power and maintain it. The crucial question is the extent to which these differences are bridgeable. Here the institutional design school has an important point to make: given different institutional design, leftists and rightists would find the incentives for collaboration much higher.

Moreover, the key problem in Ukraine under Kuchma was not that left and right could not ally, but that neither could ally with the center. This is harder to understand than the absence of a left–right coalition. A left–center or right–center coalition would form a substantial majority in parliament and could make that branch much more assertive. Again, we must ask why the institutions are not designed differently, and again, the answer concerns the interests of the prevailing elite and their ability to win key battles. In Chapters Seven and Eight we will see that the tendency of parties across the spectrum to fragment is not inevitably caused by societal fragmentation. Instead, it will be shown that particular institutional arrangements, some of which are unique to Ukraine, and many of which were promoted by Kuchma, considerably lower the incentives for party cohesion. The 2006 parliamentary elections provide evidence that different electoral laws would have significantly different effects on the party system.

In sum, the argument presented here acknowledges the utility of societal and formal institutional approaches, and builds on these approaches. However, I argue that both arguments are incomplete. Societal fragmentation and shortcomings in institutional design could be much more easily dealt with in the absence of an underlying imbalance in power. That imbalance gives an ambitious individual or faction the ability to pursue nearly unlimited authority, and to use institutional and societal weaknesses to build that power.

Ukraine in the Post-Soviet Region

While it is obvious that the answers to these questions are crucial for the future of Ukraine, the relevance of this study goes far beyond Ukraine. One of the most striking aspects of post-Soviet governments is the extent to which they converged in their politics after adopting widely different systems in 1991.[18] After the Soviet Union collapsed, the post-Soviet states created a variety of institutional designs for the building of democracies, and they started with varying degrees of democracy. By 2003, except for the Baltic states, all had converged into a relatively uniform set of political arrangements, characterized by extremely powerful presidencies, weak political parties, manipulated elections, constrained media, and what might be called "machine politics" on a massive scale.

A post-Soviet "model" of "hyperpresidential" democracy has emerged, characterized by the use of democratic forms and practices to attain fundamentally undemocratic politics. There has been, not surprisingly, a substantial number of studies examining the Russian case by itself. But without understanding other cases as well as we understand the Russian one, we will have no basis for comparison, and no ability to ascertain which phenomena are idiosyncratic aspects of a particular society, and which are general trends across states.

Equally striking is the departure of three states, Georgia, Ukraine, and Kyrgyzstan, from the norm in 2003–4. By understanding why Ukraine, which moved as far toward genuine liberal democracy as any of these states, was drawn into this model of hyperpresidentialism, and then rejected it, we will gain an insight into the nature of all the political regimes in the region, and a better understanding of the forces that lead to this sort of political system. We will also better understand the vulnerabilities of this model.

This kind of "electoral authoritarianism," in which "free but unfair" elections are used not to check the government, but rather to increase its power and legitimacy, seems to be growing even beyond the Soviet Union. Many of the new democracies of the "third wave" of democratization have followed this path. Rather than denying the virtues of democracy or extolling the necessity of authoritarianism, as have past autocracies, these polities have adopted democratic ideologies and institutions, but still manage to avoid real political competition. They are systems in which power tends to concentrate rather than disperse.

Ukraine has much in common not only with Putin's Russia and Nazarbayev's Kazakhstan, but also with Fujimori's Peru, Chavez's Venezuela, and Estrada's Philippines. As several of these examples indicate, these governments tend to be highly stable up to a point—and then to collapse amid chaos. When all legitimate or orderly means of transition are short-circuited, unplanned and hence unstable transition is the only variant remaining. For these reasons, an understanding of Ukrainian politics is an important route to understanding a much broader category of important cases—the hyperpresidential failures of the "third wave" of democratization.

Implications for the Theory of Democratization

Equally significant are the implications of the Ukrainian case for the theory of democratization. An enormous amount of research has been conducted on the prerequisites, the processes, and the institutions required for successful democratization. An anatomy of a country that has had two reversals of trajectory should help us sort out the strengths of these various explanations. The factors that led Ukraine to be ripe for democratization, even under authoritarian rule, need to be understood. Of particular importance in Ukraine and comparable cases are arguments about institutions.

Much of the recent literature on democracy, but also some of the oldest, has focused on "institutional design." We have already outlined the argument that an institutionalist approach provides an incomplete understanding of politics in Ukraine and similar countries. We do not conclude from this that rational choice approaches are not useful. Instead, we hope to show how a better understanding of power politics can add to the literature on democratization.

The Plan of the Book

This introduction has sketched out the main arguments of the book and the theoretical approaches that will be used to examine them. The next two chapters develop these ideas in much more detail. Chapter Two will examine the literature on institutions and democratization. This literature is well established in the field of comparative politics and has been applied across a variety of postcommunist states. The goal of analyzing this literature will be to put Ukraine's problems into broader context.

This literature review will be concerned with two questions in particular. First, what relationship between the parliament and the executive is most conducive to building stable democracy? Essentially, this question has been boiled down to the question of whether presidential systems (those with a separate, directly elected head of government) are more conducive to democratization than parliamentary systems (those in which the leader of the parliament is also head of government), or whether some hybrid is preferable to both. Second, there is considerable research, and a greater degree of consensus, on what sort of electoral system is most likely to yield a stable governing majority. This literature sheds a good deal of light on why Ukraine's parliament has not consolidated, and why there are no easy solutions.

Chapter Three will develop the theoretical argument. It links together the four themes that were highlighted above to help us understand why power in Ukraine could become so concentrated and what might prevent such concentration in the future. The chapter will elaborate the links between social cleavages, institutional design, power politics, and the Soviet legacy in producing a system that was vulnerable to authoritarianism. A different set of arrangements—some of which were adopted in 2004—would likely lead to a more balanced system.

Chapter Four begins the empirical analysis with an overview of the main institutional developments in Ukraine since 1991. It is a rather selective political history of the independence period, highlighting events that will be significant in subsequent chapters (such as the adoption of the constitution) and neglecting other aspects of Ukrainian politics (such as the dispute over the status of Crimea) that are less relevant to this book. For those unfamiliar with politics in Ukraine, this chapter will help to make the chapters that follow it intelligible. It will describe what the succeeding chapters seek to explain: Ukraine's move to semiauthoritarianism.

Chapter Five will examine the argument that democratization in Ukraine is severely hampered by the lack of societal cohesion. This argument implies that democracy is impossible in Ukraine until there is a fundamental narrowing of societal cleavages and the formation of a coherent "Ukrainian nation" that includes the vast majority of the country's citizens. There can be no doubt that Ukraine's societal cleavages have important effects on the development of democracy in the country, but this chapter will show that the effect on the parliament is much more limited than many believe. Unlike some other authors, I do not focus on general arguments about the need for a unified "Ukrainian idea." Rather I look to see what verifiable connections can be established between societal divisions and political outcomes. We find persuasive evidence that regional/linguistic/ethnic cleavages did not obstruct alliances in the parliament. Instead, traditional left–right cleavages dominate. As long as the center was dominated by Kuchma, no democratic majority coalition could emerge. Such a coalition became possible following the Orange Revolution.

Chapter Six begins our analysis of Ukraine's formal institutional framework, focusing on the constitution. It applies to Ukraine broader findings in the field of comparative politics on the merits of presidential versus parliamentary systems of government. The most important question is how the 1996 constitution, by creating a presidential-parliamentary hybrid that strongly favored the president, contributed to Kuchma's ability to obtain authoritarian control. This chapter will also consider the relationship between the form of government and the party system, where Ukraine faces some particularly difficult dilemmas. There is some reason to believe that the shift of power toward the parliament will replace the problems of Kuchma's reign with a new, but equally dangerous set. The new institutions may be prone to stalemate, which is hazardous in new democracies.

Chapter Seven continues the discussion of institutional arrangements with a discussion of the electoral law, the fragmentation of parliament, and the weakness of political parties. There is a considerable body of literature on the effects of different sorts of electoral laws, and considerable consensus within that literature. The main goal of designing election laws is to provide for the maximum degree of representation in society that still allows for a majority coalition to develop in order to pass legislation. As many theorists have shown, these goals are to some extent contradictory. In the 1998 and 2002 parliamentary elections, Ukraine used a hybrid electoral law that was aimed at providing the benefits of both proportional and majoritarian laws. In practice, this law yielded the negative aspects of both laws rather than the positive ones. This is readily explainable. In 2004, looking forward to the 2006 elections, a fully proportional law was passed. This chapter will argue that the shift to a fully proportional system, while not without its disadvantages, probably suits Ukraine best, especially as power is shifted toward the parliament.

One problem with the literature on institutional design is that it treats the electoral law as the sole institutional influence on the structure of the party system and on the ability to form a functioning coalition in parliament. Therefore, Chapter Eight considers another level that will prove to be equally important: the rules of procedure in the parliament. Most theorists find that the electoral laws do not create incentives for parties to fragment; rather, they vary in their provision of disincentives to fragmentation. The same type of analysis can be applied to parliamentary rules of procedure, particularly the rules for recognizing distinct "factions" and the powers given to those factions. In Ukraine, parliamentary factions have been able to split into very small groups without losing their official status or perquisites. Because party leaders have had little ability to sanction defectors, party cohesion is further undermined. Moreover, some rules have actually provided a positive incentive to divide parties. In sum, then, there are identifiable changes in the parliamentary rules of procedure that would increase party cohesion, reduce the number of parties, and quite likely increase the parliament's ability to pass legislation. Some of these changes were adopted in 2004 and went into effect in 2006, though their effects are as yet difficult to assess.

By the end of Chapter Eight, we will have examined in considerable detail both the societal and institutional sources of Ukraine's slide toward authoritarianism, and we will have seen that many important questions remain unanswered. Chief among these is the inconsistent strength of institutions and rules. Chapter Nine shows how the power of the executive branch allows it to skew seemingly impartial rules in its favor. The executive branch has been able to intervene with resources that are not envisioned in the constitution or electoral law, and hence are characterized in this chapter as "informal power." These include the control of tax and law enforcement, as well as other regulatory duties assigned to the executive branch, which when applied selectively can provide incredibly powerful levers (positive and negative) over the behavior of other actors. They also include the power of patronage, which is especially powerful in a state with a unified system of government, little or no civil service protection, and a long history of the authorities telling people how to vote. This array of levers can be applied to common voters, judges, and legislators. In a system that is on paper only moderately tilted in the president's favor, these extralegal powers tipped the balance overwhelmingly in the president's favor.

Looking forward, reducing these de facto powers will be essential if liberal democracy in Ukraine is to be consolidated. In discussing constitutional reform in 2004, supporters of Yushchenko sought to maintain the level of presidential power that Kuchma enjoyed. While it was tempting to give Yushchenko, "the good guy," as much power as Kuchma, "the bad guy," such a practice would raise troubling questions for the future. Changing the constitution has reduced the de jure power of the president, but the effect on the president's de facto powers remains unclear. Moreover, it seems possible that the prime minister may now have enough power to pursue these tactics. Perhaps dividing the resources used for power politics between president and prime minister will reduce the use of these tactics, assuring that a tainted preelection process as occurred in 1999 and 2004 will not be repeated.

In Chapter Ten, we broaden the focus to consider an array of other countries that have developed forms of electoral politics that in their essentials are quite similar to those of Ukraine. In fact, the use of democratic means to achieve nondemocratic ends is a widespread practice among the states of the "third wave" of democratization. In the former Soviet Union, we see that almost all of the states outside the Baltic region have developed this form of rule, despite having adopted an array of institutional arrangements after 1991. This convergence indicates that there are powerful factors promoting this practice. Examinations of Russia, Kazakhstan, and Kyrgyzstan show how three states that at various times were considered strong candidates for democratization have gone the same route as Ukraine. Kyrgyzstan, like Ukraine, has now begun to move tentatively back toward liberal democracy. Their presidents have used many of the exact same techniques that Kuchma used in Ukraine. Ukraine's form of politics is not unique to Ukraine.

Demonstrating that the patterns we see in Ukraine exist elsewhere is important both for our understanding of Ukrainian politics and for the development of democratization theory more broadly. For Ukrainian politics, this finding counters the notion that Ukraine's problems are unique, and are the result of uniquely Ukrainian conditions. Such arguments, which imply that lessons from other countries cannot be applied to Ukraine, deprive us of the perspective that can lead to both a better understanding of Ukraine, and, perhaps, possible ways to improve the quality of democracy there. Finding a pattern across countries is also important for the democratization literature because it shows that instances where democratic means are used to produce undemocratic outcomes are not isolated or unique.

This potential is inherent in every democracy. When practical political power, for whatever reason, becomes overconcentrated in the hands of one individual or group, formal institutional checks on the abuse of power lose their potency. Checking powerful actors requires both de jure and de facto power. This basic point was emphasized by Madison in his discussion of the U.S. Constitution, but the lesson has seemingly been forgotten by modern democratization theorists, who have tended to let formal rules substitute for a genuine balance of power.

Finally, the conclusion (Chapter Eleven) will consider both the origins of "electoral authoritarianism" and the sources and implications of the Orange Revolution. In addition to summarizing the main assertions of the book, the conclusion will present a series of questions that are raised in this book but not fully answered by it. Foremost among these is the implication of the changes that occurred in 2004. Is the replacement of Kuchma by Yushchenko by itself sufficient to promote the consolidation of liberal democracy? Does the resurgence of Viktor Yanukovych and the Party of Regions mean that democracy is working, or that it is doomed? What effects can key institutional changes be expected to have? Has the emergence of Ukrainian "civil society" trumped the regional divisions that were also evident in the election? Clearly the Orange Revolution has vastly improved the chances for enduring liberal democracy in Ukraine. But it has not automatically created that outcome. The conclusion, therefore, evaluates the reforms adopted in 2004 and lays out an agenda for further reforms that are essential to consolidating democracy in Ukraine. Much remains to be done. Just as the hopes of 1994 were dashed by subsequent events, the full implications of 2004 remain to be determined.

2

Institutions and Democracy
Questioning the Connections

The collapse of communism, first in Eastern Europe in 1989 and then in the Soviet Union in 1991, instigated the need to create new political systems in twenty-eight states. Every one of these states declared the intention of building liberal democracy. This "third wave" of democratization[1] provided both an opportunity and a challenge to scholars of democratization and political institutions. The challenge was to provide advice on how these new states might succeed in their democratic aspirations. The opportunity was that this new group of democratizing states, adopting a variety of institutional arrangements in a variety of conditions, would considerably increase the empirical base of knowledge on democratic institutions and democratization.

This book is partly concerned with the question of what sort of institutional arrangements might lead to more genuine liberal democracy in Ukraine. However, it is also skeptical of this line of inquiry, because in Ukraine, much of what is obviously important happens outside of formal institutions and in contradiction of the formal rules. Therefore, this chapter reviews the considerable progress made by the literature on institutions, while pointing out important questions that are left unanswered.

Prior to addressing questions of institutional design, we need to clarify what we mean by "democratization." The word "democracy" is used so broadly that its meaning is sometimes unclear. Defining democracy has become more difficult, as a number of postcommunist regimes have arrived at systems that are neither fully democratic nor fully authoritarian. By labeling all the postcommunist regimes "in transition to democracy," observers may have assumed more about the processes under way in those states than is warranted. Therefore, the chapter begins by discussing the nature of democracy and democratization.

The chapter concludes with a discussion of what institutional approaches do *not* do. Most important, formal institutional approaches—those that deduce behavior from institutional constraints and actors' interests—are much better at specifying the results of a particular set of institutions than they are at explaining why and how that set of institutions emerged. Historical institutional approaches—which explain the development of institutions in terms of the process by which they developed—are much more appropriate for this task. Therefore, we use historical institutional approaches in a way that complements rational choice approaches, even though these approaches are sometimes seen as contradictory.[2]

A focus on historical process is essential in understanding how institutions have evolved in post-Soviet states. Moreover, formal institutional explanations are premised on the assumption that institutions constrain behavior. To some extent, this is a useful approach. In many environments, however, actors are not tightly constrained by the rules. To the extent that this is true, formal institutional approaches will not help us to explain outcomes. We need to understand what factors determine why institutions constrain behavior more in some situations than others. That has been the central question in post-Soviet Ukraine.

Qualifying the Notions of Democracy and Democratization

As the "third wave" of democratization proceeded in the 1990s, students of democracy and democratization became increasingly troubled by the growing number of regimes—including Ukraine—which possessed some of the crucial attributes of democratic rule, such as regularly held elections, but seemed undemocratic in important ways. In addition to problems with freedom of the press, rule of law, and corruption, the most basic democratic shortcoming seemed to be the absence of serious competition for power. Philip Roeder was among the first to point this out, arguing that the post-Soviet states had developed a variety of authoritarian models of rule. Roeder classified these regimes as variants of authoritarianism, rather than as variants of democratization.[3] As a result, the literature on comparative politics has developed some qualifications of the terminology of democracy, as well as several different ways of categorizing regimes that possess some but not all of the characteristics of democracy. Out of this discussion emerge three points that are central for understanding post-Soviet Ukrainian politics.

First, when Western scholars and lay people discuss "democracy," they usually mean "liberal, constitutional democracy." But while liberalism, constitutionalism, and democracy often go together in the West (Fareed Zakaria states that they go together so frequently that we imagine there is no other sort of democracy[4]), they are distinct phenomena and do not necessarily coincide. Thus, we need to consider what a democracy might look like if it is not liberal, or constitutional. Second, observers, scholars, and governments have tended to equate democracy with elections, in the belief that even if elections did not by themselves equal liberal democracy, they would promote all the other things that constitute liberal democracy. Finally, there has tended to be a teleological assumption that every polity that rids itself of authoritarianism is headed toward (liberal) democracy, and that liberal democracy is the natural endpoint toward which political systems inevitably evolve.

In contrast to these generalizations, more recent literature points out that much of what we value in liberal democracy comes not in "democracy" per se, but in its "liberal" nature. Without liberal characteristics, democracy can look much like the authoritarianism that preceded it, or can descend into chaos. Similarly, the holding of elections does not necessarily produce responsive government or good government. More important, elections do not by themselves force the system toward greater openness, or to become more liberal. Moreover, regimes that have some democratic characteristics are not necessarily headed inexorably toward further democratization or toward the creation of liberal democracy. Not only can these "partial democracies" (there is considerable disagreement on how to label them) revert to authoritarianism, as has long been recognized, but they can persist as partial democracies indefinitely. In other words, these intermediate forms of government are their own type, and need to be analyzed as such, rather than as a transitory phenomenon between authoritarianism and democracy. The following three sections take up these points in more detail.

Democracy Versus Liberal Democracy

The reminder that democracy and liberal democracy are not the same thing has come from numerous scholars, the most notable of whom include Guillermo O'Donnell, Fareed Zakaria, and Thomas Carothers. The central point in all of these arguments is that many states that are labeled "democratic" primarily due to the holding of regular and at least partially free elections lack many of the crucial attributes that we often associate with liberal democracy.

Robert Dahl, whose definition of democracy has perhaps been the most influential in recent decades, contends that democracy entails:

1. Elected officials
2. Free, fair, and frequent elections
3. Freedom of expression
4. Alternative sources of information
5. Associational autonomy
6. Inclusive citizenship[5]

For O'Donnell, many states commonly regarded as "democratizing" have taken one step toward forging liberal democracy by democratically electing a government. They have not, however, created two other fundamental components that characterize more meaningful democracy: institutions and representation.[6] The main concern with institutions, O'Donnell argues, is whether the democratic institutions in a country are "really important decisional points in the flow of influence, power, and policy."[7] By determining which agents may participate in the process (and determining how such agents are selected), by constraining the "range of feasible outcomes,"[8] by inducing patterns of representation, by stabilizing the expectations of representatives and agents, and by lengthening the "time-horizons" of participants, institutions create the predictability and stability needed for political actors to make deals that they have an incentive to stick to. Institutions also create incentives to act within the bounds of the rules rather than going outside them. Without such institutions, politics descends into "the hell of a colossal prisoner's dilemma," in which power is wielded and political decisions made by "other nonformalized but strongly operative practices: clientelism, patrimonialism, and corruption."[9] This characterization fits Ukraine's politics from 1995 to 2004 quite nicely.

Zakaria focuses on the illiberal conduct of many of the regimes that have been elected democratically. "It has been difficult to recognize this problem because for almost a century in the West, democracy has meant liberal democracy—a political system marked not only by free and fair elections, but also by the rule of law, a separation of powers, and the protection of basic liberties of speech, assembly, religion, and property. . . . Democracy is flourishing; constitutional democracy is not."[10] While the election of governments makes them democratic in a very narrow sense, they lack most of the traits we generally associate with democracy. Following James Madison's analysis of the U.S. Constitution, Zakaria sees democracy and constitutional liberalism as not only different but also fundamentally in tension with each other: "Constitutional liberalism is about the limitation of power, democracy about its accumulation and use."[11]

Zakaria faults analysts for failing to distinguish between "democracy," which means only that governments are elected, and its constitutional and liberal variants, which are much more narrowly defined and much more valued. Constitutional liberalism, he argues, is not about the process by which leaders are selected, but about the fact that the government is designed to protect the individual against coercion, and the fact that it is characterized by the rule of law.[12] In sum, Zakaria asserts that to call a regime "democratic" is to say very little about it. "If a democracy does not preserve liberty and law, that it is a democracy is a small consolation."[13]

Carothers goes further than Zakaria or O'Donnell, asserting that we should not even be talking about these regimes in terms of democracy. His point is not that they are in no way democratic, but that to focus on their level of democracy or on their progress on an assumed path to democracy provides little help in understanding how politics actually works in these states. Referring to countries in what he calls the "gray zone," because they are neither fully democratic nor fully authoritarian, Carothers states that: "By describing countries in the gray zone as democracies, analysts are in effect trying to apply the transition paradigm to the very countries whose political evolution is calling that paradigm into question."[14]

Each of these three authors has developed alternative categories with which to characterize these states.[15] O'Donnell calls them "delegative democracies," a term that has been profitably applied to Ukraine by Paul Kubicek.[16] "Delegative democracies rest on the premise that whoever wins election to the presidency is thereby entitled to govern as he or she sees fit, constrained only by the hard facts of existing power relations and by a constitutionally limited term of office."[17] The regime is democratic in the sense that it was elected more or less fairly, but it is neither liberal nor constitutional, because the constitution and other formal rules place little meaningful constraint on the president's power.

Zakaria coined the term "illiberal democracy," conveying many of the same general ideas as O'Donnell: the government can be termed democratic because of the way that it is elected, but the way that it governs does not include most of the things we associate with liberal democracy. Zakaria sees such a system as heavily majoritarian, in that whatever individual wins a presidential election, however narrowly, can rule unchecked, and can often subsequently expand presidential power further.[18]

Again, Carothers goes further, abandoning the word "democracy" altogether. He introduces two categories of "gray zone" regimes, "feckless pluralism" and "dominant power politics." In the former type, found most commonly in Latin America, there is a good deal of political freedom and there is alternation in power, but participation is limited largely to voting, and politics overall is perceived as uniformly corrupt. In "dominant power politics," "one political grouping—whether it is a movement, a party, an extended family, or a single leader—dominates the system in such a way that there appears to be little prospect of alternation of power in the foreseeable future."[19] Ukraine under Kuchma appeared to be subject to the second pattern, that of a dominant power eliminating the chances for real competition. Ukraine under Yushchenko, many Ukrainians fear, could take on the first pattern, in which one corrupt regime replaces another.

Do Elections Make Democracy?

A second question raised in recent research is the relationship between elections and democracy. There has been a considerable tendency among scholars, governments, and international organizations to equate elections with democracy. For example, G. Bingham Powell states: "There is widespread consensus that the presence of competitive elections, more than any other feature, identifies a contemporary nation-state as a democratic political system."[20] As the discussion above indicates, there is increasing recognition that while elections may mean democracy in some very limited sense, they do not constitute the kind of liberal constitutional democracy that is assumed to be the goal of reformers. Many would now go further, questioning whether elections can always be expected to lead toward more liberal, more constitutional democracy.[21]

Carothers asserts that "the belief in the determinative importance of elections" is one of the core assumptions of the democratization paradigm.[22] "[I]t has been assumed that in attempted transitions to democracy, elections will be not just a foundation stone but a key generator over time of further democratic reforms."[23] In dominant-power regimes, there tend to be "dubious but not outright fraudulent elections in which the ruling group tries to put on a good-enough electoral show to gain the approval of the international community while quietly tilting the electoral playing field far enough in its own favor to ensure victory."[24] In such a system, elections no longer provide the check on elected officials that one generally expects. Because rulers can hold power by manipulating the process rather than by responding to voters' preferences, elections do not force incumbent leaders to bend to the will of the voters. By holding elections that are at least partly free and competitive, rulers create the impression that they have a democratic mandate, and hence that they rule legitimately in the name of the people. Zakaria (p. 42) states: "Illiberal democracies gain legitimacy, and thus strength, from the fact that they are reasonably democratic." Thus elections, rather than constraining rulers or making them accountable, can actually empower and legitimate them, and make them less accountable.

Zakaria focuses as well on a different problem, that of populism run amok. He points out that Alberto Fujimori in Peru experienced an increase in popularity when he disbanded the parliament. Similarly, Vladimir Putin in Russia found widespread support for appointing, rather than electing, regional governors. Moreover, in states with weak parties but strong regional or ethnic divisions, it is much easier for politicians to organize their support along ethnic or regional divisions, a tendency that strengthens rather than weakens these divisions and can make reaching political compromise very difficult.

As an example, Zakaria points out that many of those "democrats" who sought to dislodge Slobodan Milosevic from power in Serbia did so not because he was too nationalist, but because he was not nationalist enough.[25] Countries that have created systems that are too democratic—rooted too much in electoral politics with no other checks on power—have tended to descend into tyranny.[26] There is a strong tendency in such situations for usurpation, in which strong presidents use their considerable power to seize even more power, going over the heads of legislatures and courts to popular referenda when necessary.[27] "[T]he problem with these winner-take-all systems is that, in most democratizing countries, the winner really does take all."[28]

Both O'Donnell and Zakaria point out that elections are only one of the necessary checks on the abuse of power, and not necessarily the strongest. O'Donnell argues that crucial to institutionalized democracy is not only "vertical accountability" between elected and voters, which is achieved through elections, but also "horizontal accountability" across a "network of relatively autonomous powers (i.e., other institutions) that can call into question, and eventually punish, improper ways of discharging the responsibilities of a given official."[29] An example of such "horizontal accountability" is the "checks and balances" system built into many constitutions. Without such horizontal checks, there may not be enough countervailing force to continuously nudge rulers down the path toward democracy. Alexander Motyl goes further, questioning whether countries such as Ukraine and Russia have a sufficiently developed state to produce the rule of law on which horizontal accountability rests.[30] Elections may be necessary to increase the level of democracy, but they are not by themselves sufficient. O'Donnell is very skeptical that delegative democracy can be thought of as a move toward liberal democracy: "Even if [delegative democracy] belongs to the democratic genus, however, it could hardly be less congenial to the building and strengthening of democratic political institutions."[31]

Democracy as Telos

Many analysts have assumed that every overthrow of an authoritarian government represents the beginning of a trek toward democracy. We tend to assume that everyone wants democracy, and that efforts to achieve it will eventually succeed. This view has been asserted perhaps most famously by Francis Fukuyama, who writes that liberal democracy represents the "end point of mankind's ideological evolution" and the "final form of human government."[32] Thus, we have tended to assume that any country moving *away* from authoritarianism is therefore moving *toward* liberal democracy. Typical of this assumption is the way that states that are no longer moving toward democracy are characterized as having "stalled" democratization. The implication of the term "stalled" is that the process is halted only temporarily, and that its eventual outcome is not in doubt. In the first two "waves" of democratization, reversion to authoritarianism was common enough. Observers of the "third wave" have only belatedly focused on the possibility that a partially democratic system might be an enduring form of politics with its own characteristics, and worth investigating in its own right.

Carothers states the position succinctly: "Many countries that policy makers and aid practitioners persist in calling 'transitional' are not in transition to democracy. . . ." In contrast to the standard notion that elections would slowly force a liberalization of other aspects of postauthoritarian regimes, he finds that "such profound pathologies as highly personalistic parties, transient and shifting parties, or stagnant patronage-based politics appear to be able to coexist for sustained periods with at least somewhat legitimate processes of political pluralism and competition."[33] This can happen not only under the "dominant-power" regime, but also under "feckless pluralism," in which alternation in power does not lead to progressive liberalization or reform, but simply to a change in the beneficiaries of state patronage and corruption. That this is possible in Ukraine is clearly considered likely by citizens, many of whom see the teams of Viktor Yushchenko and Yulia Tymoshenko as little better than the Kuchma regime. Carothers concludes that "what is often thought of as an uneasy, precarious, middle ground between full-fledged democracy and outright dictatorship is actually the most common political condition today of countries in the developing world and the postcommunist world. It is not an exceptional category."[34]

O'Donnell makes much the same point, distinguishing between institutionalized regimes and enduring ones. Even though his delegative democracies suffer from poor institutionalization, they can be enduring forms of government. "In many cases there is no sign either of any imminent threat of an authoritarian regression, or of advances toward representative democracy."[35] He views democratization as occurring in stages. The first stage is the democratic election of a government, and the second the institutionalization of a consolidated regime. "Nothing guarantees that this second transition will occur. New democracies may regress to authoritarian rule or they may stall in a feeble, uncertain situation. This situation may endure without opening avenues for institutionalized forms of democracy."[36]

What Kind of Democracy Is Ukraine?

Writing in 2002, Bohdan Harasymiw was blunt about Ukraine's situation: "The odyssey on which Ukraine embarked in 1991 is often referred to as a transition to democracy. That is simply wishful thinking."[37] The creation of categories such as "illiberal democracy" and "delegative democracy," as well as Carothers's effort to move beyond the terminology of democracy altogether, raises the question of whether Ukraine under Kuchma could be called a "democracy" at all, whatever adjectives are used to qualify the term. While Ukraine in the post-Kuchma era seems more easily characterized as democratic, it cannot yet be called a "liberal" democracy or a "consolidated" democracy. Ukraine's case for being called a democracy, without qualification, rests primarily on the fact that it has held regularly scheduled elections.

Holding elections, however, is not sufficient: even the Soviet Union held elections, which were entirely uncompetitive. To be a democracy even in the most basic sense, elections must not only be held regularly, but also must be competitive, free, and fair. Yushchenko came to power only when an election that was manifestly unfair was overturned in the streets and the courts. The 2006 parliamentary elections, while not perfect, were genuinely free and fair. The question is whether future elections will also be free and fair, or whether 2006, like 1994, will in retrospect appear as an anomaly.

There is a tendency in the literature for a lot of "slippage" on the questions of freeness and fairness of elections. Definitions of democracy always specify that elections must be free and fair, but most observers, in labeling countries democracies, focus on the incidence of elections, ignoring the question of whether they are free or fair. This is understandable because, as Ukraine shows, deciding whether an election is free and fair is much harder than saying it took place. Unfortunately, Western scholars as well as international organizations have generally adopted the standard of "innocent until proven guilty." Unless there is widespread and massive electoral fraud, and it is easy for everyone to see, and there is documentary proof, observers and scholars are reluctant to declare elections unfree or unfair. And so countries get a very dubious label of "democratic," based on elections whose problems are serious but at least partially obscured. Yet in Ukraine and a great number of other countries, elections have been progressively less free and less fair. The details of how ruling groups manipulate the election process will be discussed in Chapter Nine. Here, it is sufficient to say that Ukraine's case for being labeled a democracy rests on its elections, and that these have been only partially free and partially fair. Ukraine's claim to being a liberal democracy, even if strengthened by the Orange Revolution, remains weak.

Institutions and Democracy: Key Questions

From the time of Aristotle, political research has considered how the institutional form of government affects the qualities of government. Perhaps the most influential analysis was that of James Madison, primary author of the *Federalist Papers*, who condensed much earlier thought into the central notion that the point of political institutions is to prevent a "majority faction" from being able to abuse the rights of the minority. Building on Montesquieu, Madison and his colleagues contended that the separation of powers into three branches was the most reliable means of producing government that could be effective but not tyrannical. However, the Federalists did not believe in the view, often advanced today both implicitly and explicitly, that institutions themselves preserve liberal democracy and that well-designed rules lead directly to publicly minded behavior by rulers. Rather, the goal of separation of powers was to provide for mutual checks among the different parts of government and different interests in society, such that one group could not gain a preponderance of political power. In this view, the virtue of politicians was irrelevant as long as the institutions were designed properly. This approach has been labeled "democracy without democrats."[38]

The philosopher Immanuel Kant summarized the sentiment of this school of thought:

> [T]he problem of setting up a state can be solved even by a nation of devils (so long as they possess understanding). . . . [T]he constitution must be so designed that, although the citizens are opposed to one another in their private attitudes, the opposing views may inhibit one another in such a way that the public conduct of the citizens will be the same as if they did not have such evil attitudes.[39]

In recent decades, theorists of political institutions have sought to reduce much of democratic theory to the study of formal institutions. Their logic is simple: political actors' motives are fairly uniform, and can be assumed to center on gaining and retaining political office. Political actors are also assumed to be rational, though exactly what this means has been debated. Most broadly, the rationality assumption simply means that actors know their preferences, that their preferences are not self-contradictory, and that actors are able to evaluate the likelihood that different courses of action will lead to their desired goals.[40] If so, then politicians' likely behavior within a specific set of constraints could be predicted with some degree of confidence. Dennis Mueller asserts: "If institutions do not 'make the man,' they do, in combination with his goals, determine his behavior."[41] If so, then political institutions can be designed to induce the sort of outcomes that are deemed to be desirable.[42] Thus Giovanni Sartori calls his book on institutional design *Comparative Constitutional Engineering*. He sees institutions as "mechanisms that must 'work' and must have an output of sorts."[43] Key goals include representation of a wide variety of societal interests, alternation in power of political parties, the existence of strong political parties, and creation of sufficient consensus within government to avoid political stalemate. In many respects, the greatest challenge is to foster the most diverse possible representation of interests that still allow stable and effective government, rather than producing stalemate, and perhaps conflict and overthrow of the system. As Powell argues, this tension is inherent, and a tradeoff must be made.[44]

In the context of the "third wave" of democratization, the literature on political institutions in the 1990s focuses on two key issues. The first concerns the relative merits of parliamentary versus presidential forms of government. To some extent, parliamentary systems are considered to be more representative but more subject to stalemate or instability, while presidential systems are more likely to create strong governments, but if that goes too far, to lead to authoritarianism. In Ukraine, this dilemma is acute. A presidential form of government has evolved toward authoritarianism, but a new arrangement with a weakened presidency may lead to stalemate.

The second question is the relative merits of different electoral laws. Here the debate is over the strengths and weaknesses of majoritarian versus proportional systems, which are held to have a significant effect on the nature of the party system in the country and hence on the effectiveness and stability of parliament. Majoritarian systems, in general, are those in which candidates are chosen in single member districts (as in the U.S. House of Representatives and the Canadian or British House of Commons), with the candidate who wins a plurality of votes winning the seat. In theory, such laws should lead to two-party systems, in which one party has a clear majority. In proportional systems, citizens vote for parties rather than candidates, and seats in the parliament are allocated according to the percentage of votes each party receives. Such laws often lead to parliaments in which no single party holds a majority, and postelection coalition-building must take place for a majority to form. This, presumably, induces compromise among competing parties, rather than giving a single party complete control.

This second issue has been at the center of political debates in Ukraine. A loosely majoritarian design produced exactly the opposite of the standard predicted effects in 1994.[45] In subsequent elections, Ukraine sought to capture the benefits of both forms of laws, by using a mixture of majoritarian and proportional rules. As we will see however, this hybrid introduced the weaknesses rather than the strengths of both systems. In 2006, Ukraine moved to a fully proportional system. This chapter considers both of these questions in general, and shows how they are relevant to Ukraine. Subsequent chapters will examine in much more detail the evolution of constitutional arrangements and of electoral laws in Ukraine.

Presidential Versus Parliamentary Rule

One of the issues raised in O'Donnell's work on delegative democracy is the tendency for strong presidents to become even more powerful, to the point where they dominate all other sources of political power. A similar point is made by Carothers in his "dominant power" model. These arguments touch on a much broader debate in the field of comparative politics on the dangers of presidential forms of government. Beginning with Juan Linz's article "The Perils of Presidentialism," scholars have debated the virtues of presidential versus parliamentary forms of government.[46] The essential question is which form is more likely to lead to consolidated democracy. The examples of the United States and the United Kingdom, two of the oldest and most stable democracies in the world, indicate that both forms are compatible with democracy. Both the United States, the archetypal presidential system, and the United Kingdom, the archetypal parliamentary system, have preserved democracy. Nonetheless, Linz argues, examining primarily the experience of Latin America, presidential systems in new democracies are likely to lead to continual accretion of power by the president until the executive is so powerful that the system loses its democratic characteristics.

As many authors point out, presidential and parliamentary systems pursue two goals that are inherently in tension: representativeness and decisiveness. The question, as Arend Lijphart phrases it, is: "To whose interests should the government be responsive when the people are in disagreement?" In the "majoritarian" view, the answer is that the government should follow the will of the majority. In the "proportional" view, the answer is, in Lijphart's words "as many people as possible."[47] Similarly, Shugart and Carey pose the tension as one between "efficiency" and "representation." The former is promoted by a low number of parties (as in a two-party presidential system), which is "efficient" in the sense that it provides clear choices to voters (since positions are laid out prior to the elections, and there is no postelection coalition-building). "Representation," in Shugart and Carey's view, is promoted through multiparty systems, which allow for a broad range of interests to be represented.

The more divided a society is, the more these goals will clash. By putting executive power into a single president who is elected by a majority, presidential systems are "majoritarian" in that they overrepresent that majority and underrepresent minorities. In other words, there is something of a "winner take all" quality. Parliamentary systems, in contrast, are designed to require bargaining among different parliamentary parties to form a coalition that supports a chief executive. By requiring the consent of some minority parties for formation of a government, the system is seen as more representative of minorities, and therefore less majoritarian.

It should be noted, however, that these are general tendencies that will depend on the specific powers given to the president and parliament as well as on the nature of the party system. In parliamentary systems with majoritarian electoral laws for parliament, such as Canada and the UK, the overall system is very majoritarian, because there is no institutional check on the parliament. The winning party simply names the prime minister and can safely ignore the minority. Thus the Canadian system has been called "the friendly dictatorship."[48]

Defining Presidential and Parliamentary Systems

We can broadly define presidential and parliamentary systems. Linz characterizes a presidential system as one in which "an executive with considerable constitutional powers—generally including full control of the composition of the cabinet and administration—is directly elected by the people for a fixed term and is independent of parliamentary votes of confidence."[49] Shugart and Carey similarly define a presidential system as one that includes:

- The popular election of the chief executive
- Fixed term of office for the chief executive and the parliament (as opposed to terms of office depending on confidence votes)
- The prerogative of the president to choose cabinet members and direct their work.[50]

In contrast, a parliamentary system , in Linz's definition, is one in which: "the only democratically legitimate institution is parliament. In such a regime, the government's authority is completely dependent upon parliamentary confidence."[51] The key points are:

- The chief executive is chosen by the parliament, rather than directly by the voters.
- The duration of the term of chief executive and parliament are not fixed, depending instead on the maintenance of a parliamentary majority, and subject to a vote of no-confidence.

While there is consensus in "textbook" definitions of presidentialism and parliamentarism, hybrid structures such as that in Ukraine, which has both a president (who is not merely a figurehead) and a prime minister (PM), cause difficulties. Some have labeled the Ukrainian system under Kuchma a "presidential-parliamentary system," acknowledging that it is a hybrid. Theoretically, the PM played a significant role in managing the cabinet. But since the PM was chosen by the president, and could be fired by the president, the cabinet was effectively controlled by the president.[52] In cross-national studies of postcommunist regimes, Ukraine was routinely categorized as presidential. We use that categorization in this book to cover the period up to 2006. Constitutional changes that went into effect in early 2006 transformed Ukraine into a "parliamentary-presidential" system. That arrangement, like its predecessor, has both a president and a prime minister. In the parliamentary-presidential system, the PM is chosen by the parliament rather than by the president.

The Case for Presidentialism

Presidential forms of government are held to have five primary political advantages.[53] First, the president is highly visible, and thus a single individual can be viewed as responsible for policies. In parliaments, in contrast, it is often hard to sort out who is responsible for a particular policy. It can be quite difficult for the average voter to identify exactly who is making policy.

Second, partly as a result of this higher visibility, presidents are seen as being more accountable: in a presidential system, the president cannot "pass the buck." Voters hold him or her accountable for what happens in the country. In contrast, it is argued, with several parliamentary parties, and hundreds of individual members of parliament, it is difficult for voters to identify whom to blame when things do not go as they wish. While it may be that presidents get both more credit and more blame than they deserve, this accountability increases voters' sense of efficacy.

Third, horizontal accountability is built into a well-designed presidential system. By dividing authority to make and implement policy between two branches of government (the separation of legislative and executive powers familiar to any student of U.S. politics), there are "checks and balances" built into the system. The parliamentary system, in contrast, is seen as having very little possibility for balance, since all the authority, both legislative and executive, derives from the parliamentary majority. In a parliamentary system, there is no institutional base from which to challenge the executive apart from the majority that put it there. A British or Canadian prime minister can be checked only by losing an election or by a rebellion within his or her party.

Fourth, the presidency is seen as playing the role of an arbiter, using executive power to forge a consensus when none emerges from a divided parliament. This might be seen as its primary advantage in Ukraine, where the need to help push legislation through a badly divided parliament has been a frequently used argument for building a strong presidency.

Fifth, a powerful president with a clear mandate may be more able to introduce and sustain dramatic economic reform. In contrast to the third and fourth arguments, this view sees the presidency as relatively unchecked, and able to overcome antireformist sentiment from old-guard holdovers in the legislature. This argument is made not universally, but with specific reference to the post-Soviet cases. In this view, the primary goal is not building liberal democracy, but instigating economic reform.[54] This argument has particular relevance to the Russian and Ukrainian cases, where Yeltsin, Putin, and Kuchma justified their increasing power in terms of the need to implement economic reform. This argument was often greeted warmly in the West.

The Case for Parliamentarism

The case for parliamentarism stems from different assumptions than those in the case for presidentialism. Whereas promoters of presidential rule see the primary threat to good government in fragmented and stalemated parliaments, advocates of parliamentarism see the danger in institutional conflict between the executive and legislative branches. This institutional conflict, especially if it is worsened by partisan conflict, can lead to impasse.

Critics of presidentialism point to three primary dangers. The first is authoritarianism, or any of the unsavory versions of democracy discussed above. These can occur when a powerful president is able to rule with relatively little limit on executive authority. The second problem is that with two separate bases of national political authority (the executive and the legislature), there is bound to be conflict over whose agenda takes primacy. The third problem is that, with two separately elected national authorities, final responsibility for policy is shared, and accountability is therefore blurred. Hence, one can argue that the presidential system offers less accountability than the parliamentary model. If presidential and parliamentary elections are held at different times, and according to different election laws, as is generally the case, it is inevitable that the executive and legislature will come to power with different perceptions of their mandates and of the policies that will serve their reelection interests.

All of these problems are possible even when the executive and legislative branches are controlled by the same party. The problems with presidential systems are dramatically increased when different parties control the executive and legislative branches. With differently timed elections, and different election rules, this is not at all unlikely. Even in the United States, with its very narrow political spectrum, control by one party of both houses of the legislature and the executive is relatively rare. By dividing power across parties this way, critics of presidentialism argue, presidential systems have a built-in tendency toward partisan deadlock, in which the party controlling the legislature and the party controlling the executive work to block each other's priorities. Such obstructionism can stem from genuine disagreements or from the electoral advantages of denying the other side success.

In a parliamentary system, according to advocates of this type of system, power is shared through the coalition-building process, but unified once a government is formed. Coalition governments cannot rule unchecked, because they must keep junior partners in the coalition. Because the group that controls the legislature also controls the executive, institutional conflict between the two branches becomes nearly irrelevant, and it is impossible for the two branches to be controlled by different parties.

Recently, the bulk of opinion among political scientists seems to be in favor of parliamentarism, though there is no consensus.[55] M. Steven Fish, for example, refutes the finding that presidentialism is more conducive to reform, by showing an inverse relationship between presidentialism and economic reform in the postcommunist states.[56] Rather than trying to resolve this theoretical debate, it is much more important to recognize a more fundamental point: the question ultimately is empirical rather than theoretical. The cases for the two different approaches are based on two different notions of what the danger is. Advocates of parliamentarism worry about interbranch conflict and about hyperpresidential rule. Advocates of presidential systems worry about stalemate within the parliament and resulting instability.

Since there are numerous successful examples of both types of systems, and numerous failures of both types, it seems dubious to argue that one system is inherently superior. Rather, the key point for practitioners of "institutional design" should be to figure out which problems are more salient in a given situation, and once a choice of system is made, how to guard against its inherent dangers. When a parliamentary system is chosen, design of the electoral law to maximize the likelihood that a stable majority will emerge is essential. When choosing a presidential system, ensuring that both president and legislature have incentives to compromise is crucial.

Presidentialism Versus Parliamentarism in Ukraine

Parliamentary and presidential systems have different strengths and are intended to solve different kinds of problems. The fundamental challenge for Ukraine is that it has experienced the problems to which *both* types of constitutional arrangement are vulnerable. Ukraine's parliament has generally been badly fragmented, such that passing decisive legislation has been nearly impossible. This has motivated the shift toward increasing presidential power in creating a post-Soviet constitution, and more recently has driven Viktor

Yushchenko's claim that the presidency needs more power. However, Ukraine is equally plagued by the dangers of presidentialism: institutional conflict between the executive and legislature has been endemic, and even though the parliament has been fragmented, partisan deadlock between executive and legislative branches has been substantial.

Ukraine's institutional problems have not been explored in sufficient detail. Subsequent chapters will probe the factors that lead to fragmentation of parliament, executive-parliamentary conflict, and the accretion of presidential power. It will become clear that many of Ukraine's problems indeed stem from its institutional arrangements. This does not mean, however, that solutions are simple.

While presidentialism is not necessarily inappropriate for Ukraine, the arrangements in Ukraine from 1995 to 2006 gave the executive so much power that it had little need to compromise with the legislature. Instead of becoming an honest broker for a divided parliament, as advocates of presidentialism predict, the Ukrainian executive has had every incentive to undermine legislative unity. As long as the legislature is stalemated, the president rules unimpeded.[57] As a result, we will see, tipping the balance of power more toward the parliament was necessary, even if the measures adopted in 2004 are not ideal.

However, shifting power toward the parliament is no panacea. What good can come of giving more power to a parliament that is chronically stalemated? In order to make the system work, that too would need to change. One reason parliament is stalemated, I shall argue, is that with no real power vis-à-vis the executive, there is little to be gained in return for the sacrifices that must be made to forge coalitions. To that extent, giving the parliament more power will itself create incentives to form durable ruling coalitions. Early evidence from the new rules adopted in 2004 indicate that this is already taking place.

We shall see (in Chapter Eight) that much of this problem stems from a level of institutional rules that is generally ignored in the literature on institutional design: the rules of parliamentary procedure. Several salient aspects of the parliamentary rules discourage coalescing of parties and encourage fragmentation. Moreover, to the extent that the executive seeks to prevent coalescing, the parliamentary rules make it very easy to achieve that goal. Finally, the parliament has been so badly fragmented because of an electoral law that minimizes incentives for preelection coalition-building, undermines the construction of strong parties, and gives elected members minimal incentive to forge coalitions or to stick with them.

In sum, then, the standard institutional arguments do indeed apply to Ukraine, but not if applied simplistically. The choice of a presidential versus a parliamentary system is crucial, but it would be silly to argue that one system will doom the country while the other will automatically produce democracy. There are multiple necessary conditions for the development of liberal democracy. In reviewing debates about the virtues and shortcomings of the two types, it is more important to grasp the requirements for each to work well, and the threats to it, than to try to figure out which form of rule will be a silver bullet that will solve all problems.

For Ukraine, as for any other country, neither form of government will work well without the establishment of a well-functioning parliament. To switch to a parliamentary system, as some have advocated, without fixing the parliament, would be disastrous. To maintain a presidential system, without fixing the parliament and curtailing executive power, is likely to be equally unproductive. Legislatures are at the center of every liberal democracy in the world, and there is no reason to believe that any constitutional setup will allow Ukraine to prosper without a functioning legislature.

Parliamentary Electoral Laws: Proportionality Versus Majoritarianism

No aspect of institutional design has received greater attention than electoral laws, and only a very broad sketch of an enormous literature can be offered here.[58] Electoral laws can have an immense effect on the party system in a country, on the degree of fragmentation or cohesion of the parliament, and hence on the parliament's ability to legislate effectively. Moreover, "compared to other components of political systems, electoral systems are the easiest to manipulate with specific goals in view."[59]

The study of electoral laws, while usually carried out distinctly from the debate over presidential versus parliamentary forms of government, in fact has important implications for both. How well either system performs will be strongly influenced by the situation in the parliament. Presidentialism, for example, is seen as especially problematic when elections do not yield a majority party. In a presidential system, therefore, electoral laws that emphasize, above all, the formation of a parliamentary majority are essential. Parliamentarism also relies on the formation of a parliamentary majority, but this can happen through a postelection coalition process rather than through the elections themselves. Since either form of government relies on a functioning parliament (though each has different requirements) the institutional rules that define the composition of the parliament are vital.

Studies of election laws have focused on two archetypal systems, the single-member district (SMD) plurality system (e.g., that used to elect the U.S.

House of Representatives and the British or Canadian House of Commons) and the proportional representation (PR) system used in electing legislatures in Germany,[60] Israel, and Poland, among many others. In practice, there are many variants of these two schemes. The two systems are subject to Duverger's law and Duverger's hypothesis, respectively. Together, Duverger's law and hypothesis find that SMD plurality election laws lead to two-party systems (Duverger's law) while proportional representation laws lead to multiparty systems (Duverger's hypothesis).[61]

In two-party systems, one party or the other is virtually guaranteed a majority in parliament, such that coalition formation is not an issue. In PR systems, it is more likely that no single party will win a majority, and that a coalition will be required to form a working majority. The primary benefit pointed to by supporters of PR is that it allows for representation in parliament of a much broader array of political forces, forcing winners to compromise with losers and preventing minorities from feeling disenfranchised. We can think of plurality systems as forcing political groups to form semipermanent alliances prior to elections, while in PR they form more temporary alliances after elections.

Mixed Electoral Systems

Ukraine confounded this analysis in 1998 and 2002 by using a mixed system: 225 deputies were elected in SMDs based on plurality voting, while another 225 were elected on party lists according to PR (this system is still used in Russia).[62] This hybrid, rare until the 1990s, has become increasingly popular in the "third wave" democracies. As Erik Herron and Misa Nishikawa have shown, it is difficult to model the expected outcomes of this system using the standard assumptions.[63] A growing literature finds, unsurprisingly, that there are no generally predictable effects for the variety of "mixed systems."[64] Instead, whether the systems behave more like proportional systems or more like plurality systems depends on how the two components are combined.[65]

For example, in the German "compensatory" mixed system, citizens vote for both a district-level representative and a party. But the seats are not divided equally between the two parts of the ballot. Instead, after the single-member districts are allocated, additional seats are awarded to parties so that their *totals* conform to the results of the proportional portion of the election. Thus, the system functions essentially as a proportional system, and is usually classified as such. In a mixed system such as that used in Ukraine (in 1998 and 2002) and in Russia, the SMD portion has equal influence over the distribution of power among parties. Parties therefore can make winning SMD seats a significant part of their strategy for controlling parliament, as did the pro-Kuchma United Ukraine bloc in 2002.

Advocates hold that mixed systems have "the promise of providing the best of both the dominant nineteenth- and twentieth-century worlds of electoral systems."[66] From proportional systems, it is contended, they take the ability to represent sizable minorities and a tendency to build party cohesion. From plurality systems, it is contended, they take strong representation of local and regional interests and an incentive for members to serve constituents. A more cautious view, however, is that the two portions of the mixed system "contaminate" each other, so that neither portion functions as it would in a pure SMD or pure PR system.[67]

Strengths of Proportional and Single-Member District Elections

As was the case with the debate over presidentialism versus parliamentarism, plurality and proportional electoral systems are intended to serve different ideals of democracy, and to avoid different pitfalls. Plurality systems, by creating (in theory) a two-party system and hence guaranteeing a parliamentary majority, have both the benefits and drawbacks of majoritarianism: they create a clear winner, with a majority to pass legislation, that can be held accountable at the next election. In presidential systems, the existence of a clear parliamentary majority to bargain with the president and provide a check on executive power is viewed as essential. On the other hand, creating a clear winner also creates a clear loser, and can severely overrepresent a narrow majority. At the level of the district, a party that wins 51 percent of the vote wins 100 percent of the seats; and at the level of the parliament, a party that controls 51 percent of the seats has 100 percent of the legislative power. In states with relatively fragmented societies or with substantial minorities, it can mean that some parties that represent substantial portions of the population have no chance of ever coming to power or influencing legislation. The strength of proportional systems is that they allow such minority parties to have an influence through their potentially crucial role in the coalition-building process.

The other key difference between plurality and proportional systems concerns to whom members of parliament "owe" their seats. In a party-list proportional system, the party organization determines an individual's placement on the list, and hence his or her likelihood of entering parliament. The virtue is that, because members are dependent on party leadership for their seats, party discipline ought to be high, which is usually helpful for passing legislation. However, members of parliament in this system have no specific "constituents" more narrowly defined than the entire electorate. Therefore, representation of local concerns is minimized, and individual citizens have no particular member to contact with their concerns. In contrast, in single-member districts, members owe their seats to the local constituents who elect them. This, it is argued, gives them a much more substantial interest in being responsive to the concerns of those constituents, and in the United States, Canada, and the United Kingdom, members and their staffs spend a good deal of time on exactly this. However, because legislators in the United States can be elected by local voters even if these legislators displease the party leadership, single-member districts are held to provide for weaker party discipline, and therefore to require "log-rolling" in order to get legislation passed.

These generalizations should be taken with a good deal of reservation. Many of the supposed effects of both systems are, on close inspection, effects not of the general system, but of other rules. An important example is party discipline, which is very high in the plurality SMD system in Canada and the United Kingdom, and very low in the plurality SMD system in the United States. Clearly, the electoral system does not determine party discipline. Rather the nomination rules that control who can be a party's candidate in a given constituency are decisive. In the United States, representatives must reside in the district they aim to represent, and disputes over who will be a party's candidate are resolved by voters, in primary elections, rather than by the party leadership. In the United Kingdom, in contrast, anyone can represent any constituency, and party leaders determine which party members will run in which districts. Thus, the British practice of assigning party leaders to "safe" seats has much more in common with the PR practice of putting leaders at the top of the list than it does with the primary system used in the United States.

Similarly, the level of party discipline is heavily influenced by a more microlevel factor that is not inherent to either system: rules about switching parties. In systems where an individual holds the "mandate" for a seat in parliament, the member can switch parties without losing the seat. In other systems, however, the seat belongs to the party rather than to the member, and a member who quits the party forfeits the seat. As we will see in the case of Ukraine, this factor is as crucial as choice of electoral law in understanding the problems in parliament and the possible solutions.

The Problem of Weak Political Parties

In one important respect, the mainstream literature seems unable to grasp the nature of Ukraine's problems, and in this area we will need to strike out on our own in developing explanations and prescriptions. The problem concerns the incredible weakness of political parties in Ukraine. While most literature on electoral laws focuses on resolving the problem of forming a parliamentary majority, Ukraine has needed to solve a prior problem: the weakness of political parties in general. The mixed system was adopted in Ukraine in part with a view to solving both problems at once. This is a tall order, not envisioned in the considerable literature that has been used to design and analyze these systems. This issue will be treated at much greater length in Chapter Seven. But it is important to note that the literature on institutional design and on electoral systems does not really address the problem of forming political parties. Nor does it consider how various electoral rules will work in systems without a recognizable "party system."

The literature on electoral systems does have much to say about the influence of electoral laws on the evolution of existing party systems. However, none of this theory considers the question of how different electoral provisions will influence the formation of parties where no parties exist. Previous scholarship should not be faulted for this, for the question has rarely arisen empirically. Moreover, it seems reasonable to take for granted that when a state becomes democratic and prepares to hold elections, parties will form spontaneously to contest them, and that once they do, conventional approaches to electoral systems will apply.

At least in the case of Ukraine, the problem of party system formation turns out to be very different than the problem of the evolution of an existing party system. Put simply, it is not inevitable that parties will come to dominate the electoral scene. In Ukraine, politicians have used ad hoc alliances and personal resources, as well as permanent parties, to contest elections. Some electoral arrangements may have a much stronger effect than others in forcing electoral activity into parties, as opposed to other possible avenues for vying for office, such as loose electoral alliances or individual resources. Ukraine thus presents problems for analysis that go beyond the solutions provided by the conventional literature.

Two important points result. First, application of the standard findings from the literature on electoral systems leaves crucial puzzles (such as the weakness of the party system) unsolved. We must therefore be willing to explore some new theoretical ground here. Second, however, it would be wrong to conclude that conventional theory "does not apply" to Ukraine. Within important limits, it does indeed apply. The problem in applying this theory to Ukraine so far is that it has been done without much attention to detail. For example, the single-member portion of the mixed ballot has been advocated on the grounds that this format will tend to reduce the number of parties, as indicated in Duverger's law. However, Duverger's law does not state that *entire countries* will develop a two-party system. It says that each *constituency* will develop a two-party system. This will result in the entire country going to a two-party system *only* if the country is sufficiently homogenous that the same two parties emerge victorious across all the districts. Given what we know about Ukraine's regional diversity, Duverger's law predicts not a two-party system at the national level, but a multitude of parties, each of which is one of the two strongest within its region, but may be utterly absent elsewhere.

What the Institutional Design Literature Does Not Tell Us

The literature on institutional design tells us a lot, but much of what we want to know is beyond its scope. If scholars of Ukrainian politics have tended to pay too little notice to the findings from the broader study of institutional design and comparative democratization, scholars of institutional design have probably applied their strongest findings too universally, and underestimated the influence of factors not included in their theories. The argument here is not that theories that apply elsewhere do not apply to Ukraine. On the contrary, most of them apply as well to Ukraine as to other countries, as long as they are applied carefully. The problem is that there are some key questions that these theories simply do not address, and are not intended to address. In this respect, two issues arise that will appear throughout this book. First, theories of institutional design can reasonably attempt to predict the *effects* of different arrangements, but they cannot predict the *causes* of those arrangements. Second, institutional theories assume that all the key political processes occur within formal institutions. To the extent that politics is noninstitutionalized (in other words, the rule of law is weak) formal institutional theories are less applicable. These two issues turn out to be related.

Theories of institutional design specify the relationship between a set of formal institutions and certain outcome (e.g., single-member district plurality electoral systems lead to two-party systems). They do not, and in fact cannot, explain why one set of institutions is chosen over another. In other words, they can explain the effects of formal rules but not the causes. This is readily acknowledged by leading scholars in the formal analysis of institutions. George Tsebelis, for example, argues that there cannot be a rational choice theory of institutional design, because the design of the institutions is an art and its laws are "unknowable."[68] While scholars tend to write in the abstract as though the discussion for institutional rules in a given country is driven by some abstract notion of what would produce the best government, to the actors actually making the rules, it is often the pursuit of political power that motivates decisions.[69] Thus, Tsebelis argues that institutions should not simply be considered objective "inherited constraints," but rather are the "objects of human behavior."[70]

Advances in our understanding of the effects of different institutions actually promote this, because "Knowing precisely what kinds of outcomes an institution will produce transforms voting over outcomes into voting over institutions."[71] There are many examples of this in Ukraine, including the struggle over election laws. Since the effects of different electoral laws on different political forces have been readily predictable, discussions of electoral law have focused on who would gain or lose seats, rather than on what might lead to effective government.

A broader problem with focusing on the effects of formal institutions is that much of politics occurs outside of institutions. We may tend to underestimate this because in most Western states politics is highly institutionalized, but there are clear examples of this even in stable democracies. For example, despite many rules trying to limit its influence, money has a profound effect on politics, both in terms of winning elections and in terms of influencing legislators and bureaucrats between elections. Efforts to stem that influence have been made for 200 years, but have only been partially successful.

In a state undergoing fundamental institutional change, much less is circumscribed by formal rules. Accordingly, therefore, much more is potentially solved through noninstitutional means. Such means include not only the use of money, but the use of violence. Everyday legislation is "nested" within laws about how legislation is made, and how legislators are elected. These rules in turn are nested within a constitutional order. As long as that constitutional order is robust, everything else can follow from it. But where does the constitutional order come from, and how robust is it? In Western democracies such as the United States, Canada, and the United Kingdom, we take these matters for granted. In the postcommunist states, these are not hypothetical questions.

The study of politics in a weakly institutionalized setting has long been the purview of the field of international relations rather than comparative politics. But the problems faced in postcommunist states are not theoretically dissimilar. At crucial times in Moscow, Kyiv, and elsewhere, vital institutional decisions have been determined by the ability of different actors to apply physical force. In other words, a domestic version of "balance of power politics" has prevailed. In Russia, the military's decision to side with Yeltsin rather than Rutskoi and Khasbulatov in 1993 ushered in a new order and a new constitution. In Ukraine, when the security forces sided with Kuchma and one group of legislators, a challenge by another group of legislators was defeated. When the security organs refrained from involvement in 2004, the outcome changed drastically. Again, this is not unique to post-Soviet states struggling for democracy: both the United States and England had full-blown civil wars to determine which institutional rules would prevail.

In this vein, Michael McFaul argues that the success of postcommunist democratization has been largely determined by the balance of power between reformers and autocrats. He contends that democracy emerges only where reformers hold a disproportionate share of power, and that where power is balanced stalemate persists, as in Ukraine.[72] This view rejects the "democracy without democrats" perspective discussed above, and premises the creation of democracy on imbalance, rather than balance, of power.

To understand post-Soviet Ukrainian politics we need to understand "power politics" as well as institutional design. Institutional design will help us understand the effects of different arrangements. Power politics will tell us why certain rules have been adopted and why the rules do not apply equally to all actors. In the following chapters, these explanations are intertwined. If we want to explain the adoption of a particular rule or set of rules, we need to understand both the predictable effects of those rules and the ability of certain actors to win the contest over the rules.

3

Power and Institutions

Overview of the Argument

The previous chapter reviewed several different strands of literature on political institutions and on democratization, and referred briefly to how some of these concepts apply to Ukraine. The purpose of this chapter is to move from the general to the specific; to present a coherent explanation of how politics in Ukraine worked under Kuchma, and to indicate what will need to change if the Orange Revolution is to lead to liberal democracy.

The explanation developed here is not simple or unicausal. There is no single factor that causes liberal democracy in general, nor is there a single factor that has inhibited its emergence in Ukraine. As the previous chapter indicated, liberal democracy is a complex phenomenon that consists of several factors, including free and fair elections, a high level of political participation, independent media, organized parties, rule of law, and institutionalization of democratic practices. It stands to reason that such a multifaceted phenomenon will be explained (or have its absence explained) by more than one variable.

The explanation advanced here links four factors: societal fragmentation, institutional design, power politics, and the absence of revolutionary change. These factors are listed in Figure 3.1. Societal fragmentation is a problem, but not an insurmountable one: it simply raises the standards for institutional design. Institutional design is also a problem, but it cannot be understood in isolation from societal fragmentation, since societal factors influence the effects of different institutional designs. Institutional designs that work well in other countries will not work well in Ukraine.

Institutional design, however, is at the mercy of power politics, which influences both how the rules are written and how they are enforced. By power, we mean the resources actors possess that can influence the behavior of other actors, by altering their incentives. Formal powers are those that are legally recognized, such as the authority for elected officials to determine certain policies. Other powers are not legally recognized, such as the ability to bribe or threaten another actor, or at the extreme, the power to kill. Both matter in the conduct of politics.

Figure 3.1

Outline of the Argument: Causes of Electoral Authoritarianism in Ukraine

1. Societal Fragmentation

2. Institutional Design
    a. Constitutional Design (strong presidential system)
    b. Electoral Law
    c. Rules Governing the Functioning of Parliament

3. Power Politics
    a. In Implementation of Laws (selective law enforcement)
    b. In Writing the Laws

4. The Nonrevolutionary Nature of Political Change in Ukraine

Note: As the previous chapter indicated, there are several labels for describing such "hybrid regimes." The label "electoral authoritarianism," is used here because it stresses the role of elections in promoting authoritarianism, rather than democracy, and because it stresses that regimes such as Ukraine's under Kuchma are more accurately labeled authoritarian than democratic. The term is used by Larry Diamond, among others. See "Thinking about Hybrid Regimes," *Journal of Democracy* 13, no. 2 (April 2002): 24.

There is no way that the rules can be productively rewritten until it is in the interest of the most powerful actors in society. Now that those rules have been rewritten, the path is open to new patterns of politics. However, as the Orange Revolution vividly demonstrated, much in Ukraine is still determined by power politics. At the root of the problem, therefore, has been the concentration of de facto political and economic power in a single place: the executive branch of government.

How did power get so concentrated? It was already heavily concentrated under the Soviets, and without a genuine revolution in 1991, independent Ukraine inherited this system. A combination of historical circumstances and shrewd calculation allowed the people who controlled these assets under the Soviet system to weather the changes of 1991 with their power substantially intact. A main question for post-2004 Ukraine is whether the division of executive powers between the president and prime minister will reduce the potential for power politics, or simply lead to a new battle for control of the executive branch.

If we focus on the Kuchma era, and ask why liberal democracy eroded, we can begin with two broad categories of answers. The first is that Ukrainian society is too divided to build effective democracy. The second is that the institutions are poorly designed. I argue that both of these factors are operative, and that they interact. The regional fissures in Ukrainian society would not be so salient were it not for the election law. The literature on election laws is quite clear on the limitations of certain kinds of systems. In particular, single-member district elections do not have the same effects in regionally divided societies as they do in homogeneous societies. Regional cleavages mean that whatever the election law, Ukraine will likely have a multiparty parliament. The reality of a multiparty system clashes with the choice of a presidential system, which has been found to work poorly in multiparty systems. While societal cleavages present a problem for institutional design in Ukraine, these problems are not insurmountable.

Therefore, a large part of the explanation for the erosion of liberal democracy in Ukraine is in the design of institutions, which are easier to change than the composition of society. The effects of institutional problems were seen in the inefficacy of the parliament and in the ease with which President Kuchma usurped power. Both the constitutional arrangement of powers between president and parliament and the electoral laws needed to be changed. It is not clear, however, that the changes agreed to in December 2004, and which went into effect in early 2006, will make a substantial improvement. Moreover, parties and the parliament have functioned poorly in part due to two other levels of rules: those that influence the level of control party leaders have over members and those that control the operation of the parliament itself.

Rule **of** *Law versus Rule* **by** *Law*

Any focus on formal rules in Ukraine, however, must answer this question: how can we say that the rules matter in a country in which they are often ignored? The answer is that institutional rules matter even when they are not enforced uniformly. In Ukraine, the rules are not uniformly ignored, but rather are enforced selectively. The difference is crucial. Uniform irrelevance of the laws breeds anarchy and chaos. Selective enforcement, on the contrary, leads to concentration of power in the hands of those who choose how and on whom to enforce the laws. It has been said that Ukraine does not have "rule of law" but "rule *by* law." We need to examine how informal power, such as patronage, control of the economy, and control of law enforcement leads to selective law enforcement. It is essential, therefore, to strengthen both the vertical and horizontal checks on executive power, not simply to write more rules. Where there is massive imbalance in de facto power, even the best rules will do little good.

Assessing de facto power is essential because it explains not only why the formal rules are selectively enforced, but why a particular set of formal rules favors certain actors. One example is the power legally accruing to the president in the constitution. In 1996, when Ukraine's post-Soviet constitution was finally adopted, almost all power was on Kuchma's side: he credibly threatened that if he was not given extensive powers by the parliament, he would take even more authoritarian powers through a referendum.

Similarly, the constitutional changes adopted in December 2004 reflected the existing balance of power: Yushchenko had thousands of people in the streets, and was threatening a revolution. But Kuchma still had enough votes in the parliament to deny Yushchenko a legitimate path to the presidency. So Kuchma was able to deny Yushchenko a complete victory. Thus, the pact reached at that time cleared the way for Yushchenko to come to power, but protected the interests of others by diluting the power of the presidency. The result was one that neither side sought. Rather, it reflected the distribution of power at that time. It is perhaps ironic that Kuchma sought to enhance presidential power in the first instance and to limit it in the second.

The Tendency for Power to Accumulate

Crucial to the accrual and exercise of de facto power is the mutually reinforcing nature of economic and political power in the post-Soviet environment. This is not unique to Ukraine or even to the former Soviet Union. With economic and political power heavily concentrated, and with the two more easily interchangeable in Ukraine than in many other countries, those who held one kind of power could obtain the other, use it to get more of the first, and so on.

The result of all of this can be stated succinctly: in Ukraine, power has tended to concentrate very quickly—those that have it get more and more. This is the most fundamental difference between Ukraine and a liberal democracy. The ways in which power gets dispersed and divided—fair elections, sources of wealth independent of the state, a free market—are present in Ukraine very weakly if at all. Thus, under Kuchma, Ukraine developed something that resembles the "machine" politics that persisted for decades in many American cities, in which the existence of essentially democratic institutions nonetheless allowed powerful machines to rule nearly unchecked. This tendency toward concentration of power is the key criterion by which politics in Ukraine must be judged after the Orange Revolution. Only if it becomes much more difficult to concentrate power will we regard the Orange Revolution as heralding genuine change. Otherwise, it will simply mark the transfer of power from one group to another, perhaps less odious, group.

Concentration of Power as a Soviet Legacy

This prompts us to ask how it was that opponents of liberal democracy had sufficient de facto power to write the formal rules to their liking and to enforce them selectively. In terms of structure, they were able to do so because they had more power. But this phenomenon is better understood in terms of process. In Ukraine in 1991, there was never a political revolution in which de facto political power was fundamentally reordered. In contrast to more successful countries to the west, there was no "roundtable" or "pacting" process in which new institutions were negotiated between the existing elites and those in opposition.

The new rules were made by the old elites, who, while forced to make certain concessions, were able to maintain key positions. Most important in the long term was that the existing elites maintained control over economic assets. The mutually reinforcing nature of political and economic assets allowed those who had control over these in the Soviet era to maintain and strengthen their control in the post-Soviet era. Given the original distribution of power in Ukraine in 1991, the partial opening of the system made it easier, not harder, for those with power to consolidate it. This phenomenon, where partial reform of a system with concentrated power leads to continued concentration of power, is not unique to Ukraine. Having summarized the argument, we can now present it in more detail.

Societal Fragmentation as a Challenge

Various authors have located the major problem for building liberal democracy in Ukraine in the country's deep societal cleavages. The salience of regional voting patterns, augmented by threats of secession, brought these problems to the fore in late 2004. Arguments vary concerning the precise causal mechanism that links societal division and problems for building liberal democracy, but there is widespread belief that the problem is formidable for Ukraine. The problem will be examined in depth in Chapter Five, but here we will summarize the problem and its link to the overall argument.

We can focus on a relatively narrow question concerning societal cleavages and the building of democracy in Ukraine: Do societal cleavages make it impossible to design institutions that will provide for a functioning parliament and functional political party system? This question is rooted in the assertion that it is not possible to build liberal democracy without a well-functioning legislature and a structured political party system.

The challenge that Ukraine's societal divisions create is this: because the society is so divided, it naturally elects politicians and parties that have little in common with one another. This presumably impedes creation of a stable parliamentary majority that can legislate and check presidential authority. Societal divisions might impede effective democracy in three ways. First, in the creation of parties, it makes it more difficult for parties to develop into mass-based parties as opposed to narrow special-interest ones. Second, in the behavior of parties following elections, it makes it more difficult for them to build nationwide as opposed to regional groupings, and more difficult to form a parliamentary majority. Third, in elections themselves, the difficulty in forming parties that are strong across the entire country means that a single-member district plurality election law will not tend to consolidate the party system.

The problem can be seen by examining the various efforts over the years to force Leonid Kuchma from power. The first such movement arose after Kuchma's link to the murder of the journalist Heorhiy Gongadze was made public. It appeared that if he fell, rightist parties, broadly characterized as nationalist and pro-market, and based primarily among Ukrainian-speakers in western Ukraine, would come to power. The left, strongest in Russian-speaking regions of eastern Ukraine, and led by the communists, supported Kuchma rather than see their enemy come to power. Similarly, when the parliament was controlled by the left in the mid-1990s, the rightist (western Ukrainian) parties supported increased presidential power, which greatly aided Kuchma. Simply put, both left and right (which seem to equate with eastern and western Ukraine) saw Kuchma's authoritarianism as a lesser threat than the success of their adversaries. The inability of reformist Viktor Yushchenko and socialist Oleksandr Moroz—both avowed opponents of Kuchma—to join forces to oppose him in 2001–2 illustrates the seriousness of the problem.

Once the leftist Moroz and the populist Yulia Tymoshenko joined forces with Yushchenko, it became much easier to put pressure on Kuchma. Were they not unified, Yushchenko might not have won the 2004 election, or have been able to successfully challenge the fraud that occurred. Had they unified sooner, Kuchma might have been defeated in the 1999 presidential election. Similarly, once Tymoshenko and Yushchenko fell out, in September 2005, the reform coalition was unsustainable. The same dynamic allowed Viktor Yanukovych, Kuchma's designated successor, to return to power in 2006 after being seen as politically dead in 2004.

However, without denying the significance of Ukraine's societal divisions, there is reason to question whether they alone are responsible for the fragmentation of political parties and of the parliament, for two reasons. First, there are many other states with considerable ethnic, regional, linguistic, and political cleavages that nonetheless manage to create stable party structures and functioning parliaments. As various authors have pointed out, the homogeneous "nation-state" of the textbooks is largely a myth; nearly every state in the world is divided in some way, and many of them are liberal democracies. Belgium, Canada, Spain, and Switzerland are four notable cases of linguistically and regionally divided societies with robust parliamentary democracies. In other words, while Ukraine's differences are substantial, there is little comparative evidence that Ukraine is more divided than other societies that have built liberal democracy.[1]

Second, because Ukraine's political institutions were poorly designed, we must consider whether different institutional arrangements would provide greater incentives for diverse political forces to coalesce for the sake of gaining power. If one considers either the incredible range of parties involved in some governing coalitions (e.g., in Italy or Israel) or the incredible range of opinion included in the parties of two-party systems (e.g., moderate versus fundamentalist members of the Republican Party in the United States), it seems worth considering whether more powerful institutional incentives might induce both consolidation of parties and more reliable coalition building in Ukraine's parliament.

Even if societal cleavages can be overcome, they will have serious implications for how different institutional arrangements will perform and for what kind of institutional design will work best. Ukraine's regional cleavages make it clear that a two-party system will not result even from strong institutional measures designed to create one. Therefore Ukraine will not have a two-party system. However, comparative research indicates that presidential systems work best with two-party systems.[2] We must conclude that the presidential form of government is ill-suited to building liberal democracy in Ukraine.

Institutional Design

If Ukraine is to build a successful democracy, whether its format is presidential or parliamentary, it is essential that a functioning parliament be created. By a functioning parliament, we mean one in which fairly stable parliamentary majorities are created and in which the parliament as an institution constitutes a substantial counterweight to presidential authority. Those two requirements are linked, for a parliament that has no majority, and therefore is mute as an institution, cannot provide a check on the executive branch. And in a parliament that has little real power, there is less incentive to make the compromises needed to form a majority.

Constitutional Design: The Problem of Multiparty Presidentialism

The absence of a parliamentary majority in Ukraine has been widely viewed as a justification for expanded presidential authority. However, extensive presidential authority is itself a cause of parliamentary weakness. As has been discussed extensively in the theoretical and comparative literature, the stronger the executive, the less incentive for parliamentarians to compromise in order to form a majority coalition. Assuming that the differences between different parties and politicians are genuine, they will need significant incentives to compromise to form a governing coalition. The question is especially relevant for those parties that will not lead the coalition. Because joining a coalition might have strategic costs in terms of maintaining one's ideological distinctness in the eyes of the voters, there are good reasons to avoid the necessary compromises unless the benefits are substantial.

The less power and privilege that accompanies the formation of a parliamentary majority coalition, the less reason there is to pay the costs. In a normal parliamentary democracy, there are significant benefits to taking part in the governing coalition. For the party leading the coalition, payoffs include control of the legislative agenda and of the executive branch of government. With all this power to gain, it is relatively easy to exchange some of it with smaller parties in return for their support in building and maintaining the coalition. Thus, junior parties are often rewarded with control over certain ministries, and some of their priorities are often included in the legislative agenda of the ruling coalition.

What incentives have there been to create a coalition in Ukraine? Until 2006, the parliament had almost no power over the composition of the cabinet. The most prominent incentive for coalition formation was thus absent. Because the parliament as a whole has had little ability to enforce its legislation if the president disagrees, it is pointless to make substantial sacrifices to gain such authority. In sum, then, the very existence of a strong presidency reduces the chances of maintaining a parliamentary majority. The two should not be seen as independent of one another. Nor should the absence of a parliamentary majority be seen only as a justification for strong presidential power, and not as an effect of presidential power. In 2006, parliament gained control over the appointment of much of the cabinet, dramatically increasing the incentives to form a majority.

If the absence of a parliamentary majority is a justification for increased presidential power, it stands to reason that the president has an incentive to prevent or obstruct the formation of such a majority. As we will see, there are plenty of examples of such behavior in Ukraine. Several efforts to form a center–right majority were foiled through pressure by Kuchma on individual members, at the very same time that Kuchma was arguing that the absence of such a majority demonstrated the need for stronger executive powers. Such behavior can only be explained by the president's stake in an ineffectual parliament. It is not clear that this incentive has diminished under the new arrangements.

All of these ways in which presidential authority undermines the construction of parliamentary majorities demonstrate why multiparty systems are seen as ill-suited for presidential forms of government.[3] With a multiparty system and a strong president, the required coalition among the parties may never occur, causing the system to break down. With a two-party system, a majority in parliament is guaranteed. If the majority party is the president's party, undivided rule is produced. If the opposition wins, there can still be bargaining between the parliamentary majority and the president over legislation.

In sum, Ukraine's strong presidency is inherently problematic for the construction of liberal democracy. It will be quite difficult to build a two-party system in Ukraine, and both logic and empirical evidence indicate the difficulty of building a functional multiparty presidential system. For multiparty presidentialism to work successfully, substantial progress must be made in the consolidation of parties, which would at least begin to make the formation of a legislative majority more likely. Does this mean that Ukraine cannot build liberal democracy with a presidential system? We will not reach so categorical a conclusion, but the problems in doing so are substantial.

In December 2004 a partial reform was adopted in which control over the prime minister and government is to be shared by the president and parliament. The division of executive power between the president and prime minister and the increased influence of the parliament over the cabinet will be substantial barriers to the reestablishment of electoral authoritarianism. Conflict between the president and prime minister, and stalemate within the executive branch, is now a more significant danger.

Parliamentary Election Laws

Even with the shift to a parliamentary-presidential system, the party system will need to be consolidated in order for the parliament to function effectively. An ineffective party system, in some authors' opinions, is even more dangerous in a parliamentary system than in a presidential system, because there is no president to fall back on when the parliament functions poorly. Moreover, it will be difficult to convince many that a parliamentary system can function in Ukraine until the parliament itself shows more promise than it has so far displayed.

A detailed analysis of parliamentary election laws will be presented in Chapter Seven. Here we summarize the argument. Ukraine's 1998–2002 election laws appear as though they were designed to elect a highly fragmented parliament, especially in light of the societal cleavages in the country. In fact, it is important to recognize that the laws were as much a result of political compromise as of conscious design.

The laws in place for the 1998 and 2002 parliamentary elections almost guaranteed not only a multitude of parties but also a multitude of independents in the Ukrainian parliament. In these elections, Ukraine used a mixed system (similar to that used in Russia) in which half of the 450 members were elected in single-member districts (SMDs), and half were elected on party lists (proportional representation [PR]). Ideally, each part of this system would provide a benefit: the PR portion would strengthen parties, and create an incentive for elites to invest in parties, while the SMD portion would provide strong incentives to merge. In practice, Ukraine got the worst of each system, not the best. The SMD portion allowed a large number of independents in, while the party list system removed pressures for party consolidation.

The SMD plurality portion of the ballot is ill-suited to Ukraine for two distinct reasons. First, as mentioned above, conditions in Ukraine are far from those required for the SMD plurality system to achieve its primary benefit, a two-party system. Regional divisions ensure that different parties will be strong in different regions, such that even if a two-party system develops in the Donbas and in Galicia, the parties will not be the same in the two regions. Thus, even if a two-party system were created in each region, coalition building would still be required. This negates the main advantage of the SMD system.

Second, the SMD system is especially pernicious in Ukraine because it undermines the building of strong parties. One of the "footnotes" to Duverger's law (concerning the tendency for an SMD election law to lead to a two-party system) is that the law applies only where parties are already strong, such that independent candidates have little chance. Such a situation accompanies SMD plurality systems in the United States and United Kingdom, but not in Ukraine. In Ukraine, prominent individuals have more of the key resources for elections—name recognition and money—than any party has. Given such a starting point, the SMD portion of the ballot tended to perpetuate that situation. With up to a quarter of the parliament consisting of independents, constructing a stable majority has been severely hampered. Keeping independents in a coalition requires a continuing series of individual inducements. This requires extensive "log-rolling," bribery, or coercion.

Fourth, while the "mixed system" was intended to give Ukraine the benefits of SMD plurality systems and proportional representation, it in fact yielded the worst of both. In part, this is due to the conditions in Ukraine already discussed, but in part it is inherent in the mixed system. The idea was that the PR portion of the ballots would help build parties, and allow the representation of minority interests, while the SMD portion would provide a strong incentive for parties to merge (or at least not to split) to succeed in that portion of the ballot. There is some evidence that this was working.[4] At the same time, it is clear that the system also contributed to the fragmentation that hampers the parliament. As already discussed, the SMD portion contributed more to the election of independents than to the coalition of parties, and the 4 percent threshold of the PR portion was so low that it further undermined party consolidation.

In sum, there are a variety of obvious ways in which Ukrainian election laws have contributed to the inefficacy of the parliament. This increased Kuchma's ability to augment his power in two ways. First, with the parliament ineffective, many people viewed increased presidential power as the only alternative to deadlock. Second, even when many in parliament became worried about Kuchma's behavior, the parliament was ineffective in checking his power. With different electoral laws, the electoral process could force parties to consolidate the broad range of societal opinion, rather than translating it wholesale into the parliament. The 2006 election indicates that this is indeed happening: only five parties entered parliament.

The Missing Dimension of Institutional Analysis: Rules on Parties and the Parliament

Given the immense political science literature on how the design of the constitution and of the electoral laws determines the nature of politics in a given country, it is surprising that little attention is given to other rules that influence party formation and consolidation. Rules governing how parties are formed and how they relate to their members exist in every country, and are so mundane that they are rarely studied in depth. In the former Soviet Union, however, we have seen these rules manipulated to serve the interests of strong presidents. Perhaps the most common ploy is to create relatively high burdens for parties to be officially registered, and to require frequent reregistration of parties, as a way to make it harder for opposition parties to stay registered. This particular tactic has not yet been used in Ukraine, but it shows how rules concerning parties can have an important effect.

In the case of Ukraine, the prominent issue is how parties relate to their members in parliament. Perhaps more destructive than any aspect of the election law has been the absence in the parliament of what is known as the "imperative mandate," in which individuals elected on party lists are required to remain members of that party, or else surrender the seat. Because the seat belonged, until 2006, not to the party that wins it but to the individual member, parties have had little ability to control their members once they are in parliament. Because they cannot "deliver" the votes that they ostensibly control, they cannot be reliable coalition partners or be treated seriously as bargainers. Their primary lever to maintain the votes of those elected on their lists is the threat to leave the individual in question off the party list at the next election. However, since many parties have not lasted more than one election cycle, that threat has not amounted to much. In essence, not only those elected as independents, but all those elected on party lists, have been independents once they enter the parliament.

This appeared to change with the new rules adopted in December 2004. Beginning with the parliament elected in 2006, members who leave their party will surrender their seats (the imperative mandate). This will not by itself guarantee party discipline because deputies may still be able to vote against the party line without actually leaving the party (there was ample evidence of this in the early days of the new parliament). But it is an important step toward strengthening the party system and facilitating the construction of majority coalitions.

The way that parliamentary business is conducted also influences the incentives and disincentives for parties to coalesce or to fragment. Typically, one would assume that parties that divide would lose resources in parliament, or at least not gain any. But because each party or "fraction" receives funding, staff, and membership on the presidium, parties that split into two receive more of those benefits as two small parties than as one big one. A strictly rational choice analysis would predict that parties would fragment to the smallest possible size in order to maximize the number of party leadership slots and staff funding available. Thus, the once-powerful Rukh split into three factions, two of which barely maintained the fourteen deputies necessary to maintain official status. The shift to a full PR system and the adoption of the imperative mandate should eliminate this problem.

To some extent, weak parties have become a self-reinforcing tendency in Ukraine. Because many parties are new, and have little to contribute in terms of money, organization, or reputation, individual politicians gain little from them. Similarly, prominent politicians have little to lose if they abandon their party. Indeed, because their party may not exist at the next election, they have little reason to invest in it. These incentives ensure that many parties indeed will remain weak, poor, and shallowly rooted in society. This further undercuts the incentives to take them seriously, and so on. This problem—the formation of political party systems where none exists—has received insufficient attention in the political science literature, in part because researchers have always assumed that parties will form spontaneously to represent societal interests. However, as many cases in the former Soviet Union and in the "third wave" more broadly indicate, strong parties do not form spontaneously in many instances. A thorough analysis of the conditions that lead to the development of strong party systems is beyond the scope of this book, but the problem is an important one. In this study, it is sufficient to note that institutional rules, such as electoral laws and the rules of parliament, can play an important role in creating the incentives for political elites to build strong parties as opposed to pursuing other avenues of influence. The adoption of a fully proportional electoral law will certainly channel more political activity into parties, but this will not necessarily lead to strong parties. They might still be created by powerful individuals for a given election, and then neglected.

Power Politics and Weak Institutions

In Ukraine, as in any other state, political disagreements are resolved through the application of power of various types. In some cases, what counts as power is strictly limited by law. For example, in a legislature, power is defined primarily by the number of votes one can muster. In other cases, there is almost no limit on what counts, as occurs in cases of civil war. If we are to understand the potential for genuine democratization in Ukraine, it is essential to understand how institutions and power are linked to one another.

Above all, it is important to recognize that institutional rules and raw power are interdependent. While in a stable rule-governed state it seems that rules define what counts as power, it is also the case that power defines how the rules are written. To take an example from perhaps the most rule-governed and stable polity in the world, power in the U.S. Senate is defined by rules that accord each senator one vote, and that allot two senators to each state. Why does a state such as Alaska with fewer than a million inhabitants have the same representation as California, which has 34 million, making the U.S. Senate one of the least representative elected bodies in the world? The answer is based on the distribution of power over 200 years ago, when neither California nor Alaska was a state: At the Constitutional Convention in 1787, the small states had the power to scuttle the formation of a new constitution unless some nonrepresentativeness was built in to augment the power of small states.[5]

To take a more recent example from the United States, rule changes on the legality of certain types of campaign contributions (known as the McCain-Feingold law) have altered the power that different actors are able to exert in the system. In turn, those rule changes were the result of a certain constellation of political power.

In the post-Soviet states, institutional rules are confusing, poorly enforced, and often incomplete. This situation resulted from the transition from Soviet rule. It was impossible to change the rules over night, yet the rules in place from the Soviet period were ill-suited to running any kind of democracy. The rules, therefore, became less relevant.

The key question in such cases is: how are disputes resolved in institutionally weak environments? The answer has to do with power. What other resources can actors bring to bear to have ambiguous rules interpreted in their favor, or to rewrite rules in their favor, or to gain the most of whatever resource (such as votes) is defined as legitimate power by the rules?

In Ukraine, these different resources lay disproportionately in the hands of the president of the country, and in the second half of the 1990s, President Kuchma was able to take an initial advantage in power and expand it considerably. He used his de facto (informal, "practical," rather than theoretical) power to institute rules that gave him more formal powers. He was able to use those formal powers to gain informal power, and so on, in a self-reinforcing cycle.

Imbalance of power is the fundamental factor that has prevented Ukraine from becoming a liberal democracy, and that must be overcome in the post-Kuchma era. Moreover, rather than having a dominant equilibrating or "balancing" tendency, in which smaller power centers in society tend to ally to challenge a potentially dominant actor, in Ukraine the tendency is toward concentration, rather than balance, of power. Those with de facto power use it to change the formal rules (to gain more de jure power), and those with de jure power use it to acquire de facto power. Equally important, many independent actors will choose to side with the stronger power rather than the weaker, calculating that it is better to join the winner and share in the spoils than to challenge him and risk losing everything. As a result, the powerful become more so, and those with lack of access to resources find themselves increasingly shut out.

The president's power in Ukraine stems from his control over the executive branch, which is by far the most developed of Ukraine's three branches. Because it is charged with executing and administering the laws of the country, the executive branch can alter the incentives of other actors. The inability of the legislature or the courts to check presidential power stems in part from the fact that those institutions are themselves underdeveloped, and in part from the fact that they control very little in the way of direct means of influence over other actors. For this reason, the restructuring of powers between the president, prime minister, and parliament that followed the Orange Revolution is essential. Even if the president and prime minister both seek to use their executive powers to coerce other actors, they are likely to work against one another. A brief summary of the executive's de facto powers below, which until 2006 were held solely by the president, will suffice to make the point, and the problem will be examined much more closely in Chapter Nine.

- *Law enforcement:* The executive branch controls law enforcement in the country. This makes it possible for politically motivated selective law enforcement to bolster the president's position and undermine that of those who oppose him. Not only can the president instigate unfounded investigations and criminal charges against his adversaries, but he can ensure that his allies, however criminal, are spared such inconvenience. While we associate such malfeasance with President Kuchma, there have been credible accusations of such protection by President Yushchenko as well.[6] Both of these tactics can induce self-interested elites to either support the president or at least avoid obstructing his plans.

• *Administration of regulations:* In addition to criminal law enforcement, selective enforcement of all types of civil codes from building and fire codes to taxes can have much the same effect. The president can harass opponents with administrative investigations, charges, hearings, and fines, while allies can be given a "free ride" in Ukraine's burdensome regulatory environment. It is important to recognize in this respect that Ukraine's notoriously complex tax code and regulatory regulations make selective enforcement a much more powerful tool. Because of the complexity, which international organizations such as the World Bank have consistently complained about, it is nearly impossible for a firm to be in total compliance with every regulation at all times. Hence, there is a built-in reservoir of charges to be leveled against the economic interests of any adversary of the administration. Selective law enforcement therefore often does not require falsification of evidence or false charges, either of which could run into trouble with assertive judges. Instead, by creating a system where everyone is guilty of something, all the power lies in the hands of those who decide whom and what to investigate, and whom to prosecute. Under Kuchma, these powers were firmly in the hands of the president. They will now be divided between the president and prime minister, though how this will function in practice is unclear. They have played an important role not only in undermining the financing of rival movements and in creating economic incentives for individual politicians to support the president, but also in stifling the free press. Independent and opposition news outlets have been among the most notorious targets of arbitrary enforcement of arcane regulations, often with devastating effect.

• *Control over the media:* Under Kuchma, the presidential administration was able to control the media not only through selective enforcement of regulations, but through state ownership of a substantial portion of the most widely available media in Ukraine, most notably major television and radio stations. In media owned by the state, Kuchma was able simply to appoint managers and editors who guarantee favorable coverage both in the amount given the president versus the opposition and in the content of that coverage. Perhaps the most significant change in Ukrainian politics since the Orange Revolution has been the genuine freeing of the media from government pressure. It remains to be seen if that will last.

• *Control over the election process:* The president appoints the head of the Central Electoral Commission, which is in charge of overseeing all of the country's elections. That this position is held by a political appointee obviously bodes ill for the impartial application of election laws and regulations. Ukraine actually has a fairly strong system of ensuring that observers from a variety of parties are able to monitor polling and the tabulation of returns. In 2004, a monumental effort on the part of opposition groups and international observers to take advantage of these provisions provided reliable evidence of election fraud. However, there is little these observers can do to pursue violations of the electoral law that take place in advance of polling day, and they cannot themselves decide to investigate dubious returns or declare elections invalid. Had Kuchma nominated a less loathsome candidate to succeed him in 2004, he likely would have prevailed by using methods of vote manipulation that could not be easily seen.

• *Control over patronage:* All of the above-mentioned levers yield power over elites, but a key aspect of Kuchma's ability to maintain a veneer of political legitimacy was his ability to win elections, either for himself, for parties that support him, or for referenda that changed laws in his favor. These require votes, and while control over the Central Election Commission helps to avoid investigation of skewed voting results, large-scale falsification of elections is difficult to hide. It is crucial, therefore, to be able to do at least well enough in elections to keep the scale of outright fraud manageable. Control over government jobs, and the exchange of those jobs for electoral support (otherwise known as patronage), was crucial to Kuchma's political survival. The evidence of massive and well-organized efforts to use the enormous state payroll to ensure substantial pro-Kuchma voting turnout is too widespread and well-documented to be doubted. This potential has not diminished. Yushchenko and subsequent incumbents will find themselves powerfully tempted to use the same tactics, and there remains little to stop them until a serious civil service system is put in place. Yanukovych and his successors as prime minister will have the same incentives. While outright vote-rigging appears to have diminished between the 2004 and 2006 elections, voting patterns as well as anecdotal evidence indicate that patronage is widely employed to influence voting.

State Control over the Economy

The extraordinary powers held by the executive branch might not yield such power were it not for extensive state control over the economy. Corruption in state-owned enterprises is not, of course, unique to the former Soviet Union, but the extent of state ownership in these countries makes the problem especially pernicious. Under the Soviet Union, nearly the entire economy was owned by the state, and Ukraine has privatized only slowly. In Ukraine entire firms and industries are or were owned by the state. These industries include the notoriously lucrative and corrupt natural gas sector, the arms industry, which is a major source of hard currency, and many large enterprises. State ownership yields political power in a variety of ways. First, profits can be siphoned off into the coffers of the president and his supporters, either to finance political campaigns or to buy loyalty. This can happen either on an ongoing basis or through the process of privatization. Second, while in the long-term privatization should reduce the power of the executive branch, in the short term, the ability to determine who wins prized assets, and how much they pay, can yield both political leverage and incredible financial gains for the executive. The privatization of Kryvorizhstal in 2004 to Kuchma's son-in-law and a key political ally is a good example. Third, the ability to subsidize certain state industries can either reward political allies or punish adversaries. In sum, selective application of the laws is as relevant in administering state-owned firms as in other areas of administration. One asset held by the state is especially useful in influencing parliamentarians and judges: state ownership of many of the finest apartments in Kyiv. Especially for judges, with low nominal pay, the ability of the state to offer or withdraw housing is a powerful lever. This might be a weaker lever in the case of individuals with independent sources of wealth, but, as stressed above, almost no source of wealth in Ukraine is beyond the reach of law enforcement, codes administration, and tax administration.

The post–Orange Revolution rearrangement of the executive branch will likely dilute the president's economic power more than his law-enforcement power. A range of ministries has influence over the economy, and many of these are now controlled by the prime minister and by ministers who are nominated by the parliament, rather than the president. Thus, 2005 saw battles between Prime Minister Tymoshenko and President Yushchenko for control over the economy, including over the political use of that control. While this was not the best arrangement, it was an improvement over a situation in which one actor could use these assets without any struggle. The major concern when Yanukovych returned as prime minister in August 2006 was whether his control over economic ministries would allow him to gather the extent of economic power that Kuchma had, and if so, whether he could then use this power to undermine institutional checks on his power.

The Reinforcing Nature of Political and Economic Power

Political power and economic power in Ukraine are connected in part through state ownership in the economy, which creates some possibility for those with political power to turn it into economic power. But the influence runs the other way as well. In a society in which most people are impoverished, money can be very influential. Moreover, both the status and enforcement of laws governing the use of money in politics (e.g., campaign finance laws, enforcement of bribery laws) is incredibly weak. Therefore, actors who have accumulated wealth can relatively easily convert it into political power, most notably by obtaining a seat in the Ukrainian parliament, which has been compared to the New York Stock Exchange as the center of the country's business dealings. As a result of this dual link between economic and political power, the two reinforce one another and tend to become nearly synonymous, as they have in Russia. The advantage for the wealthy in becoming politically powerful is not unique to Ukraine, as demonstrated by the Bush family in the United States, or Silvio Berlusconi in Italy. But in Ukraine there are no significant barriers to using money to gain political power, and there is an extraordinary capacity to use political power to make money.

This connection between money and political power has important consequences. Because economic power yields political power, one way to erode an adversary's political power is to attack his or her economic base. The executive branch has a huge advantage in this regard, for all the reasons outlined above. Moreover, because economic power and political power are connected, the highly concentrated nature of political power tends to cause a highly concentrated distribution of economic power, as the authorities use their power to grab more for themselves and to exclude others, regardless of whether the primary motive in doing so is economic or political. This is perhaps the key difference between states such as Ukraine and states that have achieved liberal democracy: in liberal democracies, the connections in both directions between economic and political power are loose enough so that one does not simply translate into the other, and since both economic and political power tend to be comparatively widely distributed, no one has enough power to easily seize that of others. In Ukraine, this is precisely what has happened. Kuchma's successors will be just as tempted to pursue these strategies as was Kuchma. Murky dealings in the energy sector indicated that Yushchenko's associates were quite willing to use their government power and connections to control lucrative businesses.[7]

The mutually reinforcing nature of economic and political power has gained increasing attention in the literature on comparative politics. Joel Hellman, for example, contradicts the standard assumption that the economic "losers" from the first stage of economic transition are the actors most likely to halt further reform. Instead, as Hellman shows in a persuasive cross-national study, those who benefit economically from the first stage of transition, when economic arrangements are in an intermediate zone between plan and market that yields extraordinary profits for some actors, seek to halt further reform in order to "freeze" the economy in this highly lucrative intermediate position. To the extent that they are able to do so, their continuing ability to extract monopoly rents and other extraordinary profits increases their political power. This combination of factors, he argues, leads to a "partial reform equilibrium," by which he means that partial reform may not be a midpoint in an inevitable transition, but a situation that is very stable in its own right. Powerful economic interests gain political power, and use it for further economic gain, a phenomenon that Hellman and others refer to as "state capture" by economic interests. There are some things to quibble with in applying the concept of state capture to Ukraine. Most notably, it is not clear whether economic interests captured the state or the state captured economic interests. Ultimately, to the extent that the two become one and the same, the distinction is perhaps unimportant. But it is worth emphasizing that in Ukraine, of the two sources of power, state power has come to dominate. It is easier for the state to capture economic assets or to dispossess its enemies of them than it is for wealthy individuals or groups to penetrate the state. The state dominates in Ukraine in large part because its power is concentrated so heavily in one hierarchical structure, the executive branch.[8]

A similar argument is made by Anders Aslund, Peter Boone, and Simon Johnson, referring to what they call "the under-reform trap."

> [I]t is now clear that many former Soviet bloc countries have become trapped in a rent-seeking equilibrium. Slow and ineffectual reform created the opportunity for corrupt bureaucrats and politicians to become entrenched and extract bribes from firms. High inflation offered huge temporary rents, and the longer it lasted the richer the rent seekers became. Slow privatization facilitated extortion by government officials.[9]

The Effect of a Unified State Structure

Presidential power in Ukraine is concentrated even further by virtue of the fact that Ukraine is a unitary state. In contrast to federal states, there is no division of powers between national, regional or state, and local governments. Rather, the assumption is that national laws and national level authorities supersede and overrule regional and local counterparts. As a result, there is no limit to the jurisdiction of the national executive branch, and no place for strong alternative centers of power to easily build up. Ukraine is not unique in this regard; both France and the UK have heavily centralized states (but both also have well-developed alternative centers of power stemming from other sources). The importance of federalism as a check on national power was important not only in the design of the U.S. Constitution, but in the formation of the German Constitution after World War II, in which it was argued that it would be much more difficult for authoritarianism to reemerge if alternative bases of de facto administrative power were created at the level of the *Länder* (states). We have seen the phenomenon in Russia, where Vladimir Putin successfully made the position of governor an appointed rather than an elected post, removing a major check on his power.[10]

In Ukraine, the question of federalism has been discussed in terms of the regional diversity of the country, where federalism has been seen as a way of giving greater recognition and autonomy to Ukraine's diverse regions. Many have seen federalism as a means to secession, rather than as a source of checks and balances. Nationalists and statists, therefore, including both Presidents Kravchuk and Kuchma, have placed a high priority on maintaining a unified state. Less noticed, however, is how the unified state leaves the power of the executive undivided, reaching from Bankivska Street in Kyiv down to every city, town, and village in Ukraine. One example is illustrative of the broader phenomenon. Ukraine's schools are governed by the Ministry of Education in Kyiv. The centralization of the system means that every teacher in every school in the country, not to mention the administrators and janitors, is an employee of the Ministry of Education, appointed by the president. Any of those roughly 600,000 employees can be fired if they displease their supervisor, which in some cases has been defined as voting "incorrectly." With patronage power undivided territorially, not only is the president's power massive, but there is a reduced basis for an alternative power center to be built on a separate regional patronage structure.

Similarly, the unified structure of the state concentrates the president's power over law enforcement. Rather than having federal, regional, and local police forces, every police force in the country is part of the central Ministry of Internal Affairs. The direct line of authority from local law enforcement to a politically appointed minister makes it easier for selective law enforcement to be practiced in the president's favor and more difficult for other actors to make use of this resource.

It should be clear, then, that this argument about federalism is not based on the notion that law enforcement or patronage would be less politically motivated in a federal system—there is simply no reason to believe that. Rather, the argument is that in a federal system, administrative powers such as patronage and selective law enforcement are divided between local, regional, and federal authorities, and hence there is some built-in tendency (though certainly no guarantee) for these powers to be divided between different political interests, providing the basis for competition between opposing centers of power rather than the concentration of power within a single actor or network.

Machine Politics in Ukraine

To summarize, the extraordinary informal power held in the executive branch constitutes a major barrier to the development of liberal democracy in Ukraine. This power stems not primarily from the formal institutional design of presidential powers as laid out in the constitution, but from the executive branch's de facto hold on the levers that shape the incentives of other political actors. While some powers were deliberately given to the president in the hope that a strong president would bring speedy reform, many other powers were inherited in the state apparatus left over after the collapse of the Soviet Union. A primary goal of this book is to show how the various aspects of the Ukrainian system have combined to produce the results that we see. It is therefore important to try to characterize this combination of extraordinary "informal" and "de facto" powers possessed by the executive branch.

Overall, Ukrainian politics since the late 1990s can be characterized as "machine politics," with certain analytical similarities to the practice in some U.S. cities in the nineteenth and twentieth centuries of politics that is usually linked with that term.[11] Informally, one might define "machine politics" as a form of politics in which the state is turned into a giant machine for collecting votes, such that political control is perpetuated indefinitely until some external shock causes a change in power. The term "machine" is appropriate here because there has been, especially under Kuchma, a certain logic and regularity to the operation of the system. Over time, it can become highly regularized into a nearly bureaucratic set of practices. Indeed, in several U.S. cities, the "machine" itself was viewed as the most defining political institution in the system. Specifically, machine politics in Ukraine today consists of three main features, which have endured past the Orange Revolution:

- Use of state jobs to gain votes (patronage);
- Use of selective law enforcement to punish adversaries and create impunity for allies;
- Use of control (administrative or ownership) over the economy and over law enforcement to bring in wealth either for personal gain or for reelection.

To some extent, these tactics are used even in the most liberal democracies.[12] For example, the practice of giving high government jobs to political supporters is well-established in U.S. politics. The key difference, however, is the scope. In the United States, the top levels of officials are "political appointees," while the hiring and firing of the vast majority of government employees are conducted through the civil service system, which was instituted precisely to protect against patronage politics.[13] Thus, patronage in the United States can gain a candidate the support of a relatively small number of influential, wealthy, and ambitious people, but it cannot by itself cajole massive numbers of state employees to vote in a certain way.

There are, of course, differences between machine politics in other contexts and that practiced in the former Soviet Union today. Two of these are worth highlighting. First, in the United States, politicians were always limited in their ability to control the press. The muckraking tradition in American journalism coupled with the independent financial base for many newspapers made it more difficult to control the press, and there were virtually no state-owned media. So while there were always pro-machine newspapers, opposition newspapers, often with financial support from beyond the jurisdiction of the machine, continually challenged the machines.

Second, and perhaps more important, the most powerful political machines in U.S. history were always based in a single city, and could therefore always be challenged from outside. There was never a successful attempt to build a nationwide political machine in the United States. Such a project was inherently limited not only by the political diversity of the country, but by the relatively limited role of the state in the economy, and by the presence of a federal system, which produced alternative bases of power. Because political machines in the United States were locally based, they were often challenged by law enforcement either at the state or national level, which were beyond the machine's control.

In Ukraine, while Kuchma's ability to control the press was nearly complete, it was not enough to preserve his machine's power. Ukraine's regional diversity, so widely viewed as a barrier to democracy, emerged in 2004 as a source of liberal democracy: no matter how much power Kuchma accumulated over the press and over people, the western part of the country simply was not going to vote for a machine boss from Donetsk.[14] Similarly, the fact that an entire region of Ukraine detests Yushchenko is an important barrier to his becoming too powerful.

The Nonrevolutionary Nature of Political Change in Ukraine

If it was so easy for Ukrainian elites to maintain and consolidate their power following the collapse of the Soviet Union, two related questions arise. First, how did this machine come into being? Second, how did this machine develop in countries such as Ukraine, Kyrgyzstan, and Russia, while other post-Soviet states (e.g., the Baltic republics) as well as other postcommunist states developed more open and liberal democracies? The answer to both questions lies in the nature of the transition from communist rule.[15] In Ukraine and most of the other post-Soviet states, the primary transition in 1991 was to national independence. In terms of politics, and especially in terms of institutions, change was evolutionary rather then revolutionary. The effort to build a separate state trumped the effort to completely change the political institutions, the structure of the economy, and the political elite in the country. The assumption made by many external observers as well as many inside the country was that those changes could be made over time once the new state was set up.

However, as the discussion in the previous chapter indicated, overturning authoritarianism did not produce an automatic transition to democracy. Further liberalization did not occur automatically. In Ukraine, the Soviet elite maintained most of their power after August 1991, and they had little interest in a thorough reform of the system. In contrast, the more liberal elements of society, such as the "national democrats," did not gain substantial power in 1991. Nor did these "national democrats" put a high priority on liberalization. They focused instead on establishing sovereignty, building the state, and strengthening national identity. Thus, a door was opened in 1991, but for various reasons Ukraine was unable to walk through it. Once a new system began operating, that door had closed by 1995. In other states, such as Poland, the Czech Republic, and the Baltic states, the fall of communist regimes was seized upon quickly. Roundtable talks were held, new constitutions were written, and new authorities were elected. In some of these states, rapid regime change was combined with rapid change in economic ownership, which also tended to distribute power away from those who had always held it. As a result, powerful constituencies for further reform developed in these countries. In Ukraine and similar cases, power remained in the hands of those who sought to block reform altogether or to create partial reforms that created vast opportunities for enrichment.

The comparative politics literature on transitions has focused increasingly on the *process* of change, rather than on the structural prerequisites. Karl and Schmitter contend that "the mode of transition from autocratic rule is a principal determinant of whether democracy will emerge."[16] Various researchers have focused on the role of "founding elections" in promoting further liberalization.[17] Simply put, the sooner new elections (especially parliamentary) are held after a change in regime, the more likely it is for further reform to occur. The logic of such an argument is simple. At the time of the regime change, the existing elite has been rejected and is often in disarray, especially if it has been organized by a communist party that is now defunct or banned. At this time, the playing field between new parties and regrouping old forces is relatively level. However, the longer the old forces are left in power after the regime change, the more able they are to reorganize, to close off access to new parties, and to write rules that advantage themselves.

A similar argument is made by Hellman and others about economic change. Hellman finds that the biggest backlash against reform occurs not in countries that liberalize quickly, but in those that liberalize slowly. In countries where economic reform comes quickly, constituencies develop that benefit from the new arrangements, and seek to defend them and push them even further. Thus, even in states such as Poland and Hungary where leftist (reformed communist) forces returned to power in subsequent elections, they made little effort to turn back liberal reforms. In contrast, countries that reformed slowly developed an economic "gray area" between plan and market that allowed well-placed actors to get richer than they could either in a fully planned or fully marketized system.

A prominent example in Ukraine was the de facto liberalization of the money market combined with profligate monetary policy and a continuation of low-interest government loans to firms. Those who had access to low interest loans during high inflation could easily convert the loans into dollars. They could then wait until the Ukrainian currency depreciated further. Once this happened, a fraction of the dollars were sufficient to pay off the loan in devalued karbovanets. The currency trader could pocket the difference. When inflation was running 100 percent per month, those with access to government loans could double their money in a month (while passing the costs to the state budget). This could occur only with this transitional mix of market and nonmarket mechanisms, and with bad monetary policies. Those with access to these loans had powerful incentives to prevent either full liberalization or a return to state planning, and once this system started, they had a lot of money with which to influence politicians.

Why was there no fundamental political revolution in Ukraine in 1991 to go along with the revolution of national independence? A good deal has been written on this question, and only a sketch has been provided here. The simplest explanation is that forces supporting both independence and reform felt that they could not pursue the two goals simultaneously. Given this dilemma, they had to give first priority to establishing independence. From Ukraine's previous bid for independence at the end of World War I, many had taken the lesson that division among Ukrainians was fatal to the cause of independence. So when a group of leading communists, led by Leonid Kravchuk, was willing to take Ukraine into independence in return for an evolutionary change in domestic politics and economics, nationalists and national democrats took the deal.

This was probably not unreasonable, for it did not appear at the time that nationalists by themselves would have the power to seize the state and gain independence from the Soviet Union. Indeed, had the nationalists first taken over the state, support for independence in parts of Ukraine might have been much lower. So while much of Ukraine's lack of reform can be traced to the tactical decision made by nationalists to sacrifice a political revolution to guarantee national independence, they should not be judged too harshly, because this was probably the most they could get in 1991. This dilemma was not faced by liberalizers in the Baltic states, where support for independence was much less contested than it was in Ukraine. For this reason, many authors point to Ukraine's fragmented or weak national identity as the reason for its lack of deeper economic and political reform. While this explanation is sometimes overemphasized, there is undoubtedly some validity to it, especially in considering the options open to political reformers in 1991.

Because Ukraine's independence left most domestic arrangements intact, the old elite had little trouble in transferring their power resources from the old system to the new one. Ironically, the new arrangements actually magnified many of their existing powers. For example, without rapid privatization, Soviet-era factory managers simply became post-Soviet factory managers. But with a partially marketized economy and ties to the world economy, they now had options for enrichment that did not exist previously. In the confused legal environment of the early 1990s, they could sell assets abroad for hard currency and pocket the proceeds. Or they could privatize assets to themselves and their close associates at cut-rate prices. Similarly, state bureaucrats in the old system simply moved to the new system, but the partial liberalization of the economy gave many of them vastly increased opportunities to demand bribes and kickbacks. Most significantly, perhaps, there were no new parliamentary elections until 1994. This gave existing elites plenty of time to make the transition to the new system, and to put rules in place that would make it more difficult to oust them. This helps explain why there was essentially no change from the law used to elect the Soviet parliament to that used to elect the first post-Soviet parliament in 1994.

The maintenance of power was closely intertwined in economic and political spheres. Powerful business people used their money and their patronage to secure spots in parliament. State officials used their power over firms, universities, tax collection, and so on, to accrue great wealth. The inability of the new state to govern itself meant that bureaucrats used their official authority largely for their own enrichment. Even schools and universities were subject to the trend, as school officials sold everything they could, from entrance spots to diplomas, and pocketed the proceeds. While privatization of firms proceeded slowly in Ukraine, privatization of the state took place quickly and thoroughly.

Summary

This chapter has laid out a general scheme of the problems in Ukrainian politics. To recapitulate, the origins of the system lie in the concentration of political power in the Soviet system, which was transferred largely intact to the executive branch in independent Ukraine. This initial predominance of executive power has been maintained and exaggerated by the inability of the parliament to provide a sufficient institutional counterweight. Initially, this was due to ideological fragmentation as well as to the electoral law. At the root of the system is the concentration of de facto political power in the executive branch. It is not yet clear that the political and institutional changes ushered in during the Orange Revolution will cure these fundamental problems, but there is reason for hope.

4

The Evolution of Ukrainian Politics, 1989–2006

Many strands of institutional analysis focus on "path dependence," the notion that choices made at one time limit the range of choices down the road. In other words, once society chooses and moves along one path, it cannot go back to choose a different path. To the extent that this is true, understanding the historical evolution of Ukrainian political institutions is essential to understanding how Ukraine has gotten to its present state and why certain alternatives are difficult to achieve.

Adam Przeworski has straddled this argument. The main thesis of his important book *Democracy and the Market* is that countries in postauthoritarian transitions are all in the same situation because events in them "are determined by a common destination, not by different points of departure."[1] Przeworski also admits, however, that new institutional arrangements almost always reflect the existing balance of power.[2] We see this clearly in Ukraine, where the distribution of political power in 1991 was very different from that in most of the East European states at the time of their "revolutions" in 1989. In Ukraine, power was still held almost entirely in the hands of the Soviet bureaucracy, and opposition groups were weak.

This chapter therefore serves two purposes. The first is simply to provide an overview of the emergence and evolution of Ukrainian politics and political institutions since 1989.[3] This overview should be useful especially to readers who have limited familiarity with these events. The second purpose is to try to connect in a single coherent narrative events that in subsequent chapters will be dealt with in distinction from one another for analytical purposes.

The most important theme of this chapter is that there was not a political revolution in Ukraine in 1991 when the Soviet Union collapsed. To state the case so starkly perhaps exaggerates the point, but it is necessary to qualify the widespread assumption that August 1991 marks a fundamental watershed in Ukrainian politics. In 1991, Ukraine suddenly became independent of Moscow and took an increasingly independent course. However, in the

1990s political change in Ukraine was as much evolutionary as revolutionary. Moreover, while there has been considerable evolution away from strictly Soviet institutions and forms of politics, that evolution has occurred not as a break from those institutions and forms, but as a modification of them. Speaking in 2001, Leonid Kuchma said, "Ukraine virtually lives in accordance with the laws of the former Ukrainian Soviet Socialist Republic."[4]

Two examples, which will be discussed in more detail below and in subsequent chapters, illustrate this basic theme. First, Ukraine's Soviet constitution remained in effect until 1996, when a new one was adopted. While the old constitution was amended repeatedly between 1991 and 1996, that course of action (amendment of the Soviet constitution rather than rejection of it) meant that both the process of the amendments, and the overall constitutional framework, continued to be constrained by the Soviet document, which cannot be considered "neutral" in any respect. Even the new 1996 constitution was adopted according to the methods prescribed in the Soviet version. This requirement had important effects on which actors had a say in the process and which did not. This stands in stark contrast to the "roundtable" talks held in some other postcommunist societies to open up the political process and to start from scratch in designing postcommunist constitutions.

Second, in part because the Soviet constitution remained in force, the *Verkhovna Rada* (literally "Supreme Council," or parliament) that had been elected under the Soviet regime in 1990 remained in office until 1994. Therefore, in both the institutional form and the personnel inhabiting key positions, there was no break at all in the legislature of Ukraine. It was this group that inhibited many proposed reforms in the early 1990s, and chose not to change the election law for 1994. Those interests continued to obstruct reform. In other words, the decision to retain Soviet institutional forms and personnel after independence in 1991 was not only a decision to change things gradually, but a decision to limit how far reform might go. These choices were not made by misguided reformers, but by self-interested actors who were already in power in the late Soviet era. That elite was never ejected from power. Just as scholars of U.S. politics attribute much concerning the current political arrangements to the decisions of "founding fathers" more than two centuries ago, the actions of elites of the late Soviet and early post-Soviet era have continued to condition politics in Ukraine.

The Demise of Soviet Rule in Ukraine, 1989–1992

After coming to power in 1985, Mikhail Gorbachev slowly loosened the constraints on political discourse in the Soviet Union. Gorbachev sought to use criticism of the existing system as a way to overcome the tremendous bureaucratic inertia that was impeding his efforts to restructure the economy (perestroika) and acceleration of economic growth (*uskorenie*).

In Ukraine, that inertia was immense. In many respects, Ukraine and the Communist Party of Ukraine (CPU) can be viewed as the birthplace and stronghold of Brezhnevism, the conservative and corrupt form of government that Gorbachev was trying to overcome. Brezhnev had risen through the party ranks in Dnipropetrovsk, as had Volodymyr Shcherbitsky, the conservative head of the CPU and member of the Soviet Politburo.[5] The leaders of reform in the Soviet Union came out of Moscow and Leningrad (now St. Petersburg). In contrast, Kyiv, Dnipropetrovsk, and other Ukrainian cities were controlled by old style conservatives who were very effective at preserving their privileges even as economic growth slowed.[6]

Perhaps the most important aspect of the Soviet form of government, when considering it as a basis for a democratic successor, is that the Soviet system was based on the monopoly of power by the Communist Party, rather than a system of checks and balances.[7] On paper, the Soviet Union had executive, legislative, and judicial branches. But there was no doctrine of the separation of powers. The opposite doctrine, unity of power, prevailed. Institutionally, that monopoly on power was exercised through a massive state bureaucracy, which was controlled by the powerful vertical authority structures of the Communist Party of the Soviet Union. There were no horizontal checks. This bureaucracy was passed intact from the Soviet Union to independent Ukraine, where it came under the control of the president.

Along with a hypertrophied executive structure, the Soviet Union possessed a weak and politicized judicial branch. Following Soviet insistence on monopolized rather than divided power, the judiciary was seen as serving, and not constraining, executive authority. In neither theory nor practice was there any notion that the judiciary protected citizens from the government or served as a safeguard against abuse of power. This institution as well was passed intact from Soviet to post-Soviet Ukraine.

Political power in the Soviet Union was legitimized by pseudodemocratic legislatures such as the USSR Congress of People's Deputies and the Verkhovna Rada of Ukraine. While these legislative bodies had little real power under Brezhnev, under Gorbachev they started to gain legitimacy as elections became more competitive and the Communist Party's monopoly on control weakened. In the Baltic states initially, and later in Ukraine, nationalists sought seats in republic-level parliaments as a way to pressure Soviet elites. But while these legislatures were used by opposition politicians to undermine the Soviet regime, they were not set up to be organs of democratic governance.

In elections held in 1990, candidates critical of the Soviet regime captured roughly 125 seats in the 450-seat Ukrainian parliament, despite the fact that the Rukh movement was registered too late to participate.[8] In popular terms, this performance was seen as a great success. In institutional terms, however, the result was fundamentally conservative, for the process would continue to be controlled by the existing elite. While this election can be seen as marking the "beginning of the end" of the communist monopoly on power in Ukraine,[9] it also marks the beginning of the process by which members of the old elite transformed the system without surrendering their positions in it. As Wolczuk points out, the Communist Party actually increased its representation in the parliament in this election.[10] Roeder emphasizes that "*The most important determinant of the subsequent development of these* [post-Soviet] *institutions was the composition of the parliamentary body elected in 1990.*"[11] Thus, the fact that opposition forces showed their growing strength was less significant than the de facto majority retained by orthodox forces.

Attitudes in Ukraine toward the Soviet government in Moscow remained ambiguous. In a spring 1991 referendum, Ukrainian voters declared themselves to be in favor of both Ukrainian sovereignty and continued membership in the Soviet Union. This contradiction in views continued to characterize both public and elite opinions after independence. Nonetheless, the parliament became the center of "official" criticism of the Soviet government and the one institution of the Ukrainian government open to political opposition.

The government of the country was characterized by a parliament with little experience and a powerful bureaucratic apparatus. As Ukraine began to take a line distinct from that of Moscow in 1991, and to gather to itself more and more of the powers previously held by the central government, the speaker of the parliament naturally emerged as the de facto head of government and head of state. Once the Communist Party dissolved, there was no check on the executive branch.

Even prior to the coup attempt in Moscow in August 1991, Ukrainian opposition leaders, dominated by the nationalist opposition movement Rukh, faced a dilemma. Ideally, Rukh would have preferred a revolution in which Ukraine became independent from Moscow and the existing elite was overthrown in Kyiv. However, because the communist elites were still well entrenched, they could not be overthrown, and their support was crucial to obtaining independence. If declaring independence meant that the elite would be ejected from power, then they would have no interest in it. The reformers' dilemma only intensified with the crisis in Moscow.

The elites had their own interest in breaking away from Russia. To the extent that the Soviet and Russian governments were coming under the control of serious economic and democratic reformers, it was in the interest of economic and political elites in Ukraine and the other republics to separate themselves from Russia. They did this not as an act of rebellion or revolution, but as a reactionary effort to preserve and extend their control over economic and political power in their regions. For Ukraine's elite, independence was a way to resist the unwelcome reforms being forced on them by Gorbachev. Thus, in the Ukrainian parliament, many deputies associated with the *nomenklatura* voted for independence, with only those most strongly committed to the unity of the Soviet Union and the preservation of communism opposing it.

Well aware that previous efforts to obtain Ukrainian independence had failed in large part due to the inability of the Ukrainians to form a united front, Rukh and others acquiesced in an implicit deal that allowed the existing elite to remain in power, at least temporarily, in return for a decisive break with Russia. In retrospect, it is possible to trace the lack of genuine reform that plagued Ukraine after 1991 to this decision, but it is not clear that the opposition had a better choice. Given the uneven strength of the opposition movement across the country, it seems unlikely that an effort to oust the ruling elite would have succeeded, and the result might well have been that neither democracy nor Ukrainian independence were achieved. Taras Kuzio argues that given Ukraine's weak national identity, there was no basis for a national revolution in 1991. Instead, he contends, nation-building would have to follow rather than precede national independence.[12] It therefore made sense to achieve independence on whatever terms were available. Moreover, it seemed reasonable to believe that separation from Russia would inevitably lead to democracy in Ukraine, since many believed that communism and authoritarianism were imposed from Russia, and had little indigenous support in Ukraine.

The groups that spearheaded the drive for independence were more concerned with the nationalist agenda than with the democratic agenda. Almost all of these groups were based in western Ukraine, and among their leaders were many former political prisoners who had been sent to the gulag primarily due to their nationalist activities. There was no contradiction between the national agenda and the democratic agenda—in many ways they were complementary. The freedom of Ukrainians to worship as they wished and to publish their political views was closely related to the national agenda. But in cases where the two agendas did conflict, the national agenda was likely to triumph.

The strategy of the Ukrainian elites is also worth noting, because they did not simply react to changing circumstances, but actively took advantage of them. By allying themselves with the nationalists in declaring independence, they were able to rid themselves of oversight from Moscow, thus acquiring full control over the economic and political resources of the republic. The success of the communist elite in co-opting many of the dissidents' demands was ruefully acknowledged by Vyacheslav Chronovil in 1991, when he was asked during the presidential campaign about the differences between his platform and Kravchuk's. He replied, "Nothing. Except that my program is thirty years old, and Kravchuk's is three weeks old."[13] By rejecting communist power (and banning the CPU), cagier elements of the entrenched elite gained credentials as nationalists and as reformers, and created at least some outward signs of a genuine revolution. They remained in full control of all economic and administrative levers, which meant that they, and not the national democrats, would control the pace, scope, and direction of any future changes in the country. This turned out to be crucial. As Roeder says of all the post-Soviet states: "The institutions employed in 1990 for 'democratization' of the Soviet system allowed politicians to shape the means by which they would be held accountable for their actions."[14]

In the election held in December 1991 for a president of the new country (a newly created position, to be discussed below), in which the leading candidates were Leonid Kravchuk, the sitting speaker of the Verkhovna Rada and Vyacheslav Chornovil, the leader of the Rukh movement, Kravchuk defeated Chornovil in a landslide. Kravchuk, the former ideology secretary of the CPU, showed how effectively the old *nomenklatura* could make the transition to new *nomenklatura.* By not only quitting the Communist Party but also jumping to the pro-independence movement, and declaring independence, Kravchuk managed to disassociate himself from his recent past, and to recast himself as a moderate nationalist. The ease with which Kravchuk made the transition is shown by the fact that in the 1994 presidential election, he gained large majorities in the parts of western Ukraine that voted almost unanimously for independence. Other elites throughout Ukraine did the same, embracing the notion that communism had been imposed from without and that they had had little to do with it, a myth that they bolstered by rapidly surrendering their party memberships. The Verkhovna Rada banned the CPU.

Institutionally, the evolution of the Ukrainian state apparatus from August to December 1991 laid the groundwork for problems that continue to plague the country to this day. As has already been mentioned, independent Ukraine inherited from Soviet Ukraine what appeared to be a pure model of parliamentary government. With no formally identified prime minister, the speaker of the parliament emerged as the de facto head of government, and there was no head of state. Following the declaration of independence, there was a rush to create all the formal trappings of a state, to leave no doubt domestically or internationally that this was a truly sovereign state that would have state-to-state relations with other states, including Russia.

In the fall of 1991, there were genuine doubts as to whether the state would actually become fully independent of Russia. The international community was withholding recognition until after the December independence referendum, and the Yeltsin government in Moscow was working feverishly to prevent complete state sovereignty for Ukraine. Ukraine's new institutions were thus created in haste. The primary goal was not to design the institutions of an effective liberal democracy, but to create the most convincing presentation to the international community that this was indeed an independent state. Therefore, the office of president was created as an official trapping of an independent state. Also in the fall of 1991, the office of prime minister was created to head the government, which meant that in a matter of months Ukraine went from having no separate head of the executive branch to having two.

Over the next decade, conflict between the president and prime minister over prerogatives plagued the exercise of executive power in Ukraine. In creating two powerful new offices, no workable constitutional provisions were made for either of the new offices or for the existing organs that were presumably giving up some responsibility to them. Thus from 1991 until the establishment of the 1996 constitution, Ukraine had a four-headed government, with executive authority unclearly divided among president, prime minister, parliament, and parliamentary speaker.

The creation of the institution of the presidency did not occur in a vacuum, a theme that recurs often throughout this book. Many members of the Verkhovna Rada, while understanding that a head of state was necessary, were concerned about surrendering their prerogatives, which at that point were enormous. Therefore, in creating the presidency, they instituted important levers by which the parliament could maintain control over the government. These included the parliamentary right to veto executive decrees, the right to override a presidential veto with only a simple majority vote (which effectively means no presidential veto), the right to reject the appointment of key ministers, and the right to dismiss the entire cabinet. The president had no right to dissolve the parliament or call new elections.[15] Kravchuk complained to the parliament: "You want to put the president in a position where he would be walking around like a puppet, consulting with everyone about what he should do. That is not appropriate."[16]

The institution of prime minister was created to divide executive power even further. While the president would be head of state, the day-to-day workings of the executive branch would be controlled by the prime minister, who would be responsible to both the president and the parliament. This experiment with a "hybrid" presidential-parliamentary system was disastrous, despite being superficially based on the successful French model.[17] Because

the prerogatives of the separate offices were not clearly delineate
was still no new constitution) and because there was, moreover, no fu
ing court system to sort things out, there ensued a pitched battle for c ..trol over the prime minister and the cabinet, with the prime minister trying to carve out some space for independence while the president and parliament each sought greater control at the other's expense.

The experience of Leonid Kuchma, prime minister from October 1992 to September 1993, illustrates the nature of the problem and shows why Kuchma, upon becoming president in July 1994, resolved to subordinate the prime minister to presidential authority, a task that took him a further four years. In mid-1992, the parliament forced out Vitold Fokin as prime minister because he was seen as too close to President Kravchuk. Kuchma was chosen because he was viewed as being more independent of Kravchuk, and therefore more easily controlled by the parliament.[18] Instead of having a cabinet at odds with parliament, Ukraine now had a cabinet at odds with the president, which worked no better. Kuchma, as prime minister, sought independence from both overseers. In November 1992, he persuaded the parliament to grant him special powers for six months to enact drastically needed economic measures. He was given the power to issue decrees (subject to parliamentary veto) thus acquiring in important respects more power than the president, to whom he reported. Simultaneously, however, the parliament granted itself greater authority over selection of ministers and gave the cabinet authority over some functions previously held by the president. By increasing its own power over the cabinet and by giving the cabinet new powers, the parliament was seizing power at the president's expense.[19] Before long, Kuchma, at odds with both the parliament and President Kravchuk, resigned in September 1993.

In making these changes, the parliament was making essentially constitutional decisions with a simple majority vote. This parliament, it should be recalled, consisted entirely of members elected under Soviet communism, many of whose democratic credentials were dubious at best.

To summarize, two forms of continuity between Soviet and post-Soviet Ukraine are crucial for our analysis. First, there was little turnover in elites, in contrast to many of the states in Eastern Europe and the Baltics, that have had more sustained democratic transitions. Second, there was substantial institutional continuity, despite the creation of the posts of president and prime minister. These processes were controlled by the parliament, which refused to surrender its legally dominant role. Perhaps the most important distinction between the East European states and Ukraine was that in the East European states pro-democracy forces were powerful enough to force change.[20] In Ukraine, the opposition was not merely disorganized and divided, but it desperately wanted something that only the entrenched powers could grant: independence. It was thus in a much weaker bargaining position than was the case in other countries.

Given the political constellation of forces in Ukraine in 1991, "revolutionary" political change was impossible. Instead, the "new" forms of government were chosen by the same people, in much the same institutional setting, that had decided things under the Soviet regime.[21] To say that these people sought to retain their positions would understate the situation. Rather, they used their existing power to seize even more control. To speak of "institutional design," in the sense of sitting down with a blank piece of paper to figure out the "best" form of government for the country, is something of a myth even in the best of circumstances, but Ukraine did not even approach this myth.

The Road to Parliamentary and Presidential Elections: 1993–1994

The political crisis that followed Kuchma's resignation in September 1993 was resolved temporarily by an agreement between President Kravchuk and the parliament that both would stand for reelection in 1994, the parliament in the spring and the president in the summer. The outcome of these elections was a highly fragmented parliament, with the largest single bloc (but far short of a majority) controlled by the relegalized Communist Party of Ukraine. Kuchma, the former prime minister, defeated Kravchuk, the incumbent president. These elections, and especially the presidential contest, constituted the high point of Ukrainian democracy until 2006.

There were substantial shortcomings in the laws by which the parliamentary elections were conducted, but the elections themselves were widely viewed as being free and fair. The plethora of candidates (an average of more than thirteen for every seat) made it very difficult for voters to know who was a viable candidate and who was not. A large number of incumbents either chose not to run or else lost, in many cases being replaced by other elites who had accumulated the economic resources needed to triumph in the new conditions.

The 1994 elections indicated that Ukraine was moving toward competitive elections. At the time Kuchma won the presidency, there was no fear that he was not a democrat. Rather the fear was that he would be very pro-Russian, which worried many in Ukraine and in the West. This election, therefore, sets the backdrop for the key problem addressed in this book. The puzzle is not just that Ukraine became authoritarian, but that it did so after the democratic elections of 1994.

Part of the explanation lies in the parliament elected in 1994, and in the institutional gridlock that emerged. The immobility and corruption, as well as the leftist dominance, that characterized the 1994–1998 parliament, helped convince many that increased executive power was necessary for reform to succeed. The problems with parliament were in part directly attributable to the election law.

As a result of the electoral law, which compounded rather than mitigated regional divisions, the parliament elected in 1994 had no chance of forming a working majority (the problems with that law are detailed in Chapter Seven). The largest coalition, formed by the CPU, the Socialist Party, and the Agrarian Party, controlled 118 seats after the first two rounds of balloting.[22] The next largest coalition was the national democrats (Rukh and its allies), who together controlled just 35 seats. The largest "bloc" of candidates was the 163 unaffiliated candidates who had been elected solely on their local power base. This group was referred to in the Ukrainian media as the *boloto* (swamp) due to its amorphous character.[23] With the parliament ineffectual, attention increasingly focused on revising the division of power between the president and parliament.

The 1995 "Law on Power" and the 1996 Constitution

Under Leonid Kuchma, economic affairs improved slightly. While gross domestic product continued to drop, inflation came under control as the state reduced its emission of currency. Viktor Yushchenko, who at that time was head of the National Bank of Ukraine, deserved much of the credit. Yet the parliament continued to block any substantial efforts at privatization and continued to enact irresponsible budget measures.[24] To many in the West as well as within Ukraine, the problem increasingly seemed to rest with parliament. Not only was the parliament fragmented, but its largest group was leftist (the speaker, who tightly controlled the agenda, was Oleksandr Moroz of the Socialist Party). Because no one was optimistic about the prospects for a fundamental change in parliament, many, including former president Kravchuk and Kuchma, supported shifting power from the parliament to the president. Kuchma made this a high priority in his inaugural address:

> Without a doubt, the conditions, without which reforms or any movement forward are impossible, are the formation of a strong and effective state power. This envisages strengthening of a single executive vertical structure as the fundamental instrument for implementing statewide policy. At the same time, relations between all branches of power should be stabilized.[25]

His justification was that strengthening the presidency would break the deadlock between the executive and legislature and circumvent the logjam in parliament. Russia's redistribution of powers in its 1993 constitution seemed to provide a good model (leaving aside the fact that the process by which the Russian constitution was revised was of dubious legality).

The distribution of powers was essentially a constitutional question, but at this time Ukraine was still operating under a modified version of its old Soviet constitution.[26] Kuchma recognized that he was unlikely to achieve the two-thirds vote in parliament required to adopt a new constitution, and was impatient for change. So while constitutional discussions continued, he sought to pass (with the normal parliamentary requirement of a simple majority) a package of measures subsequently known as the "Law on Power," to revise the distribution of power in the system.

Kuchma proposed putting the prime minister and Cabinet of Ministers under the control of the president (the proposals are discussed in more detail in Chapter Six). The parliament, not surprisingly, rejected this plan. Kuchma, in order to pressure the parliament, threatened to take the matter to a referendum. The proposed referendum, in addition to considering the "Law on Power," would contain a vote of no confidence in the parliament. While there was no legal provision for such a vote, the parliament was immensely unpopular, and recognized that, legal or not, this referendum would give Kuchma political cover to dissolve the parliament. Under this threat, the "Law on Power" was adopted in July 2005.

A similar process was repeated regarding the constitution in 1996. With the "Law on Power" due to expire in June 1996, and progress on a new constitution moving slowly, Kuchma used the same tactics again. He put forth a draft constitution that gave the president powers roughly similar to those in the "Law on Power." When parliament balked, he threatened a referendum to adopt an even less balanced arrangement. Again, there was no legal or constitutional basis to amend the constitution through a referendum, but parliamentarians understood that, in practical terms, Kuchma could get away with this. The parliamentary speaker, Oleksandr Moroz, chose what he perceived as the lesser of two evils, and ramrodded the new constitution through parliament.[27]

At each step of this process, Kuchma went outside of the existing legal framework to force the confrontation into areas where he had greater de facto power. When he could not successfully pass a new constitution, he sought instead to circumvent the whole constitutional process by passing the "Law on Power." Then, when he could not get the law that he desired through parliament, he threatened to use extralegal means, namely, the referendum (there was no provision in the constitution for legislation via referendum).

That he ended up not needing to do so is immaterial. What is significant is that he made the threat and that it was obviously considered credible. Having succeeded in 1995 with these tactics, he used them again in 1996. The existing constitution clearly specified that the constitution could be amended only by parliament. Nonetheless, Kuchma successfully threatened to ignore that requirement if he did not get his way.

As a final measure to put pressure on the parliament, Kuchma planned to put to a referendum not the most recent draft compromise, but rather an earlier version that gave him much more power. This was a masterful tactical stroke. While he could get a very favorable constitution passed via a referendum, doing so would have provoked a substantial backlash from parliament, and may have endangered the subsequent legitimacy of the new constitution. Instead, he offered to accept a slightly less imbalanced constitution if the parliament would approve it through constitutional methods. The threat of "war" was used to achieve an agreement, which, because it was reached through constitutional means, had increased legitimacy.

The way in which the constitution was adopted was much more important than its content. Ostensibly, this was a constitutional process, in the sense that it took place within the constraints of the existing constitution. And yet, at critical junctures in the process, Kuchma was able credibly to threaten to go outside the constitutional process. This, not the advent of a constitutional order, was the key outcome. Two related points emerge from these facts. First, there is significant variation in the ability of legal rules in Ukraine to constrain actors. Second, the actors powerful enough to make the rules apply to others but not to themselves will prevail in political conflicts.

While many saw the adoption of the 1996 constitution as a triumph for Ukrainian democracy, because the new document was superior on paper to what it replaced, it was in fact the beginning of the end of constitutional government, for the process by which it was adopted showed that constitutionalism as a form of government—a form in which no actor can seriously consider disregarding the constitution—was losing ground. When the constitution can be ignored by the president, or when he can credibly threaten to ignore it, the quality and details of the constitutional provisions lose their importance.

The 1998 Parliamentary Elections

The period from the adoption of the constitution in June 1996 until the parliamentary elections of 1998 was one of great hope in Ukraine. In addition to gaining a new constitution that promised effective and stable government, Ukrainians gained a new currency, the *hryvnya*, under the supervision of Viktor Yushchenko, head of the National Bank of Ukraine. Despite these achievements, however, progress both in politics and the economy seemed unable to gain momentum.

A new "mixed" election law was adopted for the 1998 elections (the details are discussed in Chapter Seven), but it led to familiar results: the parliamentary leadership was controlled by leftist parties, but the parliament as a whole was controlled by no one. Again there was no majority coalition or party, and the parliament was fragmented into numerous small factions. By early 2000, the chaos and fragmentation would again lead Kuchma to seek to fundamentally revise the constitutional order in Ukraine.

After the 1998 election, months passed before a parliamentary leadership could be elected and the parliament could begin its work. For reasons that are still unclear, the center-right parties were unable to come to agreement. Part of this fractiousness centered on disagreement over whether to support or oppose President Kuchma. Some of the "national democratic" parties sought to form an opposition majority, while many of the independents, under the strong influence of the presidential administration, were determined to build a pro-presidential majority. Rivalry between rightists and centrists over who would gain the all-important speaker's position was also an issue. Finally, a deal was brokered between leftist and pro-presidential deputies to select Oleksandr Tkachenko, head of the small, left-wing, Agrarian Party, as speaker. It apparently took a great deal of pressure and no small amount of bribery to put together the 226 votes to install him, along with several pro-Kuchma centrists in deputy speaker slots. While the majority that put Tkachenko in power could not be sustained, no new majority could be mustered to oust him, so he remained in power. Reform would continue to lag, the parliament would continue to lack effectiveness, and the public would continue to lose confidence in the institution.

The 1999 Presidential Election

By 1999 Kuchma's leadership had become a central question, but left–right and regional cleavages continued to divide the various opposition groups. Kuchma's tactics in the months before the election showed that he had learned much from Boris Yeltsin's 1996 reelection campaign in Russia, and several of Yeltsin's campaign strategists came to Kyiv to advise Kuchma. Well in advance of the elections, efforts to control the media were stepped up. Newspapers that were critical of Kuchma had a variety of measures taken against them by the executive apparatus. It was relatively easy either to force a newspaper to close or to use the threat of such measures to persuade editors to modify their coverage. State-controlled television and radio also came under tighter control, with Kuchma given increasing coverage and his opponents largely ignored.

Opposition to Kuchma became a focal point in the campaign. Four opposition candidates, two on the right and two on the left, formed an alliance, promising that three of them would drop out and support the fourth. The four candidates were Vyacheslav Chornovil, the former dissident and leader of Rukh, Yevhen Marchuk, former head of the Security Service of Ukraine and former prime minister, Oleksandr Moroz, head of the Socialist Party of Ukraine (SPU), and Volodymyr Oliynyk, mayor of Cherkassy. The allies to some extent represented incompatible constituencies, leading to considerable skepticism that the alliance would last. It was easier to agree that an alliance was needed to defeat Kuchma than to agree who would lead it. While Oliynyk was somewhat less prominent, each of the other three had some claim to be "the" candidate, and each had long-standing presidential ambitions. No one was surprised, therefore, when the alliance collapsed.

As in 1994, the election used a two-round runoff formula. Considerable polling data, in addition to reasoned analysis, indicated that Moroz was the most likely to beat Kuchma in the second round (and probably would do so). Moroz led the Socialist Party, but was regarded as more of a "social democrat" than a socialist, and was not closely linked to the communists. This made him more tolerable to rightists and nationalists. His solid nationalist credentials and a rare reputation for honesty made him an even stronger candidate across multiple constituencies. However, he could not defeat Kuchma if he did not reach the second round. Thus, the fragmentation of forces in the first round, and especially the fragmentation of leftist forces, became crucial. Kuchma's hope was that he would face Petro Symonenko, the unreformed communist, rather than Moroz, in the second round.[28] While Moroz could compete with Kuchma for both center and right, Symonenko could do neither.

In a highly fragmented first-round vote, Kuchma finished first and Symonenko, rather than Moroz, finished second. This result is largely attributable to the steadfast unwillingness of other candidates to drop out in favor of Moroz. Again, opposition fragmentation made Kuchma's path easier. Kuchma did not simply passively benefit from this fragmentation, but rather promoted it, most notably by covertly funding the campaign of Natalia Vitrenko of the Progressive Socialist Party in order to split Moroz's socialist vote.

Securing a second-round contest against Symonenko guaranteed Kuchma's victory. Even in the western regions of the country, where he was least popular and had polled most poorly in 1994, he dominated the vote. While Kuchma was seen as bad, Symonenko was anathema to many, both due to his loyalty to the Communist Party and to his apparent support for rejoining Ukraine to Russia.

The Path to Hyperpresidentialism: The Fallout from Kuchma's Election Victory

Kuchma stated during the election campaign that, if reelected, he would seek to increase the president's power. Thus the 1999 presidential election created the scene for yet another confrontation between the president and the parliament. The immediate cause of the conflict was the parliament's refusal to reapprove Valeriy Pustovoitenko as prime minister.

According to the constitution, a newly elected (or reelected) president was required to have his candidate for prime minister approved by the parliament. Therefore, Prime Minister Valeriy Pustovoitenko had to be reconfirmed. On December 14, 1999, the parliament voted 206 to 44 in favor of Pustovoitenko, with 21 abstentions, 10 deputies not voting, and 169 members not present.[29] Because the constitution required a majority of *all* deputies (226 of 450), not just a majority of those present, for confirmation, this seemingly positive vote was in effect a rejection of Pustovoitenko.[30]

In response, Kuchma immediately threatened to discipline the parliament by reducing its powers or even dismissing it. "If there is a constructive majority let [the parliament] work until 2002. If there is no such majority, the country does not need this parliament."[31] He threatened a referendum on, among other things, a declaration of "no confidence" in the current parliament and a constitutional revision giving the president the right to dismiss parliament. Even though such a referendum seemed to contravene the constitution, the threat was taken seriously. Kuchma's close ally, Oleksandr Volkov, had already funded a campaign to collect sufficient signatures for a referendum. Kuchma's threat had the intended effect on centrist and rightist parties in the parliament, and work began on constructing a pro-presidential majority coalition. Such a coalition had always been theoretically possible, but had never materialized, due to a mix of institutional disincentives, political disagreements, and petty jealousies.

This assault on parliament was closely intertwined with another development: an effort by rightist and centrist deputies to forge a pro-presidential majority in parliament that would eject the leftist leadership team led by Tkachenko. Kuchma's desire to weaken the parliament stemmed in part from its inability and unwillingness to pass legislation acceptable to the president. The willingness of the center-right parties in parliament to make the compromises needed to form a coalition was driven in large part by their desire to avoid another constitutional showdown with Kuchma.

Both processes accelerated in January 2000. On January13, eleven center-right parties announced the formation of a coalition that would include a majority (241 of 450) of members of parliament. The coalition, led by former president Leonid Kravchuk, was explicitly aimed at becoming a "pro-presidential" majority. Kravchuk appealed to Kuchma to promise to allow the parliament to continue in its existing form. It is important to note that this appeal was made despite the fact that neither the constitution nor any law gave the president the right to disband the parliament, or any right to amend the constitution through a referendum. Kravchuk's appeal shows that even at this early stage, many in parliament recognized that extra-constitutional means were very much a part of the game.

Following the formation of the majority, two dramas unfolded. The first concerned Kuchma's plans to change the constitution through a referendum. The new majority coalition sought to persuade Kuchma that measures to weaken the parliament were no longer needed, since Kuchma now had a majority favorable to him. He was unmoved: on January 15, he signed a decree scheduling the referendum for April 16. Perhaps Kuchma was not confident that the majority would last. It seems, however, that he had already made up his mind to pursue a more decisive solution, amendment of the constitution.

The second drama concerned the struggle for domination of the parliament, which quickly spiraled out of control. On January 18, at the opening of the new session of the parliament, the new majority put to a vote a resolution electing a new leadership. The motion was passed, but Viktor Omelych, the head of the parliament's Ethics and Standing Order Committee, charged that nine electronic voting cards of absent deputies had been used. As a result, the vote was rendered invalid. It is difficult to assess the veracity of Omelych's accusation in this instance, but in general the practice of voting on behalf of absent colleagues was widely acknowledged. The new majority's effort to take control of the parliament was temporarily stymied.

When the vote to replace the leadership was declared invalid, the center-right majority coalition left the parliament in protest, depriving parliament of a quorum. In the following days, the majority coalition sought to push through changes in procedure, most notably the institution of roll-call voting, which would make it easier to vote the leadership out. When Tkachenko's team repeatedly rebuffed these attempts, the majority coalition raised the stakes. On January 21, the 241 deputies of the new majority coalition met in the Ukrainian House in central Kyiv, declared their gathering the legitimate parliament, and passed resolutions ousting Tkachenko's leadership team. The remainder of the deputies (those loyal to Tkachenko, mostly leftists) continued to meet in the parliament building, declaring that they were the legitimate parliament. The parliament effectively split in two.[32]

The split put Kuchma in a position to tip the balance of power. He was able to resolve the crisis to his liking because only the executive branch could resolve the dispute. One might expect the question of which parliament was the legal one to be a matter for the courts. Instead, the executive branch jumped into the conflict, via the Ministry of Justice. When the new majority, still meeting in the Ukrainian House, passed measures depriving the old leadership, still in the parliament building, of bodyguards, cars, and telephones, it was up to the executive to decide whether or not to implement these measures. On February 4, Kuchma signed into law two bills passed by the new majority, in effect recognizing this group, not the leftist rump in the parliament building, as the legitimate parliament.[33] On February 8, officers of the Security Service of Ukraine, along with members of the majority coalition, took over the parliament building and ejected the leftists. It was a much more peaceful version of what had happened in Russia in 1993. Initially, the leftist deputies boycotted the parliament under its new leadership, but when they realized their boycott was being ignored and that it deprived them of any influence, they acknowledged their defeat and returned to parliament.

The key factor in deciding this conflict in favor of the pro-Kuchma forces was Kuchma's control of the "means of coercion," in particular the Security Service forces that led the new majority back into the parliament building. Had Kuchma supported the other faction, he easily could have had the Security Service eject the new majority from the Ukrainian House. He could have chosen to enforce the measures passed by the leftist leadership rather than the center-right group. Had some portion of the police, interior, or military forces ignored Kuchma's views, and gone to the defense of the leftist faction, the situation might have resembled the standoffs that occurred in Moscow in 1991 and 1993. The parliamentary split, combined with Kuchma's reliable control over the executive branch, put him in complete control. This episode shows how, prior to 2004, Kuchma was able to resolve such crises to his satisfaction.

The 2000 Constitutional Referendum

The parliamentary crisis played into Kuchma's hands in his effort to force a highly questionable revision of the constitution. Despite their recent and bitter battle, both the left and center-right leaders in parliament initially opposed the referendum (in a rare display of institutional unity in Ukraine), and attempted to block it. Ex-speaker Tkachenko said that the referendum had "no other goals than installing an unlimited presidential authority, destroying the parliament, and limiting the rights and freedoms of all Ukrainian citizens."[34] First, the parliament passed a moratorium on referenda (which Kuchma vetoed). Ivan Pliushch, the new parliamentary speaker, was more restrained in his rhetoric, but opposed any changes that would require new elections,[35] and stated that the referendum was unconstitutional.[36]

Articles 155 and 156 of the 1996 Ukrainian Constitution specify procedures for amendment of the constitution, and clearly do not allow referenda as such a means.[37] Those articles specify that amendments to the constitution must first be approved by a two-thirds majority of the parliament. This had been clearly spelled out in order to avoid the situation that had arisen in 1995 and again in 1996, where Kuchma threatened to hold a constitutional referendum. Presumably, by formally setting out provisions for amendment that excluded referenda, the matter was foreclosed. That Kuchma's 2000 referendum plan succeeded, even against constitutional measures designed specifically to prevent it, is powerful evidence of the weakness of constitutional order in Ukraine.

Serhiy Holovatyi, an independent member of parliament, petitioned Ukraine's Constitutional Court, arguing that the planned referendum violated the constitution. On March 29, the Constitutional Court issued its ruling, finding two of the six questions on the referendum unconstitutional, and allowing the other four to go forward. It ruled that the president could not disband the parliament, and that the parliament could not be disbanded by a referendum. It also ruled that the constitution could not be amended by referendum. In invalidating this portion of the referendum, the court, on the surface, delivered a blow to Kuchma's plans.

But what the court took away from Kuchma with one ruling, it gave back with another, bizarre ruling. Speaking for the court on March 29, Judge Pavlo Yehrafov asserted that the referendum was binding on the parliament.[38] The "logic" behind this ruling was that since the constitution makes no provision for a "consultative" referendum, by default the referendum must be binding.[39] This was asserted by the court despite the fact that the referendum itself was based on a Soviet-era law. "This is not and cannot be a consultative referendum. It has an imperative character. The Verkhovna Rada, the Cabinet of Ministers, and the presidential administration must implement and adhere to the results."[40] In other words, the referendum could not directly change the constitution, but it could do so indirectly, by legally obliging the parliament to do so. If the people passed by referendum a resolution to change the constitution, the court ruled, the parliament was legally obligated to enact the corresponding legislation. The ruling gave Kuchma exactly what he wanted: its convoluted logic effectively allowed the constitution to be modified by referendum, despite specific constitutional provisions to the contrary.

Once the referendum was legalized, there was little doubt about how it would turn out. Polls showed large majorities in favor of all the provisions, and it is not hard to understand why. The recent implosion of the parliament, on top of widespread perceptions of corruption in the parliament, led many voters to support Kuchma's efforts to "fix" the parliament. Moreover, the

Constitutional Court ruling effectively removed the charge that the referendum was unconstitutional. The state apparatus used every means at its disposal to ensure passage of the four remaining questions, and allegations of fraud were widespread.[41] Zakarpatskia Oblast in western Ukraine reported 97.93 percent voter turnout, and over 90 percent "yes" votes on all four questions.[42] Overall, all four provisions were passed with more than 80 percent of the vote. A typical tactic was to threaten employees of government agencies, including schools, with the loss of their jobs if they did not vote "yes."[43]

With passage of the referendum, focus shifted to two problems that were envisioned immediately after the Constitutional Court's ruling: First, what if the parliament did not pass legislation to amend the constitution along the lines of the referendum? Second, the referendum did not contain actual text of changes to the constitution, or even specify which articles needed to be amended. So someone had to figure out exactly what needed to be amended (it was estimated that at least thirty-two articles should be changed) and draft the actual text of the amendments.[44] The presidential representative to parliament, Roman Bezsmertnyi, envisioned a "constitutional crisis" after the referendum," a view later shared by leader of the majority and former president Leonid Kravchuk.[45] Kuchma threatened to amend the constitution by fiat if the parliament did not do so.[46]

On July 13, 2000, Kuchma's bill to amend the constitution passed in the parliament on its first reading with 251 votes. While Kuchma's supporters were clearly pleased, the vote foreshadowed the battle to come: in order to pass on its second reading, a bill amending the constitution must have 300 votes (two-thirds of the members). Yury Murashev, chairman of Ukraine's Helsinki Committee, stated, "Attempts to blackmail deputies into amending the constitution in the name of a 'tongue-less' public are leading Ukraine down the same path as Kazakhstan, Uzbekistan, and Belarus."[47]

The Gongadze Affair

With Kuchma very close to winning his battle to revise the constitution, a crisis arose that supplanted the constitutional question on Ukraine's political agenda and halted further work on constitutional revision. On September 16, 2000, a journalist named Heorhiy Gongadze disappeared. Journalists in Ukraine had been routinely subject to harassment and intimidation, so initially there was nothing new here. When Gongadze's body was discovered, decapitated, the sense of outrage grew. Very questionable handling of the body and the autopsy created the impression that someone was trying to hide something, and suspicion focused on Kuchma's government. The true crisis did not ensue, however, until the Socialist Party leader Oleksandr Moroz released tape recordings, apparently made in Kuchma's office, in which Kuchma could be heard, in rather foul language, ordering the interior ministry to get rid of Gongadze.

The "Melnychenko" tapes, as they have come to be known (named for the Security Service officer apparently responsible for making and releasing the recordings), initiated a crisis in Ukrainian politics that really ended only in 2004. From this point on, efforts by oppositionists to oust Kuchma gained increasing prominence. The Gongadze affair represented a watershed in two respects. First, those in opposition to Kuchma became increasingly able to put aside their differences to collaborate on forcing his ouster. Second, Kuchma's popularity began a downward trend that culminated in the Orange Revolution.

However, in the short term, left–right differences allowed Kuchma to continue to divide and rule. Both left and right attacked him, but the key unanswered question was who would come to power if he were deposed. As long as the answer was Viktor Yushchenko, the nationalist and market-oriented prime minister, the communists supported Kuchma. They preferred a corrupt and authoritarian Kuchma in power to any kind of nationalist/liberal. For his part, Yushchenko steadfastly avoided forming a common front with other opposition forces, rejecting not only the hard left, represented by the CPU, but also Oleksandr Moroz's socialists and the influential Yulia Tymoshenko, who was wealthy and charismatic, but also populist and tainted by corruption. Yushchenko, Moroz, and Tymoshenko joined forces only in 2004, and when they did they brought Kuchma down.

Parliamentary Elections, 2002

The parliamentary elections that were held in April 2002 were widely viewed as a referendum on Kuchma. If parties in opposition to Kuchma could gain a majority of seats in parliament, they could begin to put serious pressure on him, not only legislatively but also by seriously investigating the allegations of his misdeeds. That would require, however, not only that these parties collectively win a majority, but that they be able to put aside their differences. The election was carried out according to the same "mixed system" that had been used in 1998, with half of the seats allocated according to party lists and half in single-member plurality districts.

The most significant development in this period was the emergence of two new political "blocs," or coalitions of parties. Kuchma and his supporters organized Za Yedinu Ukrainu (For a United Ukraine). This marked the first time that a president in Ukraine clearly linked himself with a party (though Kuchma did not declare himself to be a member). This party had all the resources of the state at its disposal, and therefore had the advantages of extensive favorable media coverage, coercion of state employees, and ample money. The party did not have a particular ideological agenda, but rather was the "party of power." Most of its candidates were government officials or businessmen close to the government. Its campaign strategy was based on using state money and state control of the media to persuade voters, and on using patronage to coerce them.

Viktor Yushchenko, former head of the National Bank and former prime minister, formed Nasha Ukraina (Our Ukraine), an alliance of previously fragmented rightist parties united primarily in their opposition to Kuchma and convinced that the best person to lead the campaign to oust him was Viktor Yushchenko. The emergence of Our Ukraine was significant in that it appeared to overcome the fatal weakness of the Ukrainian right: its tendency to split. Many felt that a united rightist bloc would win enough seats to be able to play a key role in forming a parliamentary majority, and that Yushchenko would be well placed to run against Kuchma for the presidency in 2004. Yushchenko's swelling popularity was recognized by other anti-Kuchma forces, including the SPU, led by Moroz, and the "Bloc of Yulia Tymoshenko." Yushchenko, however, was reluctant to adopt a decisively anti-Kuchma position, perhaps fearing the sort of coercion (including imprisonment) that had been inflicted upon Tymoshenko, or perhaps being reluctant to make deals that he might later regret. For whatever reason, the success of bringing the right together did not carry over into the formation of a "united front" of anti-Kuchma forces across the spectrum. This occurred only later, in 2004.

In many respects, the election was a victory for Yushchenko and a defeat for Kuchma, but again, Kuchma's control of state resources prevented the victory from being anywhere near complete. Our Ukraine considerably outpolled United Ukraine in the party list vote (Our Ukraine won 23.5 percent to United Ukraine's 12.0 percent, with the Communist Party finishing second with 20.0 percent). This implied that if they went head to head, Yushchenko could defeat Kuchma or a chosen successor. Moreover, as the winner in the party list vote, Yushchenko's bloc was seen as the "winner" of the elections, and seemed in a strong position to form a majority coalition.

The elections could be called fair only in the broadest stretching of that term. While the results were not falsified wholesale, the preelection advantages yielded by the application of state resources on behalf of United Ukraine were dramatic. They were supplemented by strategic coercion of voters, and in some cases fraud, in key places (the details of this will be discussed in Chapter Nine). It was not easy for such measures to have a large impact on the party list vote, but in close single-member district races, the ability to manipulate a few thousand votes could easily shift a seat from the opposition to Kuchma, and international observers reported a multitude of such cases, using a fascinating variety of methods.[48]

As a result of their advantage in the single-member districts, the single largest bloc of delegates turned out to belong not to Yushchenko's Our Ukraine, but to Kuchma's United Ukraine. In the ensuing battle to win control of parliament, a familiar scenario was played out. The opposition had a great deal of difficulty uniting behind a parliamentary leadership slate. At the same time, Kuchma was able to use various sorts of coercion to begin picking off members from opposition parties and winning their support for his candidate for speaker. As a result, on May 29, 2002, a pro-presidential majority coalition under the speakership of Volodymyr Lytvyn was announced.

The Orange Revolution[49]

The 2002 parliamentary elections and their aftermath helped polarize Ukraine's political landscape. The blatant use of "administrative resources" and outright fraud clarified the increasingly authoritarian nature of Kuchma's regime.[50] This helped galvanize opposition forces behind Viktor Yushchenko, whose performance in the election solidified his status as leader of the opposition.

Late that year, the Melnychenko tapes further undermined Kuchma's standing, when it was revealed that he had approved the sale of Kolchuga passive radar systems to Iraq. While it appears in retrospect that the weapons were never delivered, the revelation set the U.S. government, previously rather tolerant of Kuchma's behavior, firmly against him. It also solidified the perception in Ukraine that Kuchma was gathering power not for the purpose of building the state, but to enrich his friends.

By early 2004, two major uncertainties dominated Ukrainian politics. First, who would the "party of power" run against Yushchenko? Many suspected that Kuchma would find a way to avoid the constitutional two-term limit. An opinion was obtained from the Constitutional Court stating that, since Kuchma's first term had begun before the 1996 constitution was adopted, Kuchma's first term did not "count." Ultimately, however, Kuchma chose not to run, and instead put forth Prime Minister Viktor Yanukovych, former governor of Donetsk Oblast.

A second issue that dominated the early maneuvering was an attempt to revise the constitution to substantially reduce the powers of the presidency. In May 2004, the parliament voted on a proposal to amend the constitution to transfer many of the president's powers to the prime minister. For Yushchenko and his supporters, the plan was an obvious effort to gut the presidency in anticipation that Yushchenko would soon win that office. It was also feared that an enhanced prime minister's position would become an alternate means for Kuchma to extend his rule (with no term limit). The motion attracted the support not only of many of the pro-Kuchma factions, but also of the communists and socialists, both of which had long supported a shift to a parliamentary system. For the communists, this would represent a return of power to the soviets (councils), a long-held tenet of their ideology. However, despite all this support, a small number of deputies from the "party of power," surprisingly, defected, narrowly defeating the measure. These defections may have stemmed from Yanukovych, who assumed that he would win the presidency, and could not have been any more pleased than Yushchenko at the prospect of reducing its powers. With this bill defeated, and a very strong presidency on the line, the campaign intensified.

The campaign was full of intrigue.[51] State controlled media nearly excluded Yushchenko from coverage, while running hagiographic stories on Yanukovych. Various plans to commit voting fraud and to falsify the results were revealed well in advance. The use of open violence and judicial manipulation by Kuchma's camp to steal a mayoral election in Mukachiv left no doubt what was in store for November. By summertime, opposition leaders were planning to protest the results of the elections.[52] The intrigue climaxed in September, when Viktor Yushchenko was taken to a Vienna hospital suffering from dioxin poisoning. It remains unclear exactly who perpetrated the crime, how they did it, or whether it was intended to kill Yushchenko or merely incapacitate him, but the effect was to further polarize the situation. The last scene in the preelectoral campaign was provided by Russia's president, Vladimir Putin, who spent two days in Kyiv the week before the first round, explicitly endorsing Yanukovych and appearing along aside him at a Soviet-style military parade.

In the first round of the election, on October 31, Yanukovych was declared the winner, less than 3 percent ahead of Yushchenko, with a host of minor candidates far behind. Since neither candidate received 50 percent, the second round would be held three weeks later, on November 21. Even prior to the first round, both sides were gearing up for the protests that were soon to engulf the capital. A week before the first round, over 100,000 protestors gathered at the Central Election Commission (CEC) to demonstrate their strength and to insist on a fair vote count. Barricades were erected around the building and water cannon deployed. The very close vote in the first round indicated either that Yanukovych and his team had not yet deployed all of their tricks, or that they were in much more dire straits than anticipated. Both of those things turned out to be true.

In the second round of the election, reports of fraud streamed in from around the country from two distinct armies of observers, those trained by the opposition parties and those provided by the Organization for Security and Co-operation in Europe and related international organizations. Even publicly available information, such as the alleged 95 percent voter turnout in Donetsk Oblast, pointed to massive fraud. Early in the day on November 22, the Central Election Commission announced that Yanukovych had won, with 49.5 percent of the vote to Yushchenko's 46.6 percent. Putin quickly congratulated Yanukovych on his victory, but almost no one else was willing to accept it.

Within hours, the Orange Revolution was underway. Kyiv's Independence Square (Maidan Nezalezhnosti, which came to be referred to around the world simply as "the Maidan") filled with orange-clad protestors. While many marveled at the initiative of people to protest and at the organization of the opposition in providing logistical support, the role of various parts of the elite in spurring the protests has gone underemphasized.[53] Key groups in the elite either refrained from obstructing the protests, or sent messages guaranteeing the safety of protestors, or encouraged them in other ways. Without this participation, sometimes active, sometimes passive, the Orange Revolution might well have failed.[54]

For example, early on November 22, the Kyiv City Council, led by the powerful and popular mayor, Oleksandr Omelchenko, issued a statement rejecting the legitimacy of the elections. Besides contributing legitimacy to the protests, the statement sent a signal that protestors would not be hampered in Kyiv. There was almost no effort to prevent protestors from getting into Kyiv from around the country, from moving around the city on public transportation, or from massing in the city center. This stood in stark contrast to the 2001 "Ukraine without Kuchma" protests, which were foiled in large part by blocking roads, halting trains, and obstructing access to central Kyiv. Someone made very conscious decisions not to repeat these successful tactics. In the following days, representatives of the Security Service of Ukraine, presumably a key part of any plan to quash the protests, spoke to crowds on the Maidan, urging lawful behavior on the part of the security forces, and implying that force would not be deployed. Moreover, most of the major media outlets issued emotional announcements that they would no longer broadcast biased news, as they had been in recent years, and began giving prominent coverage to the protests.

Other elites defected in short order, leaving Yanukovych's position untenable. On November 29, Yanukovych's campaign manager, Serhiy Tyhypko resigned, admitting that large-scale election fraud had taken place.[55] On the same day, President Kuchma himself announced support for a rerun of the second round of the election, destroying what remained of Yanukovych's position.[56]

While it became increasingly clear that Yanukovych's "victory" would not stand, it was not clear how to get from the prevailing impasse to a Yushchenko presidency. Most of the key actors were committed to a solution that remained within the existing legal framework, but it was unclear how legally to invalidate the results announced by the CEC. One alternative would have been to step outside the rules, and negotiate an elite "pact" as had been done in Poland in 1989. Another would have been the seizure of power by Yushchenko's supporters, a genuine revolution. The final resolution remained within existing rules, but also had elements of "pacting."[57]

On December 3, Ukraine's Supreme Court provided a legal way forward (and struck a blow for judicial independence in the country) by ruling that the election had been fraudulent, and that the second round would be rerun on December 26. However, for that to happen, new legislation had to be passed setting the rules for the election and reconstituting the CEC. At this point, Kuchma's supporters reasserted themselves in the parliament, conditioning their votes on the necessary election legislation on constitutional changes weakening the presidency. Their proposal threatened to split the opposition. Some in the opposition, most notably the socialists, supported the constitutional changes, and therefore were happy to side with Kuchma's supporters to pressure Yushchenko. Others, most notably Yulia Tymoshenko, opposed such a compromise, and advocated using the hundreds of thousands of people in the street to force the authorities to cave in. Ultimately, Yushchenko reluctantly agreed to the compromise. This opened the path to his presidency, but also gave Kuchma much of what he had sought back in the spring of 2004. The big loser, of course, was Yanukovych, whose last hopes of gaining the presidency were fading away.

The second round was rerun on December 26, and Yushchenko won, with 52 percent of the vote to 44 percent for Yanukovych. That Yanukovych garnered such a substantial share of the vote, even after having been completely discredited, demonstrated that much of the country remained steadfastly opposed to Yushchenko, and highlighted the challenges that lay ahead of him.[58]

Post-Revolution Ukraine

The Orange Revolution led to a period of optimism in much of Ukraine bordering on euphoria (although it should be kept in mind that in much of eastern and southern Ukraine, where voters supported Viktor Yanukovych, even after his attempts to steal the election became clear, the Orange Revolution was seen as a disaster). It appeared the Kuchma and Yanukovych were decisively defeated, that Russia had finally been ejected from Ukraine's internal politics, and that Ukraine was on a short path toward membership in "the

West," potentially including membership in the World Trade Organization, NATO, and the European Union. Viktor Yushchenko was feted around the globe for his courage.

By mid-2005, however, Yushchenko was under fire. By October 2005, the "Orange Coalition" had collapsed in mutual recrimination. By March 2006, Viktor Yanukovych and his Party of Regions had risen to take the largest share of votes (30 percent) in parliamentary elections. Our Ukraine finished third, with only 12 percent of the vote, far behind the parties of Yanukovych and Tymoshenko. Negotiations to form a parliamentary majority lasted nearly four months. Yushchenko and Tymoshenko were unable to agree on formation of a cabinet. Then the Socialist Party deserted the "Orange Coalition" as well, forging a coalition with the Party of Regions and the Communist Party to elect Oleksandr Moroz speaker of parliament. However, even that coalition could not forge an agreement to form a government before a constitutional deadline passed. Yushchenko could either dissolve parliament and call new elections, or agree to form a government with his nemesis, Viktor Yanukovych as prime minister. Understanding that new elections would likely weaken his Our Ukraine party even further, Yushchenko finally agreed to form a coalition with the Party of Regions, and nominated Yanukovych to be prime minister. Less than two years after the Orange Revolution, Viktor Yanukovych was returned to the position of prime minister, with considerably greater powers than the office had under Kuchma.

The inability, or rather unwillingness, of Yushchenko and Tymoshenko to reforge their 2004 partnership alienated their supporters. The 2006 parliamentary elections devastated Yushchenko and his Our Ukraine party. In the eyes of many voters, the leadership of the reform movement had shifted from Yushchenko to Tymoshenko. Disgust at Yushchenko's willingness to form a coalition with Yanukovych rather than Tymoshenko led many to question his ability to win reelection as president in 2009.

While at the time, most attention focused on the collapse of the Orange Coalition and the anguish this caused for its supporters, two other developments were more important with respect to the analysis in this book. First, Ukrainian politics became competitive again. The 2006 parliamentary elections were the most free and fair in Ukrainian history (though patronage continued to influence many votes). Control of the parliament was genuinely up for grabs. While many in the West were disappointed at Yanukovych's resurgence, it in fact indicates that the key facet of democracy may have been achieved: the ability of those who are defeated at one point in time to continue to compete, and to have hope of winning in the future.

Second, the institutional basis for politics in Ukraine changed dramatically, due to deals reached in 2004. The parliamentary election of 2006 was carried out according to a fully proportional election law, which had a powerful effect on party formation and consolidation. Presidential power was drastically reduced, with much control over the cabinet shifted to the prime minister, and, by extension, to the parliament. The intense bargaining that followed the 2006 election was ugly, but it did not differ significantly from what Germany had experienced the year before. It was a sign of the new importance of the position of the prime minister. These changes showed some promise of removing the institutional shortcomings that had led to authoritarianism under Kuchma, as the rest of this book shows.

It remained unclear, however, how those institutions would work in practice. It will take some time to determine whether the constitutional adjustments adopted in 2004, which went into effect 2006, will solve old problems, and whether they will create new problems. The results are not predetermined but, rather, will depend in large part on the interests of powerful actors and on the power they can wield in pursuing those interests. As the conclusion will point out, many things did *not* change in the Orange Revolution.

The beginning of this chapter stressed that Ukraine did not undergo a political revolution in 1991. Perhaps the 2004 Orange Revolution provided the changes that Ukraine needed. However, one might also fear that 2004 will, in retrospect, resemble 1994, in which competitive elections appeared to herald a rapid move to liberal democracy, but led instead to a lost decade.

Appendix 4.1: Key Figures in Ukrainian Politics, 1991–2006

Chornovil, Taras—Former dissident and political prisoner, head of Rukh movement, 1989–2000; killed in a suspicious automobile accident.

Fokin, Vitold—Prime minister, November 1990–September 1992.

Kinakh, Anatoliy—Prime minister, April 2001–November 2002; previously head of the presidential administration.

Kostenko, Yuri—Head of one branch of Rukh movement after 2000 split; previously minister of environment.

Kravchuk, Leonid—President, 1991–1994; previously speaker of parliament.

Kuchma, Leonid—Prime minister, October 1992–September 1993; president, July 1994–December 2004.

Lazarenko, Pavlo—Prime minister, May 1996–July 1997; convicted in the United States and Switzerland on money-laundering charges.

Lytvyn, Volodymyr—Speaker of parliament, 2002–2006.

Marchuk, Yevhen—Prime minister, June 1995–May 1996; also head of the Security Service of Ukraine, chair of the National Security and Defense Council, minister of defense.

Masol, Vitaly—Prime minister, 1987–1990, June 1994–April 1995.

Medvedchuk, Viktor—Head of presidential administration under Leonid Kuchma; head of Social Democratic Party of Ukraine (United); leader of "Kyiv clan."

Moroz, Oleksandr—Speaker of parliament, 1994–1998, 2006; head of Socialist Party of Ukraine.

Pliushch, Ivan—Speaker of parliament, 1991–1994, 2000–2002.

Pustovoitenko, Valeriy—Prime minister, July 1997–December 1999; later minister of transportation.

Symonenko, Petro—Head of Communist Party of Ukraine, 1993– ; finished second in 1998 presidential election.

Tarasyuk, Borys—Foreign minister, 1998–2000, 2005– ; previously ambassador to NATO.

Tkachenko, Oleksandr—Speaker of parliament, 1998–2000.

Tymoshenko, Yulia—Minister for Oil and Gas, 1996–1997; deputy prime minister 1999–2001; leader of the Orange Revolution, prime minister, January–September 2005.

Yanukovych, Viktor—Governor of Donetsk Oblast, 1997–2002; prime minister, 2002–2004, 2006; presidential candidate, 2004; previously governor of Donetsk Oblast.

Yushchenko, Viktor—Head of the Central Bank of Ukraine, 1993–1999; prime minister, December 1999–April 2001; leader of the Orange Revolution; president, 2005– ; head of Nasha Ukraina political bloc.

Zviahilsky, Yukhim—Prime minister, September 1993–June 1994.

Appendix 4.2: Political Leaders of Ukraine, 1991–2006

Presidents

Leonid Kravchuk	1991–1994
Leonid Kuchma	1994–2004
Viktor Yushchenko	2005–

Prime Ministers

Vitaly Masol	1987–November 1990
Vitold Fokin	November 1990–September 1992
Leonid Kuchma	October 1992–September 1993
Yukhim Zviahilsky	September 1993–June 1994
Vitaly Masol	June 1994–April 1995
Yevhen Marchuk	June 1995–May 1996
Pavlo Lazarenko	May 1996–July 1997
Valeriy Pustovoitenko	July 1997–December 1999
Viktor Yushchenko	December 1999–April 2001
Anatoly Kinakh	May 2001–November 2002
Viktor Yanukovych	2002–December 2004
Yulia Tymoshenko	January 2005–September 2005
Yuri Yekhanurov	September 2005–March 2006
Viktor Yanukovych	August 2006–

Speakers of Parliament

Leonid Kravchuk	To December 1991 elections
Ivan Pliushch	December 1991–April 1994
Oleksandr Moroz	April 1994–March 1998
Oleksandr Tkachenko	May 1998–January 2000
Ivan Pliushch	January 2000–March 2002
Volodymyr Lytvyn	April 2002–March 2006
Oleksandr Moroz	March 2006–

5

Societal Divisions and the Challenge of Liberal Democracy in Ukraine

A great deal has been written about Ukraine's ethnic, linguistic, and national cleavages, and much of it has raised the question of whether these cleavages are an obstacle not only to democracy in Ukraine, but to the continued existence of the state. Especially in the early 1990s, a variety of well-informed authors warned of the danger that ethnic violence could rip Ukraine asunder much as it had Yugoslavia.[1] The prospect of the Ukrainian state fragmenting territorially was raised again in late 2004 during the Orange Revolution. While the threat of secession quickly subsided, the sharp regional polarization of the vote reinforced the notion that Ukraine has a deeply divided society (see Map 5.1 on next page). The effects of Ukraine's domestic cleavages on its efforts to build democracy remain poorly understood, in large part because discussions of societal cleavages and institutional design have been carried out in isolation from one another. In this chapter and the next, we show how societal cleavages and institutional design influence each other in Ukraine.

Why Are Societal Cleavages Important?

The issue of societal cleavages is important to this book with respect to four specific questions, each of which is considered in this chapter. First, what effect do societal cleavages have on the political party system? While most theories of electoral laws find that the number of "effective parties" depends primarily on election laws, a considerable minority finds that social cleavages are also important factors. In this view, a greater number of societal cleavages increases the minimum number of parties possible in a system.[2] Therefore, before discussing electoral systems in the next chapter, we need to explore the degree of societal fragmentation. Second, to the extent that cleavages exist in society, how easily are they bridged by political parties? An analysis of voting patterns in the Verkhovna Rada will examine this question. Third, to what extent do the cleavages influence the efforts of the executive branch to consolidate power? Finally, what conclusions can we draw

Map 5.1

2004 Presidential Election, Vote by Regions
Second Round Runoff

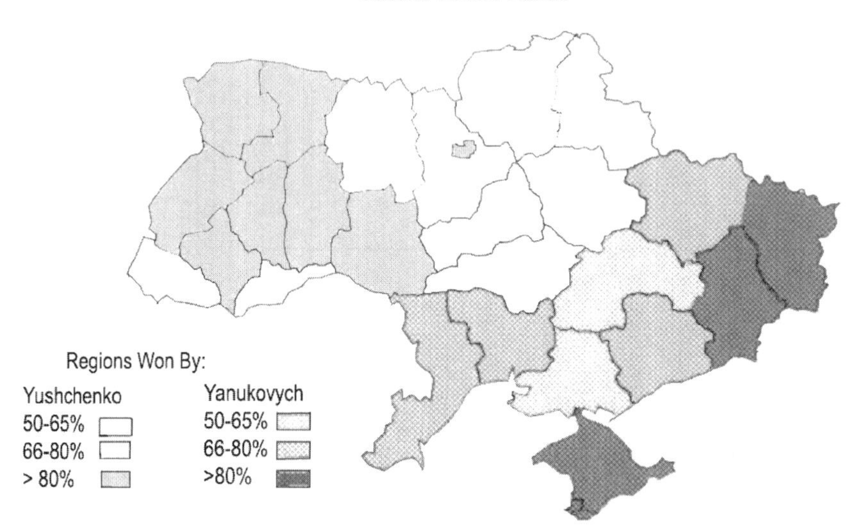

about the debate over institutional reform? Do Ukraine's societal cleavages make certain institutional arrangements more or less likely to succeed?

To summarize the chapter's findings, Ukraine's societal cleavages present significant challenges for the political system, but they do not make liberal democracy impossible or even unlikely. However, these cleavages have significant implications for what kind of institutional rules are likely to work best. Ukraine's regional differences make it unlikely that a two-party system will emerge even under the most clever institutional design. It is likely that even ideologically similar political attitudes will be represented by different parties in different regions. There is no reason why cross-regional alliances between ideologically similar parties cannot be forged by elites in parliament, and, indeed, this appears to happen more often than is commonly believed. This has important implications for institutional design. The left–right cleavage has actually been more difficult to bridge. Kuchma shrewdly exploited this left–right cleavage, relying on the fact that both left and right feared each other more than they feared him.

For institutional reform, two clear conclusions emerge from a discussion of societal cleavages. First, since a two-party system is unlikely to emerge even under very restrictive electoral laws (single-member district plurality system), it makes sense to accept that a multiparty system is inevitable and to tailor the electoral laws accordingly. Second, if Ukraine is bound to have a multiparty system, it ought to have a parliamentary form of government:

numerous authors have shown that multiparty systems are ill-suited to presidential rule.[3] If this is true (and the finding is not controversial), then Ukraine's efforts to build a presidential democracy appear doomed. Thus, Ukraine's domestic cleavages do not make liberal democracy impossible, but they probably constrain the institutional forms that it might take.

Characterizing Ukraine's Cleavages

Ukraine's ethnic, linguistic, regional, and political cleavages have probably received more attention than any other aspect of contemporary Ukraine.[4] Among the key questions asked in the literature are: (1) What is the nature of Ukraine's societal cleavage structure? and (2) What implications do these cleavages have for nation- and state-building? There is a fair degree of consensus on the nature of Ukraine's cleavage structure, but very little consensus on its prospects for the future or implications.

To simplify, we can view Ukraine as having partly overlapping regional, linguistic, and ethnic cleavages.[5] We say "partly overlapping" because there tends to be a strong, but not complete, correlation between region, ethnic identification, and language use. In western Ukraine, people are more likely to speak Ukrainian and to identify themselves as ethnic Ukrainians than are people in eastern or southern Ukraine, who are more likely to identify themselves as ethnic Russians and as Russian speakers. However, there are significant qualifications to this generalization, the most important of which is the large number of people, especially in central and eastern Ukraine, who identify themselves as ethnic Ukrainians but tend to speak Russian.

In the literature that has emerged on this topic, a considerably more nuanced view has developed. For example, various authors have developed multiregional categorizations to supplant the standard "east–west" dichotomy, which may obscure as much as it reveals.[6] The western region of Galicia, comprising Lviv, Ternopil, and Ivano-Frankivsk oblasts, is quite distinct from the rest of western Ukraine, and is not representative of that much larger part of the country, as is often assumed. Similarly, research has shown that mixed ethnic identification and mixed language use are rather common in Ukraine, complicating our views of those phenomena and of their influence on politics.[7]

Cleavages in the Ukrainian Parliament

While there clearly are significant cleavages in Ukraine, their effect on organized politics remains insufficiently explored, outside of the question of regional voting patterns. The most important question here is the extent to which Ukraine's societal cleavages explain the fragmentation and weakness of the parliament.[8] For governing, the results of elections only partly determine outcomes; the ability of elites to forge compromises across groups is essential even in homogeneous societies. Extending that question, we must ask whether societal cleavages are so deep that forming a functional parliamentary majority will necessarily be difficult or even impossible. While there has been an extraordinary amount of survey research on Ukrainian public opinion, there has been little attempt to examine how it is manifested in parliament. This is odd, since there is wide consensus that parliamentarians in Ukraine are not tightly bound by their constituents' opinions.

Two partially competing hypotheses are examined here, representing different understandings of what drives politics in Ukraine's parliament. The first hypothesis is that politics is driven by regional, ethnic, and linguistic issues. The second is that politics is driven by left–right differences. The two are not necessarily mutually exclusive. It is possible that they overlap: that people of one region or one ethnic group tend to support one end of the political spectrum. It is also possible that both are salient, but that one is more salient than the other. Is linguistic/ethnic identity stronger or weaker than left/right identity? How much?

To answer these questions, this section of the chapter examines the voting records of various political factions during the spring of 2000. We choose this period to examine because, in the parliament elected in 2002, presidential pressure on the parliament may have overwhelmed any tendency toward regional or ethnic fragmentation. If that fragmentation is not present in this earlier period, we can be more confident in the conclusion that it can be overcome. The goal is to examine the extent to which factional voting overlaps with the regional bases for the factions' support. Do factions that base their support primarily in the east vote the same way? Do those from different regions tend to vote differently? To what extent do factions with similar left/right orientations vote similarly? Which of these two cleavages seems to dominate?

Conceptual and Methodological Issues

In studying cleavages in Ukrainian society, scholars have run into a tangle of conceptual and methodological problems around the definition of different aspects of identity and the distinction of one aspect from others. These problems create substantial difficulties for the interpretation of empirical information.

First, surveys on linguistic identity and ethnic identity tend to work with exclusive categories, while the reality in Ukraine is one of blending and mixing.[9] It is possible, for example, to use a survey to discover what language a person speaks "at home" and hence to categorize that person as a speaker of that language. In reality, the majority of Ukrainians have some facility in both languages, and in practice there is a fair amount of mixing of the two languages. This mixing of identities creates a dilemma for the researcher. Either one forces people into categories that exaggerate differences (e.g., defining people as "Ukrainian speakers" or "Russian speakers" when they are both, or defining people as ethnically "Ukrainian" or "Russian" when they define themselves as mixed), or one ends up with huge numbers of people in "mixed" categories that do not allow distinctions to be made.

Second, as noted above, there is a significant but not complete overlap between three cleavages in Ukraine: ethnic, linguistic, and regional. There is even some overlap between these divisions and left–right cleavages: the most prominent leftist party (the communists) derives its support disproportionately from Russian speakers in eastern and southern Ukraine, while rightist parties are weakest in those regions and strongest in the west, where use of the Ukrainian language and self-identification as Ukrainian are highest. The overlap in cleavages makes it difficult to say in any given case which cleavage or cleavages is causing a particular effect, although statistical techniques such as multiple regression can help in this regard. Lowell Barrington, for example, relies on multiple regression to show that there is a regional dimension to Ukrainian politics distinct from ethnic or linguistic issues.[10] Paul Kubicek characterizes this gap in attitudes between eastern and western Ukraine as "enormous."[11] Rather than try to sort out all these issues, the analysis that follows concentrates on regional identification. Region has been found to be a powerful correlate of voting in Ukrainian elections.[12] The question is how directly that cleavage is transmitted into parliament, or to what extent parliamentary politics cut across the regional divide.

The regional distinction can be seen in proportional list voting in the 2002 parliamentary elections (see Table 5.1). All of the major parties gained a disproportionate share of their vote in one region, and were largely ineffective in at least one region. Most notably Kuchma's United Ukraine, despite its incredible resources (see Chapter Nine) was even more heavily dependent upon the eastern region than was the Communist Party.

This regional difference was even more pronounced in the 1999 presidential elections, in which Leonid Kuchma's margin of victory came almost entirely in the west of the country, where, despite widespread dissatisfaction with Kuchma, most voters considered the communists a greater evil (see Table 5.2 page 109). This "lesser evil" explanation is confirmed in the 2002 parliamentary elections, in which Kuchma's United Ukraine bloc received only 4.4 percent of the vote in the west.[13]

These cleavages were unchanged by the Orange Revolution. As Map 5.1 on page 104 shows, voting in the rerun of the second round of the 2004 presidential

Table 5.1

Regional Distribution of Parties' Support, 2002 Parliamentary Elections

	Percentage of party's overall proportional representation vote received in:			
Party/bloc	East	South	Central	West
Our Ukraine	10.6	5.9	25.8	57.6
United Ukraine	56.7	14.9	16.3	11.9
Communist	49.1	26.9	17.7	6.3
Tymoshenko	14.5	6.6	36.9	41.9
Socialist	26.1	11.9	53.1	8.9
Social-Democratic Party of Ukraine (United)	37.9	27.6	18.4	16.1

Source: Ukrainian Central Election Commission data; author's calculations.

Note: Rows may not total to 100 percent due to rounding. In this and the other tables in this chapter, the regions are divided up as follows: east—Chernihiv, Dnipropetrovs'k, Donetsk, Kharkiv, Luhansk, and Sumy oblasts; south—Kherson, Mykolaiv, Odesa, and Zaporizhzhia oblasts as well as Sevastopol City and the Crimean Autonomous Republic; central—Cherkasy, Kirovohrad, Kyiv, Poltava, and Vinnytsa oblasts and Kyiv City; west—Chernivtsi, Ivano-Frankivs'k, Khmel'nyts'ki, Lviv, Rivne, Ternopil, and Volyn oblasts. The regions are not equal in the number of voters; hence, the tendency by all parties for high reliance on the east and low reliance on the south. Numbers of voters in the 1998 parliamentary elections were: east—8.7 million; south—4.7 million; center—6.6 million; west—5.5 million.

elections was highly polarized regionally. By 2006, little had changed. The parties that had supported Yushchenko in 2004 (Our Ukraine, Socialist Party, Tymoshenko Bloc) won the same regions and combined to win the same overall proportion of the vote as Yushchenko had in 2004. Similarly, those forces that had supported Yanukovych in 2004 (Party of Regions, Communist Party) won the same proportion of the overall vote and the same regions as Yanukovych had in 2004.[14]

There can be little doubt that there are serious regional differences in Ukraine. The question remains, however, whether this societal cleavage is transmitted directly into the parliament, or whether electoral laws and parliamentary politics help to bridge the gaps in society.

Even determining the regional origin of members of parliament is difficult. For 225 members (half of the parliament elected in 1998 and 2002) the matter seems straightforward: they were elected in territorially defined districts. However, a candidate could run in any constituency where he or she could collect sufficient signatures to be nominated. So knowing where a candidate was elected tells us something about the electoral pressures that candidate might have catered to, but it does not necessarily tell us where that candidate was from (in fact, few candidates ran in districts where they did not live or had not lived previously).

Table 5.2

Regional Breakdown of Vote, 1999 Presidential Election, Second Round

	East	South	Central	West
Kuchma	52.4	49.3	50.5	85.5
Symonenko	47.6	50.7	49.5	14.5

Source: Ukrainian Central Election Commission data; author's calculations.

For the other half, elected on party lists, the task is even more difficult. All of these candidates had residence information listed with the Central Electoral Commission. But a disproportionate number of them listed residences in Kyiv because they were party elites or governmental officials and residing in Kyiv. So to use this measure would wipe out any possibility of finding an east/west divide in parliament, because many politicians from every region would be defined as from Kyiv.

However, there is a partial if not fully satisfactory solution, which is adopted here. Rather than focusing on individual legislators, we focus on parliamentary factions. In the party list section of the ballot, voting is highly regionalized: parties that did well in the west did poorly in the east, and so on (see Tables 5.3 and 5.4). So parties can be identified in terms of region, even if individual members cannot. Since, as will be discussed below, voting in parliament (at least in the period in question) was largely along party lines, we can achieve a reasonable assessment of the situation by examining it in terms of parties rather than individuals.

There are some problems here as well, because parties and "factions" in parliament come into and out of existence frequently. This analysis uses data from the 1998–2002 parliament, but because of shifting faction composition, we do not have election data on all the factions present in the sample of parliamentary votes (see Table 5.4). For the others, we must rely on data from single-member districts (see Table 5.3): by looking at members in the faction elected in single-member districts, we can see where they were elected. Together, these two indicators give us a good idea of where different factions' support was based. In the cases where both indicators are available for the same faction (Communist, Socialist, Greens, National Democratic Party, Rukh), they tend to give consistent results, increasing our confidence about the factions for which only single-member district data are available.

Data: Regional Cleavages in the Verkhovna Rada

Tables 5.3 and 5.4 show the regional bases for different factions' support. The differences are substantial. Most important for our purposes, we can

Table 5.3

Party Support Across Regions: Single-Member Districts, 1998 Parliamentary Election

			Rukh							Revival			
	Communist Party of Ukraine	Socialist Party	(Kos-tenko)	(Udo-venko)	Rukh total	Green	National Democratic Party	Social-Democratic of Ukraine	Reforms	Regions	Batkivsh-china	Trudova	Solid.
East	19	1				1	8	2	1	9	8	12	4
South	11	2				1	3	5	1	4	1	7	1
Central	6	2	3		3		4	4	3	10	4	4	5
West	1		7	3	10	1	2	5	4	9	3	2	4
% from East	51	20	0	0	0	33	47	13	11	28	50	48	29

Source: Rada Web site http://guru.rada.kiev.ua:2000/, accessed June 20–25, 2000, author's calculations.

Note: Regional origins and parliamentary faction affiliation of the single-member district deputies on April 6, 2000. Independent deputies and vacant seats not included.

Table 5.4

Support Across Regions (Selected Parties[1]): 1998 Proportional Representation (PR) Voting
(% of each party's PR vote gained in various regions)

	East	South	Center	West
Communist Party of Ukraine	46.2	24.4	22.1	7.3
Rukh[2]	18.1	7.0	22.0	53.0
Socialist Party of Ukraine/Peasants[3]	22.8	12.5	49.9	14.8
Greens	43.5	14.5	25.7	16.3
National Democratic Party	46	17.6	37.7	27.8

Source: Ukrainian Central Election Commission data; author's calculations.
Notes:
1.Only the five parties that passed the 4 percent threshold in the 1998 parliamentary elections and were still active in the parliament in June 2000 are included here.
2. The Rukh faction divided into two factions in 1999.
3. The Socialist/Peasants faction was disbanded in early 2000. Many of its members continued to serve in the Socialist faction.

identify four factions (Communist Party, National Democratic Party, Batkivshchina [forerunner of the Tymoshenko Bloc], and Trudova) as deriving at least 40 percent of their support from the eastern region of Ukraine, which has the highest concentrations (outside Crimea) of ethnic Russians and Russian speakers. If one focuses primarily on the ethnicity/language question, rather than on the region, one could focus on a group including Crimea, Sevastopol, Donetsk, Kharkiv, and Luhansk, where Russian-speaking populations are most numerous. The results do not differ substantially, but they would indicate slightly greater dependence of the Communist Party on this bloc of regions, and slightly less dependence of the other three parties.

Does Region Drive Parliamentary Voting?

Clearly, voting for parties is strongly affected by region. The question is whether these differences continue to manifest themselves in parliament. *If parliamentary politics in Ukraine are driven by regional differences, we should see those parties dependent on votes from eastern Ukraine voting similarly.* This is examined by looking at controversial roll-call votes in the Ukrainian parliament from the months of March, April, and May of 2000 (after the Communist/Socialist coalition had lost the leadership of the Rada). The figures in Table 5.5 indicate how often various parties voted together on sixty-eight roll-call votes, representing every roll-call vote in the months of March, April, and May 2000 in which at least 100 deputies voted for and against the measure. The point of

Table 5.5

Frequency with Which Ukrainian Political Parties Vote Together, Sixty-eight Roll-Call Votes, March–May 2000 (%)

	CPU	Rukh-K	SPU	Green	NDP	SDPU	Reform	Regions	Rukh-U	Batkiv.	Trudova
Rukh-Kostenko	19.1										
Socialist Party of Ukraine	92.6	17.6									
Green	1.4	76.5	8.8								
National Democratic Party	1.4	73.5	8.8	95.6							
Social-Democratic Party of Ukraine (United)	4.4	70.6	4.4	92.7	92.6						
Reform	22.1	64.7	25	77.9	69.1	67.6					
Regions	2.9	72.1	10.3	95.6	88.2	91.2	69.1				
Rukh-Udovenko	10.3	69.1	13.2	80.1	75	75	63.2	75			
Batkivshchina	14.7	69.1	13.2	85.3	82.4	80.1	64.7	85.3	67.6		
Trudova	2.9	72.1	10.3	95.6	97.1	94.1	69.1	94.1	75	83.8	
Solidarnist	11.7	58.8	5.8	80.1	79.4	14	61.8	79.4	66.2	73.5	83.8

Source: Rada, http://guru.rada.kiev.ua:2000/; accessed June 20–25, 2000, author's calculations.

selecting cases this way was to eliminate cases that were not controversial[15] and to maximize variation in the sample: when every faction votes the same way, we gain no insight into the differences across them.

Regional Voting Patterns Do Not Dominate in Parliament

The results are somewhat surprising. They show that the parties that were strongest in eastern Ukraine did not vote as a bloc: Batkivshchina (Yulia Tymoshenko's faction) voted with the Communists only 14.7 percent of the time, and the National Democratic Party (NDP) and Trudova factions were almost always opposed to the Communists, voting with them only 1.4 and 2.9 percent of the time, respectively. Even more surprising, the two factions of Rukh, with heavy support in the west and strongly identified with Ukrainian nationalism, voted with the Communists somewhat more often than did the other "eastern" parties (Rukh-Kostenko 19.1 percent of the time and Rukh-Udovenko 10.3 percent of the time). Only the Socialist faction consistently voted with the Communists (92.6 percent of the time). The Socialists, however, had only moderate support in eastern Ukraine (22.8 percent of their proportional representation [PR] vote,[16] and only one member from a single-member district [SMD] constituency there), and instead depended heavily on central Ukraine (49.9 percent of their PR vote, and two of their five SMD members).

Batkivshchina, Trudova, and NDP, the other three parties that relied heavily on support from eastern Ukraine, voted with each other over 80 percent of the time, often in conjunction with parties based in other regions. For example, the NDP voted with Rukh-Kostenko, based almost exclusively in the west, 73.5 percent of the time.

In sum, there were two opposing forces among parties that were elected primarily in the east, and they rarely worked in concert. These two forces were roughly equal in size: at the time studied here, April 2000, the Communist faction had 115 members, while Batkivshchina, Trudova, and NDP combined had 96, indicating a somewhat even divide in strength among "eastern" forces in parliament.[17] Both of those forces found their most frequent allies in other regions, including the western region of Ukraine. Alliances between west and east are particularly significant because those are the two regions most often seen to be in opposition.

The Salience of Traditional Left–Right Cleavages

A focus on left–right cleavages works better to explain voting patterns. If we interpret the left–right hypothesis to mean that parties at opposite ends of the

Table 5.6

Left–Right Orientations of Factions in Ukrainian Parliament, 2000

Left	Center	Right
Communist	National Democratic Party	Reforms Congress
Socialist	Social Democratic Party of Ukraine (United)	Rukh-Kostenko
	Greens	Rukh-Udovenko
	Revival of the Regions	
	Trudova	
	Batkivshchina	

Sources: Paul D'Anieri, Robert Kravchuk, and Taras Kuzio, *Politics and Society in Ukraine* (Boulder, CO: Westview, 1999), 158; Alexander Ott, *Parteien und Machtstrukturen in der Ukraine von 1991 bis 1998* (Cologne: Verlag Wissenschaft und Politik, 1999), 137; and analysis of faction/party programs.

spectrum will vote together least often, it is only partly confirmed. Categorization of parties as left, center, and right, is presented in Table 5.6. As indicated in Table 5.5, the most strongly rightist parties (the two Rukh factions and Reforms Congress) consistently voted together, as did the two leftist parties (the Communist and Socialist Parties).[18] These left and right parties rarely vote together. It is interesting to note that the rightist parties each vote more often with the centrist coalition than with each other.

This pattern is explained by a third cleavage that will be discussed below: support or opposition to President Kuchma, which became an increasingly salient factor over time, and which by 2003 was *the* defining factor in Ukrainian political alignments. This will also explain why the far right parties voted with the far left more often than ideology would predict: they shared an antipathy to Kuchma and had a common interest in blocking some of his measures.

To summarize, there is relatively little evidence that language, ethnic, or regional issues are driving forces in the Ukrainian parliament, or that they prevent tactical alliances between ideologically compatible groups. Most of the voting behavior occurred along left–right, rather than regional, cleavages. This does not mean that there are no regional and linguistic identities in the parliament. On the contrary, the fact that parties tend to be identified largely with particular regions means that there is a strong regional flavor to much of what is going on. But on difficult issues, parties from the same regions do not vote together. So despite the strong regional flavor of Ukraine's party system, parties in parliament are driven primarily by left–right rather than by linguistic or ethnic issues. The conclusion will address the reasons for this state of affairs and their implications.

Leonid Kuchma Between Left and Right

The ability of Kuchma to prevent his enemies from uniting went far beyond normal parliamentary politics. The content of the 1996 constitution, which will be detailed in the next chapter, provides a central example. The rightist forces were willing to transfer power from the parliament to the executive not because of any principle or belief about good constitutional design, but because the left controlled parliament at that time. The right was more concerned with weakening the left than with building strong institutions. Kuchma shrewdly facilitated this decision by granting nationalist parties some of their key goals on language and symbolic issues. By splitting the left from the right, Kuchma triumphed.

Kuchma used the same tactics, but switched allies, when faced with the growing popularity of rightist Prime Minister Yushchenko in 2001. Kuchma's centrist allies in parliament allied with the communists against Yushchenko, abandoning the center–right alliance that previously existed. The communists opposed Yushchenko more than Kuchma, so they went along, even though this strengthened Kuchma's hand even further.

The pattern continued in protests in early 2002 following revelations concerning the Gongadze case. The Gongadze case had little effect on left–right differences in the parliament, but divided center and rightist parties along their support or opposition to Kuchma.[19] Despite growing opposition to Kuchma from all sides, the left and right were never able to form a "popular front" to get rid of him. The socialists, led by Moroz, were willing to work with the rightists, but the communists continued to refuse. Expressing his contempt for Viktor Yushchenko, Communist Party of Ukraine (CPU) leader Petro Symonenko stated that Yushchenko's team and that of the president were "one and the same."[20] This continued a dynamic in which, if it looked as if Kuchma might fall and the right come to power, the communists would back Kuchma.

The 2002 Parliament

The data presented above help to explain why Leonid Kuchma was so successful in fending off challenges from parliament. They show a distinct left–right division in parliament. By placing himself between the left and right on key issues, Kuchma was consistently able to forge an alliance with one against the other. From the perspective of the right, Kuchma, however problematic, was preferable to the left, and vice versa. At the same time, even the right itself found it difficult to maintain a unified position, prompting one observer to state: "Kuchma seems securely in power today, as other Soviet

Table 5.7

Orientations of Ukrainian Political Parties, 2003–2004

	Left	Center	Right
Pro-Kuchma		United Ukraine, Social Democratic Party of Ukraine (United), Party of Regions (plus smaller oligarchic parties)	
Ambivalent	Communist Party		Our Ukraine
Anti-Kuchma	Socialist Party	Bloc of Yulia Tymoshenko	

holdovers have been throughout Ukraine's 10 years of independence, for a simple reason: Liberal democrats here fight more among themselves than against their foes."[21]

However, the occasional alliances between left and right became increasingly frequent after 2000, finally being cemented in the 2004 presidential election and the ensuing protests. Kuchma's self-aggrandizement increased the salience of a second dimension of political preferences: whether one is pro- or anti-Kuchma. This created a two-dimensional policy space. The first dimension was the left–right one, discussed above, which entails positions on economic issues as well as positions on national identity and foreign policy orientations. The second dimension was the orientation toward Kuchma himself and his rule of the country. As Table 5.7 indicates, these two cleavages cross-cut one another. Only the centrist (oligarchic) factions consistently supported Kuchma. Oddly, the farthest left and right groups, the communists and Yushchenko's Our Ukraine, were most ambivalent about Kuchma, perhaps because both feared that the other would strike an alliance with him.[22] The Socialist Party and the Tymoshenko Bloc, which lay between the communists and Our Ukraine on the left–right spectrum, lay outside them on the pro/anti-Kuchma spectrum. These two groups announced after the 2002 elections an unwillingness to align with the pro-presidential factions, and later were most dedicated to forcing Kuchma from office.[23]

Previously, the distance between left and right had exceeded the distance between either of those groups and Kuchma. However, as the confrontation between branches increased, Kuchma's distance from both left and right increased, while he held on to a considerable group in the center. As the "Kuchma" dimension continued to increase in salience, it made more sense for left and right to ally against him. Early signs of this alliance were visible in the 2002 parliamentary elections and in the policies of the Socialist Party of Ukraine (SPU) and the Bloc of Yulia Tymoshenko. In the 1998 parliament,

Tymoshenko's Batkivshchina voted consistently with the pro-presidential parties, and was generally thought of as leftist. The SPU was unabashedly leftist, voting over 90 percent of the time with the CPU. In other words, the left–right cleavage dominated the 1998 parliament, as indicated by the data presented above. Following the 2002 parliamentary elections, Yushchenko strongly considered joining the pro-presidential factions to form a majority. By late 2002, however, both the Socialists and Tymoshenko's Bloc had reached an informal alliance with the right opposition bloc Our Ukraine. Indeed, a more formal alliance may have been formed at this time had not Viktor Yushchenko hesitated to ally formally with Tymoshenko and Moroz.[24]

Following the 2002 parliamentary elections, the pro/anti-Kuchma axis increasingly dominated. Even the CPU considered joining the anti-Kuchma alliance, though it backed out as it became apparent that Yushchenko would be the alliance's candidate in the 2004 presidential election. In late 2002, for example, Moroz, Tymoshenko, Symonenko, and Yushchenko issued a joint declaration concerning the "beginning of a state revolution in Ukraine."[25] A lasting alliance, however, did not materialize. Symonenko ruled out the idea that the four might put forward a single presidential candidate, saying "One needs to take a realistic look at things: It's impossible to propose a single candidate from such different forces."[26] In sum, at key junctures both the left and the right put their ideological antipathy toward one another ahead of their mutual opposition to Kuchma and to the abuse of power that characterized his regime. Both were willing to ally with Kuchma at the expense of their adversary, and Kuchma deftly exploited this tendency.

Assessing the prospects for the 2004 presidential election, Yuri Kostenko, leader of the Ukrainian People's Party (one of the splinters of Rukh), expressed considerable confidence that, in contrast to the past, rightist and moderate leftist forces (including the Socialist Party and the Bloc of Yulia Tymoshenko) could unite behind a single candidate, but he remained skeptical that the Communists could be brought on board, despite the fact that the latter's chances of winning appeared even lower in 2004 than in 1999. The Communists continued to prefer Kuchma to the right.[27] Symonenko acknowledged the Communists' dilemma in 2002. The Communists, he said, hope to collaborate with other opposition groups while opposing Yushchenko's presidential candidacy, and simultaneously warning the opposition against allowing "the ruling regime to use ideological differences between opposition groups [to pursue] its dirty and greedy interests."[28] He preferred an alliance of leftist groups that would oppose both Yushchenko and Kuchma.[29] Ultimately, he ran in the 2004 election, coming in a distant third to Yanukovych and Yushchenko in the first round, and playing almost no role in the events that followed. The Communist Party won only 3.7 percent of the vote in the

Table 5.8

Shifting Alliances in Ukrainian Politics, 2000–2006

Communists allied with Kuchma/Party of Regions	Rightists allied with Kuchma/Party of Regions	Rightists allied with Communists
Dismissal of Yushchenko as prime minister, 2001	Formation of parliamentary majority, 2000	Support for proportional election law, 2000–2001, 2004
Approval of constitutional change, 2004	Vote for Yekhanurov as prime minister, 2005	Distribution of committee chairs in Rada, 2002*
	Nomination of Yanukovych as prime minister, 2006	

*Our Ukraine, the Socialist Party of Ukraine, the Communist Party of Ukraine, and the Tymoshenko Bloc agreed on a distribution of chairs among them and sought to get it passed, but failed. See Radio Free Europe/Radio Liberty, *Newsline* 6, no. 100, Part II, May 30, 2002.

2006 parliamentary election, indicating that it may at last be a spent force in Ukraine.

By the end of 2003, the Yushchenko–Tymoshenko–Moroz alliance had consolidated, with Yushchenko claiming: "The effectiveness of the opposition Three, its unity, and respect for the mutual commitments of its participants—all of these strengthen our confidence in victory."[30] At the same time, the chances that the Communist Party would ally itself with this group seemed as distant as ever when the CPU provided the crucial votes supporting the first reading of Kuchma's May 2004 constitutional provisions.[31]

Shifting Alliances

We have seen that, depending on the interests at stake, all of the major forces in Ukrainian politics have been able to align with almost any of the others. To demonstrate this, we can list the crucial issues since 2000 on which tactical alliances have been struck between various groups (see Table 5.8).

These political maneuverings indicate that a categorical statement about the effects of cleavages on party coalitions is not possible. Clearly, it was very difficult to form an alliance against Kuchma. For several years, left and right could not come together. But when the stakes were high enough, as Kuchma became more authoritarian and the 2004 election approached, various parties made the necessary compromises. Thus, while coalition-building in Ukraine is difficult, it is not impossible. This was made even more clear in early 2005 after the Orange Revolution, when Yushchenko was able to win over many of the formerly pro-Kuchma deputies in his efforts to get his cabinet approved. In September 2005, alliances had shifted again, with Tymoshenko opposing Yushchenko, and Yushchenko allying with his former nemesis, Viktor Yanukovych. The negotiations over a parliamentary majority coalition and a government following the 2006 parliamentary elections saw several combinations put forth as realistic possibilities:

1. Tymoshenko Bloc, Our Ukraine, Socialist Party (the "Orange Coalition")
2. Party of Regions, Socialist Party, Communist Party (the "Anti-Crisis Coalition," which elected Oleksandr Moroz speaker of parliament)
3. Party of Regions, Our Ukraine, Socialist Party, the coalition that finally formed a government with Yanukovych as prime minister.

That Yushchenko and Yanukovych could join forces is powerful evidence that the regional cleavages that so sharply define voting in Ukraine do not define postelection bargaining. In the 2006 bargaining, only two combinations were considered impossible: An "East–East" coalition of the Party of Regions and Tymoshenko Bloc and a "grand coalition" that would include either the Tymoshenko Bloc or Our Ukraine and the Communists.

Implications of Parliamentary Voting Patterns

Two important conclusions emerge from this analysis of left–right divisions in the parliament. First, Ukraine is a more "normal" country than has typically been appreciated, in that it is dominated primarily by a left–right cleavage. The regional differences have exactly the effects predicted by theorists of comparative electoral systems such as Duverger and Neto and Cox: political parties are defined both by region and ideology, such that common ideological positions will be represented by different parties in different regions.[32]

Second, nothing in Ukraine's societal cleavages makes a majority coalition impossible. This point is echoed by Roman Solchanyk, who states: "it is fairly clear that regionalism and, in particular, ethnicity and language, although important, do not amount to the 'great divide' that some had detected."[33] This is the crucial point, for the contrary argument was used by Kuchma, and accepted by many in the West, to justify continuing expansion of presidential power. Two tenuous pro-presidential majorities were formed, one in 2000 and one in 2002–3. Barring active measures by Kuchma to prevent it, a more stable, opposition-led majority could have been formed following the 2002 parliamentary elections. Equally important, parties from across the political spectrum have shown the ability to form alliances when it serves their interests. In 2006, a much more robust coalition was formed, even though it took a great deal of negotiation. Moreover, as we will see in subsequent chapters, other measures could substantially increase the likelihood of forming and maintaining a stable majority.

Societal Cleavages and the Design of Ukraine's Institutions

While Ukraine's societal cleavages do not form an insurmountable barrier to creating either a liberal democracy in general or a working parliamentary majority in particular, they do have important implications for the design of Ukraine's institutions. While these points will be explored in greater detail in the following chapters, we summarize the implications here, as a way of concluding this discussion. Three points in particular result from the finding that regional divisions tend to lead toward a greater number of parties than would occur in a homogenous society. First, there is little chance of creating a two-party system in Ukraine, so design of electoral laws should focus more on creating the most effective multiparty system possible. Second, it follows that there will almost certainly be post-election coalition-building in order to create a majority in parliament. Therefore, the rules within the parliament that govern coalition building and party control over deputies should be carefully constructed. Finally, and perhaps most controversially, if Ukraine cannot have a two-party system, it should not have a presidential form of government.

If we assume that Ukraine's regional differences are not easily surmountable and will not simply evaporate in the short term, then no election law will lead to a two-party system. As Duverger and others point out, a single-member district plurality system will lead to a two-party alignment within each distinguishable region. Only when a country consists of a single homogeneous space will this create two parties at the national level. "A two party format is *impossible*—under whatever electoral system—if racial, linguistic, ideologically alienated single-issue, or otherwise incoercible minorities (which cannot be represented by two major mass parties) are concentrated in above-plurality proportions in particular constituencies or geographical pockets."[34] Therefore, even if Ukraine were to adopt the strongest election law possible to reduce the number of parties, a multiparty system would still result, and postelection coalition-building would be needed.

However, this finding does not mean that Ukraine should simply adopt a full PR system and move on. As Neto and Cox show, both the number of cleavages and the electoral law have an effect on the number of parties, and their interaction tends to have a multiplicative effect.[35] In other words, Ukraine's regional divisions are likely to increase the number of parties under any electoral rule. "A polity will have many parties only if it both has many cleavages and has a permissive enough electoral system to allow political entrepreneurs to base separate parties on these cleavages."[36] Thus, a copy of the German electoral law would likely lead to a higher number of parties in Ukraine than in Germany. The implication for electoral law design is that even under a full PR system, a relatively restrictive version might be needed to keep the number of parties reasonable. It is worth noting, however, that in both the 1998 and 2002 parliamentary elections, a relatively small number of blocs was elected to parliament under the PR portion of the ballot (eight in 1998; six in 2002). The number of parties elected did not by itself present a serious obstacle to the construction of a majority coalition. In 2006, even the very low 3 percent threshold was high enough to eliminate many parties, leaving only five parties to negotiate a coalition.

Second, if a two-party system is impossible or nearly so, building and maintaining coalitions after elections will remain a crucial part of the process. In this, Ukraine has been rather deficient. Following the 1998 parliamentary election, haggling over the speakership went on for months, and once a speaker was elected, the coalition that had elected him collapsed. In 2000, under heavy pressure from Kuchma, a new majority was formed that ousted the leadership chosen in 1998, but the new coalition was ephemeral, and simply crumbled once its main task—ousting the leftist parliamentary leadership—had been accomplished. A second coalition was built, again with great difficulty and with significant pressure and inducements from the president, following parliamentary elections in 2002. This coalition was hardly a stable majority, for it held together only in some situations. In 2006, the process of building a coalition was characterized by intense bargaining, defection from existing agreements, and the threat of new elections. While this process and it results were widely criticized, it did eventually produce a coalition through democratic means.

Electoral laws will not remedy the difficulties in post-election coalition-building, though they might help. Only in two-party systems, of which there are few in the world, is coalition-building unnecessary. In all other systems, including most of the prospering liberal democracies of Western Europe, coalitions are formed and maintained by bargaining after elections. As we will see in Chapter Eight, the rules of the parliament will determine whether this will occur more successfully in Ukraine. For example, greater control by party leaders over party list seats should help prevent members from abandoning their party and undermining their coalition. The amendments that went into effect in 2006 appeared to improve the situation on this score, but it remains uncertain how they will function in the long run.

Third, if it is correct that, due to its societal cleavages, Ukraine is very unlikely to develop a two-party system, then there is serious reason to doubt that it can build a functioning democracy under a presidential system. This startling conclusion stems from applying to Ukraine a finding that has pertained across the world. The point will be explored in greater detail in the following chapter, and is only summarized here.

The bulk of opinion in political science, citing what Juan Linz called the "perils of presidentialism," finds that in new democracies, presidential systems are likely to lead to an aggrandizement of presidential power that undermines democracy.[37] There remains debate on that question, however, and increasingly, scholars are offering less categorical answers, saying instead that "it depends." Especially when democratization must be accompanied by rapid economic reform, many have advocated the concentrated power of presidentialism as a means of overcoming entrenched interests that often can hamper reform in parliament.[38] Ukraine demonstrates the validity of both arguments. Many reformers, both within Ukraine and in the West, welcomed the strengthening of Kuchma's powers as a means of overcoming the leftist parliament (as they welcomed Yeltsin's defeat of Russia's leftist parliament). Kuchma's abuse of power, however, convinced many of those same people that the presidency must be reined in.

What that discussion has missed, however, is another much less controversial finding: for presidential systems to avoid conflict and breakdown, the country in question must have a two-party system. For a variety of reasons, scholars argue, coalition-building among multiple parties is nearly impossible when the right to choose the government is not present as an incentive for parties to compromise. And while Brazil may be establishing a counterexample, all stable presidential systems in the world have two-party systems. Moreover, faced with a fragmented parliament, presidents are more likely to circumvent the parliament than to build a majority coalition. This has certainly been true in Ukraine. Therefore, whatever one thinks of presidentialism in general, it seems clear that it is unsuited to Ukraine, where the societal cleavage structure makes a two-party system unlikely even with the strongest of electoral laws.

These arguments imply that unless the bargain struck in late 2004 effectively moves the country toward a parliamentary system, the problems Ukraine experienced under Kuchma are likely to recur. This conclusion goes against the standard American practice of categorizing leaders as "good" or "bad" and seeking simply to have the "good" ones in power. The United States supported Kuchma over the communists, and then supported Yushchenko over Kuchma. However, as Americans should know better than anyone, the institutional context matters. Global experience indicates that, sooner or later, an unchecked presidency and a fragmented parliament will lead Ukraine back into a situation similar to that under Kuchma. If multiparty presidentialism is to be preserved in Ukraine, serious thought will have to be given to the problem of how this model, which has failed nearly everywhere else it has been tried, can be made to succeed in Ukraine.

Conclusion

This chapter has made no attempt to answer in the abstract the question of whether Ukraine is "ready" for democracy. Instead, that question has been answered by inquiring about the identifiable effects of societal cleavages on politics. Unless we can identify some essential part of liberal democracy that is made impossible by societal divisions, we cannot conclude that those cleavages are an insurmountable obstacle to democracy. There are, of course, examples of countries with strong linguistic, religious, or ethnic cleavages that function well as democracies, including Belgium, Canada, Switzerland, and Spain. Closer to Ukraine, the Baltic states, with divisions between titular nationality groups and ethnic Russians or Russian speakers, have surmounted the problem. Even Ukraine itself provides ample evidence: in the post-Soviet period the issue of linguistic and ethnic conflict has receded in importance, and while concerns remain, there are fewer chances of violence or secession than is the case in several of the liberal democracies mentioned above (e.g., Spain). Supporting this argument is much broader research on societal attitudes in Ukraine, which demonstrates that Ukrainian attitudes toward government support the building of democracy.[39]

However, Ukraine's differences, most notably considerable ideological differences between left and right and the continued salience of regional identities, have important effects on politics in the country and on what type of institutional arrangements are likely to succeed. Again, Ukraine is not unusual in this respect. Every country in the world has institutions tailored to its particular challenges. In the case of the divided societies mentioned above, federalism and consociationalism have been the remedies of choice. Ukraine has shown that it does not need these to cohere as a state.[40]

This chapter has shown two important effects of Ukraine's divisions. First, different cleavages seem predominant at different levels. At the level of elections, regional effects have a strong influence. This holds for both presidential and parliamentary elections. Within the parliament, however, left–right cleavages outweighed regional factors (and then were themselves overshadowed by conflict over Kuchma himself). It seems likely that in the post-Kuchma era, ideological cleavages will continue to dominate politics between elections, while region will continue to influence voting behavior. However, there will be a powerful incentive for all political parties to try to overcome their regional boundaries, because those that do will have the potential to increase their support considerably.

Second, the cleavage structure has an important intervening influence on the effects of different institutional arrangements. Electoral laws have different effects in divided societies as compared with homogeneous ones. Ukraine is almost certainly destined to have a multiparty system because there is no known electoral system that leads to a two-party system in a regionally divided state. Ukraine therefore should adopt appropriate rules to make the best of this reality. This might include not only electoral laws, but rules for forming and breaking coalitions within the parliament. More important, given the widely held view that the combination of multipartism and presidentialism is unlikely to yield stable democracy, Ukraine should adopt a parliamentary system. It remains unclear whether the partial shift toward parliamentarism following the Orange Revolution will suffice to avoid the dangers of multiparty presidentialism.

The task for the following chapters, therefore, is to further explore the formal institutional context in which Ukrainian politics operates. This chapter has allowed us to understand the societal constraints within which Ukraine's institutions must operate because it is crucial to discuss formal institutions not in the abstract, but with regard to the realistic limitations that are present. Two vital questions that emerge from this chapter will motivate the next two chapters. First, how do Ukraine's constitutional arrangements—most important, the distribution of power between the president and parliament—influence politics in the country? Second, how do lower-level institutional arrangements, including electoral laws and rules concerning parliament's function, mesh with the societal realities outlined here? There is no reason, as this chapter has shown, why bridging Ukraine's societal divisions requires a substantial impairment of liberal democracy. We must continue to dig, therefore, to identify the sources of electoral authoritarianism in Ukraine and to begin to suggest how its resurgence might be prevented.

6

The Constitution and Executive-Legislative Relations

In the previous chapter, it was shown that Ukrainian society is divided, but not hopelessly so. Ukraine's internal divisions create substantial challenges for forming the type of political compromises on which liberal democracy depends. Most important, Ukraine's pattern of regional and political cleavages indicates that it will likely have a multiplicity of political parties. However, little support was found for the proposition that Ukraine cannot sustain democracy. On the contrary, alliances have bridged not only Ukraine's regional divisions, but also, more recently, its ideological divisions.

If this conclusion is correct—that Ukraine can build representative democracy, but that there are tendencies toward division—then the design of institutions will be crucial. Institutions shape the incentives of political actors, and thus determine whether the organs of government will overcome societal divisions or exacerbate them. In this chapter and those that follow, we consider the design of institutions, with particular reference to two questions. First, to what extent have Ukraine's institutional arrangements created balance among the leading branches of government? Second, to what extent have Ukraine's arrangements created the conditions in which a stable parliamentary majority is likely to arise?

In institutional terms, the analysis must begin with the constitution, within which other institutions are "nested."[1] The electoral laws, laws on political parties, and rules of parliament, which will be considered in subsequent chapters, must all fit within the constitutional framework, at least in theory.[2]

Ukraine, along with all the other members of the Commonwealth of Independent States except Moldova, has had a strongly presidential form of government, though its presidency is now more constrained under the December 2004 amendments.[3] The choice of a presidential system differs both from the modal choice in the West European democracies, and from the most notable successes in postcommunist Eastern Europe, such as Poland, Hungary, and the Czech Republic. Is it a coincidence that, at least at first glance, those postcommunist states that have chosen strong presidential systems are less democratic than those that have chosen parliamentary government? Even if presidentialism is linked to weak democracy, as Gerald Easter has shown,[4] we must ask what is causing what. Is it that presidentialism impedes democratization, or that less democratic polities are more likely to choose the presidential form of government?

In this chapter, I aim to show that Ukraine's 1996 constitutional arrangements contributed to giving the president so much power that he had little incentive to collaborate with parliament. Moreover the legislative power given to the president reduced the likelihood that parliament would form a stable governing coalition. However, Ukraine's problems are only partly in the constitutional realm. In terms of institutional design, the choice of electoral laws and the internal rules of the parliament have had as much impact as the constitutional division of powers. Equally important, the extraordinary power held by Kuchma stemmed only in part from the formal rules. His power was also based in the informal powers he accrued, which will be discussed in Chapter Nine. Therefore, while the constitutional changes that went into effect in early 2006 are a step in the right direction, they will likely be insufficient by themselves to produce stable democracy in Ukraine. This is an important warning for those tempted to think that the Orange Revolution and the accompanying constitutional revisions are a complete solution to Ukraine's political problems.

The chapter begins with a summary of the process by which the Ukrainian constitution was adopted, and a consideration of the alternatives that were presented. Kuchma was able to gain formal power in the constitution because he already had considerable informal de facto powers of the presidency. The chapter then examines in more detail the case made by Juan Linz and others that presidential power is dangerous for new democracies. I will show that nearly every problem pointed to by critics of presidentialism manifested itself in Ukraine. Finally, the chapter considers potential arrangements that might more evenly balance power in Ukraine.

Overview: The Tortured Birth of the Ukrainian Constitution

Kataryna Wolczuk and Bohdan Harasymiw have provided thoroughly researched analyses of the adoption of the Ukrainian Constitution, from the first "concepts" for a constitution that were developed even before Ukraine's independence to the final document agreed upon amid last-minute chaos in 1996.[5] There is little to add empirically to their thorough analyses. Here we raise points that are relevant to the specific questions raised in this chapter, namely, the choice of a presidential system and the division of powers between the president and the parliament.

As Wolczuk stresses, there was much going on in Ukrainian constitution-building besides an attempt to build the perfect foundation for liberal democracy in Ukraine.[6] A primary goal for many was to establish the symbolic basis of a new state. In this respect, the constitution was seen as a genuinely "constituting" document, meaning that the document itself and the process of drafting it were important founding acts of the Ukrainian state. In that sense, the constitution was to be more than simply a "fundamental law" upon which all other law would be built. Many of the key debates on which actors focused their efforts and expended their political capital centered not on the ideal basis for liberal democracy, but on the nature of the state being created. For example, many "national democrats" were willing to grant immense authority to the president in return for establishing Ukrainian as the sole "official" language of Ukraine.

At the same time, every actor involved in the process was interested in preserving or augmenting his/her own political power.[7] The *nomenklatura*-based communists and ex-communists who dominated the Verkhovna Rada sought to maintain the power that the parliament had in Soviet times. They therefore preferred a parliamentary system, which was roughly what Ukraine had at the time of independence. Ukraine's presidents, first Kravchuk and then Kuchma (and later Yushchenko), sought to implement a strong presidential system that served their interests. Kuchma was able to prevail due in part to his ability to win over the nationalists, and in part to his ability as president to wield informal power that far outweighed what the parliament could muster.

While the constitution was a "founding" document in a symbolic sense, it was not at all a founding document in a political sense. It was not written on a "blank slate" by a group of actors who joined together to form a new political system. Unlike the "round table" discussions that took place in Poland, in which representatives of the opposition were granted a role in constitution-drafting that went beyond any elected office that they held, the Ukrainian Constitution was drafted *within* the constraints of Ukraine's Soviet constitution. In this respect, we can most clearly see that what took place in Ukraine was not a political revolution. It is worth a brief digression to examine why Ukraine took this path (see also Chapter Four).

Unlike in Poland or in the Baltic states, there was division in Ukraine concerning the desirability of breaking away from the Soviet Union. One strategy of the nationalist opposition throughout the late Soviet period was to work within the law. Those following this strategy held peaceful protests, and ran for seats in parliament when allowed, but did not seek to overthrow the existing order, which would likely have been futile. Instead, their strategy was to use means that even the communists could not claim to be illegal, and to try to continuously expand the range of what was considered legal within the communist system.

Rather than being viewed as an overthrow *of* the Supreme Soviet, Ukrainian independence was declared *by* the Supreme Soviet, and the fact that it was declared by the Supreme Soviet was a major source of its legitimacy. Similarly, at the international level, in December 1991, Kravchuk established Ukraine's independence from the Soviet Union not by rejecting the validity of the 1922 Union Treaty, but by working within the provisions of that treaty to abrogate it.

To reassert a point already discussed in Chapter Four, Ukraine's declaration of independence, and its subsequent constitutional process, remained *nested within* the Soviet Ukrainian Constitution of 1978. There was no new discussion of what kind of group should draft the constitution, or what kind of process should be used to adopt it. Instead, the process was governed by the Soviet-era constitution: The constitution could be changed by a two-thirds vote of the parliament. But since there were no new "founding" elections for parliament, the new constitution would be written and approved by the old Soviet parliament. Ultimately, that parliament could manage only a series of amendments. As Andrew Wilson demonstrates, Ukraine's constitutional arrangements prior to 1996 were so confusing that labeling the form of government was itself a challenge.[8]

For much of the period from 1991 to 1996, therefore, the process of drafting a constitution made little progress. There was a fundamental conflict of interest between the leftists in parliament, who sought to retain the system of Soviets, and nationalists and the executive, who sought a presidential system. The constitutional process was closely intertwined with everyday politics. For example, Ukraine's democratic reformers opposed the creation of a strong parliamentary system, which is what democrats in most of Eastern Europe sought. Why? As long as there was no new election to refound a postcommunist parliament, a parliamentary system would empower the opponents of reform and even of statehood. Instead, they sought to outflank the left by weakening the parliament and giving more power to the president. The power of this logic is demonstrated by the fact that most West European and American supporters of reform in Ukraine (and Russia) also advocated strengthening the powers of the executive at the expense of the legislature. In this way, the arrangement of electoral rules within constitutional provisions was reversed: the debate over the new constitution became tightly constrained by the composition of the elected parliament.

Origins of the 1996 Constitution

The adoption of the 1996 constitution defined the legal environment in which Kuchma was able to exercise such considerable power.[9] Therefore, in this chapter we examine in more detail how that process was shaped. Two salient points emerge. First, the various actors had many immediate goals apart from building the perfect constitution in some abstract sense. Second, disagreements were resolved in terms of who could most credibly threaten to defeat the others if the constitutional process failed.

The process was rather chaotic, especially toward the end. The chaos stemmed from the absence of any definitive agreement on what the process would be. In most constitutional processes, the first thing agreed upon is the rules by which the constitution will be drawn up and adopted. In Ukraine, critical aspects of the rules of the game were contested throughout the process. Because the process (including the question of who participates) can have a major bearing on the outcome, it is expected that different actors will contest it. To have the rules of adoption still undecided as the constitution is being drafted and adopted, however, means that there is no agreed-upon basis for proceeding. In the absence of rules, as Hobbes pointed out, "clubs are trumps." In such situations, the actors with the most power resources will tend to emerge victorious, and this case was no exception.

A succession of constitutional commissions had been working on drafting a Ukrainian constitution since October 1990—well before Ukraine's independence. The first was a parliamentary commission, reflecting the dominance of parliament at that stage. However, this commission barely changed in its composition through 1994, despite the rather dramatic political changes in Ukraine, including the independence of the state and the end of communism.[10] Only in October 1994 was a new constitutional commission appointed, headed by President Kuchma and parliamentary speaker Oleksandr Moroz, who could not agree even on basic procedures.[11] However, the composition of this second commission—the president appointed half its members—served to achieve an important shift in power in constitutional politics. No longer was the parliament preeminent.[12]

The 1995 "Law on Power"

With the constitutional process moving very slowly, Kuchma sought a quicker solution. In August 1994, he issued a decree subordinating all government administrations to the president.[13] In November 1994, he proposed a law titled "On State Power and Local Self-Government in Ukraine."[14] Generally known in its final form as the "Law on Power," this legislation would provide a temporary resolution of the key problems of the division of power until a new constitution could be adopted, while avoiding questions of the form of the state, symbols, and language.[15] Because the proposed changes were normal legislation, rather than constitutional amendments, they required only a simple majority vote in parliament to be adopted. This might expedite the process, but it also created the odd situation where normal legislation superseded the constitution.

Kuchma's initial plan called for subordinating the prime minister to the president (including giving the president the right to dismiss the parliament) and removing parliamentary influence over the prime minister.[16] This would allow the president to put his own people in the cabinet instead of having to placate the parliament. The prime minister and ministers would be more dependent on the president, and would have only one master rather than two. Kuchma also sought the right to dissolve the parliament under some conditions.[17] Overall, the proposed shift toward a fully presidential system was "radical."[18]

Many members of parliament were willing to allow the change in control over ministerial appointments, recognizing the need to make the government more unified. There was widespread opposition to allowing the president to dissolve the parliament. In April 1995, parliament asserted its power and expressed its discontent by passing a motion of no confidence in Prime Minister Vitaly Masol.[19] Kuchma refused to appoint a new government, waiting until a new law was passed that would allow him to do so without parliamentary approval.

When the parliament resisted, Kuchma forced a showdown, threatening to hold a nonbinding referendum on the public's confidence in the parliament and the president, which Kuchma would likely win.[20] The two sides finally reached a compromise that gave Kuchma his primary objective, the exclusive right of the president to form the government, but excluded provisions for the president to dissolve parliament or for the parliament to impeach the president.[21]

However, because the new measures contradicted the existing constitutional provisions, sixty-nine articles would have to be suspended for the new law to go into effect. Thus, Kuchma was unable to fully circumvent the need to win a two-thirds "constitutional" majority in parliament, which the communists could easily prevent. A second showdown ensued.[22] Kuchma said he would implement the new law regardless of whether the relevant articles of the constitution were suspended, and he again threatened to hold a referendum, this time going so far as to schedule a date.[23] Again, a compromise was reached in which Kuchma got most of what he wanted: parliament voted to suspend the relevant articles for a year, until a new constitution could be adopted.[24]

From the "Law on Power" to the Constitution

Ultimately, however, the crisis was not averted. In the spring and summer of 1996, the standoff of 1995 was repeated over the new constitution. There continued to be conflict over how the constitution was to be adopted—by parliament, by referendum, or both. How the constitution was to be adopted would significantly influence what kinds of provisions would prevail. With the impending expiration of the "Law on Power" in early June, a crisis approached. Kuchma again seized the initiative and capitalized on his relative popularity over the parliament.

Following the 1995 "Law on Power," the process for adopting a constitution was changed again. Having made little progress in five years of work, leaders saw little chance of arriving at a finished constitution before the "Law on Power" expired. They formed a much smaller "working group" to compose a first draft. A new draft was ready by October 1995. Despite widespread dissatisfaction with the draft, the overall constitutional commission approved it as a starting point by a vote of twenty-two to twenty.[25] A new subcommittee dominated by presidential appointees was appointed to modify this draft.[26] This time-pressured ad hoc revision of the process was not neutral in terms of the politics of the new constitution. Each improvised change in the process gave the presidential administration a stronger role in drafting the document.

This new group produced another draft in March 1996, which in Kuchma's words would "end Soviet power in Ukraine forever."[27] It would allegedly transform the system from the unified power of the Soviet system to a system of checks and balances. In reality, however, this draft would have created a strongly presidential system, with few serious checks on the executive. It gave the president the powers to appoint the holders of most government, judicial, and military offices, to appoint the prime minister and the cabinet, to issue decrees with equal status to parliamentary legislation, to initiate legislation, to name the heads of oblast and raion state administrations, and, most crucially, to dissolve the parliament if it failed to approve the government's program twice in sixty days.[28]

By ending Soviet power, Kuchma meant that local "self-government" would be appointed by the central administration, thus building the "administrative resources" that would be widely used later.[29] The powers over appointments of various officers as well as local and regional administrations would give the president massive patronage power reaching far down into the government and into local government. On a practical level, this would make it very difficult for challenges to arise. Powers to issue legislation by decree meant that there would be no need or incentive for the president to compromise with the parliament. There was no mechanism to resolve contradictions between presidential decrees and parliamentary legislation. However, it was clear what would happen when the president and parliament fundamentally disagreed: parliament would be dissolved. In such conditions, the president would have no reason to compromise, and the parliament would have no grounds on which to stand when it disagreed with the president.[30]

This draft of the constitution also included provisions on symbolic issues —national symbol, flag, and anthem—that were in line with the desires of the "national democrats." For our purposes, these issues are not crucial, but Kuchma's adoption of the nationalist position at this time indicates his strategy for building a coalition of support for his constitution. He would unite with the right against the left. More important, however, he would not compromise on the extent of power he was going to get in order to gain the approval of the right. Instead, he yielded on symbolic issues that were considered essential to nationalists but were irrelevant to the building of real political power in the country.

The parliament, with the leftist contingent at the forefront, rejected this draft. The Communist Party of Ukraine advanced several alternative drafts, which gave parliament much more power over cabinet appointments, and looked more like the much-amended Soviet constitution that had been found unworkable. The Communists even proposed a referendum of their own, in order to force Kuchma and the right to pay more attention to their position.[31] Even many on the center and right of the political spectrum had serious reservations about the extensive presidential powers Kuchma proposed. The provision for a bicameral legislature evoked the most unanimous opposition. It became clear that this draft would never be approved by the parliament. A Temporary Extraordinary Commission, yet another ad hoc change in the process, then produced a compromise document that slightly tempered the degree of presidential dominance in the constitution and eliminated the provision for a bicameral parliament.[32]

Adoption of the Constitution

The 1995 "Law on Power" was due to expire in June 1996. Without a new constitution, the system would, in theory, revert to the situation in place prior to the "Law on Power." Kuchma took advantage of this deadline to force a showdown. On June 26, he declared he would put the constitution to the people in a referendum in September if the parliament did not approve one rapidly. In planning the referendum, however, he scrapped the most recent compromise, and reverted to a previous draft with far greater presidential power and a bicameral parliament.[33] Thus, he gave the parliament the choice of approving a pro-presidential constitution through constitutional means or having a much more radically pro-presidential constitution imposed on it by presidential fiat. It was a classic case of "heads, I win; tails, you lose." Kuchma's ability to structure the alternatives under consideration, combined with his ability to carry out a referendum despite parliamentary opposition and the absence of a legal basis for it, made his position impregnable.[34]

The political reality faced by the parliament was that it could either fight a losing battle on the referendum, and face imminent dissolution, or accede to the president's wishes. Beginning on June 27, 1996, Moroz began a twenty-three-hour session of the parliament that lasted into the morning of June 28. While Moroz did not side with Kuchma, he sought to preserve the parliament (and his own position), even in weakened form. So he rammed compromises through the parliament, voting on controversial measures repeatedly (over ten times when necessary) until agreement was reached.[35] At last, all of the articles were approved, and the entire document was approved with 315 votes (in excess of two-thirds). A constitution was thus passed barely forty-eight hours after Kuchma's ultimatum.

Power Politics and Institutional Design

The process by which the constitution was adopted was driven not by abstract notions of institutional design, but by calculations of power politics. Power considerations dominated the goals pursued by the various actors, and power determined how disagreements were resolved. This occurred first when Kuchma circumvented the entire constitutional process by passing the "Law on Power." This move turned on its head the notion that standard legislation is "nested" within, and constrained by, constitutional measures. Instead, he was using regular legislation to trump constitutional provisions.

Second, when he could not get the law that he desired through parliament, he threatened to use unconstitutional means, namely, the referendum. That he ended up not needing to do so is immaterial. What is significant is that he made the threat, and that it compelled the parliament to submit. The threat was obviously considered credible (meaning that he would get away with holding a referendum and would win it, as he later demonstrated in 2000). Third, he was able and willing to ignore what should have been a substantial check on his power: the one-year limit on the "Law on Power." Instead, having succeeded the year before in forcing capitulation with a threat of unconstitutional action, he did the same thing again. Again, those who opposed this measure felt that they would be unable to resist.

Finally, Kuchma threatened that, if he went to a referendum, he would put forward a constitution maximally favorable to him.[36] In other words, he structured the alternatives so that the parliament had some incentive to vote "voluntarily" for the new constitution. Indeed, in subsequent years, there has been no questioning the legitimacy of the Ukrainian Constitution. Parties within and outside Ukraine have routinely invoked it, and complained when they feel it has been violated. This level of legitimacy might not have been obtained had Kuchma not been able to force the parliament to vote on it.

The role of the "national democrats," or the right wing in the Ukrainian parliament, in this process was also significant. Kuchma was able to secure their support for strong presidentialism in part because they sought to place power anywhere but in a parliament controlled by the left, and also because he was willing to accede to their demands on the key nationalist issues of language, flag, emblems, and anthem. As Wolczuk points out, once the provision for a bicameral parliament was removed from the draft constitution, the rightist parties actually urged Kuchma to circumvent the parliament and put the document to a referendum.[37] The right was still more concerned with winning partisan battles with the left and with pro-Russian forces than with building a balanced constitution. It is not that they were unconcerned about the imbalance in the drafts under consideration, but that given other goals, they were willing to compromise on the distribution of power.

The big losers in this process were the leftist and pro-Russian forces (which overlapped to some extent). The fact that the communists and socialists, the most direct descendents of the Soviet-era Communist Party of Ukraine, were to a large extent shut out of the final process, may be seen as accomplishing in 1996 what should have happened in 1991—the adoption of a new constitutional order without the participation of the old members. In that sense, the less procedurally and legally pristine aspects of the process (i.e., threats to hold illegal referenda) might be seen as both necessary and justified. Certainly, Kuchma and many on the right viewed the situation this way.

But the continued participation of the left was important up until the very end, and led to a very different result than would have obtained had they been excluded from the beginning. Had the communist and socialist forces been excluded all along, the right would have been correspondingly much stronger, and therefore would not have had to make the deal that it did with Kuchma. In other words, Kuchma used the specter of the left to subdue the democrats on the right as much as he used the right to subdue the left. Only with the left present did the right need to give the president such extensive power.

Thus, the constitutional process of 1996 did *not* represent the delayed founding of a state that should have taken place in 1991. Rather, it represented yet another incremental evolution along a continuum that saw the Soviet Ukrainian apparatus transformed into a new, nearly as powerful, pseudodemocratic apparatus. If the adoption of the new constitution represented the defeat of the old Communist Party, the victors were not the dissidents or the democrats, but rather the apparatchiks. The executive branch established itself as the dominant power in Ukraine, with meaningful competition from neither parliament nor the judiciary.

In contrast to the notion of a "round table," which opens up the constitutional process to a broad range of interests, the Ukrainian process remained closed. To the extent that the 1996 constitution represented a revolution, it was not a liberal democratic revolution, but an executive-dominated one. Few noticed at the time, because most reformers and observers were so relieved that the country finally had a constitution and that it did not empower the communists. However, by demonstrating that he had enough power to overcome the established rules of the game, in 1995 and 1996 Kuchma was already building the machine that became widely recognized in 1999 and after. Here we must disagree with Harasymiw, who characterizes the 1996 constitution as producing "weak president, weak parliament, weak political parties."[38] It reflected a strong presidency and produced a strong president, which became increasingly evident in the coming years.

Parliamentarism Versus Presidentialism

In examining the provisions of the 1996 constitution, several aspects are significant in terms of the distribution of power and the incentives that resulted from the document. Various aspects of the constitution are notable in other contexts, but are not examined here. By far the single most important aspect of the constitutional arrangement in Ukraine, developed in 1991 but reinforced by the 1996 constitution, is the adoption of a presidential form of government. As was discussed in Chapter Two, there is considerable argument that the basic decision between a presidential and a parliamentary system has important effects in the political evolution of new democracies. Our discussion here focuses on the effects of the choice of presidentialism in Ukraine, and on the rather extreme version of presidentialism adopted.

The Problem of Definitions: Is Ukraine a Presidential System?

The existence of the position of prime minister creates some confusion in defining the Ukrainian system from 1996 to 2006 as "presidential." Oleh Protsyk defines Ukraine's system prior to the 2004 constitution amendments as "president-parliamentary," since the parliament has some formal input in naming the cabinet.[39] In narrow terms, this may be correct, but under the 1996 constitution, the parliament's powers over the cabinet were very weak, such that the president effectively controlled the cabinet. I therefore categorize it as a presidential system. This classification is consistent with definitions provided by Alfred Stepan and Cindy Skach, who characterize a "semi-presidential" system as one "where there is a directly elected president and a prime minister who must have a majority in the legislature." In the

1996–2004 setup, Ukraine's prime minister was *not* required to have such a majority, and the parliament's control over the prime minister was weak, and it therefore makes sense to classify that Ukrainian system as fully presidential. Stepan and Skach continue, defining a "pure presidential regime" as one of mutual independence, in which "the legislature has a fixed electoral mandate which is its own source of legitimacy" and the executive also "has a fixed electoral mandate that is its own sources of legitimacy."[40] This characterization fits Ukraine from 1996 to 2006. The arrangements as revised in December 2004 will indeed meet Stepan and Skach's definition of a "semi-presidential system." In more recent work, Alfred Stepan has distinguished two types of semi-presidential systems: "super-presidential semi-presidentialism" and "parliamentarized semi-presidentialism."[41] Ukraine from 2006 onward fits the latter definition.

In the "pure" presidential system, one individual holds the position of both head of state and head of government. Systems with both a president and a prime minister (a so-called bicephalous executive) are then often labeled "semi-presidential," "presidential-parliamentary," or "parliamentary-presidential," depending on the author in question and the exact distribution of formal powers.[42] However, the key question in defining systems is not what positions exist, but what powers are given to the president and to the legislature. In a true semi-presidential system, the prime minister remains reliant on the parliament for his or her position. This gives the parliament considerable influence over the operation of the executive branch. It also means that when the president and prime minister come from competing parties, "cohabitation," to use the French term, must be managed successfully to avoid stalemate. Ukraine's system prior to the 1995 "Law on Power" (as well as its post-2006 arrangements) might be defined as semi-presidential, for the parliament had more influence over the selection of cabinet ministers. Even in that era, however, the prime minister was selected by the president.

In the 1996–2006 format, however, the prime minister was dependent almost entirely on the president for his or her position. The prime minister as well as the other ministers were chosen by the president and could be fired by the president. The parliament had only the power to confirm the prime minister and some of the other ministers, and to vote no confidence in the prime minister. But it had no authority to name the prime minister or the other ministers and no control over the executive branch. Hence, using Linz's definition of a presidential system as one in which the president possesses "full control of the composition of the cabinet,"[43] we can safely define Ukraine from 1996 to 2006 as a presidential system. Similarly, using Shugart and Carey's three-part definition of "presidential government"—popular election of the chief executive, fixed terms for the executive and the parliament, and the executive's right to name the government—Ukraine was clearly a presidential system. According to Sartori's definition, the categorization is almost as clear. Sartori defines a presidential system as one in which the head of state is elected by popular vote for a defined term of office, and in which the government is neither appointed nor dismissed by the parliament.[44] The right of the Ukrainian parliament to oust the prime minister slightly undercuts labeling Ukraine as presidential under this definition, but it still fits Sartori's presidential system much more closely than his parliamentary system.

In contrast, other polities with the post of "president" (such as Poland, the Czech Republic, and Germany) are still defined as parliamentary systems because in them the head of government (prime minister or chancellor) is chosen by the parliament rather than in a direct election and because this prime minister, rather than the president, controls the cabinet and executive branch. In such systems, the president plays a mostly ceremonial and informal political role, but has little de facto institutional power (even though the president's informal powers and prestige may lead to significant political influence, as Vaclav Havel possessed in the early postcommunist years).

The popular election of the president for a fixed term is important because it means that the president is not dependent on parliamentary confidence to retain office. He or she only needs to maintain the confidence of the people to be reelected, and cannot be dismissed, except through impeachment, which in most constitutions (including Ukraine's) is extremely difficult in practice. Besides making the president completely independent of the parliament, the popular election of the president allows him or her to claim to speak for the people and to claim that the parliament is impeding the will of the people when it opposes him. Using Walter Bagehot's terminology, Linz argues that "a presidential system endows the incumbent with both the 'ceremonial' functions of a head of state and the 'effective' functions of a chief executive, thus creating an aura, a self-image, and a set of popular expectations which are all quite different from those associated with a prime minister, no matter how popular he may be."[45]

Parliaments, of course, are also directly elected, but they rarely speak with a single clear voice, and do not possess the symbolic voice of the people that the president does. The importance of this factor was demonstrated by Kuchma himself, who frequently defended his prerogatives by pointing to his popular election. For example, in rejecting calls to resign during the scandal over the Gongadze murder, Kuchma was able to point to the millions of Ukrainians who had voted for him as a reason that he could not step down. The popular election of the president and the fixed term thus combine to provide considerable insulation from attack. As Linz and others point out, however, they also reduce flexibility, making it very difficult to change course between elections. This, Linz contends, tends to turn crises of government into crises of the system.

The Perils of Presidentialism in Ukraine

As was reviewed in Chapter Two, a variety of authors have argued that presidential government is dangerous, especially for new democracies. In presidentialism, both the president and the parliament derive their democratic legitimacy directly from the people. Therefore, they are rather independent of one another, and thus prone to conflict over prerogatives, especially when the president is not from the party that controls parliament.[46] Indeed, Linz points out, when both the president and legislature claim direct democratic mandates, there is no democratic principle by which to resolve conflicts between them. Whatever formal mechanisms for conflict resolution exist in the constitution are likely to be "too complicated and too aridly legalistic to be of much force in the eyes of the electorate."[47]

Because executives are elected for fixed terms, the conflict cannot be resolved until the next election. One of two outcomes is likely, neither of which is conducive to strengthening a new democracy. If the parliament and president have roughly equal powers, stalemate can persist, and the legitimacy of the system can be cast into doubt. If the president has substantially greater power than parliament, then the president may use extraordinary measures to reduce the influence of parliament and to rule undemocratically. Ukraine has suffered both of these problems, the first in the early years under president Kravchuk, who was constrained by the parliament and shared his power with the prime minister; and the second under Kuchma, who used his considerable powers and augmented them.

Many of the other pathologies of presidentialism against which Linz warns also arise in Ukraine. First among these is the personalization of power. In vesting such extensive and visible authority in a single individual, presidentialism increases the notion of personal rule. In the early days of post-Soviet Ukraine, this was seen as an advantage: the very existence of a president of Ukraine symbolized the country's independence from Russia and the Soviet Union. Leonid Kravchuk was the embodiment of Ukrainian sovereignty at a time when many other attributes of sovereignty were still being developed. Although great power is often vested in a president, fears of excessive presidential power lead to the creation of various checks on the exercise of that power. Presidents are therefore prone to feel that, despite their considerable powers, they are constrained from doing what needs to be done. We saw this clearly in Ukraine under Kuchma: despite his extensive powers, he continually complained that he was prevented from governing for the good of the country, and therefore needed more power. This was the essence of the debate over the "Law on Power" in 1995 and the constitution in 1996, but even having won those battles, Kuchma soon (in 2000) found himself sponsoring a legally dubious referendum to increase his powers still further.[48]

The combination of direct election of the president and extensive but limited power is likely to give the president relatively low tolerance of the opposition. The danger is that, having won a plurality of votes or perhaps even a majority, the president will act as though he has been elected by all of the people, and therefore will disregard opposition from parliament. "The plebiscitarian component implicit in the president's authority is likely to make the obstacles and opposition he encounters seem particularly annoying."[49] While this popular mandate may be an important source of political strength for the president, it can also lead to a perception that opposition to his policies is somehow illegitimate and must be overcome.

Kuchma demonstrated repeatedly the view that opposition to him in parliament was illegitimate, based solely on private, oligarchic interests, in contrast to his concern with the public interest. "In such a context," Linz states, "a president frustrated by legislative recalcitrance will be tempted to mobilize the people against the putative oligarchs and special interests, to claim for himself alone true democratic legitimacy as the tribune of the people and to urge on his supporters in mass demonstrations against the opposition."[50] This is almost exactly what happened in Ukraine, with the addition that Kuchma used the referendum (in 2000) and the threat of the referendum (in 1995 and 1996), rather than demonstrations, as a means of controlling parliament.

Linz also points out that politics under presidentialism is a "winner take all" proposition. A person (or party) either controls the presidency or does not. This gives rise to zero-sum politics, whereby what is good for one actor is bad for another. Such politics is not unheard of in parliamentary systems, where one party can win a majority by itself and thus "take all," but more often, Linz contends, parliamentary systems are based on coalition governments, which lead to partial rather than total victories and defeats. A party can increase its influence by gaining seats, without having to gain a majority. Moreover, the possibility that even a leading party will have to gain coalition partners to rule should induce some moderation into electoral politics. "The zero-sum game in presidential regimes raises the stakes of presidential elections and inevitably exacerbates their attendant tensions and polarization."[51] Though Linz does not say so directly, the "winner take all" nature of presidential elections also drastically increases the incentives to manipulate the election. When a presidential election may turn on a small percentage of the votes, the ability of manipulation to change results is clear, and the gains to be made by doing so are incredibly high.

This phenomenon was vividly displayed in Ukraine in 2004. Because the powers of the presidency were so extensive, both the Kuchma/Yanukovych group and the opposition viewed the election as one they simply could not afford to lose. Both sides anticipated that the losing side would be shut out of politics, possibly forever, and that the losing leaders would likely be either exiled or imprisoned. This seemed to justify the extensive fraud used by the authorities to secure Yanukovych's election, as well as the extraordinary measures undertaken by the opposition to thwart it.

The 1999 presidential election had already demonstrated the same point in a less dramatic way. The election campaign included considerable struggle over control of the media, credible accusations of vote-rigging, and an assassination attempt (as well as the likelihood that the assassination attempt was a plot to discredit one of the other candidates). Similarly, almost immediately following the parliamentary elections in spring 2002, the unofficial campaign for the 2004 presidential election began. Because this campaign, even two years away, dominated politics in 2002, it made governing that much more difficult.

Presidential Rule and Parliamentary Performance

While Linz focuses on the ways in which presidentialism is likely to lead to instability, confrontation, and overweening presidential power, we should also take note of the effects of a very strong presidency on the parliament. The main challenge in a democratically elected parliament is the formation of a governing coalition. This becomes more complicated as the diversity of political interests represented in parliament grows. The ability to form coalitions is influenced by many factors, including the electoral laws and the rules of the parliament itself (see Chapter Seven). However, the form of political system can also have a strong effect, as numerous authors have pointed out. This is simply because the distribution of powers has an important effect on the incentives for coalition-building.

When no parliamentary party has a majority of seats, a coalition must be built with other parties. This can entail substantial costs and dangers for the parties involved. If the coalition includes parties with substantially different platforms and constituencies, the parties may alienate both their activists and their voting base in the next elections. This is especially true if the coalition agreement includes specific provisions for legislation opposed by important components of the electorate. On the other hand, if they join forces to govern with those close to them politically, it is also likely that they are collaborating with those with whom they compete most intensely for votes.

What benefit is to be gained in exchange for these risks? In a parliamentary system it is clear: the ability to govern the country, to name the prime minister and the rest of the cabinet, and to implement one's legislative agenda. Presumably, these are the goals the parties exist for in the first place. An additional benefit of participating in the governing coalition is control over the executive branch. This can have important effects on the implementation of policies, and also can provide opportunities to strengthen the party through control over governmental appointments. Moreover, most parliamentary systems have another powerful incentive to form a coalition: the threat of new elections. The rules vary across countries, but in cases where a coalition collapses, the result is either a very vulnerable minority coalition or new elections. In some cases, parties may welcome new elections as a way to strengthen their representation. But unless a party knows for sure that its lot will improve, there are powerful incentives for legislators who want to remain in office as long as possible to avoid new elections.

However, in a presidential system, especially in a system with a very powerful president, none of the positive incentives just listed operate. Regardless of the compromises parties make to form a majority coalition, parties in a presidential system will get relatively little out of it, compared with those in a parliamentary system. In a presidential system, the president retains the power to name the cabinet and oversees the executive branch. The president in such a system also maintains considerable influence over the legislative agenda, with powers that, in different systems, range from the right to veto legislation to the right to issue decrees. In Ukraine, which has a presidency that is considered very powerful, not much has been left for the parliament.

In Ukraine's 1996–2006 arrangements, the only substantial benefit at stake in forming a parliamentary majority was the ability to name the parliamentary speaker, and to have a leading voice in allocating the chairs of the various committees. If the committees played as powerful a role in drafting (and blocking) legislation as they do in the United States, this might provide a considerable incentive. But since bills are introduced not in committee, but in plenary session, the committees have little legislative power. Also, committee chairs in Ukraine are, by law, allocated proportionately according to the seats controlled by the various parties. Thus even opposition parties receive a share of the committee chair positions. And as long as the president could effectively overrule the parliament on many key issues, there was relatively little at stake in the formation of a governing majority. This helps to explain why, for almost its entire existence as an independent state, Ukraine has had a parliament with no set majority. It is not simply that the members of parliament and their parties are divided: this is true in a great many countries that nonetheless manage to form a majority. Rather, a substantial part of the problem is the lack of incentives to make the compromises necessary to form such a majority.

The difference was immediately obvious under the new rules that took effect in 2006. In 2002, once a deal to elect a parliamentary speaker was reached, coalition talks collapsed, because so little was at stake. In 2006, Our Ukraine and the Party of Regions made significant concessions, both in the composition of the cabinet and in the content of a coalition agreement, in order to get a deal done.[52] Neither got as many cabinet seats as they would have like, and both had to agree to compromises on crucial issues such as language policy and possible NATO membership. Most important, Yanukovych and Yushchenko had to overcome their personal hostility. But for Yushchenko in particular, the alternative was worse: if he dissolved parliament and called new elections, his party would likely have ended up with a diminished chance for participating in a governing coalition.

This argument illuminates the problems that face the Ukrainian state since the Orange Revolution. Many in Ukraine (and in Russia and other post-Soviet states) have seen the accumulation of more and more power by the president as a necessary response to the unfortunate inability of the parliament to work effectively. In such circumstances, with enormous problems facing the country, it has made sense to reallocate power to the executive if it cannot be wielded effectively by the parliament.

Indeed, such a solution has been advocated by many in the West, especially when it meant weakening a parliament that would be controlled by leftists. The allure of the presidential model is shown in Viktor Yushchenko's consistent support of maintaining the post-1996 presidential model rather than moving to a parliamentary form of government: "The presidential model is more effective for a country in transition. It concerns, first and foremost, the country's economy. . . . The question is whether the reform designers have convincing arguments in favor of applying a parliamentary model specifically to the Ukrainian situation. Who can estimate all the consequences, impacts and risks of this constitutional revolution?"[53]

However, the causality between weak parliaments and strong presidencies may be the reverse of what is typically assumed. It may be that rather than a weak parliament justifying (and therefore causing) an expansion of presidential powers, extensive presidential powers reduce the incentives to form a stable majority coalition in parliament.

Shugart and Carey focus particularly on this problem:

> In the first place, presidents in multiparty systems who do not have majority party support in congress have far less incentive to seek and maintain lasting coalitions than do parliamentary executives. The success of any

> given piece of legislation may depend on putting together a majority coalition, but the survival of the executive does not. For this reason, coalition building in many presidential regimes tends to be piecemeal, and the incentives offered to congresspersons particularistic.[54]

This captures very well the dynamic we have witnessed in Ukraine, and reinforces the argument that Ukraine's problems are not due to some intractable and uniquely Ukrainian factors, but rather to a relatively well-understood effect of institutional design.

Moreover, passing legislation is further impeded in a presidential system by the incentives of the nonpresidential parties in parliament: "For representatives of parties other than the president's, the logic of opposition is clear . . . : There is nothing to gain from cooperation with the executive."[55] As a result, the executive has to resort to particularistic incentives to build the temporary majorities needed to pass specific legislation.

There is also a much more direct way in which presidential power causes a weak and divided parliament in Ukraine. While Kuchma sought to construct a pro-presidential majority in parliament, such as Putin obtained in Russia, he also devoted considerable effort to preventing the emergence of any other majority. There are widespread and credible reports of Kuchma using the resources of the executive branch to convince members of opposition parliamentary factions to defect. This was most notable in the period after the 2002 parliamentary elections, when there was still a serious possibility that a majority coalition would be built around Yushchenko's Our Ukraine bloc. A number of deputies associated with Our Ukraine subsequently defected from the bloc, either to join pro-presidential blocs or to become independent. This, of course, impeded construction of a majority, which in this case was Kuchma's goal. Some of the candidates who ran on the Our Ukraine party list in 2002 apparently did so with prearranged deals with the executive to defect after the elections. In sum, the weakness of Ukraine's parliament during Kuchma's reign resulted in part from a sophisticated and carefully implemented strategy by the executive branch. This phenomenon is explored further in Chapter Nine.

Would Ukraine Be Better Off with a Parliamentary System?

Given these arguments against a presidential system, can we conclude that Ukraine would be better off with a parliamentary system? We should answer cautiously. A point made repeatedly throughout this book is that Ukraine's governmental problems are the result of a confluence of factors rather than a single one. We cannot therefore say that Ukraine's governance system would improve markedly if a parliamentary system were developed while nothing else changed. On the other hand, the establishment of a parliamentary system would be an integral part of a package of changes that would help build liberal democracy in Ukraine. As the next chapters will show, however, both the electoral laws and the internal rules of the parliament would have to change, along with the form of government, in order for the Ukrainian parliament to function effectively. So we cannot simply state that Ukraine's government would improve substantially with a parliamentary system.

On the other hand, there is considerable comparative evidence to indicate that Ukraine will have a very difficult time building democracy with a presidential system. As was discussed in Chapter Five, building multiparty presidentialism that functions well is extremely difficult. While there may be some debate, it appears that the most successful case to date has been Chile prior to 1973, a democracy that, although it endured for three decades, ended disastrously. More recently, Brazil seems to have established somewhat successful multiparty presidentialism, but the case is too recent to draw any real conclusions. While there may be debate about classifying particular cases, there can be little debate that there are very few successful multiparty presidential systems. All the stable presidential systems, most notably the United States, have two-party systems.

It is surprising that in all the discussion of institutional design in the former Soviet Union, the seeming incompatibility of presidential constitutions and multiparty politics with consolidation of democracy has received little attention, even as all of the post-Soviet states except the Baltics have developed strong presidencies and fragmented party systems. While the blind application of social science theories to the former Soviet system has led to some substantial misunderstanding, it is odd that this seeming contradiction has not received more discussion.

If we accept the argument discussed in the previous chapter that Ukraine's society has a sufficient number of cleavages that a two-party system is highly unlikely to develop, even under the most tightly constraining electoral laws, then it is difficult not to conclude that a presidential system is likely to fail. For Ukraine to successfully develop multiparty presidential democracy would require it to perform a political feat that few if any other countries have accomplished recently. This is not necessarily impossible, but given Ukraine's political track record since independence, it might not be wise to count on such superior performance.

As Shugart and Carey have found, presidential systems tend to have weaker party systems than parliamentary systems.[56] This appears to be another strike against presidentialism for Ukraine, where parties are quite weak. On the other hand, Sartori asserts that parliamentarism will not, by itself, strengthen party systems. Inchoate party systems, he argues, will remain that way unless something more powerful, such as the rise of mass-based political parties, changes them.[57] This point is crucial for Ukraine: with a weak and fragmented party system, neither presidentialism nor parliamentarism is likely to work well. Neither of these forms of government can be expected to automatically cure the problem of weak parties. Some other factor will be necessary.

The 2006 Amendments: An Initial Assessment

The deal that led to the rerunning of the second round of the 2004 presidential election included substantial changes to the constitution, which took effect in early 2006. The balance of power between the president, the prime minister, and parliament has been substantially modified. The new arrangements strike a compromise between those who sought to maintain a very strong presidency, and those who advocated a shift to a fully parliamentary system.[58]

The 2006 amendments shift power away from the president, and toward the prime minister and parliament. According to the new provisions, the prime minister will have the power to name most (but not all) of the ministers. Several key posts will continue to be appointed by the president: these include the ministers of defense and foreign affairs, the heads of the Security Service of Ukraine, the National Security and Defense Council, the National Bank, and the procurator general. Parliament will also be able to dismiss ministers individually, increasing the parliament's ability to influence policy in individual ministries. Thus, the ministers will serve at the pleasure of both the president and the parliament. The term of office of the cabinet of ministers has been changed to coincide with parliamentary, rather than presidential, elections. When a new parliament is elected, a new cabinet will be named based on the majority in the new parliament.

The cabinet, therefore, is being more closely aligned with the parliament. Ukraine is less likely to see a situation in which the cabinet is opposed by the majority in parliament, a frequent situation in presidential systems. It is correspondingly more likely to experience a situation in which the cabinet (or at least the portion named by the prime minister) is at odds with the president. This clearly was the case in the first cabinet to be named after the new rules went into effect. In that cabinet, the prime minister (Viktor Yanukovych) and several ministers were from the Party of Regions, and as such were rivals of President Yushchenko and his Our Ukraine party.

The primary virtue of these changes is that they will undermine the constitutional basis for hyperpresidential rule in Ukraine. Allowing the prime minister to appoint most of the ministers will strengthen the prime minister relative to the president. Allowing the parliament to dismiss individual ministers—without throwing out the entire cabinet and forcing a crisis—will strengthen the parliament's control over the executive branch. This will make it harder for the president to use the government to harass his or her political adversaries.

A second potential virtue is the closer alignment of the cabinet and the parliament—in other words, the move toward a parliamentary system. If the modifications work as envisioned, conflict between the branches should be reduced. A third benefit is the increased incentive for parliament to form a working majority. Giving more power to the parliament increases the incentive for different parties to strike a deal. With the prime minister naming the heads of most ministries, the possibility now exists for coalition deals to be brokered by distributing key ministerial positions to parties supporting the coalition. This is a normal part of coalition-building in most parliamentary democracies, and was evident in Ukraine in 2006. In that agreement, the entire slate of ministers was agreed upon, rather than the president and prime minister each appointing the heads of those ministries allocated to them by the constitution. Control over ministerial posts should also help to hold a coalition together.

A less optimistic view of these changes is also possible. At least on paper, the changes adopted in 2004 will create a system in Ukraine that is somewhat similar to the one prevailing from 1991 to 1995, when the parliament and president were engaged in a constant struggle for control of the government.

In that era, the prime minister was nominally in control of the cabinet of ministers, but the parliament and president shared control over the prime minister and the government. The parliament and president fought to control the prime minister, while the latter struggled for independence from both. The result, through much of the period from 1991 to 1995, was immobility. The response was the 1996 constitution, which gave immense power to the presidency.

The problem with the 2006 amendments is that rather than establishing a system of checks and balances and a separation of powers, they create overlapping powers. It appears that the new system will be prone to competition in the selection of ministers. Moreover, with the powers over actual policy unclear, we can envision a constant struggle between parliament and the president to control the actual behavior of the government.

How well (or badly) the system functions will be determined by who controls the various institutions, and how inclined they are to collaborate. If the parliament and presidency are controlled by the same forces and they stay united, we might see the president, parliament, and the cabinet working closely together. If the presidency and parliament are held by opposing forces, the danger of immobility will only increase. We can easily imagine a situation whereby the parliament, controlling most of the ministers, pursues one political line, while the president, controlling a few of the most powerful ministers, pursues a different line. Moreover, since elements of the executive branch are often deployed as political weapons, we can imagine that the bureaucracies controlled by the different branches would engage on opposite sides of such battles. There were signs of this already in 2005, when ministers appointed by Tymoshenko and those appointed by Yushchenko were involved in an undeclared war, prompting Yushchenko to fire Tymoshenko and the rest of the cabinet. With the new amendments in effect, the president can no longer resolve conflicts this way. But such conflicts between president and prime minister are quite likely to persist when the two offices are held by rivals.

Conclusion

The primary problem in Ukraine's constitutional affairs since 1996 has been the excessive formal power granted to the president. Kuchma was able to use this formal power in combination with his extensive informal powers to establish an essentially authoritarian form of rule in Ukraine. At the same time, parliament has been relatively weak (both on paper and in reality). The limited powers given to parliament undermined its incentives to work effectively, providing even further justification for strong presidential rule.

The constitutional amendments that took effect in 2006 will certainly limit the power of the president. But it remains uncertain whether they will help lead to effective government or whether they will encourage stalemate. It is difficult to predict how practices will emerge from the formal written rules. While the new constitutional provisions (and the accompanying changes to other laws) will likely reduce the president's power, it is unclear that they will build the basis for an effective parliament. In the long term, this goal is just as important for Ukraine's future.

7

The Electoral Law
Cause or Effect of Weak Parties?

A 1998 survey of Ukrainians showed how poorly the parliament was regarded by those it is meant to represent: only 7.3 percent said they "trust more than distrust" or "completely trust" the parliament, as compared with 14.5 percent who trusted astrologers.[1] Parliament is perceived as fragmented, dominated by groups that have little desire to pass legislation, and highly corrupt.

The problem with forming a functioning parliament is arguably the central problem in building liberal democracy in Ukraine. It is not possible to have liberal democracy in the absence of a functioning legislature. In turn, a parliament cannot function effectively without the ability to form relatively stable majority parties or majority coalitions. These in turn cannot be formed without functioning political parties. In Ukraine, the absence of strong parties, majority coalitions, and a functioning parliament led in the 1990s to the widespread view that power must be diverted to the executive in order for government to be effective. This augmentation of executive power was the central component of the erosion of democracy in Ukraine. The Orange Revolution placed stronger limits on the power of the president. But if the parliament cannot function more effectively, aspirations for liberal democracy in Ukraine will continue to be frustrated.

Explaining the Absence of a Majority

Ukraine has never had a durable majority coalition in its parliament. The simplest explanation lies in the fragmentation of political views stemming from regional, ethnic, and linguistic cleavages. This view was explored at length in Chapter Five, where it was found wanting. Some theorists point out that the overall structure of executive–legislative relations has an impact on coalition formation in parliament, a factor discussed in Chapter Six. Having discussed the role of societal cleavages and constitutional provisions in causing this fragmentation, we now turn to the Ukrainian electoral law as an explanation.

There are essentially two schools of thought on the sources of parliamentary fragmentation. Both examine the same two sets of factors, societal cleavages and electoral rules. One school focuses exclusively on electoral rules, finding that well-designed laws can overcome societal cleavages. The other finds that societal cleavages and electoral laws are both significant, with societal cleavages limiting the effectiveness of electoral laws.

In all of these analyses, the primary focus is on the "effective number of parties"; that is, the number of parties that consistently gains representation in parliament. The underlying assumption is that a smaller number of parties makes it more likely that a stable, effective governing coalition will be formed. The literature on political parties becomes quite technical in measuring the "effective number of parties."[2] However, in Ukraine this precision is both unneeded and misleading. While there are a large number of political parties in the country, the number that "matter" appears to be shrinking over time. Between six and eight parties were elected to parliament in the 1998 and 2002 elections, but those parties quickly fragmented, so that there were effectively many more in parliament. Thus the relationship between the number of parties *elected* and the number of parties *working in parliament* has been tenuous.

This pattern is changing with the new rules adopted since 2004. In the 2006 elections, only five parties entered parliament. Under the new rules (in particular the "imperative mandate"), parties will not be able to split once they are elected to parliament, so the standard measure should become more relevant. We say "should" because even though formal defection from parties will not be permitted, party cohesion might remain low.

Institutional Approaches

It is widely argued that electoral laws can powerfully limit the fragmenting tendencies of heterogeneous societies.[3] From this perspective, the institutional and societal explanations of parliamentary fragmentation compete with one another. The argument, based in rational choice theory, is that politicians want to come to power and that to achieve this they will do whatever is necessary, given the constraints of the system. If electoral rules make it necessary to join forces with other parties to succeed, this view argues, party elites will do so, even if it requires making compromises with other parties that they do not like. Interest in getting elected trumps ideology. Moreover, there is a natural selection aspect to the argument: those parties that make their strategic choices based on ideology rather than on the need to win office will, over time, lose support and eventually disappear. Thus, Ordeshook and Shvetsova argue that a country will have a fragmented party system only if it has *both* substantial societal cleavages *and* an election law that creates little incentive to overcome them.[4] This view implies that properly designed election laws will overcome Ukraine's societal divisions to create a more unified parliament.

Societal/Institutional Approaches

Other scholars view societal cleavages and election laws as independent determinants of the number of parties in parliament. Neto and Cox, for example, treat the number of parties in a system as a function of *both* societal cleavages and the electoral law.[5] They do not disagree that different electoral laws create different incentives for party consolidation, and hence influence the number of parties in parliament. But they also argue that the results created by a particular electoral law are likely to be conditioned by the cleavage structure in society.

At least in the case of Ukraine, this makes more sense. As we pointed out in Chapter Two, Ukraine's regional divisions strongly condition the way that Duverger's law operates. Single-member district plurality election rules will create a two-party system only in states with a homogeneously distributed population, but not in those with substantial regional differences.[6] Moreover, because independents are so strong in Ukraine, single-member district (SMD) seats tend to undermine the role of all parties by putting independents in a strong competitive position.

More specifically, Giovanni Sartori argues that the effects of all electoral laws—both SMD and proportional representation (PR) systems—are contingent upon the geographical distribution of electorates.[7] In a society that is not heavily polarized, he contends, a PR system will have centripetal (consolidating) tendencies, providing incentives for parties to merge. Competition tends to move parties toward the center rather than toward the extremes. In such situations, he predicts, PR will lead to "moderate multipartism," in which there are more than two parties, but not many more.

In a country with a polarized electorate, however, Sartori asserts that a pure PR system will lead to "polarized multipartism," in which parties tend to move toward the edges of the political spectrum rather than to the middle "thereby inducing a multipolar competition that eventually heightens systemic polarization."[8]

Applying the Societal/Institutional Approach to Ukraine

Here we follow the view that societal cleavages and electoral laws are complementary sources of the party structure. Ukraine's societal cleavages motivate elites to form a variety of parties and to split parties in a way that makes coherent governance difficult. But there is no compelling evidence that the formation of a "normal" ruling coalition in Ukraine is impossible. On the contrary, the bargaining over a coalition following the 2002 parliamentary elections indicated that the formation of a majority is possible. More recently, bargaining over the confirmation of a new prime minister in September 2005 showed that even parliamentary factions regarded as mortal enemies can join forces when it is in their interest to do so. Similarly, after the 2006 parliamentary election, even the intense hostility among the three most successful parties did not prevent a coalition from eventually being formed.

Majority coalitions can be formed in Ukraine, but given Ukraine's societal fragmentation, the challenge is more substantial than is the case in very homogeneous societies. Election laws and other rules will need to be designed more carefully in Ukraine because the obstacles to coalition-building are higher.

Thus, assessing the extent of Ukraine's cleavages and assessing the effects of various electoral laws are not two distinct enterprises, even though they must be separated for analytical purposes. What implications do the cleavages discussed in Chapter Five have for the design and effect of electoral rules? Are the cleavages so deep that a pure PR system will lead to "polarized multipartism?" If so, then Ukraine faces quite a challenge, insofar as Sartori provides no ready solution for designing electoral laws for such a polity. Fortunately for Ukraine, the situation is not so dire. As Chapter Five showed (and as Ukraine's 2006 elections indicate), Ukraine's divisions are real but not insurmountable. There are plenty of actors in the middle of the political spectrum around whom coalitions can be built.

While Ukraine has cleavages, it does not have "polarization."[9] If we examine Sartori's criteria for a society that is too fragmented for PR to work, it is clear that these criteria do not fit Ukraine. He argues that moderate multipartism is impeded only when "incoercible *above plurality* or as the case may be, *above quotient* minorities happen to be geographically concentrated or dispersed."[10] In plain English, the point is whether minorities exist in sufficient numbers (and geographic concentration) that they can sustain minority-based parties, and not be forced to choose from among the other parties. In one of the most methodologically sophisticated studies of Ukrainian voters' attitudes, Melvin Hinich, Valeri Khmelko, and Peter Ordeshook conclude: "Preferences differ, but there remains a vast middle ground that can be nurtured in search of a national compromise, if not consensus."[11]

In Ukraine, the parties that have identified themselves with specific minority groups or languages—be they Crimean Tatar or Russian—have never gained more than a small percentage of the vote. Most significantly in this regard, parties that have sought to build support primarily by focusing on the rights of Russian speakers or on unity with Russia have never been elected to parliament. Parties following a Ukrainian nationalizing agenda, such as Rukh, have seen their share of votes consistently diminish and were not represented separately in either the 2002 or 2006 parliaments. Thus, the empirical findings of Chapter Five, combined with general findings in the comparative literature, indicate that Ukraine's societal cleavages are not of the nature that would prevent formation of a party system based on five to seven major parties.

Institutions and Coalition Building

As many students of party politics have emphasized, the problem is not that institutions create strong incentives toward party fragmentation, but that the variety of public opinion makes such incentives inherent. The natural tendency is toward fragmentation, and the question is: what institutional disincentives counteract this tendency?[12] Electoral laws can provide strong incentives for parties to coalesce in order to increase electoral success. Or they can provide weak incentives, insufficient to overcome the inherent tendencies to split parties.

Underlying the institutional approach is the assumption, widespread in the comparative politics literature, that politicians are opportunistic and react to the incentives they face. Without necessarily accepting everything that the rational choice approach to political science asserts, it is certainly plausible to build our understanding of Ukrainian politics on the generalization that the vast majority of Ukrainian politicians are self-interested and concerned with gaining and holding power. Erik Herron has examined this question in great detail, finding that electoral strategy as well as policy concerns influence the decisions of Ukrainian parliamentarians to desert their parties.[13] If party consolidation makes it much easier to gain and hold power, parties and elites are more likely to seek ways to merge, whatever their differences. This was in evidence in Ukraine in the coalition formed in August 2006.

In Ukraine, we have seen a variety of institutional arrangements that provide very little payoff to party mergers and coalition-building. For each political "identity group" in Ukraine, there may well be two or more political parties—implying that cleavage structures are not the sole source of fragmentation.[14] The most extreme example is the "national democratic" constituency that originally was served almost exclusively by Rukh. Having split once in the early 1990s, when the Congress of Ukrainian Nationalists was formed, Rukh fragmented in 2000 into three factions, and a host of other nationalist parties emerged as well. While there were serious differences among the three factions, they were very near to each other ideologically and programmatically (as shown by the fact that a single Rukh existed in the first place), and voted together often in parliament. The fragmentation of Rukh in 2000 cannot be explained by regional difference or by ideological incompatibility. While there may have been genuine differences, the personal ambitions of the leaders were likely an equally strong cause. Regardless of the cause, however, leaders could find it in their interest to split only if the costs of doing so were fairly low. This low disincentive to splitting is largely an institutional factor, for it is the electoral laws that raise or lower the costs of party fragmentation.

This chapter examines two sources of the inability to form majority coalitions in parliament. First, it examines provisions of the electoral law that have reduced incentives for parties to join together. Second, parties themselves have been very weak. Most analyses of party systems begin with the assumption that parties are well rooted in society and are the main structuring forces in politics. This assumption has not held in Ukraine, where candidates have often succeeded as independents, and where parties tend to be associated with a single individual. Because parties have been weak, elites have not invested in them, and because elites have not invested in them, parties have remained weak. There have been signs since 2002 that elites are investing more in parties, but of the five parties that surmounted the 3 percent hurdle in 2006, four were so closely identified with a single individual that the names of the individual and the party were often used interchangeably.[15]

Electoral Laws

No aspect of institutional design has received greater attention than electoral laws. It is clear that electoral laws can have an immense effect on the party system in a country, on the fragmentation of the parliament, and hence on the parliament's ability to legislate effectively. Moreover, they seem relatively easy to change (compared, for example, with the societal cleavage structure). "Compared to other components of political systems, electoral systems are the easiest to manipulate with specific goals in view."[16] Therefore, a central place to look for sources of parliamentary ineffectiveness in Ukraine—and to look for cures—is the election laws by which parliament is chosen.

To briefly recap the literature reviewed in Chapter Two, studies of election laws have focused on two archetypal systems, the single-member district plurality system (e.g., that used to elect the U.S. House of Representatives and the British Parliament) and the proportional representation system used in electing legislatures in most of Western Europe, which is the most popular model. These two systems are subject to "Duverger's law" and "Duverger's hypothesis," respectively. Together, Duverger's law and hypothesis find that plurality election laws lead to two-party systems while proportional representation laws lead to multiparty systems. In two-party systems, one party or the other is virtually guaranteed a majority in parliament, such that coalition formation is not an issue. In PR systems, it is more likely that no single party will win a majority, and that a coalition will be required to form a working majority. The primary benefits indicated by supporters of PR are that it allows for representation in parliament of a much broader array of political forces and that the politics of coalition formation force governments toward moderation.

Ukraine used a single-member district system in 1994, a mixed system in 1998 and 2002, and a full PR system in 2006. The mixed system used in 1998 and 2002 is nearly identical to the system used in Russia. Half of the 450 deputies were elected in single-member districts based on plurality voting, while the other half were elected on party lists according to proportional representation.[17] The effects of mixed systems depend on the details of the provisions, and therefore are less uniformly predictable than those of pure systems.[18] At least in Ukraine, however, it appears that the mixed system retains the weaknesses of both systems as much as it does the strengths.

Election laws in post-Soviet Ukraine have had to grapple with two problems simultaneously. The first problem is the same as that in other countries: providing incentives to party consolidation and coalition formation. Ukraine has also had a second, less typical problem: the weakness of political parties in general. This combination of challenges has traditionally been neglected in the considerable literature that has emerged both to design and analyze these systems. As Robert Moser says of Russia, "The conclusion is simple, yet surprisingly absent from most of the neo-institutionalist research: context matters."[19]

The mixed system was adopted with a view to solving both problems at once; Shugart and Wattenberg call it the "best of both worlds."[20] The proportional part of the ballot was intended to strengthen parties by selecting half the parliament's seats on the basis of parties. The plurality system was intended to promote party consolidation through the mechanism of Duverger's law.

In practice, however, the measures adopted to solve one problem tended to exacerbate the other. The plurality section undermined party-building by allowing independents to thrive. The proportional component undermined party consolidation by allowing small parties a good chance of entering parliament. Thus, Sartori's assessment that the mixed system is a "bastard-producing hybrid which combines their defects," may be more accurate.[21] Ukraine needs electoral laws that do more than just provide incentives for well-developed political parties to merge. It needs to provide the conditions for the formation and strengthening of those parties. The fully proportional law used in the 2006

Table 7.1

Results of the 1994 Parliamentary Elections

Party	Seats
Right	
Ukrainian National Assembly	3
Ukrainian Conservative Republican Party	2
Rukh	20
Ukrainian Republican Party	8
Congress of National Democratic Forces	5
Democratic Party of Ukraine	2
Center	
Interregional Reform Block	4
Ukrainian Democratic Renaissance Party	4
Civic Congress of Ukraine	2
Social Democratic Party of Ukraine	2
Labor Congress of Ukraine	4
Christian Democratic Party of Ukraine	1
Left	
Communist Party	86
Peasant Party	18
Ukrainian Socialist Party	14
Independent	163
Total (112 seats remained unfilled)	338

Source: BRAMA, "1994 Election Results in Ukraine—By Alliances/Parties," www.brama.com/ua-gov/el-94vrg.html, accessed July 8, 1998.

election had a powerful effect on party formation, and even led to the admission of fewer parties (five) to parliament than the mixed system had.

The 1994 Electoral Law

Parliaments elected under Soviet election laws were elected in single-member districts, in a two-round majority system, which has many of the characteristics of a plurality system but is expected to lead much less reliably to a two-party system.[22] It is in essence a very weak version of the single-member plurality system. There is less pressure on third parties to merge, because running second in a two-round system keeps their hopes alive, while running second in a single-round system is useless. Similarly, voters have more incentive to vote for third parties in a two-round system. However, the more important result of this system in Ukraine was the election of large numbers of independents (see Table 7.1). The first post-Soviet parliamentary elections in Ukraine in 1994, which used the Soviet-era electoral law, led to a parliament in which 25 percent of the members were independents.

Duverger's law did not apply to Ukraine's 1994 election in part because the electoral law used was not the plurality law on which the theory is based. But there was a more basic problem. The preconditions for party consolidation (a relatively small number of parties) did not exist. One of the limiting factors that Duverger and others place on his "law" is that single-member plurality systems cannot be expected to consolidate highly fragmented systems. Rather, once a system has some degree of consolidation, single-member plurality rules provide powerful incentives for parties to merge until there are only two. Ukraine's "initial conditions" in its first post-Soviet elections consisted of a very large number of very small parties, with a large number of powerful independent candidates as well. The result is that the SMD format tended to encourage, rather than undermine, independents.

Understanding why this is so is important to understanding the dynamics of Ukrainian politics in the 1990s. According to standard research on electoral laws, single-member plurality systems work through a combined "mechanical effect" and "psychological effect." The mechanical effect operates on parties, and especially those that get a substantial portion of the vote but do not win many districts. Two or more of these parties have powerful incentives to merge because until they do they will be shut out of power. For example, in a system with one right-wing and two left-wing parties, the two left-wing parties, by dividing the leftist vote, will win far fewer seats than they could by merging (imagine a situation in which the two left-wing parties each get 30 percent of the vote, but the rightist party wins the seat with 40 percent). There is a powerful incentive for them to merge, because *both* parties will receive more seats than if they continue to split the vote. This is a key point: in the SMD plurality system, the merger of parties creates a whole that is greater than the sum of its parts: the merged parties gain more total seats as a single party than they would as two separate ones. Over time, the number of parties is reduced toward two, as losing parties merge to increase their chances of winning a plurality.

The "psychological" effect works not on parties, but on voters, relying on the notion that voters do not like to "waste" their votes by voting for candidates that have little chance of winning. In a single-member plurality system, it is likely that, at most, two or three parties will have a serious chance of winning any given seat (or an overall majority in parliament). Even voters who prefer some less popular candidate are likely to vote only for one of those considered to have a genuine chance. This fact is often used to explain the inability of third parties to emerge in the United States. Over time, parties that do not win seats will get fewer votes with each successive election, eventually becoming irrelevant.

Both the mechanical and psychological effects, however, depend on the ability of party leaders and voters to effectively determine which parties have good chances of winning either a particular seat or overall control of parliament. In other words, these effects depend on the party system's already being consolidated to some extent. Thus, Sartori emphasizes that the SMD plurality system can be relied on to maintain an existing two-party system, but not necessarily to create one where it does not exist.[23] In Ukraine in 1994, with a large number of very new and very small parties, it was difficult for voters and party leaders alike to accurately assess which parties were likely to win and which were likely to do poorly. The problem was compounded by the fact that the parties that appeared likely to compete strongly in one district may have differed from those that appeared promising in another district. Because no party except the Communist Party of Ukraine was strong across regions, neither the mechanical nor the psychological effect could work.

This problem was magnified even further by the strength of independent candidates. In districts where the most prominent candidates were independents rather than party members, the logic of party consolidation ceased to operate altogether. While voters still might try to avoid obvious losers, to the extent that they could be identified, there was no mechanical effect on the candidates, because unlike parties, which by merging could expect to pick up seats overall across many districts, individual independent candidates faced a zero-sum game: consolidation meant that one candidate would have to give up his or her aspirations altogether.

The 1998 Election Law

While the 1994 election law served the interests of many entrenched elites, it produced such a badly fragmented parliament that there was a widely perceived need for change prior to the 1998 elections. There were two primary goals in changing the rules of competition. First, the fact that many districts failed to meet the requirement of a 50 percent voter turnout meant that many seats were not filled for much of the parliament's term. That problem was universally recognized, and removing the 50 percent rule endangered nobody's interests. Hence it was dropped relatively easily. The second and third problems were much more difficult to tackle.

The second need was to reduce the number of independents in parliament. It was widely recognized that the centrist "swamp" of independent candidates made it very difficult to form a stable majority. But there was disagreement concerning what to do about it, as well as outright opposition to eliminating single-member districts. The simplest way to eliminate independents, in the eyes of many participants and observers, would be to shift to a pure PR system. By making members of parliament more dependent on parties for their seats, it would help to structure the parliament by increasing party loyalty.[24] This solution was finally adopted in 2004 and first implemented in 2006.

However, the designers of the 1998 law hesitated to go to a full PR system for several reasons. One was a desire to maintain some link between candidates and their local constituencies. Perhaps the most significant shortcoming of a pure PR system is that there is no regional or local representation.[25] To some, this seemed to undermine the notion of representation. It also seemed more prone to the formation of a Kyiv-based political elite that was out of touch with the rest of the country. Furthermore, it seemed less able than a district-based system to represent Ukraine's diverse regional interests. Finally, there was some concern that a full PR system would produce a proliferation of political parties that would make the forming of a working majority no easier than it had been in the 1994–98 parliament.[26]

These debates were not carried out in a dispassionate or apolitical environment. Everyone involved recognized that much was at stake in terms of which parties and which political forces would be likely to prosper under various arrangements.[27] Generally speaking, leftist parties opposed the shift away from the single-member district system because their candidates held positions of local influence under the communist system and continued to hold them. Their local power bases advantaged them in a district-based system. The leftists' position changed in subsequent debates, as the socialists and communists lost control over local positions and realized that their superior party organizations would provide an advantage in proportional representation.

The single-member district system was also favored by the growing group of less ideological businessmen who sought seats in parliament as an adjunct to their business activities. Their local resource bases also advantaged them in a single-member district system. They benefited from the opportunities for vote trading in a system where they had no hard political allegiance. They had no interest in a system that eliminated independents or made members of parliament more easily controlled by party leaders. Centrist business interests continued to oppose a full PR system all the way through 2004.

The PR system was favored more by the rightist parties, due to the peculiar conditions that they faced at the time. The overriding problem for the right was its continuing inability to marshal its forces into a single party or even a small number of parties. The Rukh movement had split (and would split again), and there was a strong tendency for rightist elites to form new parties rather than to merge, as would be required in a full single-member plurality system. In a full PR system, there was much less need for these parties to merge because simply meeting the threshold for representation (which was established at 4 percent), rather than attaining a plurality of votes in some district, was required. Not only would PR reduce the imperative to merge, but it might turn the variety of rightist parties from a liability to an advantage. Voters would have a range of rightist parties from which to choose—some more nationalist, others more focused on the free market.

Ukraine's mixed election law was not merely a result of horse-trading. There were also some theoretical arguments supporting the idea that the mixed system would help to accomplish both of Ukraine's needs simultaneously, strengthening parties and reducing their number. The PR component was intended to build political parties by making them the central actor in the system and by reducing the ability of independents to get elected. Since half the seats in the parliament would be given to political parties, there was a new and powerful incentive to organize along party lines. Moreover, since the party lists were "closed," meaning that party leaders controlled the listing of candidates, the law promised to have a consolidating effect even after the elections. Party leaders could ensure members' loyalty by threatening to move them down the list for the next election or leave them off altogether.[28]

The plurality component was designed to consolidate the party system itself, by providing an incentive for parties to merge. The idea was that both forms of logic would operate separately and simultaneously: the PR system would channel activity into the parties, and the plurality system would create strong incentives to party consolidation. If both forms of logic operated, Ukraine could expect to develop stronger parties (and to eliminate independents) and to decrease the number of parties in parliament. Presumably, coalitions would then be easier to form and more effective governance would result. By electing half of the members by PR and half in plurality single-member districts, one might expect to have more than two parties in parliament, but not many more.

Effects of the 1998 Law

Instead, the hybrid system retained the negative features of both systems rather than the positive features. The plurality system undermined parties because candidates could still run as independents, and the most prominent individuals had the incentive to pursue this route, rather than investing in party-building. Proportional representation hindered the consolidation of parties because the low (4 percent) threshold allowed even very minor parties to be admitted to parliament. Indeed, by providing multiple routes into parliament, the mixed system led to the emergence of even more parties than a pure PR system would have.

In its effects on the number of parliamentary parties, the mixed system of PR and single-member districts functions essentially as a PR system.[29] If the key process of electoral rules in consolidating party systems is the elimination of marginal parties (the so-called mechanical effect), then the relevant question is: what is the minimal success a party can achieve and still gain representation? In Ukraine's mixed system, two different hurdles exist for a party to enter parliament. However, a party needs to clear only one or the other, *not both.* Therefore, it does not much matter how high the higher hurdle is; it matters only how low the lower hurdle is because any party that can clear the lower hurdle can enter parliament. In Ukraine, a party with less than 10 percent popular support may have no chance to win any single-member district seat, but that party could easily enter parliament on the PR side, and hence have no incentive to merge with another. Thus, the "mechanical" effect of Duverger's law on the single-member district is undermined by the PR side. Similarly, the "psychological" effect is undermined by PR, because as long as a party could enter parliament with 4 percent of the vote, a vote for a weak party is not obviously "wasted" (in the sense that it is wasted if cast for a party that has no chance of gaining a plurality).

In Ukraine, the mixed system almost certainly led to a greater number of parties than a strict PR system would have.[30] A party that could not amass enough votes nationally to clear the 4 percent hurdle for admission to parliament could win a majority in a small number of districts, and gain entry that way. At the same time, while parties with distributed support might be unable to win any local constituencies, they could still cross the 4 percent threshold nationwide. In either case, the pressure to consolidate was relieved. Because a party needed only to clear one type of barrier (either the percentage threshold on the PR side or the plurality on the single-member district side), parties with different strengths could enter parliament, and parties could even tailor their strategies accordingly. While some parties might be eliminated under a PR system and others under an SMD system, all of these could survive under a mixed system. This is precisely what happened in Ukraine's 1998 elections (See Table 7.2): eight parties entered parliament by clearing the 4 percent hurdle in the PR section, while another sixteen parties (as well as 114 independents) failed to clear the 4 percent hurdle but won at least one single-member district.[31]

The 2002 Elections

In 2002, the mixed system used in 1998 was retained intact. On both sides, there was evidence of consolidation (See Table 7.3). On the proportional side, the number of parties that crossed the 4 percent threshold declined from

Table 7.2

Results of the 1998 Parliamentary Elections

Party	Percentage of proportional representation (PR) vote	PR seats	Single-member district seats	Total seats
Communist Party of Ukraine	24.7	84	37	121
Rukh	9.4	32	14	46
Socialist/Peasant Bloc	8.6	29	5	34
Greens	5.4	19	0	19
National Democratic Party	5.0	17	11	28
Hromada	4.7	16	8	24
Progressive Socialist Party	4.1	14	2	16
Social Democratic Party of Ukraine (United)	4.0	14	3	17
Independents; parties gaining less than 4 percent (total)	34.1	0	140	140

8 to 6 (with only one party receiving between 3 and 4 percent). The percentage of votes "wasted" on parties that did not cross the threshold declined from 34.1 to 19.3. On the plurality side, the number of independents decreased from 140 to 94 (though several candidates elected as party members declared themselves as independents later).[32] While the decrease in the number of independents in the parliament between 1998 and 2002 must be considered progress, independents still amounted to more than 20 percent of the parliament, and therefore made forming a lasting legislative majority challenging.

If the main goal of the PR portion of the ballot was to strengthen parties and eliminate independents, it was clearly undermined by the plurality portion. Not only were 114 candidates in 1998 and 94 candidates in 2002 (just over 25 percent and 20 percent of the parliament, respectively) able to get elected without any party affiliation, but several small parties entered through the plurality districts, reducing their incentive to coalesce to make the 4 percent hurdle. In at least two cases in 1998, parties were demonstrably punished by failing to merge. The Agrarian Party received 3.68 percent of the vote, meaning that an alliance with any of the sixteen parties that received between 0.32 and 4 percent would have put them over the threshold. Similarly, the party of Reforms and Order received 3.1 percent, and could have crossed the threshold by uniting with any of the other ten parties receiving between 0.9 and 4 percent of the vote.

Either of these factions (and their partners) could have gained roughly fourteen seats by doing so. Instead, they received none, although Reforms and Order did enter parliament through the plurality portion of the ballot. In

Table 7.3

Results of the 2002 Parliamentary Elections

Party	Percentage of proportional representation (PR) vote	PR seats	Single-member district seats	Total seats
Our Ukraine	25.1	70	42	112
Communist Party of Ukraine	21.3	59	7	66
United Ukraine	12.6	35	68	103
Tymoshenko Bloc	7.7	22	0	22
Socialist Party of Ukraine	7.3	20	3	23
Social Democratic Party of Ukraine (United)	6.7	19	5	24
Independents; parties gaining less than 4 percent (total)	19.3	0	98	98

2002, only four parties gained multiple seats in the single-member districts without passing the 4 percent hurdle in the PR portion of the ballot, and each with very small numbers.[33] In this respect, Duverger's psychological effect seems to be operating: as voters become better at predicting which parties will do well, and steer their votes away from those who have little chance of winning.

In sum, the application of the mixed system in a country with very weak parties appears to undermine both fundamental goals of the design of the electoral system. The PR component provides some incentive to join parties and some incentive for parties to merge, but both effects are undermined by the plurality section, which allows alternate routes for both parties and individuals to enter parliament. The result was a parliament (in 1998) with a large number of relatively small parties distributed widely across the political spectrum from the overtly pro-Soviet Progressive Socialists to the neo-Nazi National Socialists. The establishment of a working majority under such conditions is difficult, to say the least, and the fact that a quarter of the parliament was elected as independents only made matters worse. The electoral law did very little to reward parties that merged forces or to punish those that did not. In this important sense then, we can say that the fragmentation of the party system both in elections and in parliament is a result of electoral laws.

How could these shortcomings be remedied? In Ukraine, one frequent proposal has been to raise the threshold in the PR section of the election from 4 percent to 5 percent or even higher. Certainly, this would make a difference: in 1998, moving from a 4 percent to 5 percent threshold would have eliminated three parties and distributed forty-four seats among the six parties that received more than 5 percent (other things being equal). The bigger problem, however, is that in a system where parties themselves are so weak, the plurality component would continue to allow many independents into parliament, undermining both the incentives for politicians to structure their activities around parties and the ability to forge a parliamentary majority. This could be eliminated by going to a full PR system, though doing so would eliminate the local representation that the single-member districts allow for. Ultimately, this is the plan that was adopted in 2004 and first used in 2006.

Revised Laws for the 2006 Elections

In 2004, conditions came together for the shift to a fully proportional system. Earlier, this was impossible because Kuchma had a strong interest in maintaining a weak and fragmented policy. By 2004, however, he and his allies sought to hedge their bets against the chance that Viktor Yushchenko would win the presidential election. With Kuchma's opposition diminished, it became possible to change the law. Under the new provisions, the plurality single-member district portion of the ballot was eliminated. All 450 seats are now allotted via proportional representation. As part of the compromise necessary to reach this agreement, the threshold for entering parliament was lowered to 3 percent.

Had a full PR system been in effect in the 1998 and 2002 elections, it would likely have led to an anti-Kuchma majority, which may explain why he so resolutely voted against it. Extrapolating from the PR portion of the 1998 election, if the entire 450-seat parliament were determined by PR with a 4 percent threshold, the Communist Party (with 168 seats) and the Socialist/Peasants bloc (with 58 seats) together would have been able to form a narrow majority, probably electing a Communist speaker.[34] In 2002, Our Ukraine would have received 140 seats, the Tymoshenko Bloc 44, and the Socialist Party 40, which would have left them just short, but within close reach, of a majority. In contrast, United Ukraine, which did form a majority based largely on seats won in single-member districts, would have garnered only 70 seats, which along with 38 from the Social Democratic Party of Ukraine (United) would have left them far short of a majority. Thus, the shift to a PR system does not appear to provide a clear advantage to any particular political force. Rather it favors the large parties at the expense of the smaller ones, and assists those with stronger party identification and with the most prominent notables. This may explain why it was politically feasible to adopt this system in 2004.

In the immediate aftermath of the 2006 election, the question was, as it had been in 1998 and 2002, which parties might form a coalition. However, the atmosphere was entirely different. There was no feeling that the elections

Table 7.4

Results of the 2006 Parliamentary Elections

Party	Percentage of votes	Seats won
Party of Regions	32.1	186
Bloc of Yulia Tymoshenko	22.3	129
Our Ukraine	14.0	81
Socialist Party	5.7	33
Communist Party	3.7	21
Bloc of Natalia Vitrenko	2.9	0
Bloc of Volodymyr Lytvyn	2.4	0
Thirty-nine other parties	16.9	0

Sources: Vote percentages are from the Central Election Commission, www.cvk.gov.ua/vnd2006/w6p001.html, accessed April 11, 2006; seat totals are from Agence France Presse, "Ukraine's 'Orange Revolution' Allies Confident of Coalition," April 11, 2006.

themselves had been unfair. Nor was there the perception that, due to the large number of independents, a coalition would be meaningless. Instead, everyone recognized that a great deal was at stake. The majority coalition would name the prime minister and most of the rest of the ministers.

There was profound drama over which parties would form the coalition. Two possibilities quickly emerged (See Table 7.4). An "orange coalition" would include the parties that supported Viktor Yushchenko and the Orange Revolution in 2004—Our Ukraine, the Tymoshenko Bloc, and the Socialist Party (totaling 243 seats). Due to the relative strength of Tymoshenko's vote compared with Our Ukraine's, which surprised nearly everyone, the Tymoshenko Bloc assumed that their candidate (Tymoshenko) would be named prime minister. It had been agreed between the two parties that the one receiving the most votes would name the prime minister. To Yushchenko and some of his close supporters, Tymoshenko was an unacceptable candidate. While this negotiation dragged on, Our Ukraine explored an alliance with the Party of Regions.

An alliance between Our Ukraine and the Party of Regions was deeply distressing to supporters of the Orange Revolution, who were profoundly dismayed to think that Yushchenko could make a deal with the forces that had tried to steal the 2004 election, and to kill him. It seemed like a betrayal of the Orange Revolution. Yushchenko, however, had a history of preferring conciliation over confrontation. He had worked well as Kuchma's prime minister. Moreover, in some respects this coalition had already existed: in October 2005, Yushchenko's candidate for prime minister, Yuri Yekhanurov, had been approved by the votes of the Party of Regions, and against the opposition of the Tymoshenko Bloc. While the "orange coalition" seemed to promise a return to the ideals of the Maidan, which had been lost in 2005, some feared that it closed out eastern Ukraine from power. The Regions/Our Ukraine coalition had the virtue of bridging Ukraine's regional divide, but it seemed unlikely to lead to serious reform, and virtually certain to leave the crimes of the Kuchma era unpunished. Moreover while an "orange coalition" provided hope for a rapid improvement in relations with the West, including perhaps a clear path to NATO membership, a Regions/Our Ukraine alliance seemed likely to end those hopes.[35]

As is sometimes the case in coalition politics, one of the small parties was able to drive the final process. Oleksandr Moroz, leader of the Socialist Party, shocked everyone by taking the SPU out of the "orange coalition," and instead formed an alliance with the Party of Regions and the Communists. In return, Moroz received their support and was elected speaker of parliament. However, this coalition could not retain enough cohesion to quickly elect a prime minister and cabinet, opening up the door for Yushchenko to dismiss the parliament and call new elections. A new coalition, of Regions, Our Ukraine, and the Socialist Party, then formed a cabinet in early August 2006. Tymoshenko was left fuming and in opposition, and supporters of the Orange Revolution declared Yushchenko a traitor, but advocates of this coalition saw virtue in its cross-regional character.

The 2006 elections tell us a great deal about the role of electoral rules in shaping party and voter behavior, and more broadly about the potential for parliament to function effectively in Ukraine. Most surprising, and generally underappreciated, was the fact that with a very low 3 percent threshold, only five parties were admitted to parliament. In a comparative context, this is remarkable, since countries with higher thresholds often have more parties in parliament. We cannot make too much of the results of a single election, but this election demonstrated in principle that Ukraine's societal cleavages are indeed bridgeable—more so, it seems, than those in many other societies. With the removal of SMDs, and the increased power given to the parliament, even a very low threshold was sufficient to shift voters away from minor parties and toward those they knew had a good chance of winning. This is a promising indicator for the future, notwithstanding the ensuing difficulty in forming a coalition agreement.

These new laws will have some clear benefits for the functioning of the parliament, but will not by themselves fix Ukraine's problems. The fully proportional system will eliminate independents from parliament. This should make it much easier to build a majority coalition. It should also strengthen party leaders' ability to maintain discipline, since members that do not toe the party line can be left off the list in the next elections. Moreover, the new laws include adoption of the "imperative mandate" (see Chapter Eight). This rule requires that members of parliament elected under a certain party lose their seat in parliament if they leave the party. Exactly how this will function remains unclear. At a minimum, it will reduce the frequent party-jumping that has characterized Ukraine's parliament. At a maximum, it will give party leaders tight control over individual members, making it easier for party leaders to make deals with one another, and to deliver the votes needed to pass legislation.

However, several sources of weakness persist. While individual candidates will be forced to operate through parties, this will not automatically strengthen the parties. As we detail below, prominent individuals have tended to build parties around themselves, and then discard the parties after elections. This might well continue under the new system. On the other hand, perhaps the advantages to be gained by a well-organized "ground campaign" will create incentives to strengthen permanent party organizations. Furthermore, depending on how the imperative mandate functions, we might still see a very low level of party discipline, with members of parliament nominally remaining with their parties, but voting as independents. Finally, it is difficult to predict the long-term effects of the 3 percent threshold. The number is low enough that it will always be possible for well-financed individuals to form brand new parties rather than having to choose among the existing parties. In 2006, Volodymyr Lytvyn formed a party that immediately won 2.4 percent of the vote. Were he more popular, his party could well have succeeded. This might help the system avoid stagnation, but it will do little to promote consolidation.

Effects of the Presidential Election Law on the Party System

Thus far, we have focused on the parliamentary election law as the prime determinant of the party system. But as Shugart and Carey point out, consolidation of the party system is influenced not only by the rules for electing the parliament but also by the rules for electing the president. In particular, they argue, the majority runoff system (used in both Ukraine and Russia) does not provide incentives for parties to merge.[36] In this system, a first round election narrows the field to two, unless one candidate receives more than 50 percent of the vote. A second round between the top two candidates then determines the winner. This system creates two distinct disincentives for parties to consolidate.

First, even a party or candidate that does not win in the first round can hope to make it to the second round, and by collecting the votes of the eliminated candidates, win the election. This is exactly what Leonid Kuchma did in 1994. Even though he came in second in the first round, the votes of defeated leftist candidates helped him to defeat Leonid Kravchuk in the second round. In a single round winner-take-all system, Kravchuk would have won that election. The possibility for a second-place finisher in the first round to win the second round erodes the incentive for parties running second and third to join forces. As Robert Moser shows in examining the Russian case, however, by focusing on a final choice between two candidates, the existence of presidential elections has a consolidating effect on voting that advantages centrist candidates at the expense of the left, which thrives in fragmented parliamentary elections.[37]

Second, by participating in the first round, a candidate or party can hope to gain significant influence in the process by striking a bargain with one of the two leaders in the second round. For example, while Alexander Lebed had little chance of prevailing in the 1996 Russian presidential election, his ability to garner 15 percent of the vote in the first round made Boris Yeltsin willing to give him a cabinet position in return for his support in the second round. Yevhen Marchuk made a similarly weak and lucrative showing in the first round of the 1999 Ukrainian election. Had he dropped out before the first round, it is possible that Oleksander Moroz rather than Petro Symonenko would have faced Kuchma in the second round, and polling data indicate that Moroz might have defeated Kuchma.[38] Instead, Marchuk was rewarded with an important government post. Because party systems encompass both presidential and parliamentary elections, the dividing effects of the rules for presidential elections carry over to parliamentary elections.

The Self-Reinforcing Nature of a Weak Party System

The weakness in Ukraine's party system is self-reinforcing.[39] Once a situation is established where political parties have relatively little to contribute to individual politicians, there is not much reason to invest in party-building. If the primary assets to gaining election are name recognition and money, and if prominent politicians possess more of both of these assets than do parties, then there is relatively little reason for elites to invest significant resources in building durable parties.

For the politician with money and name recognition who simply wants to gain a seat in parliament, the simplest route (until 2006) was through a single-member district seat. Because parties are weak, they can contribute little to such campaigns. Because they contribute little, politicians invest few resources in them. And because politicians invest few resources in them, they remain weak and unable to contribute much. This is a very tight vicious circle. Sartori states: "So long as the voter is personality-oriented, so long as he merely votes for a person, parties remain labels of little, if any, consequence."[40] Even the shift to a fully proportional system in 2006 might not be sufficient to strengthen parties. It appears likely that parties will continue to be built around the careers of prominent politicians, rather than the other way around.

The Personalization of Parties

In post-Soviet Ukraine, individuals have greater name recognition than parties. The normal relationship between individuals and parties is turned on its head. Rather than politicians needing parties for their name recognition, finances, and organization, parties need prominent politicians for those things. In 2002, in two of the six electoral blocs that cleared the 4 percent hurdle, the name of the bloc's founder was in the bloc's title. These were Our Ukraine, which was officially titled "Blok Viktora Yushchenka 'Nasha Ukraina,'" [The Bloc of Viktor Yushchenko, Our Ukraine] and the "Bloc of Yulia Tymoshenko." This was not due simply to vanity on the part of the blocs' founders. Rather, both of these individuals were very popular among a specific segment of the population. The point of naming the blocs after them was to gain voter support for a bloc that would likely gain less support without the leader's name attached. There was no shortage of existing parties with platforms that were essentially compatible with Yushchenko's or Tymoshenko's views. But none of them had the level of popularity of the individuals, so in order to win as big a share of seats in parliament in possible, the rational strategy was to name the blocs after the leaders. There is little reason to believe that either bloc will survive in recognizable form after its namesake passes from the political scene.

Similarly, the United Ukraine bloc was created in 2002 not because no ideologically similar party existed. Rather it was felt that creating a new bloc from scratch, avoiding whatever negative associations existed with previous versions of pro-presidential parties, such as the nearly indistinguishable Social Democratic Party of Ukraine (United), was a winning electoral strategy. Both the creation of new parties and their naming after prominent individuals simply represent smart retail politics. The point is that successful electoral strategy in Ukraine does not require long-term building of strong parties.

Disposable Parties

Instead of investing in *parties*, Ukrainian elites invest in *elections*. Elites have found it more expedient to make small investments in "disposable parties," rather than to make large investments in permanent parties. A prominent and wealthy politician seeking to gain admission to parliament through the PR portion of the ballot might form a party or an election bloc to do so.

Once the election is over, however, what incentive remains to maintain that organization until the next election? What is to be gained by maintaining it? The party organizations themselves are not the main source of funding. At best, they are conduits, and at worst, they are irrelevant to the campaign finance process. Another potential reason to maintain the party over time is name recognition. By building a party with a strong "brand identification," one can begin building voter loyalty.

However, when none of the parties has much name recognition, not much is lost in abandoning an existing party and building a new one for the next new election. Thus, many prominent politicians have run on the lists of brand new parties or blocs. For these new parties, the fastest way to build an identity is to focus on the well-known politicians who lead the party. Once those leaders move on, the party collapses. To cite Sartori again: "The voter cannot identify himself with an abstract party image as long as the image is not provided, that is to say, as long as he is confronted with a party of mere notabilities."[41]

Moreover, relying on "disposable parties" relieves leaders of the considerable and constant work involved in building and maintaining a party organization. It also leaves them far more flexibility in choosing electoral strategies—they are not constrained by the views of the rank and file. Rather than being identified with a particular party and incurring serious costs by breaking with that party, politicians can be "free agents." In sum, there may be incentives for underrepresented societal groups to build parties as a way of gaining influence in the system, but in a system where parties start out as unimportant, there is little incentive for elites with resources to invest those resources in parties.

Disposable Parties in Operation

The ability to use "disposable parties" successfully was powerfully demonstrated in the 2002 parliamentary elections. In the year leading up to that election, a plethora of new parties was formed.[42] Thus, the election process itself induced a proliferation rather than a coalescing of parties. The two electoral blocs that were by far the most successful, United Ukraine and Our Ukraine, did not exist during the 1998 elections. Both were created expressly to provide a vehicle for the 2002 elections. Both centered on a particular political figure (United Ukraine on President Kuchma, and Our Ukraine on Viktor Yushchenko). By mid-2003, one of them, United Ukraine, had vanished from the political landscape, having served its electoral purpose.

As noted above, four of the five parties that entered parliament in the 2006 elections (as well as those that finished sixth and seventh) were based on individual personalities. It is hard to imagine that Our Ukraine, the Tymoshenko Bloc, or the Socialist Party will survive long without their leaders. Only the Party of Regions, centered on the elite from the Donetsk region, transcends its individual leader, Viktor Yanukovych. Its existence depends less on Yanukovych than on its main financial backer, the Donetsk oligarch Rinat Akhmetov.

At the same time, parties with the longest track record and most developed grassroots organizations are weakening over time. The most venerable and most thoroughly organized parties in Ukraine—Rukh, the Communist Party, and the Socialist Party—have seen their influence diminish over time. Rukh, with its constant divisions and redefinitions, is coming more to resemble the disposable parties of notables. In May 2003, Boris Tarasyuk was elected head of the largest successor to Rukh despite the fact that he had been a member of the party only since March of that year, when he abandoned the smaller Party of Reforms and Order.[43]

Similarly, Yuri Kostenko, head of the Ukrainian People's Party (another Rukh offshoot), argued in February 2005 that, having succeeded in the 2002 parliamentary elections and propelled Yushchenko to the presidency, Our Ukraine was no longer needed.[44] It is truly remarkable that, within two months of its greatest triumphs, the most popular political bloc in the country was regarded as disposable. As long as prominent politicians can jump parties so easily, they will have little reason to invest in them. By 2006, Rukh had vanished from the Ukrainian landscape, with some of its supporters in Our Ukraine, others in the Tymoshenko Bloc, and others in a variety of smaller parties. Similarly, the Communist Party appears to be headed for extinction.

Ukraine's Electoral Law Dilemma

We noted above that Ukraine needs to achieve two difficult tasks at once: it must strengthen the role of parties and induce parties to coalesce in parliament to provide a governing majority. How can Ukraine's electoral law be revised to accomplish both of the tasks at hand? Two factors make the puzzle substantially more difficult than it appears at first.

First, as mentioned above, the two goals are in some respects—though not completely—in conflict with one another. The simplest way to induce existing parties to consolidate is to institute an SMD plurality system. However, such a system undermines the effort to channel political activities into the party system, because it leaves open a great deal of room for independents.[45] Conversely, a complete PR system will force electoral activity into parties, but—depending on the exact details—might tend to provide weak incentives for party consolidation.

Second, if we define party strength as the influence parties have over individual politicians and over the electoral process, other problems arise. As Sartori points out, when a strong electoral rule is applied to a weak party system, it is unlikely to have a strong effect on it.[46] Sartori therefore finds that in countries with weak party systems, full PR systems are likely to have little effect in consolidating parties.[47] "[W]hen relatively pure PR is combined with structurelessness, neither the electoral nor the party systems intervene in the political process with a manipulative impact of their own."[48]

Thus the preexisting weakness of Ukraine's party system may reduce the power of electoral laws to change the party system. Therefore, while the shift to full PR is a step in the right direction, it is unlikely automatically to make the Ukrainian parliament an effective actor.

The situation is not hopeless. If the 2002 and 2006 election results are any indication, then the problem of party consolidation is not insurmountable. In 2002, with an electoral law that was very weak (mixed system; only a 4 percent threshold in the PR portion), only six parties were admitted to parliament under the PR system (see Table 7.3). This is significantly fewer than in 1998, and fits well within what is considered normal for "moderate multipartism." The shift to full PR with a 3 percent threshold in 2006 reduced the number of parties to five, with only two others coming close to the threshold.

It is unclear whether those results will hold in the future. One can imagine that several of the parties that met the threshold in 2006 will fragment before 2011, leaving a much larger number of successors capable of gaining 3 percent in that election. The sides in 2002, and especially in 2006, were particularly clearly drawn (and even then the "orange coalition" ran as two separate major parties, and several much smaller ones). If there is further falling out, or if the parties based on a single individual collapse, they could be succeeded by a much larger number of smaller parties. With a 3 percent threshold, there will be no powerful disincentive to such fragmentation.

On the other hand, building new parties between 2006 and 2011 will not be easy. The attention and the political resources will go to the five parties represented in parliament. New parties will find it more difficult than ever to break in. Those with prominent individuals at the head, and especially those bankrolled by wealthy supporters, will continue to find this possible. New mass-based parties will be harder to construct.

One problem will still remain: even if a small number of electoral blocs gain admission to parliament, they might fragment tremendously once in parliament. Producing a more consolidated *electoral* party system does not necessarily lead to a more consolidated *parliamentary* party system, which ultimately is the goal. The first problem can be dealt with through electoral laws, which have been discussed here, while the second problem is a function of the parliamentary rules of procedure, and will be discussed in the next chapter.

Conclusions

Several important conclusions result from this analysis of Ukraine's electoral laws. Ukraine is not doomed to illiberal democracy simply by its societal cleavages. Institutional arrangements can help to consolidate Ukraine's party system. However, the effects of electoral laws are tied up with three other independent variables that affect the results they produce. First, the overall form of government (presidentialism versus parliamentarism) has an important effect on what will work. The more power the parliament has, the greater the incentives for coalition-building. Second, the weakness in Ukraine's party system tends to be self-reinforcing, so that the new rules adopted might not have as strong an effect as hoped. Third, the internal rules of the parliament, which will be discussed in the next chapter, play a powerful role in influencing the incentives for party cohesion and fragmentation.

If the analysis in this chapter is correct, the shift to a PR system should produce optimism concerning the consolidation of the party system and hence the efficacy of the parliament. By shifting to a fully proportional system, Ukraine's elites will be forced to build parties, and its voters will be forced to think in terms of parties. However, two weaknesses remain.

First, the new rules may not be strong enough to overcome the existing weakness of the party system. Changes in the electoral law did not lead to the demise of the "disposable party" in the run-up to the 2006 parliamentary election. As long as parties are disposable, they will be weak and less effective in coalition formation. The poor performance of disposable parties in 2006 is a good sign; the continued importance of personality-based parties is a less favorable sign. Second, lowering the threshold to 3 percent may reduce the pressure on parties to merge and facilitate the success of "disposable" parties. We did not see evidence of this in 2006, but that does not mean it cannot become a problem in the future.

Because the parliament, under the constitutional changes adopted in December 2004, will have a much greater role in government formation, these two weaknesses have significant implications. The potential danger is that Ukraine will be returned to the situation it faced in the early 1990s, when parliament had more power but was effective only in stymieing the president. That was the circumstance that opened the door to authoritarianism under Kuchma.

Even taking those dangers into account, however, it is difficult not to conclude that the parliamentary election laws that went into effect in 2006 are likely to be far more effective than either of Ukraine's previous versions. There is no guarantee that the 2006 parliament will work effectively or that other problems will be avoided. But by reducing the number of independents to zero, and producing a parliament with five parties, only the smallest of which is an unlikely coalition partner, the shift to proportional representation is an important step toward building a functioning parliament, which is an essential component of liberal democracy.

8

Parliamentary Rules and Party Development

The weakness of political parties is a central problem in Ukraine. Around the world, liberal democracy is built, in one way or another, on the assumption of a strong party system. The previous chapter showed that while developing such a party system in Ukraine is possible, it will not be easy. In addition to the electoral law, the rules of the parliament will be important to whether or not strong parliamentary parties can emerge. The purpose of this chapter is to show why parliamentary rules matter, and where the problems are in Ukraine's current arrangements.

There is, unfortunately, little comparative literature on the role of legislative rules in the formation of party systems. There is an immense literature, some of it highly technical, about the rules of procedure in the two houses of the U.S. Congress. The literature leaves little doubt that these rules create incentives that powerfully influence the strategies of legislators and parties and shape the legislation that eventually emerges.[1] However, the focus has been on legislative strategies, not on strategies of party-building. Instead, the assumption is that the party system is determined by external factors and that parliamentary rules simply shape legislative strategies.

While there is a literature on party-switching between elections, parliamentary rules are not seen as a central factor in this process.[2] This perspective complements the standard literature on party systems, which views party systems as being determined by the combination of societal cleavages and the electoral law in place. Because parties are formed primarily to contest elections, it stands to reason that elections and electoral laws will play the main role in determining what strategies parties devise and which parties survive. That has been the main reason to neglect the role of parliamentary rules in party-building.

Various authors, however, open the door to a more nuanced analysis of the determinants of party systems, in two ways. First, by showing that the initial condition of the party system has an important independent effect on the influence of electoral laws, they demonstrate that the question involves more than simply cleavages and electoral laws. Moreover, they prompt us to ask what influences those "initial conditions." Second, by pointing out that the key issue, ultimately, for building liberal democracy is not *electoral* parties but *parliamentary* parties, they prompt us to investigate what happens to electoral parties when the election is over and the parliament convenes.

> [P]arties may be the real units in the electoral arena, and yet lose their "unity" in the parliamentary arena, as parliamentary parties. . . . [P]arties matter only if they display a modicum of discipline. Without parliamentary discipline, whether parties are two or more does not make much difference.[3]

Parties are formed not only to win elections but also to pass legislation within legislatures,[4] so it stands to reason that these rules as well as electoral rules would influence coalition behavior. Duverger himself argues that such rules can have important effects, showing that in France, the double-ballot majority system yielded more than ten parties under the Third Republic (prior to 1940) but only four in the Fifth Republic (post-1958). The difference, he asserts, is explained by parliamentary rules governing the minimum number of members of a parliamentary grouping (there was no minimum prior to 1940, and a minimum of thirty after 1958).[5]

This problem is profound in Ukraine, where after the 2002 parliamentary elections a relatively small number of successful electoral parties rapidly fragmented into a large number of parliamentary parties, with new parties being formed and existing ones disappearing frequently, and members constantly switching among the various factions and independent status.

Parties, Blocs, and Factions in the Ukrainian Parliament

Before embarking on the analysis in any greater depth, the role of "parties," "blocs," and "factions" in the Ukrainian parliament should be clarified. These three different entities all correspond roughly to the Western notion of a "party," yet in Ukraine they are defined distinctly and play different roles. "Parties" in Ukraine are organizations formed to contest elections and participate in politics in other ways. Each one is registered independently, has its own leadership and party platform, and so on. In this way, Ukrainian parties are similar to those in the West. However, because they are often small, and cannot do well in elections by themselves, they ally into "blocs."

Electoral Blocs

"Blocs" refer to coalitions of parties that join together *before* an election for the purposes of competing in the election. Especially when competing in proportional representation, it makes sense for ideologically similar parties to unite, both to maximize their chances of passing the threshold and to pool limited resources. In most cases, however, the parties do not actually merge into a single party, but form an electoral alliance known as a "bloc." These alliances are understood not to be permanent, as a merger is; rather, they are based on the tactical needs of competing in elections. Already, we see a partial difference between the role of parties in Ukraine and that typically understood in the West. Parties in Ukraine are formed on some basis other than winning elections, and then must ally into blocs to contest elections. This phenomenon also occurs elsewhere—Italy is one of many examples. The existence of these blocs shows why the actual number of parties in parliament may substantially exceed the number of "blocs" that triumph in the elections.

A look at two prominent blocs in the 2002 parliamentary elections illustrates this phenomenon. Our Ukraine consisted of over a dozen minor parties, none of which were actually willing to merge with each other.[6] United Ukraine consisted of nine parties:

- Labor Ukraine
- Party of Regions
- Industrialists and Enterprise Bosses
- Our Ukraine (which was the name of a party as well as bloc)
- National Democratic Party
- People's Power
- Agrarian Party
- Democratic Initiatives
- European Choice

As Andrew Wilson examines in detail, these nine went their separate ways once they had elected a speaker of the parliament.[7] The breakup of the coalition took place in part along the regional lines that the parties were built upon, with one part of the Donbas clan, led by former head of the State Tax Administration, Mykola Azarov, going with European Choice, the Kharkiv group going with Democratic Initiatives, and so on. By June 2002, barely three months after the election, five of these parliamentary factions had fewer than twenty members.

If these various parties collaborate only upon getting into parliament and then behave as independent actors, the parliament is effectively divided into the overall number of independent parties, not the nominal number of blocs selected. Since there are no means to ensure bloc loyalty (ensuring loyalty within parties is hard enough), there is no reason to consider these blocs as single parties.

Factions

Parliamentary "factions" (*fraktsia*, in Ukrainian) sometimes called "fractions," are the groups of members in which the parliament actually functions. In the parliament elected in 2006, each faction corresponds to one of the electoral blocs that passed the 3 percent threshold in the election. Two of these factions (Our Ukraine and the Tymoshenko Bloc), represent multiple parties, like the electoral blocs they are built on. Prior to 2006, however, there was not a close connection between the results of elections and the factional composition of parliament.

In any parliament, rules govern how various groupings are recognized officially and how they interact. In most parliaments, the groups under consideration are parties. In Ukraine before 2006, there were consistently independents in parliament. The parliamentary rules were designed to encourage consolidation by allowing independent deputies to join party-based groups (just as the occasional independent or third-party member in the U.S. Congress generally caucuses with one of the two major parties). Moreover, to encourage parties with small numbers of deputies to merge in their parliamentary functions even as they remained separate, some supra-party structure was needed. The result is that groups in the Ukrainian parliament were recognized as "factions," rather than parties. In this sense, "faction" did not necessarily mean a faction of a party (i.e., a subset), but nearly the opposite. A "faction" in the Ukrainian parliament was a formal grouping larger than a single party. In general, they were composed of two or more parties and several independents. In some cases, the membership of a faction could be identical to the membership of a party or electoral bloc in parliament. These rules were created in the hope that there would be fewer factions than parties in parliament, thus facilitating coalition-building and efficiency. Prior to 2006, there was almost always a greater number of factions in parliament than the number of parties elected via the proportional representation (PR) section of the ballot. The only exceptions were in the first seating of a new parliament following an election, before the parties and deputies had time to realign themselves. Table 8.1 shows the pattern of constant realignment in the 1998 parliament.

Roots of the Faction System

These parliamentary groupings had their origin in the final Soviet parliament, elected in 1990, when a number of reformist members joined together to form the "democratic bloc" in parliament. Because the Soviet system made no allowance for multiple parties, new mechanisms were invented

Table 8.1

Variation in Membership, Factions in Ukrainian Parliament, 1998–2002

	5/14/98	7/21/98	1/15/99	7/16/99	1/20/00	7/14/00	1/18/01	7/13/01	1/18/02	3/6/02
Nonfaction	36	20	26	16	25	50	45	48	47	46
Communist Party of Ukraine	119	120	122	122	115	114	111	113	113	113
Rukh	47	47	46	30	26	21	23	22	22	23
Left Center	35	33	24	24	22	17	16	17	17	17
Greens	24	24	27	23	18	17	17	17	15	16
National Democratic Party	89	87	72	30	27	23	20	16	14	14
Hromada	39	45	45	17	14	0	0	0	0	0
Progressive Socialist	17	14	14	14	11	0	0	0	0	0
Social Democratic Party of Ukraine (United)	25	25	24	26	35	33	33	36	32	32
Independents	0	26	19	19	14	0	0	0	0	0
Agrarian	0	0	15	15	15	0	0	0	0	0
Reforms	0	0	14	21	13	15	15	15	15	15
Rebirth of Regions	0	0	0	28	36	36	35	18	15	15
Rukh (Udovenko)	0	0	0	16	17	19	17	14	14	14
Batkivshchina	0	0	0	28	35	34	32	26	24	24
Trudova	0	0	0	18	23	44	48	46	38	38
Solidarnist	0	0	0	0	0	27	23	21	21	20
Regions	0	0	0	0	0	0	0	24	23	23
Yednist	0	0	0	0	0	0	0	0	20	21

Source: Laboratory F-4, "Dynamics of Factions Arrangement (During Third Convocation)," *Verkhovna Rada-Week,* no. 4, May 13, 2002. For a detailed listing of members' faction changes, chronicling every single change, see Komitet Vybortsiv Ukrainy and Laboratory F-4, *Verkhovna Rada Ukrainy III Sklykannya* (1998–2002 rr), (Kyiv: Fact, 2002), 27ff.

spontaneously when multiple groupings emerged. In the 1994–98 parliament, the faction system was institutionalized more fully to allow the large number of independents to form parliamentary groupings, or to join them. This practice, and the perceived utility of it, caused the status of factions to be enshrined in the parliamentary rules, which allowed independent deputies to form groupings for parliamentary purposes only, without having to join a party for electoral or other purposes.[8] By bringing the independent deputies into some organizational structure, the practice of forming factions helped to structure the parliament, but the effect was a relatively weak one, because members could and often did desert their factions for any number of reasons. There was very little faction discipline. Moreover, by creating an organizational structure that competed with the party structure, the faction system undermined party discipline. It was possible, and not unusual, therefore, for a faction based on a particular party that passed the 4 percent hurdle to split into two, or simply to dissolve, as the Hromada faction did in the 1998–2002 parliament.

Due to an odd set of circumstances, the threshold for official recognition of a faction was reduced to fourteen members, or roughly 3 percent of the parliament, even lower than the 4 percent required for admission into the parliament. Originally, when the faction rules were created, the minimum membership necessary for a faction to be given official status was set at twenty-five members, or 5.6 percent of the membership. However, with the move to the mixed system in 1998, some parties barely passed the 4 percent threshold, such that the smallest party who gained entry on the party list portion was entitled to fourteen seats. Because it seemed unfair for a party elected on the party list to be denied faction status in the parliament, the number of seats required for official status was correspondingly lowered to fourteen.

To prevent the fourteen-member limit from leading to the fragmentation of the larger groups, another rule was adopted at this time, specifying that only parties that had passed the 4 percent threshold could form recognized factions. This limited the number of factions to eight at that time, prevented new factions from being formed from among independents, and increased substantially the disincentives to dividing or abandoning existing parties. Deputies seeking to leave their party would have to become independent or join another party. However, independent deputies initiated a lawsuit, contending that this rule violated their constitutional rights of association. The Constitutional Court declared the rule unconstitutional.[9] As a result, any group of fourteen deputies could form an official faction, which led to the wholesale fragmentation of the parliament.

The low threshold for forming a faction, combined with the elimination of any barrier to forming new factions, led to an ongoing process of faction dissolution and formation, rendering the parliament incoherent. This incoherence led directly to the campaign to revise the constitution to give more power to the president in 2000. There was no attempt to revise the constitution to strengthen the parliament by allowing the previous limits on faction formation, or through other measures. By fostering the fragmentation and ineffectiveness of the parliament, the weak parliamentary rules led indirectly to Kuchma's push for greater power.

Parliamentary Rules and Parliamentary Fragmentation

Parliamentary rules have had a powerful effect on fragmenting parties and hence on parliaments in Ukraine.[10] They have not merely failed to create incentives to coalesce, but actually created incentives to divide parties. We focus here on three aspects of the system: the rules for party recognition in the parliament, the rules for conducting business in the parliament, and the rules determining the power of parties relative to their members in parliament. In Ukraine, in particular, these rules contributed to party fragmentation, and this effect was independent of the electoral system. The adoption of new rules for the 2006 parliament will improve the situation considerably, but the exact effect of those rules remains to be seen.

The first problem in Ukraine is the absence of any substantial disincentive to the fragmentation of factions. We can assume that there are natural incentives for parties to split. The question is what disincentives, such as a decreased chance at gaining power, prevent parties from splitting or even encourage them to merge? Leaving aside electoral politics and focusing on policymaking within the parliament, there are few identifiable benefits attached to having a larger party or faction.

Incentives to Split Parties

The second problem with the pre-2006 rules did not just represent a low barrier to fragmentation, but actually created a positive incentive. A deeper examination of the functions and prerogatives of factions indicates that there was some incentive for factions or parties to divide, making the low threshold even more significant. There existed something akin to an inverse of Duverger's "mechanical effect," in that rather than losing influence in the system by refusing to merge, the rules made it possible to *gain* influence by dividing. Attainment of faction status yielded two benefits to parliamentary groups: the right to have a faction staff at public expense, and the right to hold a seat on the presidium of the parliament, which controls the work of the parliament, including agenda formation and committee assignments. Both of these created incentives to multiply party groupings.

According to the rules, each faction had a seat on the parliament's presidium, which develops the parliament's agenda. Each member of the presidium has one vote. A party that split, therefore, ended up with two seats on the presidium in the place of one (and two publicly funded staffs in the place of one). Rather than losing influence through division, a group could gain influence over the agenda this way. The potential was demonstrated in late 1999, when leftist factions boycotted the parliament because the presidium refused to schedule debate on President Leonid Kuchma's announced plan to privatize collective farms.[11] Even though the left controlled more seats in parliament (and the leadership), rightist factions, which controlled more seats on the presidium, were able to block inclusion of the land reform plan on the agenda. In this case, a large number of small factions was able to stymie a smaller number of factions that probably controlled more seats in the parliament.

Clearly, the incentive to marshal as many votes as possible on the presidium is significant. Some observers felt that the fragmentation of United Ukraine into so many factions after the 2002 elections was in part motivated by a desire to gain additional influence over the presidium.[12] Even if membership in this group did not bring influence over the agenda, it still brought resources in the form of staff and office space.

As Sarah Whitmore points out, an alternative means of organizing the parliament was used by the majority that existed briefly in 2000. That majority shifted most control over the agenda to a "coordinating council of the majority," in which voting was weighted according to how many seats each faction controlled, in which only members of the short-lived majority coalition participated. In this system, bills were brought to the floor only after their ability to garner 226 votes was confirmed.[13] This model was an effort to shift Ukraine closer to West European parliamentary practices. It is unclear how strong a role the council of faction leaders played.

An additional incentive to fragment factions was simply the ambition of individual party elites, who, not wanting to be number two or number three in a moderate-size faction, might seek a split in order to become the head of a smaller faction. As long as he or she could bring along thirteen other members (each of whom might also increase correspondingly in importance), a new faction could be formed. The individual forming the new faction gained a seat on the presidium as well as the prestige of leading a recognized parliamentary faction. Leading a smaller faction could yield political benefits as other politicians courted the faction's support, as well as electoral benefits, through increased name recognition, and perhaps even business benefits. As emphasized above, the benefits of splitting a faction did not need to be enormously high as long as the costs were nearly nonexistent.

Ideological Sources of Fragmentation

Finally, fragmentation can be motivated by genuine disagreements on ideology or policy.[14] In some of the cases where this has seemed to be the cause (e.g., the split of Rukh in 2000), policy disagreement may have been a veneer for petty personal rivalry among party leaders.[15] In either case, however, a system that punished faction fragmentation would force leaders who disagreed on policy (or just did not like each other, or who could not decide on who should hold what position in the faction or party hierarchy) to seek to overcome those differences, rather than encouraging them to split. This tendency is exaggerated by proportional representation election rules, which give parties incentives to stress their differences from like-minded competing parties.[16] Thus the rules on faction formation played an important part in causing the most destructive aspect of Ukrainian parliamentary politics: the unwillingness and inability of leaders with similar policy positions to join forces rather than dividing.

If that were not enough, there is some evidence that the effective threshold for a faction formation sometimes effectively went below fourteen members, making fragmentation even more likely. Because faction formation was separate from party membership, it was possible for a party with more than fourteen members in its faction to "lend" some to a faction that was short of fourteen members, in return either for some support in voting or simply for money.[17] Indeed, this lending was rational and, based on anecdotal evidence, was not unusual.

In this system, the overall amount of privilege increased as parties fragmented. The overall number of seats on the presidium was not fixed, nor was the number of staff, nor the number of people who could gain the status of "faction leader." In technical terms, party fragmentation was a positive-sum game. As long as a splinter group continued to vote with its former faction, there was nothing to be lost, and much to be gained, through fragmentation. In economic terms, the Ukrainian parties were practicing the same sort of market-segmenting strategy practiced by purveyors of breakfast cereal and beer in the West. It may not have led to effective legislation, but it was rational from the participants' perspective.

To summarize, Ukraine has a problem in its parliamentary rules that is directly analogous to the dilemma it faces in choosing an electoral law. Efforts to reduce the number of independents and strengthen the role of parties have operated at the expense of efforts to reduce the number of parties and form a coherent party system. Thus, the fragmentation and inefficacy of the Ukrainian parliament will not necessarily be eliminated by a different electoral law. Even in a full PR system, parties in the parliament would continue to have some incentive and little deterrent to fragmentation. Only raising the bar for faction recognition, or eliminating factions altogether, and decreasing the benefits of segmentation would reduce these incentives.

Under the new rules that took effect in 2006, most of this is no longer possible: only those parties that crossed the 3 percent threshold in elections are recognized actors in parliament. While discipline among those parties may be low, new groupings will have to remain informal, and will not get additional resources or voting rights. Thus the incentives to fragmentation have been substantially diminished. These new rules are discussed in more detail below.

Voting Rules and Party Coherence

At some times, parliamentary voting rules also undermined party coherence in the Ukrainian parliament. In particular, the absence of roll-call voting has undermined party discipline. For much of the post-Soviet period, roll-call votes were rarely used in parliament. Instead, voting was conducted in secret, using an electronic voting system that connected deputies' desks to a tabulation system that displayed results immediately above the speaker's dais. While this system made for amusing television, as voting results appeared instantaneously, as in a game show, it helped undermine the role of parties for the simple reason that party leaders had little way of knowing whether their members had followed the "party line" or not.

Adopted in the early post-Soviet years as a barrier to the sort of pressure that the Communist Party used to ensure uniform voting, the secret ballot was adopted for the right reasons at the time. This demonstrates again the extra challenges created by the Soviet legacy. Measures that are seen as normal in liberal democracies seem particularly dangerous because they were so badly abused under communism. Transparency of voting in parliament is a case in point. While at the time it was adopted the secret ballot was necessary for the parliament to escape Soviet control, it subsequently undermined the ability of party leaders to enforce voting discipline, and the ability of voters to assess their legislators. Not only was it difficult for Ukrainian party leaders to sanction defectors, it was often impossible to know who had defected.

The ability of party leaders to "deliver" votes was impeded, and, by extension, it was much harder for leaders to strike bargains because there was no way to guarantee that a party leader could deliver what had been promised. Nor was it possible for parties to verify whether deals had been adhered to or not. Transparency is essential to the ability to verify bargains, and bargains are essential to passing legislation in a multiparty parliament. Secret voting undermined all of this.

Secret voting also undermined a key notion of representative democracy by making it impossible for voters to monitor their elected representatives, and, based on members' voting records, choose whether to vote for them again. Accusations concerning how an incumbent or party voted on one measure or another are standard in Western democracies. There is never any uncertainty. The absence of roll-call voting made it impossible to ascertain what an incumbent had actually done in parliament.

In the turmoil that followed the unseating of the leftist parliamentary leadership in January 2000, the new leadership instituted roll-call voting. This was deeply controversial, however, for it was recognized that the change was not politically neutral. It was widely anticipated that roll-call voting would strengthen the center and right parties at the expense of the left. Speaker Tkachenko, prior to his ouster, expressed the partisan nature of this issue, predicting that with a shift to roll-call voting, Ukraine would "ultimately be ruled by the IMF [International Monetary Fund]."[18] For some time after that, the parliament's Web site listed every vote, not only the votes of individual legislators but also the votes of factions. That reportage was discontinued, and while it is still possible to obtain roll-call data, they are not easily available in Ukraine.[19]

The introduction of roll-call voting has made no perceptible difference in the cohesion of the parliament—nor could it be expected to. It would be interesting to investigate quantitatively whether faction loyalty increased after the introduction of roll-call voting, but this is not possible given the absence of data from the period when it was secret.[20] Nonetheless, the adoption of roll-call voting is important for two reasons. The first is the question of democratic representation discussed above. While it is still unlikely that most citizens can readily find out how their representatives voted on key issues, the institution of roll-call voting is a step in that direction. On crucial votes, such as the effort to amend the constitution in early 2004, the bargain that resolved the postelection impasse in late 2004, and the election of the speaker of parliament in 2006, press coverage meant that the different factions' voting records, and even the votes of key individuals, were widely known and discussed.

Second, while roll-call voting will not by itself substantially increase party discipline, it is one of the necessary ingredients. To increase party discipline, it is necessary not only for party leaders to know how their members vote, but also for them to have some powerful sanction or benefit that can create an incentive to vote with the party. As noted in the previous chapter, the fact that many parties do not have extensive financial resources and often will not be around at the next election undermines the positive benefits to be offered.

Table 8.2

Shifting Results of the 2002 Parliamentary Election

	Seats	
Faction	March 31, 2002	December 25, 2002
Our Ukraine	112	102
Communist Party	65	60
Tymoshenko Bloc	22	18
Socialist Party	22	20
Social Democratic Party of Ukraine (United)	27	39
United Ukraine (and successors)	121	193

Source: Freedom House, "Nations in Transit 2003: Ukraine," www.freedomhouse.org.ua/print/news/. Accessed April 24, 2004.

The Result: Shifting Faction Membership, or "Political Tourism"

The shifting of faction membership, or "political tourism"[21] is not simply a hypothetical possibility, as we can see by comparing the composition of the parliament that was elected in March 2002 with the composition as it was later the same year (See Table 8.2). United Ukraine had split into its constituent parties, making the entire parliament less structured. More significant, however, is that this bloc of parties managed to gain seventy-two seats, or roughly 15 percent of the parliament, with no change in the election results. Clearly, the low disincentives to fragmentation and the ability of powerful actors to create incentives to change membership combined to play a powerful role in shaping the membership of the Ukrainian parliament under the pre-2006 system. In a system where the composition of the parliament should ostensibly be determined by elections, this is highly problematic on a practical level (for the voters) and also with respect to the standard political science analysis, which sees parliamentary composition as determined solely by electoral laws.

Voting Rules and Parliamentary Immobility

Immobility in the parliament can be induced by fragmenting of parties as well as by artificially raising the number of votes necessary to pass a measure. Ukraine's rules of procedure do this in important ways that not only make it more difficult to pass legislation, but also make it easier for parties and members to disguise their votes on many issues, thus undermining the shift to roll-call voting.

In almost every democracy, most legislative decisions are made by simple majority. Supermajorities are required for extraordinary measures, such as overriding a presidential veto or ratifying a treaty. However, Ukraine's rules result in a situation in which supermajority votes are necessary for a vast number of issues. Consequently, it is much easier to block legislation in Ukraine than it is elsewhere, which exacerbates all of the other problems in passing legislation.

The problem is that, in contrast to most countries, Ukraine's parliamentary rules provide in many cases for a majority not of the members present, but of the overall composition of the parliament (226 of 450 members). As are many other facets of the system, the rule is a holdover from the Soviet era. Therefore, even when far fewer than 450 members are present, many decisions still need to be passed by 226 votes. It is not clear what the reasoning behind such requirements was, but it is clear that the rules impede the passage of legislation.[22]

Depending on how many legislators are absent from a session, the requirement for 226 votes to pass a measure can require a small supermajority or a rather large one. In any event, it is often the case that a bill receives a majority of the votes cast, and yet does not pass.

This provision allows deputies and parties to further obscure their voting records. This has become especially important since the advent of roll-call voting in 2000. Requiring 226 votes to pass legislation essentially means that any parliamentarian who does not show up to vote is voting against every bill considered. This misrepresents members who could not attend the session for some legitimate reason (and, by extension, those whom they represent). It also makes it possible for parties to kill legislation without going on record as voting against it, simply by abstaining or being counted as "not present." In many cases, entire factions numbering dozens of people would be counted as not present or abstaining on certain measures. Such measures might win a majority of votes cast, but nevertheless be defeated. Yet the parties or members who blocked the measure did not have to go on record as having voted against it. This practice continued after the Orange Revolution. In August 2006, when the parliament approved a controversial measure to allow foreign (NATO) troops to conduct exercises on Ukrainian territory, nearly the entire Tymoshenko Bloc (124 of 129 members) was absent from the voting.[23]

The Adoption of the Imperative Mandate

Ukrainian leaders adopted a new provision, known as the "imperative mandate," as part of the deal to hold a third round of presidential elections in December 2004. This provision, an adjunct to the adoption of a fully proportional election law (discussed in Chapter Seven), is intended to end "political tourism" and strengthen parties, both in parliament and in elections, but as long as the parties remain weak in other ways, the imperative mandate is unlikely to have much substantive effect.

The term "imperative mandate" means that a parliamentary seat won through proportional representation belongs to the party, rather than to the individual who holds it. Seats are distributed by parties to individuals (according to their place on the party list). In such a system, an individual who leaves the party also loses his or her seat in parliament. In such systems, party defection is nearly unheard of. A parliamentarian who gives up his or her seat can expect never to serve in parliament again because a spot on some other party list would be nearly impossible to obtain. This arrangement is crucial to party discipline in some systems.

Without the imperative mandate or some other means of punishing defectors, parliamentary deputies are essentially "free agents." This has been the case in Ukraine until 2006. While the party has controlled the list at election time, once a member was admitted to parliament, the mandate was his or hers, and he or she was free to support any party or policy. Therefore, there is no automatic connection between the *electoral* party and the *parliamentary* party. The ongoing defection of party members, to the point where some electoral parties disappeared as parliamentary parties (e.g., Hromada after 1998) has been a major problem in Ukraine.

In such a system, parties get no chance to sanction defectors until the next election (by leaving them off the party list, or moving them down). In Ukraine, this sanction has been very weak because it is relatively mild and slow in coming. The period between elections means that the penalty for defection cannot be immediately assessed. The weakness of the parties (analyzed in the previous chapter) means that potentially being left off a party list in the future is not a very powerful threat. The party in question may not even exist at the next election. Moreover, because there are always other parties looking for prominent individuals for their list, elites are not shut out of parliamentary politics when shunned by their party. This phenomenon creates a vicious cycle: the weakness of parties means that individual politicians can flout their authority at relatively low cost, which contributes to the further weakness of parties and of the party system.

Many observers as well as Ukrainian elites advocated for the imperative mandate as a solution to these problems. Such a proposal was made by Our Ukraine in late 2002, responding to the ability of the pro-presidential parties to entice deputies to leave the Our Ukraine faction following the 2002 parliamentary election.[24]

With the imperative mandate, members who leave their party must leave parliament and lose their base of power and name recognition at least until the next elections. Some might still choose to do this, but only the most well-financed or well-known can assume they will succeed.

More significantly, the imperative mandate will short-circuit the widespread practice whereby substantial inducements, either political or financial, are offered to get members to switch factions. This will become impossible. The number of seats each party or faction secures in an election will be fixed. A member who abandons his or her party will not be able to join another. Instead, that party would name a new member from its party list. This will eliminate the incentives for factions to actively poach each others' deputies. In addition to stabilizing the party structure in the parliament, and linking the parliamentary party structure directly to the electoral outcomes, eliminating the free agency of deputies might substantially reduce the amount of corruption involved.

While the adoption of the imperative mandate is a step forward, it will not automatically lead to strong party discipline. Its effects on voting remain unclear, because members of parliament may vote against their party without defecting from the party. So while the formal splitting of factions and the formation of new factions with official status should effectively be halted, individual members may still vote independently, undermining leaders' abilities to make and keep bargains. This became clear only days into the seating of the new parliament in 2006. When Viktor Yanukovych was elected prime minister, only 31 of 79 members of the Our Ukraine faction voted for him, meaning that over half deserted the party leadership. Yulia Tymoshenko quickly announced that she would try to recruit these dissenters, along with others from the Socialist Party, in an "inter-faction opposition coalition." Only when party leaders have effective means of sanctioning those who reject the party line will party discipline be secure.[25]

Opposition to the Imperative Mandate

It is not hard to understand why Kuchma and the oligarchic parties opposed institution of the imperative mandate. In a system where members of parliament are free to switch parties, they are likely to be swayed by incentives. The presidential administration and the large business interests linked with the oligarchic factions had a disproportionate ability to provide incentives. Following the 2002 elections, there was an unseemly process by which Our Ukraine deputies defected amid credible reports of massive incentives (bribes) as well as disincentives (threats to members' business interests). These tactics are detailed in Chapter Nine.

To some, the imperative mandate seems undemocratic because it denies the individual member the freedom to choose his or her faction in parliament. But a stronger case can be made that it is *more* representative than a system where members are free agents. In a PR system, voters vote for parties, not for individuals. When a deputy deserts the party on whose list he or she was elected, it causes a distortion in the translation of votes into seats. As Tables 8.1 and 8.2 indicate, those distortions can be significant. The prevailing Ukrainian practice of changing the numbers of faction members after the election essentially means that the expressed preferences of the voters are being overturned by the machinations of the politicians.

Consider, for example, the 4.7 percent of the electorate who voted for Hromada in 1998. When defections of various sorts brought Hromada below the threshold for faction status, and the faction disbanded, those voters' votes were effectively thrown away. Unless one believes that voting for parties rather than for individuals is inherently wrong, then it only makes sense to uphold voting results throughout the life of the parliament until a new vote is held. Thus, the most accurate way to translate the wishes of the electorate is to maintain the party representation in the proportion that the voters established.

The free agency model is also open to considerable manipulation. It appears highly likely that, in 2002, some candidates ran on the Our Ukraine list while planning all along to defect to one of the oligarchic parties. Because the free agency system decreases transparency, it becomes more difficult for voters to assess exactly for whom they are voting when they select a particular party.

Uncertainties About the Imperative Mandate in Practice

While the analysis here indicates that the institution of the imperative mandate will provide a modest boost to building a functioning parliament, there are dangers as well. As in other areas, the most significant danger comes from an aspect of the Ukrainian system that deviates from our normal assumptions about how these institutions work.

Some in Ukraine have stated the fear that the imperative mandate will turn party leaders into potentates with few checks on their power. This is a real danger because the checks on party leaders' power that exist in many other countries do not often prevail in Ukraine. In particular, Ukrainian parties, because they are elite-based rather than mass-based, do not have an internal democratic mechanism to determine party policy.

As noted in the previous chapter, many Ukrainian parties are built around a single powerful and prominent individual. Very few of them have the sort of party rules that allow the "rank and file" to select the leader, or to eject the leader if he or she displeases them. While this varies from party to party, in general, internal accountability and democracy in Ukrainian parties is low. If the imperative mandate were highly effective, the party leader would have very strong levers over his or her deputies' votes, but the deputies would have little ability to influence the overall position of the party. In normal times, this would not be a major problem, but when a particularly authoritarian or corrupt party leader emerges, it would be very difficult to do anything about it. And while the potential for bribery of individual party members to change factions officially would be largely eliminated, the potential for bribery of party leaders who can deliver an entire bloc of votes would correspondingly increase. However, as noted above, this fear is unlikely to be realized. The imperative mandate will likely not confer such extensive power on party leaders. Indeed, they may continue to be very weak.

The broader point is that fixing one part of the system will lead to increased pressure on another part. While the introduction of the imperative mandate will be a step forward, it will likely result in a much greater focus on the internal decision-making procedures of parties. Some unforeseen difficulties will have to be overcome before the system works as smoothly as it does in most Western countries. Finally, lest we become too optimistic, we should recall that even in those countries where the system runs well, there is no guarantee against corruption or powerful party leaders.

Conclusion

This chapter has shown that a set of rules that is almost universally ignored in research on party systems has had an important effect on party fragmentation in Ukraine. Party formation and parliamentary performance cannot be explained simply by the electoral system, as powerful as that factor is. Factors "above" that level, as discussed in Chapter Six, and factors "below" that level, as emphasized in this chapter, also have an important effect.

In a variety of ways, the rules by which the Ukrainian parliament conducts its business have undermined its ability to pass legislation. They do this indirectly by undermining party cohesion, and directly by facilitating obstruction. Moreover, certain aspects of the rules substantially undermine the ability of the voters to monitor their elected representatives, although the worst of these, secret voting, has already been abandoned.

Revising the parliamentary rules of procedure will not, by itself, fix the problems with the parliament or with the overall institutional situation in Ukraine. Some measures, such as requiring only a majority of those present to pass legislation, would be an immediate improvement. The introduction of the imperative mandate for party list seats will almost certainly improve party cohesion, but only to the extent that parties constitute significant electoral resources for politicians. While the problem of "disposable parties" will remain, the combination of the fully proportional electoral law and the imperative mandate should go some way toward strengthening parties and making them more enduring.

The combination of the 1998 constitutional ruling allowing members complete freedom in forming new factions with the earlier decision to establish the minimum faction size at fourteen members created a situation where there were very low disincentives to fragmenting parties. Under a complete PR system with the imperative mandate, this problem will become irrelevant, because the link between electoral parties and parliamentary models will become much tighter.

The process of institutional reform in Ukraine will not be a simple quick fix, whereby one key aspect of the system is changed and everything else falls into place. In that sense, much of the advice proffered by Western experts over the years has been too simple. Instead, reform plans must consider the complexity of the political institutions and the natural tendency for politicians to seek ways around measures that constrain them. As we will see in the next chapter, Ukrainian politicians have been very adept at this.

9

How Power Politics Trumps Institutional Design

This chapter considers the strategy and tactics, or what we might call the "methodology," of electoral authoritarianism in Ukraine.[1] Many of these tactics have already been alluded to in the previous chapters, and an overview was provided in Chapter Three. It is necessary to show that they are not merely disconnected efforts. Rather, the various tactics employed by Kuchma to utilize executive authority to control politics in Ukraine constituted a coherent strategy that became more organized over time. A crucial question in post-Kuchma Ukraine is whether these tactics will be banished to the past or continue to lead to the concentration of power in the executive branch. While some of the sources of electoral authoritarianism were removed during the Orange Revolution, others remain as powerful as ever. The most important change is the redivision of control over the executive branch between the president and prime minister. This change alone makes it considerably less likely that a single person or clique will amass as much power as Kuchma. Whether this new system is conducive to effective governing is another matter.

The Ukrainian executive branch controls three broad categories of resources that serve as levers of political influence: control over law and administrative enforcement, control over large sectors of the economy, and patronage (control over government jobs). To some extent, the first two categories overlap, because one way of controlling the economy is through selective law and administrative enforcement. These three basic resources are highly fungible, meaning that they can be used to influence actors and to pursue goals in a wide variety of spheres. This is most true of selective law and administrative enforcement, which can be used, for example, to ensure the defection of a politician from an opposition party, to close down a troublesome newspaper, or to give crucial business advantages to an ally, who in turn will contribute to reelection efforts.

Democratic institutional design is intended to provide for rule by the governed, the accountability of elected officials, and limited government power. Elections, the separation of powers, and the rule of law are means to these ends. Elections provide for consent by the governed, and also create, through alternation of leaders in power, a check on the abuse of government authority. Other elements of the constitution as well as the separation of powers and the rule of law are intended both to maintain the powerful role of elections and to curb the abuse of power in many other ways. Rules maintaining freedom of the press ensure that government misdeeds are publicized, so that the governed can act on them. Together, these institutions should compel the government to govern in the interests of the people. Even in the most liberal democratic society, these goals are attained only approximately.

The goal of Leonid Kuchma and other Ukrainian elites has been to use various tactics to break these links, in order to remove the checks on their power. Where institutional design creates a separation of powers, they have sought to subject both the judiciary and the legislature to the control of the executive. Where the laws provide for free and fair elections, many of Ukraine's elites have sought to make elections unfair, so that they do not make the government more accountable, and especially so that continuation in power of the ruling group, rather than alternation in power, becomes the norm. They seek to curb freedom of the press to keep the public unknowledgeable about the government's misdeeds as well as to win elections.

As Roeder asserts, the central problem for the would-be authoritarian is "control of accountability."[2] The single most important goal for Leonid Kuchma and the group of elites around him was to maintain control of the executive branch. Control of the executive branch is central to holding both political and economic power in Ukraine. Because elections are a powerful source of accountability, Kuchma and his supporters strove to control them (rather than abolish them). The goal is to maintain control while presenting an impression of fair elections, from which immense legitimacy is gained both at home and abroad.

Not unique to politicians in Ukraine, these goals are present in most democracies. What varies is how far such attempts go, how they can be countered, and how much success they meet. The key question for every society that aspires to liberal democracy is not simply the design of institutions, but what happens when institutional design is confronted by power politics. In Ukraine, power politics triumphed until December 2004, largely because power was so concentrated. The discussion that follows elaborates exactly how practical power can be legitimized through ostensibly liberal institutions. The conclusion will address the prospects for change in the years ahead.

Selective Law Enforcement

Selective law enforcement refers to the political use of law enforcement activity. Excessive scrutiny of minor violations can severely hamper one's opponents, while ignoring significant violations can empower one's allies. Selective law enforcement is an all-purpose tool for coercing political opponents. It is used to shut down or to intimidate media outlets that create problems for the president. It is also used to coerce business leaders to support the ruling group and to ensure that their employees vote for it. When business owners are also members of parliament, selective law enforcement is a useful way to control their votes.

Selective law enforcement is especially easy in Ukraine's confusing legal environment. The complexity and self-contradictory nature of the Ukrainian tax and legal codes make perfect compliance nearly impossible. The variety of law enforcement bodies and their overlapping jurisdictions further confuse the situation.[3] Moreover, government corruption tends to drive firms out of the official economy, which then makes it easier to charge them with violating the law. While international organizations have often sought to persuade the Ukrainian government to reduce the complexity of the tax code and to combat corruption, they fail to recognize that it persists in part because it facilitates the control of firms and votes by the executive branch.

Creating a situation where noncompliance is the norm facilitates selective law enforcement. If everyone is guilty of something, then everyone can reasonably be prosecuted at any time, completely legally, and without it appearing repressive to the public. Survey research conducted by Simon Johnson and his colleagues has shown that government demand for bribes, rather than high tax rates or organized crime, drives Ukrainian business out of the official economy.[4] The problem is massive, with 41 percent of economic activity, according to the figures of Johnson and his colleagues, in the "shadow economy," and hence vulnerable to politically motivated persecution.[5] Focusing enforcement on those who either oppose or insufficiently support the government can turn the shadow economy into a powerful and widely applicable political lever. Such politically motivated enforcement, by all accounts, did not disappear after the Orange Revolution.

This phenomenon is demonstrated in a conversation secretly recorded in President Kuchma's office. Kuchma is overheard telling Mykola Azarov, the head of the tax inspectorate, to make sure that Azarov has some grounds for prosecuting every business leader within a particular region, and to prosecute those that do not deliver sufficient votes to the referendum campaign in 2000.[6] In theory this could be applied to every firm in Ukraine, covering nearly every voter.

Ukraine's Byzantine tax code provides numerous possibilities to accuse enterprises, including media outlets, of having violated the law and underpaid taxes. Most tax offenses are criminal rather than civil offenses, and tax inspectors do not need to take alleged violators to court; rather, they can simply arrest them.[7] The tax police have the authority to close any business found to be in noncompliance. Even if the matter could eventually be sorted out in favor of the firm by a court, by that time the firm will likely have gone bankrupt due to the disruption of its business. Fire and health inspections can also lead to the closing of a business. In fact, nearly any government body can conduct inspections of a business to look for violations. Thus, the newspaper *Den'* was inspected over thirty times in a period of thirty months.[8] Such harassment is technically within the existing legal framework, creating the impression that the closure of media outlets amounts to law enforcement rather than political control, and that the outlets affected had it coming to them.

Selective Law Enforcement and Control of Media

A good example of selective law enforcement as a means to control media is the enforcement of broadcasting licenses. During the 2002 parliamentary election campaign, the government blocked transmission of some regional television outlets because their licenses were expired. However, in some cases the licenses had been expired for two years, with no enforcement. In other cases, broadcasters continued to operate without licenses with no interference. Whether stations operating with expired licenses were shut down appeared to be linked to the editorial line they took.[9]

Another method, effective especially against the press, is the libel suit. Ukrainian libel laws put the burden of proof on the news source to prove the truth of its reporting, rather than on the plaintiff to prove libel. As a result, the printing of any serious allegations without absolute proof can be dangerous, even though, in many respects, that is a key role of the press in a liberal society. Libel judgments can easily bankrupt a news outlet, and, as with tax laws, judgments are often enforced immediately, such that even if an appeal is successful, it is often too late to do any good. For example, in 1998, the popular newspaper *Vseukrainske vedomosti* was bankrupted by a $1.75 million libel suit by the Dynamo Kyiv football club, which was controlled by supporters of Kuchma. *Kyivskie vedomosti* was sued by the interior minister, Yuri Kravchenko, and found liable for $2.5 million in damages, although that award was later overturned.[10] There are numerous other examples of similar efforts.

In practice, such tactics need to be employed only occasionally to be largely successful. A few prominent examples serve to warn every other media outlet what can happen to them if their coverage is damaging to the executive branch. These warnings lead to self-censorship, which is exactly what the government wants. The extensive use of these tactics led the Committee to Protect Journalists to name Leonid Kuchma to its list of top ten enemies of a free press in 1999 and 2001. In its 2002 Worldwide Press Freedom Index, Ukraine ranked 112 out of 139 countries in terms of government interference with the news.

Selective Law Enforcement and Control of Parliament

The same leverage can be applied against members of parliament. Particularly in the center of the political spectrum that is crucial to control of the parliament, a large number of the deputies have important business interests (this does not appear to have changed with the shift to proportional representation [PR] in 2006). While parliamentarians themselves have immunity from prosecution (something Kuchma sought to do away with), their businesses are not immune to arbitrary inspections and closures. The executive therefore has a powerful lever over businesspeople in parliament. It can confer some degree of de facto immunity from law enforcement, as well as access to choice government contracts. Therefore, some businessmen seek seats in parliament primarily because of the executive's desire to control deputies: they seek to trade their votes in parliament for favorable treatment for their businesses.

The bribery of deputies is an even more direct method of controlling parliament. Because this is clearly illegal, it tends not to be well documented, but it is so widespread and the anecdotal evidence is so varied that there is little doubt that it is a frequent occurrence. In Kyiv, those close to the parliament can recite the "going rate" for various "services," from voting on a particular bill to switching parliamentary factions. Because the executive branch and the oligarchic parties that support it have access to so much money, they are more capable of using bribery. Moreover, because the executive controls law enforcement, its bribes are sure to remain beyond official investigation. In 2000, former president Leonid Kravchuk, at that time a member of the pro-presidential Social Democratic Party of Ukraine (United) (SDPU[o]), said, "if someone is for sale, they will buy him. Here everything occurs in this manner—voting and transfers."[11]

The executive's ability to decisively sway votes in the parliament was demonstrated after the 2002 parliamentary election. Following the elections, Our Ukraine won a plurality of seats and looked well positioned to form a majority, and to name the new speaker. For several weeks, neither the opposition nor the pro-presidential forces could muster enough votes to achieve a majority. Eventually, Volodymyr Lytvyn, former head of the presidential administration and a member of the pro-presidential SDPU(o) was proposed. Opposition leaders confidently stated that they had enough votes to block Lytvyn's election. But on the day of the voting, just enough deputies defected from opposition parties to give Lytvyn 226 votes—the bare minimum needed to win a majority. Seven deputies had defected from Our Ukraine, and smaller numbers from other opposition parties. Press reports indicated that for this vote, deputies were being offered $250,000 to defect, while opposition politicians asserted that the price was $500,000.[12] Of the seven deputies who defected from Our Ukraine, six were millionaire businessmen who reported being told either to defect or be bankrupted. The seventh was the prominent politician Volodymyr Shcherban, former head of the Sumy Oblast administration, who said simply: "I didn't come here to fight with the powers."[13] One of the few parliamentarians who has spoken on the record about bribery states that "if it is not a matter of big money, then money can be brought, as it used to [be], in photocopier boxes, according to the well-known Russian model. If the amounts are big, then probably they are transferred from one foreign account (usually offshore) to another."[14]

Some of these defectors were not bribed or coerced, but, it appears, ran as "stealth" candidates, gaining spots on the Our Ukraine list while intending to defect later. The incentive for the deputies to do so was twofold: they may have been able to obtain a higher spot on the Our Ukraine list than on another list, and they may have been handsomely rewarded for their efforts.

Cash-poor parties are especially vulnerable to such efforts, because their need for campaign funds creates a temptation to give high spots on their list to significant contributors, in effect using their party list as a fund-raiser. Viktor Suslov, a member of parliament, reported in 2002 that leading businessmen wanting a seat in parliament were paying between $300,000 and $1 million for a high spot on a party list.

> If you analyze the composition of the so-called safe section in any election bloc in Ukraine, you will see that where the coalition's rating is fairly high, then the businessmen appear if not in the top five, then in the top ten, and that's a fact. It's easy to pick them out: the people who have their places on the party lists never showed an interest in politics, never worked for any party. Their appearance can be explained by only one thing: the payment of that million dollars.[15]

These problems, which may be even more prominent with the shift to the full PR system, point to the need to develop stronger parties, either with reliable independent bases for funding or with access to public funding. They also point to the importance of the adoption of the imperative mandate, which will at least restrain the ability of elected deputies to change parliamentary faction repeatedly and at no cost.

Control of Media

Control of the media was a major means by which Kuchma's group sought to avoid accountability and control elections. Above, we showed how selective law enforcement was used to eliminate unfavorable coverage of Kuchma and his supporters. However, a broader ranger of tools supplemented selective law enforcement.

Intimidation of Individual Journalists

In addition to pressure on media organizations, efforts have also been aimed directly at individual journalists. Kuchma himself was deeply implicated in the most notorious case, that of the journalist Heorhiy Gongadze, who was murdered in 2000. To summarize, Gongadze was a relatively obscure journalist, writing for a Web site (to which very few Ukrainians had access) known for its investigative reporting and its criticism of the government. After his murder, tape recordings made in Kuchma's office, and later authenticated by the U.S. Federal Bureau of Investigation, showed Kuchma ordering his interior minister to do something about Gongadze. Even if this does not absolutely prove Kuchma's involvement,[16] it shows his strong interest in repressing journalists who criticize his rule.

Among the many mysteries of the Gongadze affair is why Kuchma should have been concerned about this particular journalist. While Gongadze's criticism of Kuchma was trenchant, it had almost no audience. The decision to go after him seemed to contradict the broader strategy of leaving alone smaller outlets of criticism that have little influence on the mass public. Indeed, the existence of these small critical organizations, such as the newspaper *Dzerkalo tyzhnya* (with a circulation of just 48,000[17]), allows the government to claim that Ukraine has a free press. Thus, a government official in information policy pointed to *Dzerkalo* to prove to the author that critical newspapers were allowed to operate in Ukraine, and that accusations of government control of the press were overblown.[18]

Secret Bulletins (Temniki)

In 2002, the government's influence over media was sufficiently strong that the presidential administration began dictating content to news outlets, through secret bulletins (*temniki*).[19] The *temnik* was an eight- to ten-page daily bulletin sent from the administration of the president to major news outlets, indicating which stories were to receive prominent coverage that day, and what slant was to be given them. The *temniki* gave very precise instructions about news coverage, leaving little room for interpretation. Editors were clearly under pressure to conform, lest they be subject to the measures described above, or simply fired.

There can be little doubt about the influence of such measures. According to monitoring conducted by the Organization for Security and Co-operation in Europe (OSCE) during the 2002 parliamentary election campaign, coverage of United Ukraine averaged 21 percent of the attention given to parties, while the Bloc of Yulia Tymoshenko received just 3 percent. Moreover, United Ukraine coverage was overwhelmingly positive, and the Tymoshenko Bloc's coverage negative.[20] Similarly, "in the six weeks preceding the election, Mr. Lytvyn and Mr. Kinakh received more than seven hours of coverage on UT-1 prime time news and current affairs programs. By comparison, during the same period, Mr. Yushchenko received a total of 14 minutes despite the bloc's leading position in most opinion polls."[21] As several of the *temniki* demonstrate, the presidential administration sought to have Tymoshenko herself disappear from the news. When a criminal case against Kuchma was opened by a Kyiv judge in October 2002, five of the six main stations ignored the story altogether in their main evening newscasts, while ICTV carried the item fifth in its evening news show.[22] The goal of this policy is to have the best of both worlds: the press appeared to be free, and would thus be trusted by the public. At the same time, the content of media coverage was tightly controlled by the government.

As in the Gongadze case, however, rather than producing a more docile press, the measure induced a backlash among irate reporters. A number of prominent news anchors, such as Yevhen Hlibovitsky of TV 1+1, resigned their positions, while the journalists of the UNIAN news agency held a press conference to publicize and protest the new attempt at government control. As an effort to increase the legitimacy of the regime, the *temniki* probably backfired. In the 2004 presidential elections, control of the press failed the Kuchma/Yanukovych team in two ways. First, the overall credibility of the press was undermined, so that its biased reporting was largely ineffective. Second, at the decisive moment in the contest for power, many major media outlets refused to continue biased coverage, announced that they had been under government control, and provided extensive coverage of the opposition movement.

Ownership of Media Outlets

Ukrainian television, where over 75 percent of Ukrainians get their news,[23] was largely owned by Kuchma's government and his supporters. While Ukraine has a vast number of small and largely irrelevant local television and radio stations, there are six national television stations. Of these, one (UT-1) is owned by the state. Three others (*Novyy Kanal*, STB, and ICTV) were controlled financially by Kuchma's son-in-law, Viktor Pinchuk, who also controlled the country's largest daily newspaper, *Fakty i komentarii.* Leading figures in the pro-presidential SDPU(o) party, including Oleksandr Zinchenko, controlled the other two, Inter and Studio 1 + 1.[24] Zinchenko's defection from the pro-presidential camp helped undermine this monopoly during the Orange Revolution.

In addition to a general environment of bias and censorship, access to media during election campaigns was highly variable, though the situation improved dramatically during the Orange Revolution (see below). At the regional and local levels, many parliamentary candidates found it very difficult to gain access to media.[25]

However, control of the media could not reliably achieve the results Kuchma and his colleagues sought, in large part because the Ukrainian public is widely skeptical of the news media. Because there is little recent tradition of a truly free and activist press in Ukraine, Ukrainians do not assume that they should believe everything they read or hear. After decades (or even centuries) of total state media control, a short period of press freedom in the 1990s has not been enough to undermine public skepticism.

Patronage

Shaping opinion through control of the media is an indirect means of influencing voting behavior. Patronage is much more direct. In Ukraine, the largest source of patronage is government jobs, but state control over university places, pensions, and the quality of life for soldiers, prisoners, and hospital patients is also important. The basic technique of patronage is to exchange jobs for votes. If people vote for the incumbent, they either receive a job, or keep the one they have. This has been a widespread phenomenon worldwide.

In order for patronage to work at the individual level, it is necessary for those in power to know how each individual employee votes, or at least to create the impression that they do. This should not be possible in a system where ballots are supposed to be secret. To individuals who are concerned about losing their jobs, however, absolute certainty that one's vote is known is not required to influence behavior. Some amount of doubt that the ballot is secret may be all that is needed to influence many votes.

Patronage is most powerful in state institutions: the army, hospitals, and prisons. In the army, in the 2002 parliamentary elections, soldiers in some units simply were not allowed to vote secretly: officers checked their ballots before they were deposited. Similarly, in some prisons, inmates were required to place their ballots in the boxes in such a way that prison officials could observe the voting. Presumably, prisoners who did not vote as instructed would be mistreated. Similar behavior was observed in hospitals.[26]

For the vast majority of state employees, or those, such as students, who depend on state services, more indirect means are used to gather votes. Instead of issuing threats and determining votes at the individual level, the tactic is carried out at the precinct level. Because of the small size of precincts, many are dominated by a single institution, such as a factory, university, hospital, or school. It is therefore possible to estimate from the precinct-level returns how people in large institutions voted. Retribution can then be carried out at the group level. In one example reported to me by a voter, children at a school in Dnipropetrovsk Oblast were sent home to tell their parents that their teacher would lose her job if the parents voted against the government in the 2000 constitutional referendum. Because school populations are regionally defined, it is easy to see how the parents in a particular school voted. Those who did not vote as they were told would not be punished individually; the school to which they sent their children would be punished.

This ability to monitor voting and to punish at the level of precincts and their dominant government institutions had a particularly powerful effect in the single-member districts in parliamentary elections.[27] In a closely contested district, the ability to decisively manipulate one or two precincts out of the whole district can control the outcome and change a seat in the parliament without ever showing anything abnormal in the district-level votes that are so widely reported. All an observer would see at the district level is a close race, of perhaps 51 percent to 49 percent. One particularly clear case in 2002 occurred in District 108, where the United Ukraine candidate won by 1,695 votes. In three precincts within that district, each of which consisted of a prison, there was a 100 percent vote for the United Ukraine candidate, totaling 4,341 votes.[28]

It is not coincidental, therefore, that United Ukraine performed better in the SMD portion of the 2002 parliamentary elections than in the PR portion: in the PR portion, votes collected in this way are aggregated at the national level and have a proportionate effect on results. At the district level, however, this kind of vote influence has highly disproportionate effects. This, in turn, explains why Kuchma repeatedly vetoed changes in the 2002 parliamentary election law that would have reduced the number of seats selected in single-member districts. The results were significant, because even a small shift in the distribution of seats could tip control of parliament. With the shift to a full PR system, this road to vote manipulation will become much less powerful.

Equally important to the use of patronage is the "machine" aspect of it, the way in which it is systematically organized so that voting in local precincts can be controlled from the top of the executive branch. Such control is facilitated by the organizational structure of the Ukrainian state, which is organized on a unitary (rather than federal) basis, and is hierarchically arranged, just as was the system of soviets. The executive branch in Kyiv controls all of the ministries, as well as the armed forces. It also appoints the heads of the oblast administrations, who in turn appoint lower level officials, and so on.

In order to collect votes, therefore, all that the central authorities have to do is assign each minister or regional head a quota of votes to deliver. They then leave that individual to figure out how to provide them. That person then issues quotas to those at the next level down, and so on:

> The system of influence on the electorate is very simple—the highest executive power gives directives to those below as to how many votes they should ensure. You can't give less, otherwise you'll have to face the consequences. Then, it's just a technical side of the affair—the meeting of local authorities, then the meeting of the authorities with their staff, then necessary explanations. In general, these questions are not the problem of the state authorities, who simply need the results.[29]

How many votes can the executive branch garner this way? It is hard to determine for certain, for two reasons. First, obtaining exact figures concerning the number of government employees is difficult. Second, we cannot assume that 100 percent efficiency is possible.[30] It likely varies across category, with those most dependent or vulnerable most likely to vote for the authorities. That lack of precision should not obscure a more important point: the number of votes subject to patronage is enormous compared with what would be necessary to fight a reasonably closely contested election. An estimate of the number of votes subject to government control through patronage is presented in Table 9.1.

This list does not include hospital patients, policemen, or firemen, for which statistics are not available. When this total is compared with the roughly 29 million votes cast in the "third" round of the 2004 presidential election, we can see that over 8 percent of the vote is subject to direct manipulation through patronage mechanisms.

Following the first round of the 1999 presidential elections, Ukraine's ambassador to the United States, Anton Buteyko, was dismissed because a plurality of the votes collected at the embassy were for Yevhen Marchuk rather than Kuchma.[31] Similarly, two oblast heads, who were not as effective

Table 9.1

Number of People Subject to Direct Voting Pressure from the State

Teachers	546,600[a]
Armed forces	304,000[b]
Medical personnel	224,000[c]
Prison population	218,800[d]
Central ministries	226,985[e]
Municipal employees	77,442[e]
Tax administration	44,820[e]
Customs administration	16,438[e]
Interior troops (police)	800,000[f]
Total	2,459,085

Notes:

[a]Ukrainian Ministry of Education and Science, www.education.gov.ua. Figure is for 2001.

[b]United Nations Development Programme, http://hdr.undp.org/reports/global/2002/en/indicator/cty_f_UKR.html. Figure is for 2000.

[c]Ukrainian Statistical Committee, www.ukrstat.gov.ua/. Figure is for 2002.

[d]Ombudsman of Ukraine, www.ombudsman.kiev.ua. Figure is for 2000. A similar figure (220,000) is reported by the U.S. State Department, "Country Reports on Human Rights Practices, Ukraine," March 31, 2003, 7.

[e]Ukrainian Statistical Committee, personal communication, July 2003. Figure is for 2003.

[f]Taras Kuzio, "The Organization of Ukraine's Forces," *Jane's Intelligence Review*, June 1, 1996, 254.

in bringing in the vote as Kuchma had hoped, were dismissed. Kuchma's approach to the problem was voiced during the 1998 parliamentary elections: "Those who do not pull the carriage—we should thank them and look for new people."[32] His ally at that time, Anatoliy Matvienko of the People's Democratic Party, lamented that 60 percent of the bureaucracy was "uncontrolled" and he advocated "partizing" the bureaucracy.[33]

Voting Fraud

Outright voting fraud was less widely used in Ukraine than other tactics until the 2004 presidential elections, when it became widespread.[34] In Ukraine it is relatively difficult to simply falsify election returns because the provisions for giving opposition candidates access to monitoring polling stations and vote counting are relatively stringent and are generally enforced. Therefore, fraud is carried on through multiple voting and other similar schemes. There were reports in 2002 of voters, especially soldiers, being bussed from one district to another in order to vote en masse.[35] In districts with close races, this could easily tip the balance. In the same election, a large number of unsecured ballots were discovered in District 99 in Kirovohrad Oblast, indicating an organized scheme for large-scale fraud. The OSCE concluded that "[t]he printing of ballots was not sufficiently transparent. No official documents were made available on the process of printing, storage, transfer and delivery of the ballots."[36] More broadly, the OSCE reported that almost 12 percent of polling stations received at least 10 percent more ballots than there were registered voters in their precincts, in contravention of rules stating that no more than 3 percent extra ballots can be issued. In over 4 percent of precincts, there were at least 25 percent more ballots than registered voters.[37] A large number of surplus ballots obviously facilitates fraud.

There were other cases of outright voting fraud prior to 2004, most notably in the 2000 referendum. Some of the reported results were so lopsided that they lacked credibility, and indeed were reminiscent of votes either in the Soviet Union or in present-day Turkmenistan. Zakarpatskia Oblast in western Ukraine reported 97.93 percent voter turnout, and "yes" votes on all four questions in the 95 percent range.[38] Kuchma vetoed a law that would strengthen enforcement of election regulations.[39] In the 1999 presidential elections and again in 2004, therefore, there was considerable controversy over the staffing of electoral commissions.[40] There were also substantial allegations of fraud, and in fact Kuchma's returns exceeded those predicted by exit polling.[41]

In 2004, of course, all of these problems vastly increased. Elaborating the wide variety of schemes influencing voters, implementing fraud, and then falsifying the returns would require a lengthy separate study.[42] However, despite that extensive manipulation, the tactics failed. This requires an explanation, which will be provided at the end of this chapter.

Controlling of the Judiciary

The Ukrainian legal system provides little protection against the tactics of power politics. In a "rule of law" society, many of the abuses of power described above would likely be prevented by appeal to the courts. For example, an order to close a newspaper due to some tax infraction would be delayed by a court until the case could be heard, rather than being implemented immediately. Moreover, if such a case were baseless or politically motivated, it would probably be thrown out. In Ukraine, the judiciary provides very few barriers to executive efforts to use "administrative resources," and provides very little recourse to those who suffer them.

The sources of these deficiencies are debated, with some explanations focusing on institutional factors, such as the lack of institutional separation of the judiciary from the executive branch, while others cite normative factors, including the lack of a tradition or a strong norm of judicial independence. Whatever the causes, the fact of the executive branch's considerable influence over the judiciary is not in doubt. This section explores some of the institutional sources for that influence, as well as the manifestations.

In the Soviet system, in which government was not divided into branches, there was no notion of a distinct judicial branch. The idea that the courts exist in part to check abuse of power by the government is therefore foreign to post-Soviet Ukraine, and while there have been some signs of change, it is occurring slowly at best. Both institutionally and politically, Soviet courts were expected to help the government (and party) achieve their goals, not to interfere with them. As emphasized in Chapter Four, the evolutionary change from Soviet to post-Soviet rule has meant that no fundamental break has been made. While the 1996 constitution states the intention of an independent judiciary, little of the organization and legislation concerning the judiciary, not to mention the funding, make this a reality in practice.

Under Kuchma, Ukraine's courts were not only pro-government in an institutional sense, but they tended to be pro-Kuchma in a partisan sense. It seems, therefore, that more than just a lack of independence was at work; rather, the courts actively participated in the execution of electoral authoritarianism. While they were not at the center of its practice on a daily basis, they played a crucial role by lending legal legitimacy to many of the actions ensuring that politics were skewed in the executive's favor.

In contrast to many countries, the executive branch in Ukraine has almost sole control over appointments to and dismissals from the judiciary. Some appointments are made within the judiciary itself, but the legislative branch has no influence other than the right to appoint six of the eighteen judges on the Constitutional Court. In addition to being responsible for creating courts, the president is responsible for determining the number of judges in them, and naming administrators of courts, who have considerable power over personnel decisions.[43]

> The Constitution provides for an independent judiciary; however, in practice the judiciary was subject to considerable political interference from the executive branch and also suffered from corruption and inefficiency. The courts were funded through the Ministry of Justice, which controlled the organizational support of the courts, including staffing matters, training for judges, logistics and procurement, and statistical and information support.[44]

In essence, then, the judiciary is not an independent branch, but rather an appendage of the Ministry of Justice, which, under Kuchma, was tightly controlled by the president. As a result, the old Soviet practice of telephone calls from political leaders to judges telling them how to rule on cases continued.

A few examples illustrate the politicized nature of the judiciary (this discussion leaves out the related problem of corruption in the courts). In July 2001, Ihor Aleksandrov, director of a television station in Donetsk, was murdered, presumably for his reports on corruption in the local administration. The police charged Yuri Verediuk, a homeless person, with the murder; he was alleged to have confessed, and was convicted. However, the Donetsk Oblast Court of Appeals found the conviction wanting, and overturned it, warning that Verediuk's life could be at risk. He died shortly thereafter. The Supreme Court overturned the Appeals Court's dismissal of the conviction, and sent the case back to the Procuracy for a new investigation. That the Court of Appeals overturned the original conviction indicates that, at least in some cases, judges were willing to act independently when something appeared rotten. But even in those cases, they can be overruled by higher-level judges that are more loyal to the authorities.

In 2001, politicization of the courts was demonstrated in the Kuchma administration's efforts to have opposition leader Yulia Tymoshenko imprisoned. After Tymoshenko was arrested, a Kyiv district court judge, Mykola Znayemko, ordered her released from custody pending trial. He further infuriated Kuchma by giving the wife and mother of Heorhiy Gongadze the status of "victims of crime." Kuchma simply dismissed him, citing inefficiency in forwarding case files.[45] In late 2002, after the U.S. government found the recordings made in Kuchma's office to be authentic, a Kyiv judge opened a criminal investigation against Kuchma, but it was quickly quashed by the Supreme Court. The Supreme Judicial Council subsequently recommended the dismissal of the investigating judge.[46]

How are judges controlled? First, even the most important judges in the country, those of the Constitutional Court, do not serve life terms. Instead, they serve nine-year terms. Even those who are not appointed by the president have powerful incentives to go along with his wishes, because if they wish to get good jobs after leaving the court, they will almost certainly require the cooperation of the executive branch, where almost all such appointments lie. The poor pay of judges also makes them subject to all kinds of blandishments, from outright bribes to better apartments. Because most judgeships are controlled by the executive (and most judges can be dismissed by the president or someone appointed by him) there is little de facto basis for judicial independence.

A related problem is that judicial rulings that go against the wishes of the executive are simply not carried out. While courts can issue rulings, these must be enforced by the executive branch (the Ministry of Justice). In liberal democracies there is both a normative commitment to enforcing judicial rulings, and a fear that further action will be brought against officials who refuse to enforce such rulings. This does not occur uniformly in Ukraine, especially when political interests are at stake.[47] Similarly, on several occasions the prosecutor general has dismissed requests from opposition parties to investigate wrongdoing by public officials.

The Limits of Administrative Resources

This analysis of the resources available to the executive branch in Ukraine and the tactics used to convert those resources into legitimate authority confirms that the Ukrainian president had the potential to decisively sway key parts of the democratic process. The result is that what is designed on paper as a finely balanced and fair set of laws and procedures became fundamentally unbalanced and unfair. Leonid Kuchma augmented the resources available to the executive, and honed the techniques for applying them. Many of these same resources will be available to Kuchma's successors, though they will be divided between the prime minister and the president.

While our primary conclusion based on the data presented in this chapter focuses on the power available to the president, the second conclusion must focus on the limits to that power. Kuchma's power over elections was significant, but not total. His ability to control a certain percentage of the vote meant that any close race would go in favor of the president. This is what we saw in the 2002 parliamentary elections, when United Ukraine made up in individual constituencies what it lost in the PR portion of the ballot. However, while the tactics used to win votes could reliably shift close elections in Kuchma's favor, it is much more difficult to use such methods to overcome a very large deficit in popular sentiment. This is the lesson of the PR portion of the 2002 parliamentary elections, where despite the massive advantages of funding, press coverage, and vote manipulation in favor of United Ukraine and the SDPU(o), those parties finished well behind the opposition Our Ukraine and Communist blocs. In that respect, the 2002 parliamentary elections demonstrated the vulnerabilities that brought down Kuchma's group in 2004.

The Failure of Power Politics in the 2004 Presidential Elections

Given all the power accumulated in the executive branch, how did Kuchma fail to install his chosen successor, Viktor Yanukovych, in 2004?[48] This section provides a brief explanation, focusing on four factors. First, by picking an extremely unpopular candidate, the Kuchma team went beyond the limits of what could be achieved using previous tactics. Second, the opposition became much more united than it had been during previous confrontations. Third, Ukrainian civil society, assumed by many to be nonexistent, asserted itself in favor of democracy. Fourth and perhaps most crucial, key elements of the elite, including some on whom Kuchma and Yanukovych were depending, defected from the "party of power," facilitating the protests that came to be known as the Orange Revolution. Thus, Kuchma failed not because he was constrained by institutions, but because, in the end, he was confronted by superior power.

The Unpopularity of Yanukovych

Kuchma's strategy relied on skewing vote counts, but still required collecting enough votes to win. This became even more difficult with the nomination of Viktor Yanukovych as the candidate to replace Kuchma. The Kuchma administration was widely perceived in society to be corrupt, and was therefore very unpopular by 2004. The more specific problem was the candidate selected to represent Kuchma's group in the election, Viktor Yanukovych. Yanukovych was the sitting prime minister and former governor of Donetsk Oblast in eastern Ukraine. He managed to alienate both elites and masses. Many elites mistrusted him because he and the "Donetsk clan" from which he came appeared to want to seize as much as they could get their hands on, rather than splitting the spoils with others.

Many citizens loathed him because they viewed him as criminal and authoritarian. It was widely known that Yanukovych had two criminal convictions from the 1970s, and he occasionally used rather crude prison slang in public speeches. Many believed that electing him would move the country much closer to full authoritarianism. But many, especially in Ukraine's populous east, found Yushchenko equally unacceptable. Many observers of Ukrainian politics agree that, had a different candidate been selected (such as National Bank chairman Serhiy Tyhypko), he could have fairly and legitimately defeated Viktor Yushchenko.

It is therefore a mystery why Kuchma chose Yanukovych as the heir apparent. One factor may have been the power of the "Donetsk clan," which had succeeded more than any other regional clan in gathering votes for the pro-presidential United Ukraine bloc in 2002. It also appears that Kuchma's team believed that popularity could be manufactured through their control of the press and that voting fraud would do the rest. Neither Yanukovych nor the main strategists of his team understood that the system was still partly democratic. Instead, they behaved as if they were already in an authoritarian system in which people would simply vote for whom they were told to vote.

The Unification of the Opposition

Until 2004 the various Ukrainian opposition groups (right, center, and left) were never quite able to unite against Kuchma (as discussed in Chapter Five). In the run-up to the 2004 election, this changed decisively. The rightist forces of Yushchenko allied with the socialists of Moroz and the populist leftists of Tymoshenko behind a single shared goal: to get rid of Kuchma's group. This represented a drastic change from the situation even two years earlier. As recently as 2002, Yushchenko had entertained the idea of taking Our Ukraine into a coalition with Kuchma's United Ukraine to form a parliamentary majority. In 2004, only the Communist Party of Ukraine, among major opposition to Kuchma, was unwilling to unite with the others.

Because Yushchenko was so obviously the best choice to lead the anti-Kuchma forces into the election, other potential candidates, including Tymoshenko and Moroz, supported him rather than running against him. The result was an alliance that was cemented in early 2004 and remained intact through the election. This contrasted with 1999, when the early anti-Kuchma coalition fragmented. The 2004 coalition was not without strain, in particular, because many among Yushchenko's core supporters were very leery of an alliance with Tymoshenko. But in contrast to past episodes, objections were put aside.

The results were clear to see. Yushchenko's alliance had a well-organized effort to contest the election at three distinct stages. First, there was a campaign to win over voters and turn them out on election day. The range of parties involved in the alliance meant that different parties could work with segments of voters and regions where they were most able to succeed. Had either Moroz or Tymoshenko sought the presidency and deprived Yushchenko of their organizational support, he may well have lost the election.

Second, the opposition jointly prepared a massive effort to monitor the election vote tabulation. This effort would make fraud harder to practice and easier to discover, and led to much of the evidence that convinced the Supreme Court to overturn the election result.

Third, the opposition prepared well in advance to put protestors into the streets in the event the election was stolen. The protests were not spontaneous. Because the intention to steal the election was so obvious, the opposition had plenty of time to prepare. Most remarkable about this effort was the ability of a wide range of groups to delegate tasks among themselves and coordinate their implementation effectively.

The Emergence of Civil Society

Prior to November 2004, most people within and outside Ukraine believed that Ukraine had very little "civil society." Clearly, Kuchma and Yanukovych believed that they could steal the election and that no one would care very much. Coverage of the campaign on Ukraine's television stations was so thoroughly one-sided that even unsophisticated voters were able to see that it was manipulated. Apparently, the goal was to create a sense of inevitability that would promote acquiescence.

This election demonstrated not only that large numbers of Ukrainians were willing to become politically active, but also that they had considerable organizational capacity.[49] Organizing, training, and deploying, first, election monitors, and later, protestors, required considerable logistical capacity. There was also an impressive capability for spontaneous action: only a week before the first round, the idea of silently showing one's support for Yushchenko by wearing orange began to spread, and by the second round (three weeks later), orange ribbons, scarves, and banners were ubiquitous, showing that opposition to Yanukovych was widespread. Kuchma's control over the media could not do anything to counter the message sent by all this orange. Once organized forces got the protests started, hundreds of thousands of citizens quickly joined in.

Division Among the Elites

The role of the elites in the success of the Orange Revolution has been underemphasized, given the stirring images of citizens in the streets of Kyiv.[50] However, from the very beginning of the crisis, key segments of the elite eased the job of protest organizers, both by what they did and what they did not do.

First, there were no efforts to block access to central Kyiv. This contrasts substantially with successful efforts to foil protests during the "Ukraine Without Kuchma" campaign in 2001. In that case, state authorities used several means to squelch these protests, while almost always avoiding direct coercive repression. These means included blocking access to central Kyiv, and into Kyiv from other parts of the country. Additional means not used then, but presumably available in 2004, would have included shutting down the cell phone networks and the Internet, on which the protestors relied so heavily to coordinate their activity. Just weeks before the protests, the ability to shut off central Kyiv was demonstrated clearly during the parade celebrating the sixtieth anniversary of the liberation of Ukraine in World War II. That the level of repression declined to nearly zero in 2004 indicates that decisions were made to allow the protests to grow.

Second, unmistakable signals were sent to potential protestors that the protests would be allowed, that they would not be repressed, and that they would succeed. The most important such signal may have been the announcement, immediately after the second round of the elections, that the Kyiv City Council rejected the legitimacy of the announced results. Kyiv's mayor, Oleksandr Omelchenko, had appeared previously to support Yanukovych. His defection sent clear signals that some of the elite would support protests, and more important, that Kyiv would be "open for protest." Later, high-ranking figures in the Security Service of Ukraine (SBU) appeared on the stage at the Maidan Nezalezhnosti (Independence Square), encouraging the protestors.

As the crisis proceeded, the elite did not merely divide; rather, most of it defected to Yushchenko, so that Yanukovych was isolated. On November 29, Yanukovych's campaign manager, Serhiy Tyhypko resigned. Moreover, he admitted that large-scale election fraud had taken place.[51] Like many others, Tyhypko was trying to cut his losses in a post-Kuchma Ukraine. On the same day, President Kuchma himself announced support for a rerun of the second round of the election, destroying what remained of Yanukovych's position.[52]

The positions of the various armed forces (the military, the Security Service of Ukraine, and the Interior Ministry) were more ambiguous, but generally served to encourage protests as well. Rumors of an imminent crackdown arose repeatedly, but never materialized. The army was neutral, but this neutrality clearly played into the hands of the opposition, as it seemed to guarantee that the army would not suppress the demonstrations. Most significantly, the SBU seemed to encourage the protestors, and to ensure them that they would be safe.

The Limits of "Political Technology"

In both the Russian and Ukrainian presidential elections, much attention has focused on what has been labeled "political technology," and to the "political technologists" who implement such methods.[53] In many respects, this technology is not new. Controlling media, extorting financial support from businesspeople, using the government payroll to gain votes, and controlling the counting of votes are all time-honored methods of machine politics.

The lesson of this election, for both political scientists and politicians in the region, is that such tactics are neither omnipotent nor foolproof. The Ukrainian "party of power," along with some outside analysts, tended to overestimate the effectiveness of machine politics and "political technology." The tools of machine politics can no doubt influence votes, though the exact influence is unclear and will obviously vary from case to case. In a close election, which will tip by a small percentage of the votes, such methods can be decisive if they are available much more extensively to one side than to the other, as is the case throughout the former Soviet Union, where control of the state apparatus conveys huge advantages.

However, such tactics cannot by themselves create a winner out of just anyone. This seems to have been the misconception driving the Ukrainian party of power. They apparently assumed that their huge advantages in "political technology" would automatically deliver them the election. They may have been encouraged in this belief by the ease of Vladimir Putin's victory in Russia in 2003, where such tactics were employed extensively. The crucial difference, which appears to have gone unnoticed, is that Putin had immense personal popularity and almost certainly would have won the election even if it had been fair. In other words, "political technology," while widely applied in Russia, was probably irrelevant to the result of the election.

The problem for Yanukovych was that he had to make up a much bigger gap than machine politics and political technology could overcome. Had the party of power selected a more popular candidate, they could likely have swung the 5–10 percent of the vote needed to change the outcome of the election without resorting to outright and obvious fraud and intimidation. Picking such an unpopular candidate made the gap too big to cover, such that they had to move from "machine politics" to outright falsification, indicating a move toward full authoritarianism.

When one is required to actually falsify the voting, it becomes easier to undermine the legitimacy of the results. Both alternate vote counts and exit polls can provide evidence that the election was stolen. The widespread perception among Ukrainians that the election was fixed was the result of an abundance of clear evidence to that effect. Without such evidence of fraud, it is unlikely that postelection events would have developed as they did.

The transparent role of Russia in supporting "political technologies" in Ukraine probably also backfired. In the opinion of Russian analyst Sergei Karaganov:

> We . . . had the right to prefer one of the candidates. But we made almost all of the imaginable mistakes. Our campaigning took the form of a brazen commercial operation, which was bound to irritate even Russia's supporters in Ukraine. Moreover, political specialists managed to involve in their games even the top Russia leaders, who took a stand and hence weakened their long-term ability to influence the situation in Ukraine.[54]

In sum, we need to recognize the limitations of "political technologies." That they can tip a close election is obvious. They can skew a certain percentage of the vote without leaving enough clear evidence to undermine the legitimacy of the elections. Kuchma, still fairly popular, was able to use "political technologies" in this way in 1999. But they cannot make an unpopular candidate popular, and they are not a replacement for political *skill*, which was rarely discussed in the Ukrainian election, but was perhaps the deciding factor. The ineptitude with which Kuchma and Yanukovych exploited their considerable advantages is remarkable.

Machine Politics After the Orange Revolution

If Kuchma was able to consolidate his power and maintain it through what we have called "machine politics" and "political technologies," what potential is there to do this in post-Kuchma Ukraine? We can identify two concrete changes that will reduce the president's ability to use these tactics in the future. At the same time, we must emphasize that considerable potential for these tactics remains.

Division of Powers

The constitutional changes adopted in 2004 divide control over the executive branch between the prime minister and the president. This will make it difficult for either of them to amass the sort of power that Kuchma had. The prime minister, through his/her power to appoint most ministers, will have much of the patronage power and power of selective enforcement of regulations that Kuchma had. However, the president will retain control of the so-called power ministries, and therefore will retain some ability to use selective law enforcement. The president and prime minister will thus be able to check each other. The bad news (as already discussed in Chapter Six) is that this is a recipe for conflict and stalemate. The good news is that this division of power impedes renewed authoritarianism. We may see a situation, sometime in the future, when the prime minister uses one set of bureaucracies to pursue political advantage against a president who is using another set of bureaucracies for the same purpose.

Freedom of Media

A central strategy of Kuchma (and of other authoritarian leaders in the former Soviet Union) was to control the media. A major accomplishment of the Orange Revolution was the rejection by the media of governmental control. Once again, Ukraine has a range of privately owned media, representing various political interests. It will be very hard for any aspiring autocrat to reassemble the control over the media that Kuchma had. Ukrainian society and elites are likely to be more vigilant in the future, having seen how this process works. A good example of changed attitudes was visible in mid-2005, when Ukrainian media focused attention on the expensive lifestyle of Yushchenko's son Andriy.[55] When Viktor Yushchenko reacted angrily to such reports, he was widely criticized for attacking the media. Moreover, with media control having become much more decentralized since late 2004, it is not clear that anyone will be able to put it back together again.

The Remaining Potential for Machine Politics

Despite the changes for the better, much potential remains for "machine politics" and "political technology." The absence of an effective civil service system means that using government jobs and resources to coerce voters can continue. In the fall of 2005, there were already credible accusations that such pressure was being applied in the run-up to the 2006 parliamentary elections.[56] Similarly, the fact that regional governors are still appointed by the president rather than elected concentrates nationwide patronage power in the hands of the president, instead of dividing it among governors. If "administrative resources" played an important role in determining the 2004 presidential vote, it is not encouraging that the 2006 vote turned out almost identically.

Moreover, while control over the bureaucracies is divided, there is no barrier to the continued use of selective law enforcement and regulation for political purposes. Less than a year after the Orange Revolution, Yushchenko appeared to be using his power to refrain from prosecuting those with whom he had made political deals, while Prime Minister Tymoshenko and several others among Yushchenko's team were accused of using their control of the government to pursue various commercial interests.

In sum, we should not expect that the Orange Revolution will change the rough-and-tumble nature of Ukrainian politics, or that it will suddenly usher in honesty in government. "Power politics" will continue to trump institutional design in many cases. However, as theorists of international relations stress, power politics is very different when power is balanced among competing forces rather than concentrated in one actor's hands. Thus, the most significant effect of the Orange Revolution is that it has fragmented de facto political power in the country, both within government institutions and within society. While the tactics of machine politics will continue to be used, they are much less likely to be controlled by a single political force. This will make the concentration of power obtained by Kuchma much harder to achieve. This is not a recipe for clean politics, but it might be a recipe for less authoritarianism.

10

Ukraine in Comparative Perspective

Electoral Authoritarianism in the Former Soviet Union and Beyond

The underlying model of politics that has developed in Ukraine since 1991, labeled "electoral authoritarianism" in this book, is not unique to Ukraine. We see analogues to this model in countries around the world as well. Only the details differ, due to differing historical, cultural, demographic, and geographic situations. Recognizing that Ukraine's problems are not unique is essential both to understanding the causes of Ukraine's problems and prescribing solutions.

Because we see electoral authoritarianism throughout the former Soviet Union, we cannot conclude that the sources of Ukraine's problems lie in some factor unique to Ukraine. Neither Ukraine's history under different empires nor its present cleavage structure can account for a result that appears in other societies lacking the same factors. Moreover, to the extent that we see electoral authoritarianism in societies that did not experience Soviet-style communism, we cannot see this form of politics as rooted simply in the legacy of the Soviet experience. Certainly that experience created the preconditions, but other, noncommunist experiences can apparently create the same conditions.

By recognizing similar forms of electoral authoritarianism across societies, and by seeing strong executives in very different countries adopt the same tactics to maintain and expand their control, we are able to see the actions taken by the Kuchma government more as purposeful responses that any ambitious leader might take and less as the tools of a singularly voracious and corrupt administration, which is how Kuchma and his regime are sometimes portrayed. Whether he was voracious and corrupt is debatable, but it cannot reasonably be argued that he is unique.

This leads to an important warning about Ukraine's post-Kuchma future: we should not assume that politics after Kuchma will automatically be different. If leaders in countries very different from Ukraine adopt the same tactics, there is little reason to assume that a new leader in Ukraine cannot adopt the same tactics. It is therefore naive to believe that Kuchma's departure will put Ukraine on a direct course toward liberal democracy. That is only one possibility.

This chapter will first summarize a general model of electoral authoritarianism, building on the characteristics of strong executive control elaborated in Chapter Nine. Second, it will apply this general model to four of the post-Soviet cases, Armenia, Kazakhstan, Kyrgyzstan, and Russia. These four countries are vastly different in many ways (language, religion, size, wealth, geography) and yet they have developed political systems strongly resembling Kuchma's Ukraine. Next, in less detail, it will consider how this model fits cases outside the former Soviet Union. In very different contexts, executives adopt similar policies to augment their rule, and similar problems result. Finally, the chapter seeks some preliminary conclusions about the broader sources of electoral authoritarianism, and considers the differences as well as the similarities in the cases considered.

A General Model of Electoral Authoritarianism

Chapter Two sought to distinguish "electoral authoritarianism" from the more traditional variant by pointing out that in electoral authoritarianism, the regime is maintained in power primarily because it builds legitimacy through elections, while traditional authoritarian regimes maintained power primarily through ideology, coercion, and intimidation.[1] While some of the cases discussed below may lead us to question how distinct those two categories are, the central point remains that all of these regimes remain committed to "democratic" structures and practices. At the same time, however, they seek to avoid most of the important implications of democratic governance. This leads them to a set of tactics that were elaborated in Chapter Nine:

1. Selective law enforcement;
2. Selective administration of regulations;
3. Control over the media;
4. Control over the election process;
5. Control over patronage;
6. Control over the economy. As emphasized in the study of the Ukrainian case, these tactics arise within a particular political and institutional context, which includes:
7. A constitution giving extensive legislative power to the executive;
8. A weak and fragmented parliament;
9. A weak judicial branch (or rather the absence of a judicial branch distinct from the executive branch).

Table 10.1

Freedom House 2004 New Democracy Score and Presidential Powers

Country	Democracy[a]	Presidential powers[b]
Armenia	5.00	13.5
Azerbaijan	5.63	no data
Belarus	6.54	15
Estonia	1.92	4.5
Georgia	4.83	no data
Kazakhstan	6.25	15.5
Kyrgyzstan	5.67	15.5
Latvia	2.17	4.75
Lithuania	2.13	12
Moldova	4.88	13
Russia	5.25	18
Tajikistan	5.71	13
Turkmenistan	6.88	18.5
Ukraine (to 2006)	4.88	15
Uzbekistan	6.46	17

Notes:

[a]Freedom House, *Nations in Transit 2004*, www.freedomhouse.org/research/nattransit.htm, accessed April 29, 2005.

[b]The score for presidential powers is from Timothy Frye, "A Politics of Institutional Choice: Post-Communist Presidencies," *Comparative Political Studies* 30, no. 5 (October 1997), 547. The score is simply a count of formal presidential powers, such as the ability to dissolve parliament, to chair the National Security Council, and so on (out of a total possible maximum of twenty-seven). The score does not ascribe different weights to different powers that may in fact be more important, so it must be taken as a rough gauge rather than as a precise measurement. For the sake of comparison, the Czech Republic scored 4.75, Hungary scored 7.25, Poland scored 13, and Slovenia scored 5.5.

These nine basic characteristics can be seen through much of the former Soviet Union, and beyond.

Summarizing the State of Affairs in the Former Soviet Union

Table 10.1 tabulates the "New Democracy" scores for all of the post-Soviet states, as ranked by Freedom House from 1 (most free) to 7 (least free), as well as Timothy Frye's scores for the extent of presidential power in each state.

The countries can be separated into three groups. The first group is the democracies, including Estonia, Latvia, and Lithuania. These have scores comparable with those of established Western democracies, and the worst democracy score in this group, Latvia's 2.17, is more than two points better than the best in the next group (4.88 for Ukraine and Moldova). At the opposite end are the countries that are authoritarian in the traditional sense of the term, including Belarus, Turkmenistan, and Uzbekistan. The countries in between are what Carothers calls the "grey zone." Their democracy scores range from 4.88 for Ukraine and Moldova to Kazakhstan's 6.25.[2] These countries all have some professed commitment to democratic procedures and some credible claim to partly fair elections. Yet their elections are not fully fair, their economies are not fully free, and civil liberties remain poorly defended. We cannot conclude on this basis that all of these are characterized by electoral authoritarianism. The examination of four cases will show that this model is not unique to Ukraine.

Russia

In Russia, the governments first of Boris Yeltsin and then of Vladimir Putin have used many of the same tactics used by Kuchma's government in Ukraine. In fact, the tactics developed by Yeltsin's advisers for the 1996 Russian presidential election were brought to Ukraine for use in the 1999 presidential elections. They were subsequently developed further and used by Putin in 2003 and Yanukovych in 2004.

A very high level of constitutional authority for the president was established in December 1993, when Yeltsin successfully put a new constitution to a referendum. However, that new constitution did not establish executive power, but rather provided constitutional legitimacy for power that had been decisively seized in September of that year, when Yeltsin unilaterally (and unconstitutionally) dissolved the Supreme Soviet.

This episode is instructive because it showed that, even within a state labeled as a democracy, the Weberian question of who controls the means of violence is crucial. In the Ukrainian case, a direct resort to arms has not occurred, and when it seemed possible, in December 2004, it appeared that the executive would lose. In the Russian case, the leftist opposition in the Supreme Soviet sought to test this question when they refused to leave the Russian White House and declared themselves Yeltsin's successors. Had the military sided with the parliament, we would have a very different Russia today. It was this military victory that established Yeltsin's de facto power in the clearest way. The constitutional referendum was hardly a ringing endorsement, with the constitution being approved by a narrow majority in a vote with credible allegations of fraud and manipulation.

The 1993 Russian constitution was drafted neither by a constitutional convention nor by a group including representatives of parliament, but rather by a group appointed directly by Yeltsin.[3] The process reflected his total victory over the parliament, and in turn was reflected in the new distribution of powers. As Table 10.1 indicates, the result was a presidency as powerful in legal terms as any in the former Soviet Union, surpassing even Uzbekistan and being barely eclipsed only by Turkmenistan. Thus, M. Steven Fish labels the Russian system "superpresidential."[4] Under the 1993 constitution, the Russian president can dissolve the parliament if it rejects the president's nominee for prime minister three times. This gives the parliament a very strong disincentive to actively vet candidates for that post. Similarly, if the Duma votes no confidence in the government twice within three months, the president can dissolve the Duma and call new elections. Again, the disincentives for Duma activism are strong.[5]

A second characteristic of Russian politics has been the weakness of the parliament.[6] Russia's parliament is bicameral, with an upper chamber consisting of the heads of Russia's regions, along with a lower house elected according to a mixed system similar to that used in Ukraine in 1998 and 2002. The major difference is that Ukraine used a 4 percent threshold and Russia uses a 5 percent threshold. Unlike Ukraine, in recent years Russia has had a relatively steady majority and little difficult passing legislation.

However, the parliamentary majority in Russia has existed only at the sufferance of the executive, and is largely seen as a "rubber stamp" of President Putin's proposals. Thus, Joel Ostrow characterizes the Duma as "complete chaos, under control."[7] Ironically, while some parties have been stable (but weak), the "party of power" has gone through a series of metamorphoses of name and organization, beginning with Russia's Choice in 1993, through Our Home Is Russia, and most recently, the Unified Russia bloc.[8] These represent successive attempts by the executive branch to create a structure that could channel the "administrative resources" of the executive branch into control of parliament. That this has succeeded in Russia is not a sign that the parliament is able to be more independent of the executive, but, on the contrary, a sign that the executive has had even greater success in controlling the legislature. The benefits are stability and the easy passage of legislation. The drawback has been that Putin's power in Russia is much more difficult to challenge than was Kuchma's in Ukraine. The parliamentary rubber stamp allows Putin to further create democratic legitimacy for policies that are developed solely by the executive. In sum, Russia's parliament cannot today be described as fragmented, but it is very weak. Indeed, it has become less fragmented only because its weakness has allowed the president to forge a majority that is controlled by him.

Russia's judicial system is separated from the executive branch on paper, but often finds it difficult to act independently in practice. As in Ukraine, even when it rules independently of the government, it relies on government agencies for enforcement of its decisions.[9] Because such enforcement is far from reliable, the judiciary cannot be said to form an independent branch of government or an independent check on executive power. The absence of such an independent and assertive judiciary facilitates the selective application of law enforcement and regulation. Unlike Ukraine, however, Russia actually undertook significant legal and judicial reform in the 1990s.[10] As Peter Solomon has shown, the period from 2001 to 2005 actually saw efforts at "judicial counterreform" in Russia. This included proposals to eliminate lifetime terms for judges and to reduce the power of the Constitutional Court to invalidate laws.[11] While these proposals have so far not succeeded, they indicate continued pressure on the role of the judiciary as a check on the executive branch.

Overall, the context in Russia is quite favorable to the exercise of electoral authoritarianism. It must be emphasized that this context is not simply the result of "natural forces" but, rather, has been engineered by the executive branch, most notably when it forcibly dissolved the parliament and rewrote the constitution emaciating the parliament for the benefit of the executive. Amending the law such that regional governors are appointed by the president, rather than elected, has further solidified executive control.

All of the tactics of executive control laid out in the general model of electoral authoritarianism have been applied in Russia. For the former Soviet Union, Russia has in fact been a model for other regimes, with tactics adopted first in Russia, and then used in places such as Ukraine. The selective enforcement of laws and regulation has been implemented most notoriously to gain control over the Russian media, a process that accelerated in anticipation of presidential and parliamentary elections in 2004.

The most notorious cases, covered in great detail in the Western press, were those of the "oligarchs" Boris Berezovsky, Vladimir Gusinsky, and Mikhail Khodorkovsky. The authorities turned a blind eye to their shady business dealings when they supported the government of Boris Yeltsin, most notably by financing his 1996 presidential campaign. When they fell out with Putin, however, and media outlets owned by them criticized Putin, all three faced legal actions that forced them to surrender their assets, and criminal investigations that forced two of them to flee Russia, while the third, Khodorkovsky, was imprisoned. As is often the case in Ukraine, it cannot be said that the individuals being "persecuted" were innocent of the violations with which they were charged. Rather, the problem is that such violations were pursued selectively—only when the individuals presented a political threat to the executive branch.

In addition to the well-publicized cases against Berezovsky, Gusinsky, and Khodorkovsky, a much broader effort was undertaken to control media in Russia. Political control over state-run media was tightened, and even much smaller news outlets were challenged. After the hostage crisis in a Moscow theater in late 2002, Boris Jordan, who became director of NTV after it was seized from Gusinsky, was fired over that station's coverage of the crisis.[12] In the summer of 2003, Russia's last independently controlled television station, NTS, was forced to close in a regulatory action, and its broadcasting frequency was turned over to a twenty-four-hour sports network, controlled by individuals closely linked to Putin.

NTS was suspect in the eyes of the Putin government in part because it had become the home of many of the journalists set loose when NTV was seized, and was already in deep financial trouble before being closed. Its financial difficulties stemmed from its inability to reach an agreement with Russia's leading advertising agency, whose founder, Mikhail Lesin, had become Putin's press minister.[13] Through the combination of administrative actions and economic leverage, the Putin government was able to completely control television in advance of the 2004 elections.

Patronage is also used to ensure that candidates favored by the executive have an advantage in elections. As in Ukraine, a wide variety of public institutions is controlled centrally, and there is little to prevent employees suspected of voting "incorrectly" from being fired. In schools, universities, hospitals, and a wide range of public institutions, pressure is placed on employees to vote for favored candidates.

Perhaps even more than in Ukraine, state control over the economy has been shown to play an essential role in maintaining the executive branch in power. This was chronicled in considerable detail in the case of the 1996 presidential election. With Yeltsin's popularity ratings in the single digits only months before the election, massive efforts were made to give "oligarchs" and other business interests very favorable access to state property (through the privatization process in general and the notorious "loans for shares" scheme in particular), in return for the massive funneling back of resources by those business interests into Yeltsin's campaign coffers. The scale of the project was shown when campaign workers were caught leaving the Kremlin with half a million U.S. dollars in cash. Presumably, those interests that helped Yeltsin win reelection could expect favorable treatment in the future as well. Later, when some of those same people opposed Putin, their interests were attacked mercilessly, such that Berezovsky, Gusinsky, and Khodorkovsky, three of the most powerful and wealthy men in Russia, were stripped of most of their business holdings.

This brief overview highlights what has been shown in a vast number of detailed studies of Russian politics since 1991, and focuses on the similarities between Russia and Ukraine. Despite considerable differences in the two countries, there is substantial overlap in key aspects of the political context: weak legislature and parties, strong presidency, and weak judicial branch. More striking are the close similarities in the ways that the executive branches in the two countries have sought to convert de facto power into legitimate power by skewing the ostensibly democratic processes of elections and parliamentary legislation decisively in their favor.

Armenia

Armenia differs more from Russia and Ukraine than those two states differ from each other. It is a tiny country in terms of land area and population, and is even poorer than Russia and Ukraine. Moreover, it has spent much of the post-Soviet era engaged in a successful war to seize territory from Azerbaijan. And while there have been some political developments in Armenia that we have not seen in other post-Soviet cases, most notably the resignation under pressure of an unpopular president and a considerable level of political violence, politics in recent years has very much resembled the model of electoral authoritarianism described above.

Even prior to the collapse of the Soviet Union, Armenia and Azerbaijan were at war over the contested territory of Nagorno-Karabakh, an Armenian enclave within Azerbaijan. Armenia has been successful not only in controlling that territory, but also in taking control of a corridor linking Nagorno-Karabakh to the rest of Armenia. This war has been the central political issue in post-Soviet Armenia, and was at the root of the change of presidents in February 1998. Armenia's first post-Soviet president, Levon Ter-Petrossian, was a holdover from the Soviet era. He met massive resistance and was deserted even by his own supporters when he agreed to an Organization for Security and Co-operation in Europe (OSCE)–proposed agreement that would have left Nagorno-Karabakh technically in Azerbaijan, while under Armenian control. He had little choice but to resign. This development shows that there is some capability of public dissatisfaction to affect the ruler, but it should be stressed that the attack on Ter-Petrossian was carried out largely by the elite, and he was not removed through any formal procedure such as an election or impeachment. Moreover, the snap elections that followed, and were won by Robert Kocharian, were severely criticized by the OSCE for massive fraud.

A second major turning point in Armenia's political development occurred in October 1999 when gunmen stormed the parliament in Yerevan and murdered the prime minister, Vazgen Sarkisian, and the speaker of the parliament, Karen Demirchian, who were partners in the Unity Bloc that triumphed in the 1994 parliamentary elections. The gunmen later insisted that they acted alone, but the fact that the murders were so conducive to the consolidation of

Kocharian's powers has led to ongoing suspicion that he was somehow connected to them.

Looking more broadly at the presidencies of Ter-Petrossian and Kocharian, we see the same conditions and tactics that characterize electoral authoritarianism elsewhere in the former Soviet Union. As is the case in Kazakhstan, by 2003 it became questionable whether Armenia should be considered an electoral authoritarian government or simply a traditional authoritarian regime. Widespread and transparent electoral fraud in the 2003 presidential elections decreased the extent to which the government's authority rested upon the legitimacy conferred by elections as opposed to force and intimidation.

Especially since 2001, Armenia has seen substantial fragmentation of all major political parties, making divide-and-conquer tactics much easier. As Freedom House reports, "several politicians who could scuttle Kocharian's plans to win a second five-year term in 2003 were kept busy putting down internal revolts staged by pro-presidential activists."[14] The tactic of infiltrating pro-executive individuals into opposition parties was also practiced by Kuchma in Ukraine. The inability of opposition forces in parliament to unite, as in Ukraine, prevented the parliament as an institution from challenging presidential authority.

For example, following the attack on parliament in 1999, Aram Sarkisian was named to replace his assassinated brother as prime minister. When Kocharian sought to replace Sarkisian with someone more loyal to him, a confrontation ensued, but ultimately the parliament backed down in the face of threats to dissolve it, and Kocharian's candidate triumphed. Opposition politicians since then have tended to join forces with Kocharian, recognizing that there is little to be gained from opposing him.

Armenia's 1995 constitution gave the president the right to dissolve the legislature, a power that tends to overwhelm other provisions that might give the parliament considerable influence over the executive branch, such as the right to approve the prime minister and other ministers and to dismiss them.[15] Amendments adopted in 2003 appear to limit to six specific circumstances the president's right to dissolve parliament, but it is not clear that these limits have practical effect. In addition to power to dissolve the parliament, Armenia's president can circumvent it through extensive decree powers: presidential decrees have the status of any other legislation as long as they do not contradict the constitution. This gives the president little reason to compromise with parliament. In December 1994, Ter-Petrossian used this power to ban the major opposition party (and the party of his successor, Kocharian) by decree.[16] In 2000, Kocharian issued a decree giving himself exclusive control over high-level military appointments.[17]

Under both the Ter-Petrossian and Kocharian governments, the executive branch has had considerable control over the judicial branch. Until the 2003 constitutional amendments, the president appointed the commission that hires all judges, and more important, could dismiss them. Under the constitutional amendments adopted in 2003, the Justice Council would not be appointed by the president, but by the judges themselves.[18]

In these circumstances, selective law enforcement is relatively easy to use against opponents of the executive. Since Kocharian came to power, many of Ter-Petrossian's ministers have been charged with a variety of crimes. Politicization of the criminal justice process appeared especially salient in the investigation of the 1999 attack on parliament. Initially, a number of people, including several with connections to Kocharian, were arrested, but those who implicated Kocharian were soon released. It would appear either that the original decision to arrest those individuals, or the decision to release them, was politically motivated. Similarly, there were massive arrests of opposition supporters in the days before the 2003 presidential elections. In 1995, the Supreme Court of Armenia upheld Ter-Petrossian's suspension of the Armenian Revolutionary Federation (also known as the Dashnak Party) for six months, a period that conveniently ended just after the national elections.[19]

The process of constitutional adoption and revision has, as in Russia, been controlled by the executive through the referendum process. In 1995 Ter-Petrossian submitted Armenia's first post-Soviet constitution to a referendum, considerably augmenting the powers of the presidency. As in similar cases, there is little surprise that a constitutional process controlled by the president had this result. In May 2003, a series of amendments was enacted that purported to rein in the president's power. Opposition parliamentarians, skeptical that Kocharian's slate of amendments would in fact limit his power, sought to put forth a competing slate of amendments, to be voted on in competition with Kocharian's proposal in the same referendum. Kocharian wielded his considerable power to prevent this, threatening the legislature with dissolution if it persisted.

According to some sources, Armenia continues to have a fairly free press, although the same tactics used in Ukraine and Russia have been employed there, and pressure on the media seems to have increased in the run-up to the 2003 elections. Several examples illustrate. Ter-Petrossian was reported to have used control over newsprint sales to control the press.[20] Libel charges have been made against editors, most notably when the newspaper editor Nikol Pashinian received a one-year suspended sentence for libel in 2000.[21] Small broadcasters in particular were threatened by a law requiring that they broadcast only in Armenian, and that 65 percent of programming be original. These provisions jeopardized small broadcasters by considerably increasing their programming costs. In April 2002, the National Council on Television and Radio (whose members are appointed by the president) auctioned television frequencies, such that independent stations A1+ and Noyan Tapan were forced off the air. This left state-controlled media as the only major news source for the 2003 elections.

Within the parliament, Armenia has seen the adoption of a measure to quash dissent not seen in other cases. After an attempt by opposition parliamentarians to impeach President Kocharian in 2002, the pro-presidential majority passed a measure that would allow the removal of "unruly" deputies from the parliament. Crucially, this decision could be made by the speaker of the parliament alone. At the time the measure was adopted, this position was held by a Kocharian backer.[22] It is not clear why Kocharian's supporters found it necessary to take this measure, since their majority in parliament would guarantee the failure of the proposal to impeach the president.

The 2003 elections saw the massive use of executive branch power to secure victory for the incumbent, Kocharian. Most notably, at least 150 campaign officials of Kocharian's run-off opponent, Stepan Demirchian, were detained in the days before the election.[23] Many others were prevented from attending opposition rallies when authorities blocked the major highways into Yerevan to keep people away.[24] The OSCE reported that while the day of the election itself proceeded smoothly, there was considerable evidence both of preelection intimidation of voters and opposition supporters, and of postelection falsification of results. State resources, such as media and government facilities, were disproportionately available to Kocharian. As a result, the OSCE withheld its endorsement of the election results.[25] This represents a difference from Ukraine (prior to 2004) and Russia, where leaders were able to heavily influence outcomes without being so transparent and without incurring OSCE disapproval.

Overall, one might argue that Armenia has gone beyond electoral authoritarianism to traditional authoritarianism. The central support for such a judgment would be the extent to which Kocharian's government has resorted to outright repression and electoral fraud, rather than being limited by what can be accomplished behind a plausible veneer of liberal democracy. In 2005, Freedom House continued to label Armenia partly free, but lowered its evaluation "due to the government's violent response to peaceful civic protests in April, a broader pattern of political repression, and the authorities' increasingly unresponsive and undemocratic governance."[26] In other words, to maintain his position, Kocharian seems to be relying much less on the legitimacy provided by liberal democratic procedures and much more on straightforward repression.

Armenia is a very different country with very different politics from Ukraine and Russia, yet many of the same tactics have been used to yield some degree of democratic legitimacy without succumbing to democratic control. That these practices persisted after the overthrow of Ter-Petrossian by Kocharian warns against the temptation of associating electoral authoritarianism with particular individuals. It is a characteristic of a political system, not of particular individuals.

Kazakhstan

In Kazakhstan, President Nursultan Nazarbayev has been perhaps the archetypical pseudodemocratic authoritarian ruler in the former Soviet Union. By 2003, it became questionable whether Nazarbayev's government could even be considered an electoral authoritarian regime, as he increasingly turned to the straightforward repression that characterizes authoritarian regimes. Nonetheless, the case of Kazakhstan is interesting because, throughout the 1990s, Nazarbayev was a pioneer of some of the tactics that became typical elsewhere. Especially in his repeated use of the referendum to alter the constitution, Nazarbayev has found a technique that combines reliable control with apparent democratic legitimacy.

Nazarbayev was already the leader of Kazakhstan at the time of the Soviet collapse in 1991. Like Kravchuk in Ukraine, and several others, he waited to see the outcome of the coup in Moscow before deciding whether to oppose it. He led Kazakhstan in declaring independence, and then worked to set up the system of government it currently possesses. In terms of political context, Kazakhstan very much resembles Russia and Ukraine: the judiciary remains weak and beholden to the executive branch,[27] parties are weak, and immense constitutional authority is vested in the presidency, earning Kazakhstan a score of 15.5 on Frye's scale. The most fundamental power of legislatures, that over budgets, is severely constrained in Kazakhstan, where the parliament is not allowed to appropriate funds or to raise taxes without approval of the executive.[28]

Even so, when the parliament became too independent for Nazarbayev, he twice pressured it to disband. In the first instance, in 1993, he obtained the resignation of the parliament that had been elected under the Soviet Union in 1989. Two years later, after new elections in 1994, he used the Supreme Court, which he controlled, to rule that the 1994 parliamentary election (which Nazarbayev had organized) had been unconstitutional and that the parliament therefore had no legitimacy. When the parliament responded by trying to suspend the constitutional court, Nazarbayev unilaterally disbanded the parliament and called yet another set of new elections. He then issued a decree outlawing participation in unregistered organizations, effectively denying the right of free assembly.[29] Yet, he did all of this while solemnly asserting that he was following the requirements of democracy and the rule of law: "The law is the law, and the President is obliged to abide by the constitution . . . otherwise, how will we build a rule-of-law state?"[30]

Within this context, Nazarbayev has used many of the same techniques used by presidents in Russia and Ukraine. The selective use of law enforcement has been extremely effective, not only in controlling the media and in placing economic power directly in the hands of Nazarbayev's allies, but also more directly by eliminating challengers in elections.

The ongoing strength of clan-based political networks in Kazakhstan facilitates the construction of patronage networks and a reliable political "machine." Two relatives of Nazarbayev, his daughter Dariga Nazarbayeva and his son-in-law Rakhat Aliyev, have come to control significant parts of the media in the country as well as the security forces.[31] Furthermore, Nazarbayev has consistently strived to solidify state control of the economy. Having generated political support through privatizing state assets to loyal supporters in the 1990s, Nazarbayev then sought to rein in these increasingly powerful figures. The Agency for Strategic Planning released a plan to consolidate Kazakhstan's leading industries into several large consortia controlled by the state. Control by the state would mean, of course, control by Nazarbayev appointees. Presumably this provides an extra guarantee that those granted power by Nazarbayev will not turn on him.

However, the plan has run into some difficulties, as many of these business elites have resisted having their power curbed, and have responded by joining the opposition.[32] An attempt by Nazarbayev's son-in-law Aliyev, as head of the security service, to wrest control of key assets from leading industrialist (and energy minister) Mukhtar Ablyazov, led to a standoff, in which Aliyev was transferred to another position and Nazarbayev publicly criticized "new Kazakhs," such as Ablyazov. Simultaneously, a tender for the state-held shares in Kazakhstan's largest bank was suspiciously won by a previously unknown group rumored to be headed by Aliyev. Ablyazov and others responded by going into moderate opposition, and Ablyazov was subsequently arrested in March 2002 and sentenced to six years in prison.[33] Thus Nazarbayev has a variety of ways to control various assets, and the interlinking of political and economic power gives a fundamental advantage to the chief executive.

Like his colleagues in other post-Soviet states, Nazarbayev has sought to reduce the scope of independent media. He has done this both through formal laws that intimidate the media and through administrative harassment. In March 2001, media laws were amended to make it much easier to charge media outlets with libel. In particular, Kazakh media outlets were made responsible for the content of material either retransmitted or reprinted from international sources. Vague laws against insulting the dignity of the president—a criminal offense for which journalists have served time in prison—make it easy to prosecute those who criticize Nazarbayev or question the legality of some of his actions. Massive fines for libel charges have bankrupted some outlets.[34] The result is considerable self-censorship by journalists and editors leery of running into criminal or libel charges. As a result, Western investigations into allegations that substantial bribes were paid to Nazarbayev by representatives of Western oil firms were largely ignored in the Kazakh press.[35] In some instances, as in other countries, state-owned printing houses refused to print issues of newspapers that were deemed to be problematic.

In addition, the state controls nearly all broadcast facilities, allowing the government to shut down any radio or television station whose programming it does not like. While there are independent radio and television stations in Kazakhstan, the only ones that broadcast nationwide are those controlled by the state. The result of all this is that news coverage is highly skewed in Nazarbayev's favor.

One tactic not seen in Russia or Ukraine but used by Nazarbayev to control elections is to make it impossible for certain candidates to run. In October 1998, shortly after calling early elections, Nazarbayev's government passed a law prohibiting anyone from running for president who had a criminal conviction in the past year. Shortly thereafter, Nazarbayev's strongest opponent, former prime minister Akezhan Kazhegeldin, was charged with and convicted of participating in an illegal organization, and thus barred from running.[36] Police harassment has also been used to hamper the campaigns of opposition politicians. In October 1998, Kazhegeldin was detained by police just as he was to attend a press conference announcing his candidacy for the presidency.

It is also worth noting that the election law in Kazakhstan derives not from parliamentary legislation, but from a presidential decree. Moreover, civil servants supporting opposition politicians have been fired from their jobs.[37] This is an especially powerful lever in an impoverished country with high unemployment. Nominating petitions, mandating 170,000 signatures to run for president, required signers to include extensive personal data, including passport numbers. This contributed to the impression that the authorities would know exactly who signed petitions for Nazarbayev and who supported others. There were widespread reports of state organizations that required all workers to sign petitions for Nazarbayev. One doctor reported being admonished by her director: "I'm warning you, this is voluntary!"[38]

This control of elections has been central to Nazarbayev's strategy of rule, because he has, as is the paradoxical norm in electoral authoritarianism, used elections to avoid political competition. In May 1995, Nazarbayev proposed canceling the forthcoming 1996 presidential election and extending his term until 2000. The proposal was not approved by parliament (which had been disbanded the month before) but instead subjected to a referendum, which due to all the tactics mentioned above, would have an easily controlled outcome. Even that, however, seems not to have been satisfactory to Nazarbayev. The official results indicated that 91 percent of the voters turned out and that 95 percent approved extending Nazarbayev's term. Unofficial counts indicated that turnout was closer to 20 percent or 30 percent.[39] In the 2004 parliamentary elections, only one opposition delegate was elected, and he refused to take his position. Partly as a result of this, Freedom House now categorizes Kazakhstan as "not free."[40]

Kyrgyzstan

Kyrgyzstan is similar to Ukraine in that it was regarded as one of the most promising young democracies in the region in the mid-1990s. While it has always had economic difficulties, its government, led by a former physics professor, Askar Akayev, rather than by a career Communist Party functionary, was considered more progressive, more liberal, and more democratic than those of its neighbors in Central Asia. By 2000, however, Kyrgyzstan and Akayev had moved significantly toward the norm in Central Asia, with the tactics of Kyrgyzstan's neighbors being adopted by Akayev to retain and consolidate his power. By 2003, politics in Kyrgyzstan was not substantially different from that in Kazakhstan or Russia. In 2005, Kyrgyzstan followed Ukraine's path, when the Tulip Revolution ejected Akayev from power.

There were early signs of the potential for electoral authoritarianism in Kyrgyzstan: in September and October 1994, Akayev followed the model established by Yeltsin in Russia a year earlier, dissolving the parliament on the grounds that it "has ceased to function," and then putting a new constitution to a referendum. This new constitution and subsequent versions have vested immense legal power in the presidency (15.5 on Frye's scale), including control over all cabinet appointments except the prime minister, which requires parliamentary approval, extensive decree powers, and considerable power over the budget.[41]

Akayev also had control over the judiciary, which is a separate branch of government formally but in fact is subject to the executive. Akayev had appointment powers, and more important, dismissal powers, over all judges. The result was some blatantly political rulings: One of Akayev's main challengers, Feliks Kulov, was sentenced to seven years in prison and had his property confiscated by the same court that had previously dismissed the charges against him.[42] The International Helsinki Federation reports that "it was claimed that nearly all judges were appointed on the basis of bribes and devotion to the present regime . . . no trial of a political nature ended with a lawful ruling, and courts ignored constitutional and international provisions."[43]

By 2003, Akayev had for the fourth time resorted to one of the most uniformly used tactics of electoral authoritarianism: the revision of the constitution through an executive-led referendum. On February 2, 2003, the Kyrgyz people voted on a slate of constitutional changes that had been designed by a group chosen by Akayev. The referendum had several provisions. Among the most prominent was a change from a bicameral to a unicameral parliament. Conveniently for Akayev, this required new elections. A shift from a proportional election law to a single-member district (SMD) law undermined the consolidation of parties (because, as in Ukraine, the SMD system opened up the parliament to independents).[44] As in Ukraine, the president complained about a weak parliament, but was actually taking every conceivable step to ensure that the parliament remained weak.

The referendum also included a "motion of confidence" question on Akayev's continued rule. There is no constitutional provision for such a public vote of confidence in the president, but Akayev used the favorable results to try to put to rest a movement among opposition parties to pressure him to resign. In both the constitutional revision and the confidence vote, Akayev circumvented the parliament and evaded the problem of checks and balances by going directly to the people. With the ability to draft the questions himself, and considerable means to influence voting, a triumph for Akayev was assured.

Previous constitutional referenda were held in 1994 (to allow for amending the constitution through referendum and to create a bicameral parliament), in 1996 (to enhance presidential powers, especially over cabinet appointments), and in 1998 (in five areas, the most significant of which were removal of parliamentary immunity from prosecution, limitation of parliamentary power over the budget, and a change in the number of members of parliament).[45] It is significant that the composition of the parliament was changed three times in a decade. Most obviously, the parliament's powers were constrained. But simply by changing its composition frequently, the consolidation of that institution can be inhibited. Moreover, changes to the number of deputies or in the number of chambers can require new elections to be held, thus ridding the executive of a troublesome parliament. This might explain why the bicameral parliament was adopted in 1994 only to be dropped nine years later.

Akayev sought to control the media through a number of measures. In

1998, a new set of media laws was issued stating that the Ministry of Justice, the National Agency for Communications (NAC), and the presidential administration must approve all broadcast licenses. The laws also expanded the power of the NAC to close media outlets or ban specific programs. Most of these provisions are unconstitutional, since the constitution states that only the courts can close a media outlet, but they have been enforced nonetheless. This example points to the weakness of the judiciary in Kyrgyzstan. Uchkun, the state-run publishing house, owns the only newspaper-printing facilities in Kyrgyzstan. In the run-up to the 2000 presidential elections, Uchkun refused to print three newspapers, *Res Publica*, *Asaba*, and *Delo No.* The same three newspapers were subjected to numerous other instances of selective law enforcement. *Res Publica* was fined for insulting the "honor and dignity" of the state television network, was refused distribution through the state-controlled distribution network, and had issues confiscated from kiosks by authorities. *Asaba* attracted particular attention after its owner declared his candidacy for the presidency. It was fined $105,000, a substantial sum in Kyrgyzstan, for insulting a member of parliament. *Delo No.* had its offices raided by Interior Ministry forces, and the editor and a journalist were detained by the ministry and subjected to lengthy interrogations.[46] Visits by tax and fire inspectors to media offices are not uncommon, in some cases outlets are ordered to close.[47] In the case of *Vecherny Bishkek*, a widely read newspaper in the capital, the government simply bought the paper.

On the broadcast side, there are independent stations in Kyrgyzstan, but they are relegated to the UHF channels while all the more widely accessible VHF channels are allocated to state television.[48] In sum, there was considerable direct control, indirect interference, and intimidation of the Kyrgyz media, and it is not clear that the Tulip Revolution has substantially changed matters.[49] As in Ukraine, however, media are controlled through mostly legal channels, using existing laws and the convenient state monopoly on newspaper printing and distribution facilities. As a result, the OSCE noted in its report on the 2000 elections that state-owned media "failed to comply with its legal obligation to provide balanced and objective reporting" and that the pressure on media caused "self-censorship and a notable decrease in the number of media outlets able or willing to offer an editorial line independent of or critical of the authorities.[50] Together, all of these measures comprise what Jerzy Wieclaw of the OSCE mission in Kyrgyzstan characterized as "structural" censorship.[51]

Patronage has been a powerful tool for Akayev in controlling elections. This was seen clearly in the 2003 constitutional referendum and vote of confidence: credible reports indicated that students at Kyrgyz State University were told that they would be expelled if they did not support Akayev.[52] In the

2000 presidential elections, students at universities in Bishkek, Naryn, and Osh were told to vote for Akayev or risk failing their exams. Students in Bishkek had their passports seized to further ensure their compliance. University students in Jalal Abad had to show their ballots to university officials before placing them in ballot boxes. The students were better off than their professors, who were expected to donate a portion of their salary to Akayev's campaign and to take a leave of absence to campaign for him. Similarly, there was pressure on state employees to sign nominating petitions for Akayev, to campaign for him, and finally to vote for him. At least one village head was dismissed from his job as a result of campaigning for an opposition candidate.[53]

Elections have also been controlled through legislation that made it difficult for major opposition parties to compete. Shortly before the 2000 parliamentary elections, a new law was passed disallowing participation by parties registered for less than one year, which effectively eliminated the Ar-Namys party. The El Bei-Bechara party was banned from the election by the Justice Ministry on the grounds that the party did not state specifically on its registration forms that it intended to run candidates in elections. Thus, the second and third largest parties in the country were eliminated, in ostensibly legal fashion.[54] Authorities have also resorted to more traditional fraud: in the 2000 presidential election, a ballot box was found to have 700 votes for Akayev in it before the voting began.[55]

A shift in election procedures from a proportional representation system to a plurality single-member district system will also enhance the prospects for presidential control. As was the case in Ukraine, SMD rules, in a society with a weak party structure, tend to inhibit party consolidation. Moreover, district level votes are in some ways more amenable to the application of "administrative resources." Thus, just as Kuchma in Ukraine found going to a fully proportional system unpalatable, Akayev successfully rolled back that system in Kyrgyzstan.

However, as in Ukraine, the system came crashing down. In early 2005, parliamentary elections were held, and were widely perceived to be fraudulent.[56] These elections were required as a result of the constitutional changes pushed through by Akayev in 2003. He expected that he would be able to use the new elections to gain a pliable parliament. This indeed occurred, but the obvious unfairness of the elections spurred the protests that forced Akayev from power.

As the newly elected parliament met, protests broke out first in the regions and then in Bishkek itself. The police rapidly lost control of the situation, and President Akayev was forced to flee the country. The details of the Tulip Revolution differ considerably from those of Ukraine's Orange Revolution. The opposition in Kyrgyzstan was less well-organized, and the protests were more spontaneous. Instead of a single organization demanding Akayev's resignation, there were mobs in the streets of Bishkek. Rather than order and nonviolence, there were chaos, looting, and a few deaths. Nonetheless, the broad causes were similar. General frustration with corruption and authoritarianism, crystallized by a stolen election, and permitted by passive security forces, led to the overthrow of a government that seemed to have matters well in hand.

As in Ukraine, the euphoria of the revolution has rapidly given way to fears that the new rulers are little better than the old ones. Only a year after the Tulip Revolution, a new opposition movement was preparing street protests to force from power the president, Kurmanbek Bakiyev, who had been elected following the Tulip Revolution. Among the charges leveled at Bakiyev and his circle were that they supported the election of a noted organized crime figure to parliament and that they may have been implicated in an assassination attempt on a leading human rights advocate and government critic.[57]

Electoral Authoritarianism Beyond the Former Soviet Union

The tactics that are employed in Ukraine, Russia, Armenia, Kazakhstan, and Kyrgyzstan are not unique to the former Soviet Union. A large number of countries in Africa, Asia, and Latin America share at least some of the characteristics of electoral authoritarianism. In this section, we summarize the elements of electoral authoritarianism in Malaysia and Venezuela, to illustrate how electoral authoritarianism spans the globe. The discussion of each case is too brief to establish conclusively the degree of similarity with Ukraine and the other post-Soviet cases, but the point is to show that the same kinds of tactics and dynamic exist beyond the former Soviet Union.

Malaysia

In Malaysia, electoral authoritarianism developed directly out of colonial rule, just as in Ukraine, it developed out of Soviet rule. The United Malays National Organization (UMNO) has been the leading party in a coalition that has won every general election since 1957.[58] Mahathir Mohamad ruled as prime minister from 1991 until 2003, employing many of the same tactics seen in the former Soviet Union. His main political challenger, and one-time heir apparent, Anwar Ibrahim, was arrested on dubious corruption and sodomy charges in 1998, and subsequently imprisoned. Security forces have arrested opposition party activists in recent years. "The government gives itself an overwhelming advantage in elections through its selective allocation of state funds to supporters, use of security to restrict freedoms of expression and assembly, and partisan use of broadcast media."[59]

As in Ukraine before 2004, opposition groups openly criticize government policies and compete in elections, but they have little genuine chance of winning those elections. Moreover, the judiciary appears to have come increasingly under executive branch control, as demonstrated by the trial of Anwar Ibrahim. According to the U.S. State Department, "government action, constitutional amendments, legislation restricting judicial review, and other factors steadily have eroded judicial independence and strengthened executive over the judiciary."[60] As in the post-Soviet cases, Malaysia has a Printing Presses and Publications Act, which bans "malicious" news and has been used against critics of the government. Both state-run television and the main private stations generally support the government. All of the regional governments have their own television stations, except the one controlled by an opposition party, which has been unable to receive a license.[61] All print media must get a new license every year, making it easy for the government to close those that criticize it. The result is not that a lot publications are closed, but that they practice self-censorship.[62]

In contrast to the post-Soviet cases, executive power in Malaysia is vested in the prime minister rather than in the presidency, which is more ceremonial. This is an important distinction, for it indicates that the link between presidential forms of government and electoral authoritarianism is not a necessary one. Another important difference is that in Malaysia the "party of power" really is a political party, with a thoroughly developed party apparatus and a long history. In that sense, it is more like the party based "machines" in U.S. cities than the post-Soviet cases, which tend to take the executive branch of government as their organizational basis.

Since Mahathir's retirement in 2003, there has been considerable hope that Malaysia would embark on political liberalization. There have been some promising signs, such as the High Court's overturning of Anwar Ibrahim's sodomy conviction and the suspension in 2004 of several UMNO members for vote buying.[63] It is notable, however, that these changes were all approved by the UMNO and the prime minister. Therefore, it is still not clear that genuine challenge to the government is possible.

Venezuela

In Venezuela, President Hugo Chavez has developed a form of rule that is heavily reliant on the use of mass public opinion, as expressed through referenda, to circumvent horizontal checks on his power. This willingness to take conflict to the voters is in some respects "hyperdemocratic," but it does not lead to liberal democratic rule. Instead, it has helped consolidate Chavez's power. Like Kuchma in Ukraine, Chavez came to power (in 1998) as a popularly elected challenger promising to stem an economic collapse. Unlike the cases considered until now, Venezuela was not a state recently freed from colonial or communist rule, having been independent since 1821. It does, however, share with the other cases a meager history of liberal democracy, having endured a series of coups, the most recent of which nearly brought Chavez to power in 1992.

After coming to power through an election in 1998, Chavez quickly embarked on a program to consolidate his control of both the economy and politics. In Venezuela, the world's third largest exporter of crude oil, much was at stake. He was able to pass laws that removed much of the power of the legislature and put the judiciary under executive control. For example, a November 2000 "fast track" measure granted him extensive decree powers.[64] He accomplished this in large part through an alliance with the military, which received extensive patronage from Chavez in return for its support. He used the military to take control of the state oil company, appointing two former generals to head the company. He also appointed military allies to be presidential chief of staff, head of the secret police, and head of the tax service. Michael Coppedge therefore labels Venezuela a "delegative democracy." While it appears that a narrow majority of citizens supports Chavez's policies, he has succeeded in removing any institutional checks on his power.[65]

As we have seen in other examples, Chavez quickly appointed a commission to write a new constitution to strengthen his legal powers. This new document, which was passed via a referendum, gave Chavez the right to dissolve the legislature and would allow him to remain in power until 2013, a term in office not contemplated even in Central Asia. With a majority in parliament, Chavez was able to pass a law increasing the number of Supreme Court justices from twenty to thirty-two. Since he would appoint the additional justices, this guaranteed his control of the court.[66] At several levels, including local government, this heavy-handedness led to increasing victories for opposition forces. Chavez responded by using the parliament, which he controlled, to give the president even more power. Despite his actions, elections in 2000 were regarded as free and fair by international observers.

In 2004, Chavez's opponents were able to collect enough signatures to force a recall referendum, which was defeated. The campaign was highly contentious, and the vote was marred by credible allegations of vote-rigging.[67] Because 2.8 million signatures had to be collected to force the referendum, *la lista* is now a powerful force in Venezuelan life, with those who signed the petitions unable to get government jobs or qualify for Chavez's welfare programs.[68]

To some of Chavez's defenders, he is ultrademocratic. He is viewed as someone who attacks entrenched privilege and pursues the populist goals of the neediest (e.g., through creating "missions" in Venezuela's poorest areas, where jobs and subsidized foodstuffs are available to those who have always lived in poverty).[69] Chavez demonstrates one of the most important qualities of successful electoral authoritarianism: the ability to convince voters (and ideally international observers as well) that the limitations placed on genuine liberal democracy are worth the goals being achieved and are justifiable in light of the alternatives (the opposition).

Comparing and Contrasting the Cases: Toward a General Understanding of Electoral Authoritarianism

The cases described above demonstrate a significant overlap in the means that leaders use to stifle genuine political competition in formally democratic societies. We are prompted to ask, therefore, what these systems have in common, and what distinguishes them. It is equally important, but more difficult, to seek to identify common causes of electoral authoritarianism in these countries.

If we look at all the cases together, post-Soviet and non–post-Soviet, what they share is a chief executive who has become extremely powerful, largely by using the resources of the executive branch both to build support and to hamstring the opposition. The cases also share judicial branches that are largely under the influence, if not the direct control, of the executive. The tactics that leaders employ to maintain power are based on these two basic sources of power: control over the executive branch and the judiciary. They also share many of the same tactics: the permitting of illegal acts by supporters, arbitrary prosecution of the opposition, regulatory obstruction of independent media, and the use of patronage to win elections.

Different leaders, however, have combined these methods in slightly different ways suited to the unique conditions of each country. Armenia, for example, has a freer press than most of the other cases discussed, but more blatant election fraud. Some have also used tactics that others have not (yet) tried: Akayev in Kyrgyzstan used party registration laws to prevent opposition parties from running in an election; Kocharian in Armenia, with solid control over a parliamentary majority, instituted a rule allowing the majority in parliament to remove "unruly" opposition deputies; Chavez in Venezuela has a lucrative state oil monopoly to buy the loyalty of the country's underprivileged; Mahathir in Malaysia had a well-organized party machine.

What distinguishes these states, in differing degrees, from more traditional authoritarian regimes, is that despite their violation of many democratic norms, they have not completely abandoned the democratic process. Indeed, for some, such as Chavez, elections are crucial to their claims to power. For each of the leaders in question, a plausible claim to being democratically elected is an important part of their ability to rule. Elections are not completely falsified in these states because blatant falsification would destroy the leader's democratic legitimacy. That this is important was demonstrated to any doubters by the speed with which Viktor Yanukovych's position crumbled when it became clear that he could claim victory only through massive fraud. Similarly, in Yugoslavia (2000), Georgia (2003), and Kyrgyzstan (2005), fraudulent elections were a key catalyst in protests that removed democratic authoritarian leaders.[70] More broadly, it is important to note that the popularity of leaders remains relevant in these systems. Electoral authoritarianism is fairly stable in places such as Russia where the leadership is popular. When such popularity crumbles, however, these leaders become vulnerable. They may then have to choose between shifting to full authoritarianism and risking ejection from power.

In thinking about the fundamental underpinnings of electoral authoritarianism and the potential for reform, important differences emerge. One major difference is the role of political parties. Our examination of Ukraine found that the weakness of political parties facilitates presidential domination. In Malaysia, however, the UMNO played a central role in maintaining Mahathir in power. The role of parties there is reminiscent of parties in the classic machine politics model in American cities, where one dominant party was the organizational mechanism for distributing patronage and collecting votes. In Russia and Armenia, a different model holds: parties remain fairly weak, but strong presidents have used coalitions of relatively weak parties to control parliament.

The differences in the role of parties in these cases might not reflect an underlying difference, but different levels of consolidation of power by the rulers. In Malaysia, where the UMNO has ruled for over four decades, the rulers have institutionalized their patronage network through the party. In several of the post-Soviet cases, including Russia, Ukraine, and Armenia, we have seen an attempt to accomplish the same thing, with different degrees of success. It is telling that Yeltsin tried twice, and failed, to organize a "presidential" party or "party of power" to contest parliamentary elections and then control parliament. Putin has succeeded where Yeltsin failed, at least in controlling parliament, though it is not clear that his party, Unified Russia, also provides a basis for institutionalizing political influence and vote collecting. Similarly, Kuchma in Ukraine has tried the same thing, first with the National Democratic Party in 1998 and then with United Ukraine in 2002. Both failed to dominate elections, but Kuchma had some success in using the latter to control parliament following the elections.

In both Russia and Ukraine, the exercise of political power seems more dependent upon ad hoc and shifting networks of patronage than on any institutionalized organization. In Central Asia, the same challenge occurs, but the role played by parties, successfully in Malaysia and less so in Ukraine and Russia, appears to be played by traditional clan networks (though these clan networks can also challenge the leadership).[71] In Venezuela under Chavez, that role has been played largely by the military. We can conclude, then, that all of these leaders face the challenge of institutionalizing their networks of influence, but that they pursue different routes, based on the strongest available networks. In some countries this may be a clan structure, in others a party, and in still others the executive apparatus or the military.

Another distinction worth noting is that in Malaysia, unlike the other cases discussed here, the prime minister, not the president, dominates the political system. This difference, however, masks an underlying similarity: the chief executive has extensive constitutional power vis-à-vis the legislature and extensive de facto power through the executive branch. It is perhaps more a matter of labeling than of substance that Malaysia has a parliamentary system with a ceremonial president and vests in the prime minister powers that in other states are vested in a president. The question is an important one, because in the preceding chapters it has been argued that part of Ukraine's problem lies in its use of a presidential rather than a parliamentary form of government. The example of Malaysia does not invalidate this claim, but rather points to a broader and fundamental caution: that changing Ukraine's institutional format without somehow achieving a functioning parliament that is a counterweight to the executive will achieve little. As Ukraine shifts power from president to prime minister, this will be a central concern.

A final distinction worth noting is that, to differing degrees, these states can be considered autocracies. It might be argued that Armenia and Kazakhstan, among the cases examined here, have replaced electoral legitimacy with repression as a means of maintaining the regime in power. Venezuela is harder to classify, after the unrest of early 2003, because it is clear both that repression was used and that Chavez retains a great deal of popular legitimacy, and he has strived to maintain a degree of legality in his rule. Similarly, in Armenia, the extensive outright fraud in the 2003 presidential elections, which was recognized as such internationally, calls into question whether we should just call this an autocracy. In Russia and Malaysia, to label the regime an autocracy without qualification might distort as much as to label it democratic without qualification.

The slide of several of these countries toward all-out authoritarianism raises the question of whether electoral authoritarianism is stable, or whether it is indeed a transition point between authoritarianism and liberal democracy. More precisely, we should say that electoral authoritarianism may be a transition point on the path back to full authoritarianism from an unsustainable attempt at full liberalization. In the post-Soviet cases, it may be too early to say. Yeltsin's ability to pass his rule intact, and even strengthened, to Putin, indicates a certain stability. However, the fact that Freedom House classified Russia as "not free" in late 2004 demonstrates the widely shared opinion that it has evolved into full authoritarianism.[72] Moreover, while few envision a "colored revolution" in Russia, it remained unclear in 2006 how Putin plans to pass on or extend his rule when his second term expires in 2008.

The inability of Kuchma to pass on his rule intact raises the question whether this model can be transferred or is essentially a personal accrual of power unstable beyond any individual. The same question arises in Central Asia. In Azerbaijan, a case not studied here, President Haidar Aliyev successfully paved the way for his son to replace him. In Mauritania and Venezuela, it appears that a change of ruler will mean a change of regime, for better or worse. Only in Malaysia does it appear that electoral authoritarianism is institutionalized.

The finding that electoral authoritarianism is vulnerable is not, by itself, good news. In the cases we have examined here, it appears that either full-blown authoritarianism or internal chaos are more likely successors to electoral authoritarianism than is liberal democracy. Revolutions in Yugoslavia, Georgia, Ukraine, and Kyrgyzstan are evidence of the instability of electoral authoritarianism. But none of these cases is clearly embarked on a path to liberal democracy. In each, political competition and rule of law remain weak, and the use of "administrative resources" by the executive branch remains a key factor in politics. The most important progress has been in freedom of the press.

A Broader Perspective

In some respects, the cross-national occurrence of "electoral authoritarianism" should not be surprising, for the same kinds of tactics have been used or attempted even in much more developed liberal democracies. In the United States, for example, the practice of giving high-level government positions, such as ambassadorships to choice countries, in return for campaign support is widely acknowledged. Similarly, incumbent leaders everywhere use the visibility provided by their positions to obtain a disproportionate share of media coverage.

In more subtle ways, such as the redistricting process that governs elections to the U.S. House of Representatives, incumbents seek, often successfully, to use their current power to change the rules to disadvantage future challengers. In 2003, one of the most prominent cases arose in the state of Texas, where the Republican Party, in control of the White House and the

Texas legislature, but not the Texas delegation to the House of Representatives, believed that it could win as many as six seats from the Democratic Party before the polls ever opened, simply by redrawing districts in such a way as to create more majority Republican districts. Democrats cried foul, despite the fact that the then-existing distribution of seats was due to their own previous redistricting plans.[73]

The same kinds of problems arise in Europe as well. The most extreme contemporary case is Italy under Silvio Berlusconi. Berlusconi exemplifies, in a more limited way, many of the practices we have seen in the former Soviet Union: his rise to power was based first on his status as Italy's wealthiest person, which was built on his control of much of the country's media. After becoming prime minister, he furthered his control of media through his control of state television. Despite a series of very credible corruption allegations, he has avoided prosecution through his control over the parliament, which has continuously changed Italy's criminal procedures in ways designed to obstruct his prosecution. In Germany, the Christian Democratic Union/Christian Social Union Party under Helmut Kohl was found to be trading political influence for illegal campaign contributions, and in France, Jacques Chirac used money gained from kickbacks on city contracts to support his election campaigns. In 2004–5, Canada also experienced major corruption in the ruling Liberal Party, when money from state contracts was funneled into the party's campaign fund in Quebec.

Therefore, we should not necessarily conclude that the politicians themselves are different—that Western politicians are inherently honest and that others are not. The difference seems to be in how far politicians can go in different countries before something or somebody pushes back. That may be a powerful opposition party (or coalition) holding hearings in parliament or using corruption as a potent campaign tool; or it may be a media sufficiently independent to resist encroachments, rather than succumbing to them; or it may be an independent judiciary unwilling to countenance selective law enforcement or illegal behavior; or it might be state employees and students with sufficient legal protection to vote for whomever they choose without fear of losing their positions.

The primary difference between the liberal democracies and the electoral authoritarian regimes is that in the former, power tends to equilibrate. In liberal democracies, politicians who become increasingly powerful tend to engender increasing opposition. In electoral authoritarian systems, in contrast, political and economic power tend to centralize, such that those who initially gain an advantage can then use that leverage to create further advantage. This self-reinforcing cycle is limited only by the competence and lifespan of the ruler. The possibility of reforming these systems will be addressed in the concluding chapter.

11

Beyond the Orange Revolution

An Agenda for Further Reform

The pattern of politics that developed in post-Soviet Ukraine has been labeled "competitive authoritarianism,"[1] "delegative democracy,"[2] "machine politics,"[3] and "electoral authoritarianism"[4] (the term used in this book) by various authors. While the labels differ, the gist of the arguments is the same. The Kuchma administration in Ukraine was able to use methods that were at least nominally democratic to achieve ends similar to those of authoritarian rule. In other words, he and his supporters, the so-called party of power, were able to erode the link between elections and genuine political competition. By 2004, it was not clear whether a challenge to his appointed successor could possibly succeed.

The 2004 election, and the subsequent Orange Revolution, ended the rule of Kuchma's group in Ukraine. Following an obviously fraudulent runoff election, street protests combined with legal challenges led to the rerunning of the second round of the election, and to the victory of opposition leader Viktor Yushchenko.[5] With Kuchma and Yanukovych defeated, the path to liberal democracy again opened in Ukraine. By 2006, however, Yanukovych was triumphant again, and it was clear that the path to democracy would be rocky.

This book has developed an empirical and theoretical explanation of those developments. Ukraine's political development since 1991 has been driven by four interrelated factors: the institutional legacy of the Soviet Union, divisions in Ukrainian society, institutional design, and above all, the practice of "power politics." The central argument has been that power politics has trumped institutional design throughout the post-Soviet era.

How do these four factors stand after the Orange Revolution? The Soviet legacy has receded a bit further into the past, but it remains powerful, especially in the politicization of the bureaucracies and the judicial system. Similarly, Ukraine's regional divisions remain profound.[6] It is even possible that the Orange Revolution led to further polarization as Yushchenko and Yanokovych were themselves polarizing figures, and were identified so clearly with different regions. Therefore, the challenges for institutional design that were laid out in Chapter Five remain serious.

Changes to Ukraine's institutions have, however, addressed some of these shortcomings. The excessive power of the presidency has been substantially curtailed. The increased power of the prime minister and parliament over the government should provide for more effective checks on abuse of power. Equally important, the shift to a full proportional representation system for parliamentary elections will likely make that institution more effective.

Finally, the gross imbalance in de facto political power has been partly redressed. This was a result not only of constitutional changes but also of the end of the Kuchma administration's grip on the economy, the news media, and the bureaucracies. The reassertion of pluralism in Ukraine's media and of Ukrainian civil society means that political power is diffused much more widely today than it was under Kuchma.

In this conclusion, we assess the changes that occurred in 2004, and point out the challenges that remain. The previous chapters have identified a series of institutional weaknesses; changes adopted in 2004 (most of which went into effect in early 2006) have addressed many of the most glaring, such as the excessive power of the presidency. However, other weaknesses remain. If further changes are not made, there is a danger that some future leader—either a president or prime minister—will be able to consolidate power as thoroughly as Kuchma has. The opposite problem also remains a danger—that the new division of powers at the top of Ukraine's government will lead to stalemate and a new crisis. This chapter therefore considers an array of reforms that should be considered if a return to Kuchma's way of ruling is to be prevented in the future. The point is not to diminish what was accomplished in 2004, but rather to indicate that it should be viewed as the beginning of a process, not the end.

Power Politics Versus Institutional Design in the Post-Kuchma Era

While the Orange Revolution was inspiring and miraculous to some, Viktor Yushchenko quickly found that overthrowing the falsified election was the easy part, as compared with governing the country. He and his associates have been tempted to use the levers of power controlled in the executive branch to undermine their adversaries and to pursue personal as well as political goals. Both Tymoshenko and Petro Poroshenko were accused of doing just this. When Viktor Yanukovych regained the position of prime minister in 2006, there was widespread fear that he would abuse his control of the government as Kuchma had.

While it would appear that the shift from a presidential to a presidential-parliamentary system should diminish the potential for executive malfeasance, we know from comparative experience that machine politics are possible even in parliamentary systems (e.g., Malaysia). To the extent that Yushchenko and the parliament clash over control of the government, he will be tempted to resort to any means he can to prevail. To the extent that the parliament or the prime minister enacts measures to which Yushchenko objects, we can imagine him using the powers at his disposal to frustrate them. That he believes firmly in strong presidential power is demonstrated by his steadfast opposition to constitutional change that would diminish the president's authority.

Two important changes, however, will make it harder for anyone to accumulate the power that Kuchma had. For this reason, the potential for Yanukovych, as prime minister, to re-create Kuchma's machine is considerably diminished. The first is the redistribution of legal power away from the president. Because control over the executive branch will be divided between the president and prime minister, neither will have the same ability that Kuchma did to use government resources for electoral purposes. This does not mean that they will not try, but unless they cooperate closely, they will be likely to check one another. The good news is that such a system will be less prone to authoritarianism. The bad news is that it will be prone to stalemate.

Media freedom is a second important development that will impede machine politics in the future. The Orange Revolution led to the freeing of the Ukrainian media, and it will be very difficult for a future leader to force the media back under state control. This does not mean that Ukrainian media outlets are independent or public-minded. Most are controlled by oligarchs or large firms with their own political agendas to promote. However, in contrast to the Kuchma era, a wide variety of views is now being expressed. Moreover, outlets that criticize the government have not been harassed. Now that the media are free, it will be difficult to corral them again. Not only will they fiercely resist such efforts, but the elites that control them will also push back. As a result, the leader who tries to control the media will likely pay a high political price. Yushchenko discovered this when he harshly criticized reporters who publicized his son's extravagant spending habits.[7]

Media in Ukraine can now play the watchdog role to which they are "assigned" in democratic theory. Even if they are politically biased, media can help limit government misbehavior by investigating and publicizing it. This is a vital check on the government, especially when it is not yet clear that official law enforcement bodies are sufficiently independent to investigate wrongdoing by government officials.

Institutional Change: Assessing the 2004 Reforms

The institutional changes introduced in 2004 map neatly onto the analysis developed in this book. Chapter Six demonstrated that the distribution of power between the parliament and the president does not allow the parliament to effectively challenge the president's power. The December 2004 constitutional changes transferred substantial power to the parliament. Chapter Seven (and Chapter Five) demonstrated that Ukraine's mixed parliamentary electoral law contributed to the fragmentation of the parliament and to its inability to play an effective role. A March 2004 law changed the electoral law, so that the 2006 parliamentary elections were conducted on a fully proportional basis. Chapter Eight showed that parliamentary rules undermine party discipline and encourage party fragmentation. A December 2004 law introduced the "imperative mandate," which is designed to strengthen party discipline and make party fragmentation much less likely. These changes should mitigate the three most significant weaknesses in Ukraine's pre–Orange Revolution institutional design.

Constitutional Change: Limits on Presidential Power

The revisions make Ukraine a presidential-parliamentary system, in which the prime minister and cabinet of ministers are appointed by and answerable to *both* the president and the parliament. In the previous system, the prime minister was appointed by the president and only had to be confirmed by parliament. The prime minister then had to get the president's approval for ministerial appointments, and ministers could be dismissed by the president. In essence then, effective power over the prime minister and the cabinet was held by the president.

In the heat of the moment, it went largely unnoticed that the adopted constitutional changes are fairly similar to what Kuchma had put forward in May 2004. In other words, the result of the election—Yushchenko's winning of a weakened presidency—is one that Kuchma found acceptable all along. In that sense, he came out a winner.[8]

The timing of the term of office for the prime minister and cabinet has been changed to coincide with parliamentary rather than presidential elections. When a new parliament is elected, it will immediately be able to influence the composition of the cabinet.

While the president formally nominates the prime minister, new provisions concerning the parliamentary majority give the parliament the key voice in choosing the prime minister. The new laws stipulate that the parliament will establish a majority within thirty days of a new sitting, and that the president will consult with that majority in naming a new prime minister. In practical terms, the parliamentary majority names the prime minister because the parliament controls the chances of confirmation. The ambiguities in this arrangement were quickly tested in the summer of 2006, when Yushchenko asserted that he was not legally compelled to nominate the candidate put forward by the majority coalition in parliament. Politically, however, he felt compelled to nominate Yanukovych, fearing the wrath of the voters if he called new elections.

Control over the cabinet of ministers is now divided between the president and the prime minister. The prime minister appoints all of the ministers except two reserved for the president, but those reservations may prove to be very important. The president appoints the ministers of defense and foreign affairs. Moreover, the president appoints the heads of the Security Service of Ukraine, the National Security and Defense Council, and the National Bank of Ukraine, as well as the prosecutor general. Thus, control over key executive positions (and agencies) is divided between the president and prime minister.[9] In practice, the system worked a bit differently when first put into practice in 2006. Rather than having the prime minister and president name "their" ministers separately, Yushchenko and Yanukovych together agreed on the entire slate as part of a broader political deal.

It seems safe to predict that these new rules will undermine the constitutional basis for hyperpresidential rule as it existed under Kuchma. Dividing control over ministries and government agencies will make it much more difficult for either the president or the prime minister to use the bureaucracies to control other actors through selective law enforcement. The ability of the parliament to fire ministers individually will also strengthen parliament's oversight capacity. Parliament therefore should become a more effective check on both president and prime minister.

Potential Problems with the New Constitution

There are considerable dangers in this new system. While the new system will make less likely a return to the 1995–2004 era, it will make *more* likely a return to the 1991–95 era, when the division of executive power among president, prime minister, and parliament led to constant infighting and stalemate (see Chapter Four).[10] To summarize, the prime minister in that era was nominally in control of the cabinet of ministers, but the parliament and president also both had influence over the cabinet. The parliament and president competed for control of the prime minister, while the prime minister struggled for independence from both. The resulting immobility convinced many Ukrainians that stronger presidential power was needed. Kuchma used this sentiment to build the case for the hyperpresidential 1996 constitution.

The problem with the new constitutional arrangement is that rather than establishing clearly separate powers that can "check and balance" one another, it creates overlapping powers. This arrangement will be prone to conflict about the selection of ministers and about the direction of executive branch policy in Ukraine. At this early stage, it is impossible to say exactly how these changes will work in practice. Much will depend on the specific constellation of power. If there is a solid parliamentary majority that is supportive of the president, the system may work well. But if the presidency and parliament are held by opposing forces, or if the parliament is badly divided, the danger of immobility will increase, and calls for a new revision of arrangements will emerge.

In its first implementation, following the 2006 parliamentary elections, the following arrangement emerged: president and prime minister were from rival forces, and a narrow majority coalition existed in parliament. This did not appear to be a recipe for effective government. The success of this arrangement will depend on two factors: the ability of President Yushchenko and Prime Minister Yanukovych to arrive at some agreed-upon policy agenda, and the ability of both of them to maintain control of their forces in parliament to support that agenda.

To the extent that control of the executive branch remains a powerful political tool in Ukraine, it could become badly politicized by the new arrangements. We can envision a situation in which the president uses one set of bureaucracies to pursue his or her political interests, while the prime minister uses another set of bureaucracies to pursue his or her competing political interests. Will the Interior Ministry be investigating firms that support the president, while the Security Service harasses firms that support the prime minister? Unfortunately, this does not seem farfetched.

Matthew Shugart and John Carey, who have studied presidential-parliamentary systems extensively, find two essential conditions for the success of this form of government: a clear division of responsibilities between president and prime minister, and respect for this division by both the president and prime minister.[11] These conditions clearly do not exist in Ukraine, and it does not appear that they will emerge in the near future.

If the new system leads to stalemate, yet another crisis will ensue in Ukraine. At that point there could be renewed calls for a strengthened presidency. However, depending on the balance of forces at the time of such a crisis, a move to a fully parliamentary system could occur.

The Adoption of a Proportional Electoral Law

In Chapter Seven, we concluded that Ukraine would be much better served by a fully proportional election law than by the mixed system used in 1998 and 2002. The results of the 2006 parliamentary election offer early evidence that this system is indeed better than the previous mixed system. Proportional representation will strengthen parties and should make it easier to build a majority coalition in parliament. This, in turn, should make it easier for the parliament to be a counterweight to the president.

One potential problem with the shift to proportional representation is that the threshold for entering parliament was lowered from 4 percent to 3 percent. While in absolute terms the difference is only 1 percent, in effect the barrier has been lowered by a fourth. This lower threshold reduces the incentives for parties to merge, and will likely increase the number of parties, especially small parties, that enter parliament. In 2006, this problem did not materialize. Only five parties were elected to parliament, and problems in forming a coalition had to do with animosities among these parties, not with an excessive number of parties.

It is not easy to predict exactly what the longer-term effects will be. In 1998, two parties obtained between 3 percent and 4 percent of the vote, and in 2006, two parties obtained between 2 percent and 3 percent, so the effect may not be enormous. However, with weak parties and a low threshold, the temptation to abandon parties rather than invest in them will remain. With each party reaching 3 percent receiving at least thirteen seats in the parliament (3 percent of 450 seats is 13.5 seats), a substantial diluting effect is possible, which may have serious consequences with respect to the effort to forge a parliamentary majority. Rather than an alliance of two or three large parties in a majority coalition, we may see these small parties holding the key, which will increase their leverage still further. In August 2005, Our Ukraine sponsored a bill to raise the threshold from 3 percent to 7 percent, but it failed.[12] We should not be surprised if raising the threshold becomes an issue in the future.

The Adoption of the Imperative Mandate

The imperative mandate may emerge as a much more significant, though less visible, institutional change. Even with fully proportional representation, if deputies in the parliament remained free to switch factions at will, the parliament would almost certainly remain weak and ineffective. It would be difficult to form a coherent majority coalition and the executive would potentially remain able to undermine the parliament by enticing deputies to defect from their parties.

The imperative mandate is a logical extension of proportional representation: if citizens vote for parties rather than individuals, it makes sense that the seats "belong" to the parties, rather than to the individuals chosen to fill them. The imperative mandate will mean that bargaining among party leaders will largely replace bargaining with individual deputies. Because there will be a reliable way for party leaders to "deliver" the votes they promise, deals can be struck without the fear that the partners will not be able to deliver the votes they promise. This should facilitate coalition formation, which often relies upon promises that one party will vote for a certain program or measure that is a central interest for a coalition partner.

However, the imperative mandate may not have a strong effect on party discipline in practice. It does not require the individual deputy to vote the party line on every bill. Moreover, individuals lose their seats only if they formally abandon the party. Already in 2006, dispute arose over the exact restrictions created by the rules. One question that arose was whether a party could eject individual deputies from the party, and then reclaim their seats. It appears that the measure does not allow parties to eject members and reassign their seats, though this question may be further contested in practice and in the courts. A second question is whether the seat is "owned" by the election bloc on which it was gained, or by the party (part of the bloc) of which the individual deputy is a member.

It seems likely that many deputies will continue to ignore the wishes of party leaders, and that the imperative mandate will have a weak effect in the absence of stronger parties.[13] Considering the possibility of an "orange coalition" in 2006, the influential journalist Yulia Mostova wrote, "Unrealized hopes and frustrated ambitions among rank-and-file deputies, stimulated by bribery or simply bad character, might not only ruin the plans of the three leaders for the government and parliament, but also kill the coalition before it flies."[14] In sum, the imperative mandate is clearly a step forward, but it will not, by itself, instill party discipline.

Ongoing weakness of party discipline was shown in voting over the prime minister in 2006. Having engineered a new coalition to take control of parliament, the Party of Regions found it difficult to assemble sufficient votes in that coalition to elect Yanukovych prime minister, because several Socialist deputies did not follow their leader, Moroz, when he switched his support from Yushchenko to Yanukovych.

Nor are all of its implications necessarily positive. To the extent that the imperative mandate actually allowed parties to control their deputies, the potential danger is that party leaders would become too powerful. What leverage will rank-and-file party members have over a party leader who is either corrupt or simply disregards the wishes of the party in pursuit of the leader's own political objectives? Depending on the internal rules of the various parties, it may be easier or harder to control the party leader. In many parties around the world, party leaders are chosen by vote of the party's parliamentary delegation or by a broader party congress, and can therefore be replaced. In Ukraine, where many of the parties are built from the ground up around a single individual, such control may be more difficult.

In determining the party list for the Tymoshenko Bloc in 2006, three of Tymoshenko's trusted lieutenants had to threaten to quit the bloc in order to keep the previously pro-Kuchma oligarch Oleksandr Volkov off the list.[15] When Socialist Party leader Oleksandr Moroz defected from the "orange coalition" to form a coalition with the Party of Regions and Communist Party, not all of his deputies supported him with their votes, and at least one resigned from the party. While this kind of internal check is necessary, it needs to be institutionalized because the threat of key members to resign is not a very reliable or democratic way to govern the party. Therefore, the development of internal party democracy will be a central challenge in the new system.

The importance of the imperative mandate is more likely to emerge gradually, and in combination with the full proportional representation system, in promoting a reasonable balance of influence between party leaders and rank-and-file members. Clearly, the development of strong party organizations is essential. In other countries with the imperative mandate, discipline comes not primarily from the imperative mandate, but from the control of the party over the proportional representation election list, and over appointments to party and government posts.

In Ukraine, the mutual influence between party organizations and members remains weak. Party leaders can shift policy without close consultation with members, but members can quit the party and hope to join another. Individual members must have more incentive to work for influence within the party than to defect when they disagree with the party line. The imperative mandate may be a powerful factor in promoting that incentive, but it will not instantly cure the problem.

An Agenda for Further Reform

Those three key institutional changes, adopted in 2004 and put into effect in 2006, address three of the major institutional shortcomings highlighted in this book. However, as we have seen throughout, one of the problems in Ukraine is that institutional rules do not always constrain behavior. As Chapter Nine showed, this is in large part because various de facto powers of the executive branch could be used to circumvent or simply negate the institutional rules.

Without a doubt, some of the institutional changes discussed above will tend to reduce that problem. Because the parliament as well as the president will now be able to dismiss individual ministers, it may become much harder for the ministries to be used as political weapons. It will in particular be more difficult for the president to use selective law enforcement against individual members of parliament and their business interests.

However, most of the tools of executive dominance elaborated in Chapter Nine still exist in Ukraine, and the consolidation of liberal democracy will be much more likely if further changes are undertaken to prevent the sort of "machine politics" practiced by Kuchma. This section therefore elaborates an agenda for further reform. Some items on this list are strictly in the institutional realm, while others are in the realm of normative or cultural change, which are harder to bring about through legislation, but important nonetheless.[16]

1. Mass-Based Parties

As noted above and in Chapter Eight, Ukraine's political parties are formed around individual leaders rather than wide societal groups. This makes it fairly easy for the leaders to abandon old parties and build new ones as tactical needs dictate. As a result, political parties serve as mechanisms by which elites contest elections, but they do not serve as entities that aggregate and express mass-based societal interests. The specific danger with the adoption of the imperative mandate is that those who are already extremely powerful will become even more powerful. In other words, the goal of the imperative mandate is to strengthen parties, not just the elites that form the parties. In the absence of democratically governed parties, parliament may be controlled by a small oligarchy, consisting of the two or three party leaders who together have enough votes to form a majority. Such a narrow alliance of party leaders led to the coalition that elected Oleksandr Moroz speaker of parliament in 2006, but so far the imperative mandate appears to be weak rather than dangerous.

In order for parties to be strengthened *as parties,* and not just as vehicles for powerful elites, they will need to become based more in their rank-and-file memberships. Mass memberships can check party leaders from below through internal party election processes. When parties have larger bases among the public, the costs to elites of defecting from one party and starting a new one will increase. This is the only way to strengthen the parties without making the party leaders dangerously powerful. The resulting strengthening of the party system would help the parliament to function effectively and to check the executive branch. It would also improve the public's sense of political efficacy.

In addition to campaign finance reform, discussed below, the strengthening and democratization of parties might be accomplished through legal requirements for internal party democracy. For example, the law could require that primary elections rather than party leaders determine candidate lists. Such a change was instrumental in democratizing American political parties in the twentieth century. Alternatively, the closed list proportional representation system could be replaced by an open list system, in which citizens vote not only for a party, but for the order of candidates on the party list. Such a system is used in Turkey and Finland.

2. Campaign Finance Reform

Related to the problem of building mass-based parties is the problem of campaign finance reform. While there are laws in place limiting campaign contributions and spending, they appear to be irrelevant, judging by the enormous amounts of money, little of which was accounted for, spent in recent elections. As has been demonstrated in the United States in recent decades, campaign finance is not easy to control because both potential donors and recipients have powerful incentives to find loopholes in whatever constraints are enacted.

However, a campaign finance system does not have to work perfectly in order to significantly constrain behavior. Even a very imperfect system would be an improvement on the present free-for-all in Ukraine. The most important project for Ukraine would be to make it more difficult for candidates and parties to rely on a very small number of very wealthy donors for financial support. The goal would not be to extinguish the effect of money on politics, which is probably impossible. Rather, the main goal would be to force politicians and party leaders to pursue a broader range of funding sources. This would be another step toward broadening the base of party support. A second goal would be to even the playing field between various candidates. Finally, campaign finance reform might reduce the incentives for elected officials to extort campaign contributions from firms and wealthy individuals. Unfortunately, campaign finance reform has received little attention in Ukraine and in external analyses of Ukrainian politics. For example, campaign finance is not discussed in over a hundred pages of recommendations produced by the Blue Ribbon Commission for Ukraine in 2005.[17]

3. Election of Regional Governors and Local Administration Heads

Ukraine's unitary state structure helped facilitate Kuchma's turning of the state apparatus into a massive machine to collect votes and attack political adversaries. This reached from the top to the bottom because there was a single *vertikal* of power, in which the heads of oblasts and local administrations were appointed by the president in Kyiv. This power remains in the president's hands, and upon his inauguration, Yushchenko quickly replaced almost all of the regional heads.

If those regional leaders were elected, they would have their own bases of power, and would have much less reason to do the president's bidding. Some of them might still choose to do so, but others likely would not. This would create a built-in check on presidential power. This is especially true when we consider Ukraine's regional divisions. It is hard to imagine that all of Ukraine's regions would elect governors who are loyal to the same president.

In electing governors, Ukraine would be moving in the opposite direction from the one Russia took in 2004. In Russia, Vladimir Putin took advantage of the Beslan school massacre to gain passage of constitutional revisions allowing him to name Russia's governors. Almost every observer saw this as a major consolidation of Putin's power and as a threat to democracy.[18] Yet this system has been present in Ukraine all along.

One potential downside of electing governors, cited repeatedly by Putin, is that it allows a situation where locally popular governors can pursue corruption without the fear of being fired by the president.[19] There is no doubt some danger of this, and one can imagine elected governors in some regions resisting any changes coming from a central government they do not like. However, the best cure for corrupt local officials is effective enforcement of anticorruption laws, not a consolidation of presidential power. In Ukraine, the president has been a source of corruption among the governors, not a remedy for it.

4. Civil Service System

The use of patronage to collect votes can occur only in a situation where one can credibly threaten to fire employees for political reasons. There is a standard remedy to that problem: institution of a functioning civil service system for the majority of government jobs.[20] More generally, in Ukraine there is insufficient distinction between civil servants and political appointees.[21] In such a system, widespread in Western democracies, workers can be fired only for cause. While this often leads to complaints about the difficulty of ridding government agencies of incompetent employees, it is the only known way to eliminate the widespread use of patronage. The need to combat patronage politics was a major reason for the adoption of civil service laws in countries such as the United States.

Ukraine does have civil service laws, and has had several commissions to consider civil service reform. Yet the coercion of government employees remained even after the Orange Revolution.[22] As noted above, the division of control over bureaucracies between the president and the prime minister will mean that such power will no longer be monopolized by a single actor. This will help to produce balance in the exercise of patronage (as long as the president and prime minister are rivals, or as long as a variety of parties controls the various ministries). However, as long as patronage politics is a way of life, elections will be unfair, and one path to electoral authoritarianism will remain open.

5. Measures to Combat Corruption

Official corruption is a far-reaching problem in Ukraine, and here we can offer no comprehensive plan to combat it. It is necessary to recognize, however, that besides its deleterious economic effects, corruption facilitates concentration of power in the executive. Corruption facilitates selective law enforcement in several ways. First, corrupt government officials are vulnerable to control from above by those who can choose to expose them or to look the other way. Moreover, because corruption makes certain government posts highly lucrative, officials given those posts have an extra incentive to follow the dictates of their bosses rather than the law. Finally, corruption creates an easy way to bring money into political campaigns "off the books." This gives large advantages to those in control of the government apparatus. Corruption played a central role in Kuchma's strategy of political control. He promoted a system in which government officials were corrupt, because he could then exchange his willingness to look the other way for financial and political loyalty from subordinates.

Combating corruption will not simply be a matter of writing new rules. In some cases, there are genuine economic barriers to ending corruption. For example, it may be difficult to get teachers to stop accepting petty bribes from students if the teachers' salaries are too meager to live on. In the cases of teachers and many low-level officials, the ability to collect bribes has been a substitute for the state's ability to pay them. There are enormous fiscal implications in changing from a system where these officials are paid through bribes to one in which they are paid fully by the state.

Such widespread everyday corruption will not be eradicated by new rules, especially when corruption will prevent the new rules from being enforced. Instead, corruption is more likely to be reduced because it becomes a political liability. A more independent parliament may have an incentive to investigate corruption within the executive branch, and vice versa. Equally important, the newly freed media can play an essential role in publicizing corruption, and in doing so, making political elites pay a price for it.

All accounts indicate that corruption in Ukraine did not diminish substantially after the Orange Revolution. However, it increasingly appears to be a political liability. Throughout 2005 and 2006, press reports about the spending habits of Yushchenko's associates were perceived as very damaging. Moreover, accusations of corruption forced Yushchenko to fire some of his closest associates (notably Petro Poroshenko). Official corruption in Ukraine will be reduced as much through the vigilance of the press and opposition politicians as through any specific changes in rules.

6. Simplification of the Tax Code

One set of rules that does influence the level of corruption is the tax code. A complex tax code is not merely economically inefficient. It provides opportunities for tax inspectors to take bribes. More important, however, it opens the door wide to selective law enforcement as a means of ensuring support for the executive. This was facilitated by unpredictable changes in the tax code, some of which had a retroactive effect.[23] Yushchenko made reform of the tax code a priority early in his presidency, but progress has been limited.

As was noted in Chapter Nine, tax enforcement actions were a favorite means used by Kuchma's team to ruin the businesses of opposing politicians and to silence unfriendly media. Simplifying the tax code would make it easier for businesses to ascertain that they are in compliance, and more difficult for the government to trump up tax evasion cases against its political enemies. As added benefits, it would reduce a serious drain on the economy and create a much more favorable climate for foreign investment.[24]

7. Ability to Appeal Administrative Penalties

The use of selective law enforcement has been so powerful in Ukraine because it quickly bankrupts the firms targeted. This results from two aspects of the system. First, there is no formal hearing process that must occur before a violation is found and a fine levied or a business closed. Second, even when a firm appeals a ruling, the penalty is administered immediately. Moreover, even if a court subsequently rules for the defendant in such a case, the business in question may have suffered such irreparable damage in the interim that it has effectively been destroyed. Knowing this, businesses can easily be cowed into supporting the administration. It would be relatively easy to change the procedures by which administrative actions can be brought and appealed, but it is not clear that this is high on anyone's priority list in Ukraine.

8. Judicial Independence

As emphasized in Chapter Nine, Ukraine has the statutory requirements in place for a fairly independent judiciary. Judicial independence was further strengthened, on paper, in December 2004, when it was agreed to revise the process for appointing judges to the Constitutional Court of Ukraine. Previously the president, the parliament, and the Union of Judges each appointed six members, but because the Union of Judges was controlled by Kuchma, he in effect appointed a majority. In the new system, the president and parliament will each name nine judges.

The problem of judicial independence does not appear to be one of rules, but one of norms. "Judicial independence [in Ukraine] in the final analysis will depend largely on the conscience and courage of the judges themselves."[25] The norm established under the Soviet system was that the judicial apparatus was part of a unified state structure and an instrument of state policy. Clearly, that understanding has persisted in independent Ukraine, supported by the efforts of Kuchma to uphold it through whatever means of coercing judges proved available.

To some observers, the December 2004 invalidation of the presidential election results by the Supreme Court was a major step toward judicial independence in Ukraine.[26] This was not the first time that a judge had defied Kuchma, but in a case on which the country's future depended, the court clearly sided with the law. On the other hand, it did so in a case where the pressure from "power politics" (in the form of protesters in the streets) was increasingly on the side of the law.

Attempts to bribe judges will continue until it becomes the case that both the bribe-givers and the judges are caught and prosecuted often enough that bribery is not worth the risks. There is a normative element here as well. Ukraine needs to reach the point where judges and citizens regard those who take bribes with contempt, rather than as normal people playing according to rules they did not make. For the questions of democratization that concern this book, the continuation of some bribery of judges is less important than the political control of judges by the state. When the judiciary becomes simply one more arm of executive power rather than a check on executive power, it contributes to authoritarian behavior. The Supreme Court's decision indicated that the courts can operate as a check on the executive, but it remains to be seen whether this will become the rule or the exception.

Conclusion

It is dangerous to assume, as many have, that the Orange Revolution represents the establishment of liberal democracy in Ukraine. Rather it represents a *departure* that might or might not result in consolidated liberal democracy. Just as it was a mistake to assume in 1991 that the path to democracy for the post-Soviet states was relatively straightforward, it would be a mistake to believe that in the case of Ukraine today. The outcome will depend on choices that are yet to be made. There are still many ways in which the process that looked so hopeful in 2004 can run aground. This is so not only because in Ukraine there are still retrograde and corrupt political forces that have no intention of admitting defeat. It is also true because the institutional basis for liberal democracy is still incomplete in Ukraine.

The Orange Revolution and ensuing developments have improved the situation considerably. Power politics is now more limited, in part because political power is more evenly distributed, and in part because important institutions have been redesigned in ways that will improve their performance. However, as this chapter has highlighted, substantial challenges remain. While a return to "Kuchmism" appears unlikely, a successful transition to liberal democracy is equally in doubt.

Institutionally, Ukraine has indeed undergone something of a revolution, from a strong presidential system to a model in which power is more evenly divided between president and parliament. This institutional change has already led to a redistribution of practical political power—from a single executive to two competing powers. To borrow a concept from international relations, control of the executive branch in Ukraine appears to be moving from a "unipolar" to a "bipolar" system. The nature of politics will shift accordingly, from a focus on the will and skill of a single dominant actor to competition and collaboration between two actors who have both common and conflicting interests. The danger of aggrandizement by a dominant president is reduced; the danger of conflict and stalemate between president and prime minister is increased.

These developments in institutional design and in the de facto distribution of power are more important than the identity of specific leaders. It is certainly significant that Yushchenko, by all indications, is less venal, less corrupt, and less brutal than Kuchma. More important, in the long run, is that even if Yushchenko or some successor were inclined to follow Kuchma's tactics, it will be much more difficult to do so. Thus, the prospect of Viktor Yanukovych as prime minister was a very different prospect than the prospect of Viktor Yanukovych as president in 2004. He is much more constrained in the new system than he would have been in the old one. In sum, the institutional changes are central.

The challenge for Ukraine's leaders and citizens is to broaden and deepen reform, even in the face of growing frustration over the pace of change. There is immense work yet to be done in Ukraine, as the agenda elaborated above indicates. Yet, frustration with the results of the Orange Revolution has already built quickly. Yushchenko has found it difficult to gain parliamentary support for his reform program, and his party foundered badly in the 2006 parliamentary elections. Among citizens, many who supported the Orange Revolution felt that it had been abandoned, while those who opposed it were no happier. While the quest for liberal democracy has clearly a taken step forward in Ukraine, success promises only what Churchill famously characterized as "the worst form of Government except all those other forms that have been tried from time to time."[27]

Notes

1. Introduction

1. See, for example, Fred Weir, "Ukraine's Orange Revolution Undone," *Christian Science Monitor*, August 4, 2006, p. 6; Anatol Lieven, "Failure of the Orange Revolution is a Historic Opportunity," *Financial Times*, July 25, 2006, p. 17.

2. Samuel P. Huntington, *The Third Wave: Democratization in the Late Twentieth Century* (Norman: University of Oklahoma Press, 1991), pp. 266–67. In fact, there is some question whether Ukraine could be considered to have passed this test in 1998. It did have two successful parliamentary elections. But Huntington's test requires that the winning party in the democracy's "founding election" be defeated, and that then the new winner be subsequently defeated. By that test, Ukraine might be viewed as not having the second turnover until 2004.

3. Paul Kubicek, "Delegative Democracy in Russia and Ukraine," *Communist and Post-Communist Studies* 27, no. 4 (July 1994): 423–42.

4. Steven Levitsky and Lucan A. Way, "Competitive Authoritarianism: Elections without Democracy," *Journal of Democracy* 13, no. 2 (April 2002): 51–64.

5. See Carlos Pascual, "Don't Give Up on Ukraine," *International Herald Tribune*," August 3, 2006, at http://www.brookings.edu/views/op-ed/pascual/20060803.htm, accessed August 7, 2006. Pascual is a former U.S. Ambassador to Ukraine.

6. Adam Przeworski, *Democracy and the Market: Political and Economic Reforms in Eastern Europe and Latin America* (Cambridge: Cambridge University Press, 1991), 10.

7. Robert A. Dahl, *Democracy and Its Critics* (New Haven, CT: Yale University Press, 1989).

8. Samuel Huntington, *The Third Wave: Democratization in the Late Twentieth Century* (Norman: University of Oklahoma Press, 1991), quoted in Fareed Zakaria, "The Rise of Illiberal Democracy," *Foreign Affairs* 76 (1997): 24.

9. Guillermo O'Donnell, "Delegative Democracy," *Journal of Democracy* 5, no. 1 (1994): 58.

10. By "liberal democracy," we mean one that is characterized not only by the rule of the people but also by the rule of law, and where competition for power is such that various political forces find clear and consistent constraint on their pursuit of power. This refers not only to the state itself, which in a liberal democracy has clear limits (both de jure and de facto) on its power, but also to partisan forces within the state. Whether such a "liberal democracy" can be produced solely by institutional design, or whether it depends as well on certain characteristics in the society (such as a certain degree of consensus on basic issues) is an issue that will be discussed further below.

11. See Taras Kuzio and Paul D'Anieri, eds., *Dilemmas of State-Led Nation Building in Ukraine* (Westport, CT: Praeger, 2002).

12. See William Riker, "Implications from the Disequilibrium of Majority Rule for the Study of Institutions," *American Political Science Review* 74, no. 2 (June 1980): 475; George Tsebelis, *Nested Games: Rational Choice in Comparative Politics* (Berkeley: University of California Press, 1990); and Gary W. Cox, *Making Votes Count: Strategic Coordination in the World's Electoral Systems* (New York: Cambridge University Press, 1997), 17. Similarly, Cox focuses on the "endogeneity of electoral structure" (the notion that "if electoral laws do indeed affect the ability of political parties to survive . . . then presumably parties will seek to manipulate those laws to their own advantage") (Cox, *Making Votes Count*, 17).

13. Tsebelis, *Nested Games*, 11.

14. Riker, "Implications," 444–45.

15. Przeworski, *Democracy and the Market*, 87.

16. Bohdan Harasymiw has linked this argument to Ukraine, citing Tatu Vanhanen, *The Process of Democratization: A Comparative Study of 147 States, 1980–88* (New York: Crane Russak, 1990). See Bohdan Harasymiw, *Post-Soviet Ukraine* (Edmonton: Canadian Institute of Ukrainian Studies, 2002), 12.

17. See Taras Kuzio, *Ukraine: State and Nation Building* (London: Routledge, 1998); Pal Kolsto, *Political Construction Sites: Nation-Building and the Post-Soviet States* (Boulder, CO: Westview, 2000); Roman Szporluk, "Nation-Building in Ukraine: Problems and Prospects," in *The Successor States to the USSR*, ed. J.W. Blaney (Washington, DC: Congressional Quarterly, 1995); Andrew Wilson, *Ukrainian Nationalism in the 1990s: A Minority Faith* (New York: Cambridge, 1997); Sharon L. Wolchik and Volodymyr Zviglyanich, eds., *Ukraine: The Search for a National Identity* (Lanham, MD: Rowman and Littlefield, 2000); Kataryna Wolczuk, "History, Europe and the 'National Idea:' The Official Narrative of National Identity in Ukraine," *Nationalities Papers* 28, no. 4 (December 2000): 671–94; and William Zimmerman, "Is Ukraine a Political Community?" *Communist and Post-Communist Studies* 31, no. 1 (March 1998): 43–56.

18. This phenomenon was perhaps first noted and analyzed by Philip G. Roeder, "Varieties of Post-Soviet Authoritarian Regimes," *Post-Soviet Affairs* 10 (1994): 61–101.

2. Institutions and Democracy: Questioning the Connections

1. Samuel Huntington, *The Third Wave: Democratization in the Late Twentieth Century* (Norman: University of Oklahoma Press, 1991).

2. On the complementary nature of rational choice and historical institutionalism, see Ira Katznelson and Barry R. Weingast, eds., *Preferences and Situations: Points of Intersection between Historical and Rational Choice Institutionalism* (New York: Russell Sage Foundation, 2005).

3. Philip G. Roeder, "Varieties of Post-Soviet Authoritarian Regimes," *Post-Soviet Affairs* 10 (1994): 61–101.

4. Fareed Zakaria, "The Rise of Illiberal Democracy," *Foreign Affairs*, no. 6 (November–December 1997): 22.

5. Robert Dahl, "What Political Institutions Does Large-Scale Democracy Require?" *Political Science Quarterly* 120, no. 2 (Summer 2005), Table 1.

6. Guillermo O'Donnell, "Delegative Democracy," *Journal of Democracy* 5, no. 1 (January 1994): 57–59.

7. Ibid., 57.

8. Ibid., 58.

9. Ibid., 59.

10. Zakaria, "The Rise of Illiberal Democracy," 23.

11. Ibid., 30. Zakaria goes on to point out that "what is distinctive about the American system is not how democratic it is but rather how undemocratic it is," (39) because limits on pure democracy are necessary to protect against the abuse of power by a strong president.

12. Ibid., pp. 25–26.

13. Ibid., p. 40.

14. Thomas Carothers, "The End of the Transition Paradigm," *Journal of Democracy* 13, no. 1 (January 2002): 10. Carothers's analysis has been widely commented on. See the essays by Carothers, Guillermo O'Donnell, Kenneth Wollack, Ghia Nodia, and Gerald Hyman in *Journal of Democracy* 13, no. 3 (July 2002).

15. The effort to characterize these regimes has led to a proliferation of different labels, including, in addition to those discussed here, "façade democracy," "pseudo-democracy," "weak democracy," and "partial democracy." See Carothers, "The End of the Transition Paradigm," 10; and Steven Levitsky and Lucan Way, "The Rise of Competitive Authoritarianism," *Journal of Democracy* 13 (April 2002): 51–63. The general problem of classifying these regimes is discussed in David Collier and Steven Levitsky, "Democracy with Adjectives: Conceptual Innovation in Comparative Research," *World Politics* 49, no. 3 (1997): 430–51; and Larry Diamond, "Thinking about Hybrid Regimes," *Journal of Democracy* 13 (April 2002): 21–35.

16. Paul Kubicek, "The Limits of Electoral Democracy in Ukraine," *Democratization* 8, no. 2 (Summer 2001): 117–39.

17. O'Donnell, "Delegative Democracy," 59.

18. Zakaria, "The Rise of Illiberal Democracy," 30–32. O'Donnell, "Delegative Democracy," 60, makes the same point.

19. Carothers, "The End of the Transition Paradigm," 11–12.

20. G. Bingham Powell, *Elections as Instruments of Democracy: Majoritarian and Proportional Visions* (New Haven, CT: Yale University Press, 2000), 4.

21. It is possible to go even further still. There is a substantial body of literature, largely developed in the 1960s to deal with the first wave of democratization, but revived in recent years, positing that there are certain structural prerequisites for democratization, and that none of the other processes—elections, constitution making, liberalization, can succeed until the prerequisites are met. For a summary of this school of thought and an application to the Ukrainian and Russian cases, see Alexander J. Motyl, "Structural Constraints and Starting Points: The Logic of Systemic Change in Ukraine and Russia," *Comparative Politics* (July 1997): 433–47.

22. Carothers, "The End of the Transition Paradigm," 7.

23. Ibid., 8.

24. Ibid., 12.

25. Zakaria, "The Rise of Illiberal Democracy," 35.

26. Ibid., 39.

27. Ibid., 31.

28. Ibid., 42.

29. O'Donnell, "Delegative Democracy," 61.

30. Motyl, "Structural Constraints and Starting Points," 437.

31. O'Donnell, "Delegative Democracy," 62.

32. Francis Fukuyama, "The End of History?" *National Interest* (Summer 1989); and *The End of History and the Last Man* (New York: Free Press, 1992).

33. Carothers, "The End of the Transition Paradigm," 15.

34. Ibid., 18.

35. O'Donnell, "Delegative Democracy," 56.

36. Ibid.

37. Bohdan Harasymiw, *Post-Communist Ukraine* (Edmonton: Canadian Institute of Ukrainian Studies, 2002), 3.

38. See Michael McFaul, "The Fourth Wave of Democracy and Dictatorship: Non-cooperative Transitions in the Postcommunist World," in *After the Collapse of Communism: Comparative Lessons of Transition*, ed. Michael McFaul and Kathryn Stoner-Weiss (Cambridge: Cambridge University Press, 2004), 59. McFaul rejects the notion of "democracy without democrats."

39. Immanuel Kant, *Perpetual Peace* [1795], in Kant, *Political Writings*, 2d ed., ed. Hans Riess (New York: Cambridge University Press, 1991), 112–13. See also Kant, *Idea for a Universal History with a Cosmopolitan Purpose* [1784] in *Political Writings*, 50.

40. For a more specific, but still nontechnical, discussion of rationality, see James D. Morrow, *Game Theory for Political Scientists* (Princeton, NJ: Princeton University Press, 1994), 17–20. Morrow summarizes: "Put simply, rational behavior means choosing the best means to gain a predetermined set of goals. It is an evaluation of the consistency of choices and not of the thought process, of implementation of fixed goals and not of the morality of those goals."

41. Dennis C. Mueller, "Constitutional Public Choice," in *Perspectives on Public Choice*, ed. Mueller (Cambridge: Cambridge University Press, 1997), 124.

42. An important example of this literature, with substantial relevance to Ukraine, may be found in Mathew Soberg Shugart and John M. Carey, *Presidents and Assemblies: Constitutional Design and Electoral Dynamics* (Cambridge: Cambridge University Press, 1992).

43. Giovanni Sartori, *Comparative Constitutional Engineering*, 2d ed. (New York: New York University Press, 1997), ix.

44. Powell, *Elections as Instruments of Democracy*, 19.

45. This is a simplification that will be qualified substantially in Chapter Seven.

46. Juan Linz, "The Perils of Presidentialism," *Journal of Democracy* 1 (Winter 1990): 51–71. The literature on this question has grown considerably. See Alfred Stepan and Cindy Skach, "Constititional Frameworks and Democratic Consolidation: Parliamentarism versus Presidentialism," *World Politics* 46 (October 1993): 1–22; Gerald M. Easter, "Preference for Presidentialism: Postcommunist Regime Change in Russia and the NIS," *World Politics* 49 (January 1997): 184–211; Scott Mainwaring, "Presidentialism, Multiparty Systems, and Democracy: The Difficult Equation," *Comparative Political Studies* 26, no. 2 (1993): 198–230; John M. Carey and Matthew Soberg Shugart, *Executive Decree Authority* (Cambridge: Cambridge, 1998); Giuseppe DiPalma, *To Craft Democracies: An Essay on Democratic Transitions* (Berkeley: University of California Press, 1990); Juan Linz and Arturo Valenzuela, eds., *The Failure of Presidential Democracy: Comparative Perspectives* (Baltimore, MD: Johns Hopkins University Press, 1994); and Timothy M. Frye, "The Politics of Institutional Choice: Postcommunist Presidencies," *Comparative Political Studies* 30, no. 5 (October 1997): 523–32.

47. Arend Lijphart, *Democracies: Patterns of Majoritarian and Consensus Government in Twenty-One Countries* (New Haven: Yale University Press, 1984) quoted in Powell, *Elections as Instrumentsof Democracy,* 21.

48. Jeffrey Simpson, *The Friendly Dictatorship* (Toronto: McClelland and Stewart, 2001).

49. Linz, "The Perils of Presidentialism," 52.

50. Shugart and Carey, *Presidents and Assemblies*, 19.

51. Linz, "The Perils of Presidentialism," 52.

52. Shugart and Carey discuss also the "Premier-Presidential" model (*Presidents and Assemblies*, 49 ff), which Ukraine's system was in part designed to emulate, and still superficially resembles. However, in order for the system to be identified as "premier-presidential" rather than "presidential," there must be a clear division of responsibilities between the president and the prime minister, and this division "must be respected on both sides, instead of producing competitive dyarchy." These conditions were certainly not met in Ukraine under the 1996 constitution.

53. The first four of these are listed by Shugart and Carey, *Presidents and Assemblies*, 44. They do not list the fifth, but it is focused on in many discussions of postcommunist reform.

54. M. Steven Fish, "The Determinants of Economic Reform in the Post-Communist World," *East European Politics and Societies* 12, no. 1 (Winter 1998): 31–78.

55. Ibid., 45.

56. Ibid., 46.

57. The president's incentive to undermine parliamentary cohesion is discussed by Shugart and Carey, *Presidents and Assemblies*, 30–31. See also Mainwaring, "Presidentialism, Multiparty Systems, and Democracy."

58. A good overview of the major issues may be found in Rein Taagepera and Matthew Soberg Shugart, *Seats and Votes: The Effects and Determinants of Electoral Systems* (New Haven, CT: Yale University Press, 1999). See also Gary W. Cox, *Making Votes Count: Strategic Coordination in the World's Electoral Systems* (New York: Cambridge University Press, 1997).

59. Taagepera and Shugart, *Seats and Votes*, 4.

60. Germany is sometimes considered a "mixed system," because part of the ballot elects members in districts. But because the party list portion of the ballot is then used to create proportional final results, the proportional component controls which party rules, even if the exact identities of a relatively small number of Bundestag members are determined by the district voting. See Matthew Soberg Shugart and Martin P. Wattenberg, "Mixed-Member Systems: A Definition and Typology," in *Mixed-Member Electoral Systems: The Best of Both Worlds?* ed. Shugart and Wattenberg (Oxford: Oxford University Press, 2001).

61. Of Duverger's two assertions, one is called a "law" and the other a "hypothesis" because Duverger and subsequent authors have much more confidence in the nearly universal validity of the former, while the latter is viewed as being generally but not definitively true. See William H. Riker, "The Two-Party System and Duverger's Law: An Essay on the History of Political Science," *American Political Science Review* 76, no. 4 (December 1982): 753–66. For substantial refinement and qualification of both the law and the hypothesis, see Cox, *Making Votes Count*.

62. For a theoretically driven comparative examination of mixed electoral systems, see Federico Ferrara, Erik Herron, and Misa Nishikawa, *Mixed Electoral Systems: Contamination and Its Consequences* (New York: Palgrave, 2005); and Shugart and Wattenberg, *Mixed-Member Electoral Systems*. In Russia, the threshold is 5 per-

cent, and in Ukraine it was 4 percent in 1998 and 2002. In the fully PR system that went into effect in Ukraine in 2006, the threshold is 3 percent.

63. Erik S. Herron and Misa Nishikawa, "Contamination Effects and the Number of Parties in Mixed-Superposition Electoral Systems," *Electoral Studies* 20 (March 2001): 63–86.

64. Shugart and Wattenberg, "Mixed-Member Systems."

65. Ferrara, Herron, and Nishikawa, *Mixed Electoral Systems*, chap. 4.

66. Shugart and Wattenberg, "Mixed-Member Systems," 1. See also Matthew Soberg Shugart, "'Extreme' Electoral Systems and the Appeal of the Mixed-Member Alternative," in Shugart and Wattenberg, *Mixed-Member Electoral Systems*.

67. Ferrara, Herron, and Nishikawa, *Mixed Electoral Systems*, chap. 1. See also Herron and Nishikawa, "Contamination Effects."

68. George Tsebelis, *Nested Games: Rational Choice in Comparative Politics* (Berkeley: University of California Press, 1990), 11. He cites William Riker on this point.

69. James Mahoney, "Combining Institutionalisms," in Katznelson and Weingast, *Preferences and Situations*, 325–27.

70. Tsebelis, *Nested Games*, 9.

71. Ibid., 11.

72. McFaul, "The Fourth Wave," 59. It should be noted that the constellation of power necessary to *create* democracy is a separate question from that most likely to *maintain* it. It could take a preponderance of power to create a new set of institutions, and some degree of balance to prevent another revision.

3. Power and Institutions: Overview of the Argument

1. This point is stressed in particular by Taras Kuzio, *Ukraine: State and Nation* (London: Routledge, 1998).

2. Scott Mainwaring, "Presidentialism, Multiparty Systems, and Democracy: The Difficult Equation," *Comparative Political Studies* 26, no. 2 (1993) 198–230. For a dissenting view, see Mark J. Gasiorowski and Timothy J. Power, "Institutional Design and Democratic Consolidation in the Third World," *Comparative Political Studies* 30, no. 2 (April 1997): 123–55.

3. Mainwaring, "Presidentialism, Multiparty Systems, and Democracy."

4. See Misa Nishikawa and Erik Herron, "Mixed Electoral Rules' Impact on Party Systems," *Electoral Studies* 23 (December 2004): 753–68. The effects of the mixed system will be discussed in much more detail in Chapter Seven.

5. This is, of course, somewhat simplified, but the basic point is valid: were it not for their crucial role in adopting the constitution, the smaller states could not have prevailed on this point.

6. Roman Kupchinsky, "Ukraine: Battle Against Corruption Grinds to a Halt," Radio Free Europe/Radio Liberty, September 28, 2005, www.rferl.org/featuresarticle/2005/9/0DF313C3-32FD-4B91-B524-0D022F46F2C2.html.

7. It is hard to know exactly who benefited from the bizarre gas deal that Yushchenko agreed to with Russian negotiators in early 2006, but it is hard to avoid the conclusion that people close to Yushchenko stood to benefit immensely. The president's unwillingness to clarify the details of the agreement and the owners of the firm RosUkrEnergo contributed to the impression that he and his colleagues had something to hide.

8. See Joel S. Hellman, "Winners Take All: The Politics of Partial Reform in Postcommunist Transitions," *World Politics* 50, no. 2 (January 1998): 203–34.

9. Anders Aslund, Peter Boone, and Simon Johnson, "Escaping the Under-Reform Trap," IMF Staff Papers 48, Special Issue (2001): 88–108. The quotation here is from page 89.

10. Strobe Talbott, "The Strains of Putin's Clampdown," *Financial Times*, September 27, 2004, 19.

11. See Paul D'Anieri, "The Last Hurrah: The 2004 Ukrainian Presidential Elections and the Limits of Machine Politics," *Communist and Post-Communist Societies* 38 (2005): 231–49.

12. See B. Guy Peters and Jon Pierre, *Politicization of the Civil Service in Comparative Perspective: The Quest for Control* (London: Routledge, 2004).

13. See Ari A. Hoogenboom, *Outlawing the Spoils: A History of the Civil Service Reform Movement, 1865–1883* (Urbana: University of Illinois Press, 1968).

14. This was not impossible to anticipate. See Paul D'Anieri, "The Mitigation of Ethnic Conflict in Ukraine: The Mysterious Case of the State that Didn't Collapse," paper presented at the annual meeting of the American Political Science Association, Boston, August 31–September 3, 1998.

15. This argument echoes that of Michael McFaul, "The Fourth Wave of Democracy and Dictatorship: Noncooperative Transitions in the Postcommunist World," in *After the Collapse of Communism: Comparative Lessons of Transition*, ed. McFaul and Kathryn Stoner-Weiss (Cambridge: Cambridge University Press, 2004) 58–95.

16. See, for example, Terry Lynn Karl and Philippe C. Schmitter, "Modes of Transitions in Latin America, Southern and Eastern Europe," *International Social Science Journal* 128 (May 1991): 269–84.

17. John T. Ishiyama, "Transitional Electoral Systems in Post-Communist Eastern Europe," *Political Science Quarterly* 112, no. 1 (Spring 1997): 95–115.

4. The Evolution of Ukrainian Politics 1989–2006

1. Adam Przeworski, *Democracy and the Market: Political and Economic Reforms in Eastern Europe and Latin America* (Cambridge: Cambridge University Press, 1991), 12.

2. Ibid., 94.

3. For more extensive coverage of this period, see Bohdan Harasymiw, *Post-Communist Ukraine* (Edmonton: Canadian Institute of Ukrainian Studies, 2002); Taras Kuzio, *Ukraine: Perestroika to Independence*, 2d ed. (London: Macmillan, 2000); and Bohdan Nahaylo, *The Ukrainian Resurgence* (Toronto: University of Toronto Press, 1999).

4. UNIAN, March 6, 2001, translated by BBC Monitoring Service, March 6, 2001, accessed through Lexis-Nexis, June 8, 2004.

5. For a thorough analysis of the "Dnipropetrovsk clan" and its influence in the Soviet Union and in post-Soviet Ukraine, see *Dnipropetrovska Simia: Dovidnyk, 54 Biohrafii* (Kyiv: Fond Demokratii, 1996).

6. See Borys Levitskyj, *Politics and Society in Soviet Ukraine, 1953–1980* (Edmonton: Canadian Institute of Ukrainian Studies, 1984); and Kuzio, *Ukraine*, 43–51.

7. The differences between the Soviet system of rule by Soviets and Western parliamentarism are elaborated in Kataryna Wolczuk, *The Moulding of Ukraine: The*

Constitutional Politics of State Formation (Budapest: Central European University Press, 2001), 47–50.

8. Wolczuk, *The Moulding of Ukraine*, 67.

9. Ibid., 66.

10. Ibid., 67.

11. Philip G. Roeder, "Varieties of Post-Soviet Authoritarian Regimes," *Post-Soviet Affairs* 10 (1994): 69, emphasis in original.

12. Kuzio, *Ukraine*, 41–42.

13. *Narodna Hazeta*, no. 18 (December 1991), quoted in Kuzio, *Ukraine*, 63.

14. Roeder, "Varieties of Post-Soviet Authoritarian Regimes," 62.

15. Ihor Markov, "The Role of the President in the Ukrainian Political System," Radio Free Europe/Radio Liberty, *Research Report* 2, no. 48 (December 3, 1993): 32.

16. See Kravchuk's interview in *Pravda*, February 11, 1992, 1–2, translated in FBIS-SOV-92-029, February 12, 1992, 71.

17. Cindy Skach examines the shortcomings of the "French" model, including its role in the failure of the Weimar republic, in *Borrowing Constitutional Designs: Constitutional Law in Weimar Germany and the French Fifth Republic* (Princeton, NJ: Princeton University Press, 2006). Others have also argued that the "French" model works in France for reasons that are unlikely to obtain elsewhere. See Alfred Stepan and Ezra Suleiman, "The French Fifth Republic: A Model for Import? Reflections on Poland and Brazil," in *Arguing Comparative Politics*, ed. Stepan (Oxford: Oxford University Press, 2001), 257–75.

18. That it was viewed as unacceptable for the prime minister to be too close to the president shows how different Ukraine's system was from the French model. While the structures were similar, the politics were entirely different. In France, there is general agreement that the system works best when the president and prime minister are of the same party, and the problems arise during periods of "cohabitation" between a president and prime minister of different parties. There is no expectation in the French system that the prime minister will serve as a parliamentary check on presidential power. Yet in Ukraine this was seen as important due to the unresolved distribution of power between the branches of government.

19. Vladimir Skachko, "Three Centers of Power: Leonid Kravchuk Has Shared Power with the Government and He Is Now Prepared to Share It with Parliament and the Local Soviets," *Nezavisimaya gazeta*, November 7, 1992, translated in FBIS-USR-92-155, December 4, 1992, 111–12. See also Vladimir Buyda, "Government's Supplementary Powers Confirmed. Parliament's Commissions Instructed to Enshrine Them in Current Constitution," *Nezavisimaya gazeta*, November 24, 1993, 3, translated in FBIS-USR-92-162, December 19, 1992, 130.

20. This is Michael McFaul's thesis. See Michael McFaul, "The Fourth Wave of Democracy and Dictatorship: Noncooperative Transitions in the Postcommunist World," in *After the Collapse of Communism: Comparative Lessons of Transition*, ed. McFaul and Kathryn Stoner-Weiss (Cambridge: Cambridge University Press, 2004).

21. On the role of the Soviet elite in post-Soviet Ukraine, see Vyacheslav Pikhovshek, et al., *Politychnyi protses v Ukraini: suchasni tendentsii ta istorychnyi kontekst* (Kyiv: Agenstvo Ukraina, 1999), ch. 4.

22. The election law (essentially unchanged from the Soviet era) required not only a runoff if no candidate received a majority of the vote, but a rerun of the runoff if turnout did not exceed 50 percent of registered voters. Several seats took over a year to fill.

23. Oleg Shmid, "Vybory staly pomstoiu," *Post-Postup*, April 15–24, 1994, 1.
24. See Robert Kravchuk, *Ukrainian Political Economy: The First Ten Years* (New York: Palgrave Macmillan, 2002), ch. 4–5.
25. See "Inauguration Speech by President Leonid Kuchma at the Supreme Council in Kiev—Live Relay," Radio Ukraine World Service, July 19, 1994, translated in FBIS-SOV-94-139, 20 July 1994, 36.
26. See Wolczuk, *The Moulding of Ukraine*, ch. 5, on these plans.
27. Ibid., 228.
28. Kuchma's strategy in 1999 echoed that of Boris Yeltsin in 1996. As unpopular as Yeltsin was, his strategists correctly calculated that he could triumph against an unreformed communist, such as Gennadi Zyuganov.
29. Radio Free Europe/Radio Liberty (RFE/RL), *Newsline*, Part II, December 15, 1999.
30. Voting rules such as these have made it much harder than it might otherwise be to pass legislation. In effect, an absence, for any reason, is equivalent to a "no" vote. See pp. 185–86.
31. RFE/RL, *Newsline*, Part II, December 15, 1999.
32. RFE/RL, *Newsline*, Part II, January 25–31, 2000.
33. RFE/RL, *Newsline*, Part II, February 7, 2000.
34. RFE/RL, *Newsline*, Part II, January 9, 2000.
35. RFE/RL, *Newsline*, Part II, January 31, 2000.
36. RFE/RL, *Newsline*, Part II, February 28, 2000.
37. On the constitutional issues, see Peter Byrne, "Governing by Referendum No Way to Govern," *Kyiv Post*, January 20, 2000, p. 5.
38. Askold Krushelnycky, "Council of Europe to Debate Ukraine's Suspension," RFE/RL *Newsline*, Part II, March 31, 2000.
39. Ukrainian Center for Independent Political Research Research, *Update*, April 17, 2000.
40. Quoted in Roman Woronowycz, "Constitutional Court Rejects Two Questions of Ukraine's Controversial National Referendum," *Ukrainian Weekly*, April 2, 2000.
41. Viktor Luhovyk, "Rada Poll a No-Brainer," *Kyiv Post*, April 20, 2000, p. 1.
42. *Ukraine Today*, April 17, 2000.
43. Interviews with voters from around Ukraine, May 2000. These tactics are addressed further in Chapter Nine.
44. Ukrainian Center for Independent Political Research, *Update*, April 17, 2000.
45. RFE/RL, *Newsline*, Part II, April 11; April 17, 2000.
46. RFE/RL, *Newsline*, May 18, 2000.
47. Peter Byrne, "Rada Rubber-Stamps Kuchma Power Play," *Kyiv Post*, July 20, 2000, p. 1.
48. See Andrew Wilson, *Virtual Politics: Faking Democracy in the Post-Soviet World* (New Haven, CT: Yale University Press, 2005).
49. For detailed accounts and analyses of the Orange Revolution, see Anders Aslund and Michael McFaul, *Revolution in Orange: Origins of Ukraine's Democratic Breakthrough* (Washington, DC: Carnegie Endowment for International Peace, 2006); and Andrew Wilson, *Ukraine's Orange Revolution* (New Haven, CT: Yale University Press, 2005).
50. See James Sherr, "Ukraine's Parliamentary Elections: The Limits of Mani lation," CSRC Occasional Brief, April 21, 2002.
51. This is captured in great detail in Wilson, *Ukraine's Orange Revolution*.

52. Interviews in Lviv, June 2004.

53. See Paul D'Anieri, "Explaining the Success and Failure of Post-Communist Revolutions," paper presented at the annual convention of the Association for the Study of Nationalities, Columbia University, New York, March 23, 2006.

54. One attempt to explore the role of the security services is C.J. Chivers, "How Top Spies in Ukraine Changed the Nation's Path," *New York Times*, January 17, 2005, p. 1. For additional analysis and a critique of Chivers's view, see Taras Kuzio, "Did Ukraine's Security Services Really Prevent Bloodshed during the Orange Revolution?" *Eurasia Daily Monitor*, January 24, 2005, at http://www.taraskuzio.net/elections2004/revolution_sbu.pdf, accessed July 10, 2006.

55. Interfax, November 29, 2004; BBC Monitoring International Reports, November 29, 2004.

56. *Financial Times*, November 30, 2004.

57. See Michael McFaul, "Transitions from Postcommunism," *Journal of Democracy* 16, no. 3 (July 2005): 17–18.

58. Even if we assume that Yanukovych still benefited in the rerun from the measures that had been applied in the first two rounds, it is difficult to avoid the conclusion that most of the votes for him were legitimate.

5. Societal Divisions and the Challenge of Liberal Democracy in Ukraine

1. Roman Solchanyk, *Ukraine and Russia: The Post-Soviet Transition* (Lanham, MD: Rowman and Littlefield, 2001), 135–36. For predictions of Ukraine's collapse, see among others: "Ukraine: The Birth and Possible Death of a Country," *Economist*, May 7, 1994; Eugene B. Rumer, "Letter from Eurasia: Will Ukraine Return to Russia?" *Foreign Policy*, no. 96 (Fall 1994): 129–44; P. Klebnikov, "Tinderbox," *Forbes*, September 9, 1996; and F. Stephen Larabee, "Ukraine: Europe's Next Crisis?" *Arms Control Today*, 24, no. 6 (July/August 1994): 14–19.

2. Studies deriving the number of parties primarily from cleavage structures are listed in Octavio Amorim Neto and Gary Cox, "Electoral Institutions, Cleavage Structures, and the Number of Parties," *American Journal of Political Science* 41, no. 1 (January 1999): 149, especially note 2.

3. Scott Mainwaring, "Presidentialism, Multiparty Systems, and Democracy: The Difficult Equation," *Comparative Political Studies* 26, no. 2 (1993): 198–230.

4. Some of the more notable studies are: Domnique Arel, "Ukraine: The Temptation of the Nationalizing State," in *Political Culture and Civil Society in Russia and the New States of Eurasia*, ed. Vladimir Tismaneanu (Armonk, NY: M.E. Sharpe, 1995), pp. 157–188; Dominique Arel, "Language Politics in Independent Ukraine: Towards One or Two State Languages?" *Nationalities Papers* 23, no. 3 (September 1995): 597–622; Dominique Arel and Valery Khmelko, "The Russian Factor and Territorial Polarization in Ukraine," *Harriman Review* 9, nos. 1–2 (Spring 1996): 81–91; Lowell W. Barrington, "The Geographic Component of Mass Attitudes in Ukraine," *Post-Soviet Geography and Economics* 38, no. 10 (December 1997): 601–14; Sarah Birch, "Interpreting the Regional Effect in Ukrainian Politics," *Europe-Asia Studies* 52, no. 6 (2000): 1017–41; Peter R. Craumer and James I. Clem, "Ukraine's Emerging Electoral Geography: A Regional Analysis of the 1998 Parliamentary Elections," *Post-Soviet Geography and Economics* 40, no. 1 (January 1999): 1–26; Vicki L. Hesli, "Public Support for the Devolution of Power in Ukraine: Regional Patterns," *Europe-*

Asia Studies 47, no. 1 (1995): 91–121; Paul Kubicek, "Post-Soviet Ukraine: In Search of a Constituency for Reform," *Journal of Communist Studies and Transition Politics* 13, no. 3 (September 1997): 103–26; Taras Kuzio, *Ukraine: State and Nation Building* (London: Routledge, 1998); Taras Kuzio and Paul D'Anieri, eds., *Dilemmas of State-Led Nation Building in Ukraine* (Westport, CT: Praeger, 2003); George Liber, "Imagined Ukraine: Regional Differences and the Emergence of an Integrated State Identity," *Nations and Nationalism* 4, no. 2 (April 1998): 187–206; David Saunders, "What Makes a Nation a Nation? Ukrainians since 1600," *Ethnic Groups* 10 (1993): 101–24; Zenovia A. Sochor, "No Middle Ground? On the Difficulties of Crafting a Consensus in Ukraine," *Harriman Review* 9, nos. 1–2 (Spring–Summer 1996): 57–61; Roman Solchanyk, "The Politics of State Building: Center-Periphery Relations in Post-Soviet Ukraine," *Europe-Asia Studies* 46, no. 1 (January–February 1994): 47–68; Stephen Shulman, "International and National Integration in Multiethnic States: The Sources of Ukrainian (Dis)Unity," Ph.D. diss., University of Michigan, 1996; Catherine Wanner, *Burden of Dreams. History and Identity in Post-Soviet Ukraine* (University Park: Pennsylvania State University Press, 1998); Andrew Wilson, *Ukrainian Nationalism in the 1990s, A Minority Faith* (Cambridge: Cambridge University Press, 1997); Andrew Wilson and Valeri Khmelko, "Regionalism and Ethnic and Linguistic Cleavages in Ukraine," in *Contemporary Ukraine: Dynamics of Post-Soviet Transformation,* ed. Taras Kuzio (Armonk, NY: M.E. Sharpe, 1998), pp. 60–80; Sharon L. Wolchik and Volodymyr Zviglyanich, *Ukraine: The Search for National Identity* (Lanham, MD: Rowman and Littlefield, 2001); and William Zimmerman, "Is Ukraine a Political Community?" *Communist and Post-Communist Studies* 31, no. 1 (1998): 43–55.

5. For a general treatment of Ukrainians' "political mentality," see V.I. Chyhrynov and I.O. Polishchuk, *Politychna mentalnist ukrainskoho suspilstva: Istoriya i modern* (Kharkiv: KhIBM, 2001).

6. Sarah Birch, for example, points to five distinct regions in Ukraine, based on different patterns of historical rule in those regions. See "Interpreting the Regional Effect," 1019, especially Table 5.1. See also Lowell Barrington and Erik Herron, "One Ukraine Or Many? Regionalism in Ukraine and Its Political Consequences," *Nationalities Papers* 32, no. 1 (March 2004): 53–86; and Barrington, "The Geographic Component of Mass Attitudes in Ukraine," 601–14.

7. On the overlapping of Ukrainian and Russian identity, see Orest Subtelny, "Russocentrism, Regionalism, and the Political Culture of Ukraine," in *Political Culture and Civil Society in Russia and the New States of Eurasia,* ed. Vladimir Tismaneanu (Armonk, NY: M.E. Sharpe) 1995, pp. 189–208.

8. Various aspects of this question have been investigated: See Andrew Wilson and Sarah Birch, "Voting Stability, Political Gridlock: Ukraine's 1998 Parliamentary Elections," *Europe-Asia Studies* 51, no. 6 (1999): 1039–68; Sarah Birch, "Party System Formation and Voting Behavior in the Ukrainian Parliamentary Elections of 1994," in *Contemporary Ukraine: Dynamics of Post-Soviet Transformation,* ed. Taras Kuzio (New York: M.E. Sharpe, 1998), 138–60; and Paul Kubicek, "Regional Polarisation in Ukraine: Public Opinion, Voting and Legislative Behavior," *Europe-Asia Studies* 52, no. 2 (2000): 273–94.

9. Paul Pirie, "National Identity and Politics in Southern and Eastern Ukraine," *Europe-Asia Studies* 47, no. 7 (November 1996): 1079–104.

10. Lowell W. Barrington, "Region, Language, and Nationality: Rethinking Support in Ukraine for Maintaining Distance From Russia," in *Dilemmas of State-Led*

Nation Building in Ukraine, ed. Taras Kuzio and Paul D'Anieri (Westport, CT: Praeger, 2003), pp. 131–46.

11. Kubicek, "Post-Soviet Ukraine," 109.

12. See Sarah Birch, *Elections and Democratization in Ukraine* (London: Macmillan, 2000); Birch, "Interpreting the Regional Effect"; Andrew Wilson and Sarah Birch, "Voting Stability, Political Gridlock: Ukraine's 1998 Parliamentary Elections," *Europe-Asia Studies* 51, no. 6 (1999): 1039–68; and Steven D. Roper and Florin Fesnic, "Historical Legacies and Their Impact on Post-Communist Voting Behavior," *Europe-Asia Studies* 55, no. 1 (2003): 119–31.

13. Ukrainian Central Election Commission data; author's calculations.

14. Based on Ukrainian Central Election Commission data; author's calculations. For summary data, see "Vidomosti pro pidrakhunok holosiv vybortsiv v mezhakh rehioniv Ukrainy," www.cvk.gov.ua/vnd2006/w6p001.html. Accessed April 20, 2006.

15. The vast majority of votes were not on substantive issues or even on the agenda, but on questions to be put to various ministers.

16. The Socialist Party ran jointly with the Peasants Party in the 1998 elections.

17. Rada Web site, http://guru.rada.kiev.ua:2000/, accessed June 20–25, 2000; author's calculations.

18. Relationships among Ukraine's leftist parties are analyzed by Andrew Wilson, "The Ukrainian Left: In Transition to Social Democracy or Still in Thrall to the USSR?" *Europe-Asia Studies* 49, no. 7 (1997): 1293–316.

19. This claim is demonstrated by spatial analysis of Rada voting conducted by the Kyiv NGO Laboratory F-4. Their analysis of all of the parliamentary votes in the sixth session of the Rada (September 2000–January 2001) shows a fairly normal left/right split. Analysis of a subset of votes that occurred after the release of tapes implicating Kuchma in Gongadze's death showed two dimensions of conflict, with those on the right divided both from the CPU and from each other. See *Verkhovna Rada Week*, no. 12 (29), February 7, 2001.

20. "Symonenko ne bachit riznitsi mizh 'komandamy' Kychmy ta Yushchenka," UNIAN, as cited in www.Pravda.com.ua, February 2, 2003. Accessed March 10, 2003.

21. Sharon LaFraniere, "Split Opposition Falters in Ukraine; Divisions Help Kuchma Retain Power," *Washington Post,* April 21, 2001.

22. On Yushchenko's dilemma, see Roman Olearchyk, "In Search of a Rada Majority," KPNews.com, April 4, 2002. Accessed April 6, 2002.

23. On the Socialists' position toward working with the pro-presidential parties in parliament, see the interview with Yuriy Lutsenko of the Socialist Party in *Den,* April 11, 2002.

24. See Serhii Rakhmanin, Yulia Mostovaya, and Olga Dmitricheva, "The End of the Dead Season," *Dzerkalo nedeli,* July 27–August 3, 2002.

25. "Zayava fraktsiy bloku 'Nasha Ukraina,' KPU, SPU ta Bloku Yulii Tymoshenko: Pro fakt pochatku derzhavnoho perevorotu v Ukraini," Press Service of Our Ukraine, December 12, 2002. The declaration protested the means used by the parliamentary leadership to install Serhiy Tyhypko as director of the National Bank of Ukraine. The four groups continued to work together on the issue, with Yushchenko speaking for all of them, in proposing a compromise on December 19. See Radio Free Europe/Radio Liberty (RFE/RL), *Newsline* 6, no. 238, Part II, December 20, 2002.

26. RFE/RL, *Newsline* 7, no. 32, Part II, February 19, 2003.

27. Kostenko's views are elaborated in an interview in *Den,* June 3, 2003.

28. RFE/RL, *Newsline* 6, no. 146, Part II, August 6, 2002.

29. RFE/RL, *Newsline* 6, no. 82, Part II, May 2, 2002.

30. Viktor Yushchenko, "There Will Be a Presidential Election, Come What May," *Zerkalo tyzhdnia,* December 26, 2003–January 9, 2004.

31. See "Symonenko Khochet Referendum po Politreforme," *Ukrainskaya pravda,* www.pravda.ua, December 26, 2003. Accessed January 4, 2004.

32. Maurice Duverger, "Duverger's Law: Forty Years Later, in *Electoral Laws and Their Political Consequences,* ed. Bernard Grofman and Arend Lijphart (New York: Agathon Press, 1986), 19–42; See also Maurice Duverger, *Political Parties: Their Organization and Activity in the Modern State*, 2nd ed., translated by Barbara and Robert North (New York: Wiley, 1966), Neto and Cox, "Electoral Institutions," 149.

33. Solchanyk, *Ukraine and Russia,* 139. Taras Kuzio is more equivocal, stating that there is nothing to prevent such a situation arising in the future. See *Ukraine: State and Nation Building,* 46.

34. Giovanni Sartori, "The Influence of Electoral Systems: Faulty Laws or Faulty Method?" in *Electoral Laws and Their Political Consequences,* ed. Bernard Grofman and Arend Lijphart (New York: Agathon Press, 1986), 59.

35. Neto and Cox, "Electoral Institutions," 149. See also Peter C. Ordeshook and Olga Shvetsova, "Ethnic Heterogeneity, District Magnitude, and the Number of Parties," *American Journal of Political Science* 38 (1994): 100–123.

36. Neto and Cox, "Electoral Institutions," 155.

37. Juan Linz, "The Perils of Presidentialism," *Journal of Democracy* 1 (Winter 1990): 51–71.

38. Roman Solchanyk advocated this for Ukraine. See *Ukraine and Russia,* 119.

39. A prominent example of this line of research is James L. Gibson, "A Mile Wide But an Inch Deep(?): The Structure of Democratic Commitments in the Former USSR," *American Journal of Political Science* 40, no. 2 (May 1996): 396–420.

40. This question is addressed in Paul D'Anieri "The Mitigation of Ethnic Conflict in Ukraine: The Mysterious Case of the State that Didn't Collapse," paper presented at the annual meeting of the American Political Science Association, Boston, August 31–September 3, 1998.

6. The Constitution and Executive-Legislative Relations

1. George Tsebelis, *Nested Games: Rational Choice in Comparative Politics* (Berkeley: University of California Press, 1990).

2. "At least in theory" is an important qualification in the Ukrainian case, where "normal" legislation has sometimes trumped the constitution. The most notable example was the Constitutional Court's ruling on Kuchma's right to hold a referendum in 2000.

3. The question of whether Ukraine should be defined as a "presidential," "semi-presidential," "president-parliamentary," or "parliamentary presidential" system is discussed in depth below.

4. Gerald M. Easter, "Preference for Presidentialism: Postcommunist Regime Change in Russia and the NIS," *World Politics* 49 (January 1997): 184–211.

5. Kataryna Wolczuk, *The Moulding of Ukraine: The Constitutional Politics of State Formation* (Budapest: Central European University Press, 2001); Bohdan Harasymiw, *Post-Communist Ukraine* (Edmonton: Canadian Institute of Ukrainian Studies, 2002), ch. 2. See also Oliver Vorndran, "The Constitutional Process in Ukraine: Context and Structure," University of Birmingham Center for Russian and East European Studies, Occasional Paper 97/3 (December 1997).

6. Wolczuk, *The Moulding of Ukraine*, ch. 1.

7. This is stressed in Harasymiw, *Post-Communist Ukraine*, and Vorndran, "The Constitutional Process in Ukraine."

8. Andrew Wilson, "Ukraine: Two Presidents and Their Powers," in *Postcommunist Presidents*, ed. Ray Taras (Cambridge: Cambridge University Press, 1997), 67–105.

9. In addition to Wolczuk, *The Moulding of Ukraine*, and Harasymiw, *Post-Communist Ukraine*, the origins of the 1996 constitution are detailed in Vorndran, "The Constitutional Process in Ukraine."

10. Wolczuk, *The Moulding of Ukraine*, 119. The process from 1991 to 1994 is also described in Vorndran, "The Constitutional Process in Ukraine," 5–7 and Harasymiw, *Post-Communist Ukraine*, ch. 2.

11. Wolczuk, *The Moulding of Ukraine*, 192.

12. Ibid., 206.

13. Vorndran, "The Constitutional Process in Ukraine," 8.

14. Harasymiw, *Post-Communist Ukraine*, 65.

15. Vorndran, "The Constitutional Process in Ukraine," 2; Harasymiw, *Post-Communist Ukraine*, 65–66.

16. Vorndran, "The Constitutional Process in Ukraine," 9.

17. *OMRI Daily Digest*, part II, February 17, 1995.

18. Wolczuk, *The Moulding of Ukraine*, 192.

19. *OMRI Daily Digest*, part II, April 5, 1995.

20. *OMRI Daily Digest*, part II, April 18, May 15, 1995.

21. *OMRI Daily Digest*, part II, May 19, 1995.

22. *OMRI Daily Digest*, part II, May 26, 31, 1995.

23. *OMRI Daily Digest*, part II, May 30, June 1, 1995.

24. *OMRI Daily Digest*, part II, June 8, 1995.

25. Wolczuk, *The Moulding of Ukraine*, 197.

26. Ibid., 197–98.

27. Quoted in ibid., 198.

28. Ibid., 198–99; Vorndran, "The Constitutional Process in Ukraine," 16–17.

29. The local government provisions of the 1996 constitution are discussed in Harasymiw, *Post-Communist Ukraine*, 74.

30. This draft also called for a bicameral parliament, with an upper house representing the regions. This was viewed by many as a further weakening of the parliament, by making it much less likely that a parliament united in opposition to the president would arise.

31. Vorndran, "The Constitutional Process in Ukraine," 15.

32. Wolczuk, *The Moulding of Ukraine*, 200. Vorndran, "The Constitutional Process in Ukraine," 16–18, discusses the maneuvering within parliament over the composition of the group that would draft the new constitution.

33. Vorndran, "The Constitutional Process in Ukraine," 20.

34. For a comparative study of the use of referendums to circumvent established rules, see Mark Clarence Walker, *The Strategic Use of Referendums: Power, Legitimacy, and Democracy* (New York: Palgrave MacMillan, 2003).

35. Wolczuk, *The Moulding of Ukraine*, 204.

36. Vorndran, "The Constitutional Process in Ukraine," 26.

37. Wolczuk, *The Moulding of Ukraine*, 201.

38. Harasymiw, *Post-Communist Ukraine*, 77.

39. Oleh Protsyk, "Troubled Semi-Presidentialism: Stability of the Constitutional

System and Cabinet in Ukraine," *Europe-Asia Studies* 55, no. 7 (2003): 1077–95.

40. Alfred Stepan and Cindy Skach, "Constitutional Frameworks and Democratic Consolidation: Parliamentarism versus Presidentialism," *World Politics* 46, no. 1 (October 1993): 3–4.

41. Alfred Stepan, "Ukraine: Improbable Democratic 'Nation-State' But Possible Democratic 'State-Nation,'" *Post-Soviet Studies* 24, no. 4 (December 2005): 279–308.

42. For an attempt to distinguish between "semi-presidential" and "president-parliamentary" systems, see Mathew Soberg Shugart and John M. Carey, *Presidents and Assemblies: Constitutional Design and Electoral Dynamics* (Cambridge: Cambridge University Press, 1992), 18–27.

43. Juan Linz, "The Perils of Presidentialism," *Journal of Democracy* 1 (Winter 1990): 53.

44. Giovanni Sartori, *Comparative Constitutional Engineering: An Inquiry into Structures, Incentives, and Outcomes*, 2d ed. (New York: New York University Press, 1997), 83–4.

45. Linz, "The Perils of Presidentialism," 53.

46. Ibid.

47. Ibid., 53.

48. On the legality of the referendum, see Katya Gorchinskaya, "Ukraine Set to Vote Again," *Kyiv Post*, January 20, 2000. English versions of the six referendum questions are in the same issue of the *Kyiv Post*.

49. Linz, "The Perils of Presidentialism," 61.

50. Ibid., 63.

51. Ibid., 56.

52. The coalition parameters were outlined in Yulia Mostova, *I Tse Mynet'sia . . . Dzerkalo Tyzhnia*, 5–19 August 2006, at http://www.zn.kiev.ua/nn/index/609/, accessed August 10, 2006.

53. Viktor Yushchenko, "Reform Is Not a Game," *Zerkalo nedeli*, August 23–29, 2003. He went on in the same statement to refute the argument that he supported the presidential model because he was the front-runner for that position, and wanted to keep it as powerful as possible.

54. Shugart and Carey, *Presidents and Assemblies*, 33.

55. Ibid., 34.

56. Ibid., 177. Note that there is some disagreement on this point, for example, from Powell, who argues that presidentialism leads to a stronger party system. See G. Bingham Powell, *Contemporary Democracies: Participation, Stability, and Violence* (Cambridge, MA: Harvard University Press, 1982), 101, cited in Octavio Amorim Neto and Gary Cox, "Electoral Institutions, Cleavage Structures, and the Number of Parties," *American Journal of Political Science* 41, no. 1 (January 1999): 153.

57. Sartori, *Comparative Constitutional Engineering*, p. 42.

58. This section is based on Paul D'Anieri, "What Has Changed in Ukrainian Politics? Assessing the Implications of the 'Orange Revolution,'" *Problems of Post-Communism* (September–October 2005): 82–91.

7. The Electoral Law: Cause or Effect of Weak Parties?

1. *Ukrainian Society, 1994–1998* (Kyiv: Democratic Initiatives Foundation, 1998).

2. For the methodology of measuring the effective number of parties, see Markku Laasko and Rein Taagepera, "Effective Number of Parties: Measurement with Appli-

cation to Western Europe," *Comparative Political Studies* 12 (1979): 3–27. See also Arend Lijphart, *Electoral Systems and Party Systems: A Study of Twenty-Seven Democracies, 1945–1990* (New York: Oxford University Press, 1995). This approach is applied to postcommunist states in Robert G. Moser, "Electoral Systems and the Number of Parties in Postcommunist States," *World Politics* 51, no. 3 (1999): 359–84.

3. See Peter C. Ordeshook and Olga V. Shvetsova, "Ethnic Heterogeneity, District Magnitude, and the Number of Parties," *American Journal of Political Science* 38, no. 1 (February 1994): 100–124.

4. Ibid.

5. Octavio Amorim Neto and Gary Cox, "Electoral Institutions, Cleavage Structures, and the Number of Parties," *American Journal of Political Science* 41 (January 1997): 149–74.

6. The point was acknowledged, though not emphasized, by Duverger, and has been stated more forcefully by Gary Cox. See Cox, *Making Votes Count: Strategic Coordination in the World's Electoral Systems* (New York: Cambridge University Press, 1997), 27–29.

7. Giovanni Sartori, "The Influence of Electoral Systems: Faulty Laws or Faulty Method?" in *Electoral Laws and Their Political Consequences*, ed. Bernard Grofman and Arend Lijphart (New York: Agathon Press, 1986), 43–68.

8. Giovanni Sartori, *Comparative Constitutional Engineering: An Inquiry into Structures, Incentives, and Outcomes*, 2d ed. (New York: New York University Press, 1997), 42.

9. Ukraine's voting behavior does show polarization in a different sense of the term: the regional voting patterns in the 2004 presidential elections show clear differences between eastern/southern Ukraine and the rest. However, what is lacking is an intensity of difference.

10. Sartori, *Comparative Constitutional Engineering*, 40–41.

11. Melvin J. Hinich, Valeri Khmelko, and Peter C. Ordeshook, "Ukraine's 1998 Parliamentary Elections: A Spatial Analysis," *Post-Soviet Affairs* (April–June 1999): 183.

12. See William Riker, "Duverger's Law Revisited," in *Electoral Laws and Their Political Consequences*, ed. Bernard Grofman and Arend Lijphart (New York: Agathon Press, 1986), 30; Sartori, *Comparative Constitutional Engineering*, 47.

13. Erik Herron, "Causes and Consequences of Fluid Faction Membership in Ukraine," *Europe-Asia Studies* 54, no. 4 (2002): 625–39.

14. Vicki L. Hesli, "Issue Voting in Ukraine," paper presented at the annual meeting of the Midwest Political Science Association, April 15–18 1999, Chicago, 1–2.

15. The parties (and their leading individuals) were the Tymoshenko Bloc (Yulia Tymoshenko), Our Ukraine (Viktor Yushchenko), the Socialist Party of Ukraine (Oleksandr Moroz), and the Party of Regions (Viktor Yanukovych). Only the Communist Party, which is rapidly declining, did not lean on a particular personality. Of the others, only the Party of Regions could be expected to survive the departure of its leading figure.

16. Rein Taagepera and Matthew Soberg Shugart, *Seats and Votes: The Effects and Determinants of Electoral Systems* (New Haven, CT: Yale University Press, 1999), 4.

17. In Russia, the threshold is 5 percent; in Ukraine it was 4 percent in 1998 and 2002, and 3 percent in 2006.

18. Erik S. Herron and Misa Nishikawa, "Contamination Effects and the Number of Parties in Mixed-Superposition Electoral Systems." *Electoral Studies* 20 (March

2001): 63–86. See also Federico Ferrara, Erik Herron, and Misa Nishikawa, *Mixed Electoral Systems: Contamination and Its Consequences* (New York: Palgrave, 2005).

19. Robert G. Moser, *Unexpected Outcomes: Electoral Systems, Political Parties, and Representation in Russia* (Pittsburgh, PA: University of Pittsburgh Press, 2000), 4.

20. Matthew Soberg Shugart and Martin P. Wattenberg, eds., *Mixed-Member Electoral Systems: The Best of Both Worlds?* (Oxford: Oxford University Press, 2001).

21. Sartori, *Comparative Constitutional Engineering*, 74–75.

22. Matthew Soberg Shugart and John M. Carey, *Presidents and Assemblies: Constitutional Design and Electoral Dynamics* (New York: Cambridge University Press, 1992), 213.

23. Sartori, *Comparative Constitutional Engineering*, 40.

24. In the next chapter, it will be shown that while party list voting eliminates nominal independents from being elected, it does not, by itself, eliminate members of parliament from behaving like independents once elected. Further rules, most notably the "imperative mandate," in which a member loses his/her seat when he/she abandons the party to whom the seat belongs, are necessary to ensure that members do not behave independently of their parties.

25. Shugart and Wattenberg (*Mixed-Member Electoral Systems*) see the ability to retain local representation as one of the significant benefits of the mixed system.

26. These views were all expressed in interviews with policymakers and political scientists in Kyiv in the summer of 1996.

27. This point is made in a cross-national context in seminal electoral studies such as Seymour Martin Lipset and Stein Rokkan, "Cleavage Structures, Party Systems, and Voting Alignments: An Introduction," in *Party Systems and Voter Alignments: Cross National Perspectives*, ed. Lipset and Rokkan (New York: Free Press, 1967), 113–85.

28. Herron, "Causes and Consequences," 629–30, shows that placement on the party list did indeed influence party loyalty in the parliament elected in 1998.

29. This argument is consistent with that made by Herron and Nishikawa, "Contamination Effects and the Number of Parties."

30. In addition to the ways described here, other ways in which mixed electoral systems can lead to party system fragmentation are discussed in Ferrara, Herron, and Nishikawa, *Mixed Electoral Systems*, ch. 8.

31. International Foundation for Election Systems, www.ifes-ukraine.org/english/Elections1998/ Deputies/index.html, accessed March 10, 1999; *Ukrainian Weekly*, www.ukrweekly.com/Archive/1998/149810.shtml, accessed March 10, 1999.

32. Data from Ukraine Central Electoral Commission, http://195.230.157.53/pls/vd2002/webproc0e, accessed March 25, 2002.

33. Author's calculations based on Central Election Commission data.

34. Data from Central Election Commission; author's calculations. The totals that parties received in the PR half of the parliament were simply doubled to determine what they would have received were the entire parliament determined on that basis.

35. The need to include the Party of Regions, in order to represent eastern Ukraine in the coalition, is argued by Dominique Arel, "The Virtue of Mistrust and Regional Rivalries," paper presented at the Roundtable on Ukrainian Elections, University of Toronto, April 11, 2006, as printed in the *Ukraine List,* no. 388, April 18, 2006. Support for an "orange coalition" is articulated in Tammy Lynch, "Fancy Cars and Hope Clash in Ukraine," UNIAN, April 17, 2006; and Taras Kuzio, "Parliamentary Elections to Have Geopolitical Implications," *Kyiv Post,* April 13, 2006.

36. Shugart and Carey, *Presidents and Assemblies*, 207–13.

37. Robert G. Moser, "The Electoral Effects of Presidentialism in Post-Soviet Russia," in *Party Politics in Post-Communist Russia*, ed. John Löwenhardt (London: Frank Cass, 1998), 54–75.

38. Yulia Tishchenko, *Vybory-99: Yak i Koho My Obyraly* (Kyiv: UNTsPD, 1999), 230.

39. One should not overestimate the salience of this fact, but even in pre-Soviet Ukraine, there was some tendency to vote for independents. In the elections to the first Russian Duma in 1906, Sarah Birch shows that 65 percent of voters in regions that are today part of Ukraine voted for independents, and the leading party (the Kadets) received only 11.8 percent of the vote. See Sarah Birch, "Interpreting the Regional Effect in Ukrainian Politics," *Europe-Asia Studies* 52, no. 6 (2000): 1023.

40. Sartori, "The Influence of Electoral Systems," 55.

41. Ibid., 55–56.

42. For an overview of this process, see "2001 Political Sketches: Too Early for Summing Up," UCIPR Research Report 8, no. 1/249, January 4, 2002.

43. "Yushchenko formuye komandu na vybory. U NRU novyi lider," *Ukrainska Pravda*, May 3, 2003, www.pravda.com.ua, accessed June 10, 2003.

44. *Lvivska Hazeta*, February 14, 2005; Razom.org, February 14, 2005.

45. In addition, as noted previously, in Ukraine, such a system is likely to produce two parties within each distinct electoral region, but not necessarily overall. Nonetheless, this would still have a consolidating effect, even if more than two parties resulted.

46. In the immense literature on party systems and electoral laws, Sartori is one of the few authors who gives more than cursory treatment to the existing strength of the party system as an important independent variable. Most of the well-known analyses begin with the assumption that the party system is already somewhat well formed, and therefore can be applied to Ukraine only with caution. Sartori's analysis is therefore especially useful in understanding Ukraine and many other new democracies. *Comparative Constitutional Engineering*, 42–44; "The Influence of Electoral Systems," 55–57.

47. Sartori, *Comparative Constitutional Engineering*, 43–44.

48. Ibid., 44.

8. Parliamentary Rules and Party Development

1. For an introductory overview, see Walter J. Oleszek, *Congressional Procedures and the Policy Process*, 6th ed. (Washington, DC: Congressional Quarterly, 2003).

2. See Michael Laver and Kenneth R. Benoit, "The Evolution of Party Systems between Elections," *American Journal of Political Science* 47, no. 2 (April 2003): 215–33. Laver and Benoit see the incentives to defect (and for parties to accept defectors) as driven solely by electoral considerations, not parliamentary rules (216–18).

3. Giovanni Sartori, *Comparative Constitutional Engineering*, 2d ed. (New York: New York University Press, 1997), 177. Sartori points out that undisciplined parties are inherently more problematic for parliamentary systems than for presidential systems, because parliamentary systems have no fallback when there is no majority, whereas presidential systems have some ability to govern even in the absence of a majority.

4. Kenneth A. Shepsle and Barry R. Weingast, "Positive Theories of Congressional Institutions," in *Positive Theories of Congressional Institutions*, ed. Shepsle and Weingast (Ann Arbor: University of Michigan Press, 1995), 5–35.

5. Michel Duverger, "Duverger's Law: Forty Years Later," in *Electoral Laws and Their Political Consequences*, ed. Bernard Grofman and Arend Lijphart (New York: Agathon Press, 1986), 81.

6. "'For Our Single Ukraine': Hard Pre-election Blocking," Ukrainian Center for Independent Political Research (UCIPR) Research Update, November 13, 2001.

7. Andrew Wilson, "Ukraine's 2002 Elections: Less Fraud, More Virtuality," *East European Constitutional Review* (Summer 2002): 93. www.Pravda.com.ua/?20620-fraction-new. Accessed June 20, 2002.

8. A similar phenomenon takes place in very rare cases and on a very small scale in the U.S. Congress, when an independent is allowed to "caucus" with one major party or the other, and hence to avoid being completely shut out of committee work.

9. Constitutional Court Decision N17-rp/98, December 3, 1998.

10. The effect of parliamentary rules on party systems has received very little attention in the literature. However, rules are used to explain a wide variety of outcomes within a given legislature, and thus have received increasing attention by the "second generation" of scholars of the U.S. Congress. See Shepsle and Weingast, "Positive Theories of Congressional Institutions," 7.

11. Radio Free Europe/Radio Liberty, *Daily Digest*, December 17, 1999.

12. Interviews in Kyiv, October 2003.

13. Sarah Whitmore, "Fragmentation or Consolidation: Parties in Ukraine's Parliament," University of Birmingham, *Research Papers in Russian and East European Studies* (2002): 28.

14. Erik Herron quantifies the relative influence of policy versus electoral and party-based motivations for defections from factions in the 1998–2002 parliament. See Erik Herron, "Causes and Consequences of Fluid Faction Membership in Ukraine," *Europe-Asia Studies* 54, no. 4 (2002): 625–39.

15. On the role of personality clashes in party coalescence, see Michael Laver and Norman Schofield, *Multiparty Government: The Politics of Coalition in Europe* (Oxford: Oxford University Press, 1990), 199. That this occurs in Ukraine is confirmed by interviews conducted with members of the Party of Reforms and Order Lviv regional organization, May 12, 1999.

16. George Tsebelis, *Nested Games: Rational Choice in Comparative Politics* (Berkeley: University of California Press, 1990), 190.

17. See Vladimir Katzman, "Kapitalisty, kupite sebe po Kommunistu," *Zerkalo Nedeli*, April 18–24, 1998, p. 1.

18. Radio Free Europe/Radio Liberty (RFE/RL), *Newsline* 4, no. 14, Part II, January 20, 2000.

19. The Ukrainian nongovernmental organization Lab F-4 compiles all roll-call votes, and performs a variety of analyses of the data. But since 2000, there has been no readily available listing of parliamentary voting records.

20. Sarah Whitmore, who has spent considerable time observing the Rada firsthand, reports that both attendance and party discipline increased following the adoption of roll-call voting. See "Fragmentation or Consolidation," 23.

21. "Political tourism" is the popular term in Ukraine for the tendency of deputies to change factions.

22. The best explanation that I can imagine for this rule is that it was instituted

to prevent the parliament from being rapidly called into session to pass legislation with a narrow selection of legislators. In most systems, that possibility is ruled out by strict rules concerning the convening of parliament and by quorum requirements. In fact, Ukraine's parliament has laid out in the rules a very clear schedule for when "plenary" or voting sessions will take place and when "working sessions" will take place. It is not clear that the 226 vote requirement serves any useful purpose.

23. Personal communication from Taras Kuzio, August 5, 2006.

24. "'Nasha Ukraina' proty 'Mihratsii' deputativ," Courier.com.ua, December 12, 2002, at www.courier.com.ua. Accessed December 20, 2002.

25. Ukrainska Pravda, August 7, 2006, at www.pravda.com.ua/en/news_print/2006/8/7/6027.htm. Accessed August 15, 2006.

9. How Power Politics Trumps Institutional Design

1. Some of the research in this chapter was originally put forward in Paul D'Anieri, "Machine Politics in Ukraine," paper presented at the annual convention of the American Association for the Advancement of Slavic Studies, Toronto, November 21, 2003, and subsequently, in abbreviated form, in D'Anieri, "The Last Hurrah: The 2004 Ukrainian Presidential Elections and the Limits of Machine Politics," *Communist and Post-Communist Societies* 38 (2005): 231–49.

2. Philip G. Roeder, "Varieties of Post-Soviet Authoritarian Regimes," *Post-Soviet* Affairs 10 (1994): 65–69.

3. See Bohdan Harasymiw, "Policing, Democratization and Political Leadership in Postcommunist Ukraine," *Canadian Journal of Political Science* 36, no. 2 (June 2003): 327–28.

4. Simon Johnson, Daniel Kaufmann, John McMillan, and Christopher Woodruff, "Why Do Firms Hide? Bribes and Unofficial Activity After Communism," EBRD (European Bank for Reconstruction and Development) Working Paper, no. 42 (October 1999).

5. Johnson et al., "Why Do Firms Hide," 2.

6. "New Tape Translation of Kuchma Allegedly Ordering Falsification of Presidential Election Returns," *Kyiv Post*, February 13, 2001, p. 1.

7. Blue Ribbon Commission for Ukraine, "Proposals for the President: A New Wave of Reform," 2005, 51; available at www.carnegieendowment.org/files/BRCReport121204Eng2.pdf.

8. Human Rights Watch, "Negotiating the News: Informal Censorship of Ukrainian Television," March 2003, http://www.hrw.org/reports/2003/ukraine0303/Ukraine0303.pdf, 9. Accessed June 30, 2005.

9. Organization for Security and Co-operation in Europe/Office for Democratic Institutions and Human Rights (OSCE/ODIHR), "Final Report, Ukraine Parliamentary Elections," March 31, 2002, 15; available at www.osce.org/odihr/documents/reports/election_reports/ua/ua_pe_march2002_efr.php.

10. Human Rights Watch, "Negotiating the News," 11.

11. *Den'*, September 21, 2000, 3.

12. The $250,000 figure is cited in "Administrativnyi resurs v deistvii: spikerom Verkhovnoi Rady izbran stavlennik Kuchmy," Pravda.ru, May 29, 2002; available at http://pravda.ru/kuchma/2002/05/29/41906.html. Accessed June 15, 2004. The $500,000 figure was asserted by Our Ukraine deputy Yuriy Orobets'. See "'Nasha

Urkaina' proty 'Mihratsii' deputativ," Courier.com.ua, December 12, 2002, www.courier.com.ua. Accessed December 20, 2002.

13. "Administrativnyi resurs v deistvii."

14. *Segodnya*, March 27, 2002, 1.

15. Ibid.

16. In a case laden with intrigue, some have speculated that after Kuchma was recorded making remarks about Gongadze, those who made the tapes and were seeking to embarrass Kuchma had Gongadze killed in order to implicate Kuchma and drive him from office. This is implausible, but not impossible, and it is certainly not the most implausible theory concerning the release of the tapes, the origins of which have never been satisfactorily accounted for.

17. Human Rights Watch, "Negotiating the News," 10.

18. Interview with a director of a Department of Information Policy, Kyiv, May 5, 2003. Tellingly, the official asked not to be identified by name, even though his remarks were in no way critical of the Kuchma government.

19. The use of *temniki* is analyzed at length in Human Rights Watch, "Negotiating the News." This report is quite thorough and contains several examples of *temniki* in an appendix.

20. OSCE/ODIHR, "Final Report, Ukraine Parliamentary Elections," 15.

21. Ibid., 15–16.

22. Human Rights Watch, "Negotiating the News," 17–18.

23. OSCE/ODIHR, "Final Report, Ukraine Parliamentary Elections," 14.

24. Human Rights Watch, "Negotiating the News," 9.

25. OSCE/ODIHR, "Final Report, Ukraine Parliamentary Elections," 3.

26. I am grateful to Taras Kuzio and Erik Herron for sharing their experiences as election monitors.

27. This argument is developed and supported with considerable statistical analysis in Erik S. Herron and Paul E. Johnson, "Fraud Before the 'Revolution': Special Precincts in Ukraine's 2002 Parliamentary Election," in *The 2004 Presidential Poll in Ukraine: A Case Study in Local and International Election Observation*, ed. Ingmar Bredies, Andreas Umland, and Valentin Yakushik (Stuttgart: Ibidem-Verlag, forthcoming).

28. These figures are from Herron and Johnson, "'Fraud Before the 'Revolution'"

29. Artem Storozhenko, "From Old to New Administrative Resource. Only with Peculiarities of 2002," PART.ORG.UA-Political Network Edition, November 20, 2002; available at http://part.org.ua/eng/print.php?art=29718943, Accessed January 14, 2003. See also the interview with Volodymyr Lupatsiy and Oleksandr Chernenko, "Deja Vue [sic] or We Have Already Seen This," PART.ORG.UA-Political Network Edition, November 23, 2002; available at http://part.org.ua/eng/print.php?art=29978792. Accessed January 14, 2003.

30. The problem of enforcing patronage is discussed in Vassyl Yurchyshyn, "Investment Future of Regions Will Depend on Administrative Resource's Functioning," PART.ORG.UA-Political Network Edition, October 12, 2001; available at http://part.org.ua/eng/print.php?art=31447215; and Ukrainian Center for Independent Political Research (UCIPR), "Political Season's Blocking Sublimation," *Research Update* 7, no. 30/231 (July 23, 2001): 2–3.

31. Votes at the embassy include not only those by embassy staff, but by Ukrainians resident in the United States who voted at the embassy. It means that more than a few votes are at stake, but still not enough to sway the election. It also means that

Buteyko was punished not for the direct disloyalty of him or his staff, but rather for the general failure to collect votes as dictated by the "machine."

32. *Ukraina moloda*, April 11, 1998, quoted in UCIPR, "Political Season's Blocking Sublimation," 2.

33. *Ukraina Moloda*, April 3, 1998, quoted in UCIPR, "Political Season's Blocking Sublimation," 2. By "partizing" the bureaucracy, Matvienko meant unifying the bureaucracy with the party so that the bureaucracy could do the work of the party.

34. Fraud in the 2004 election is covered in extensive detail in Andrew Wilson, *Ukraine's Orange Revolution* (New Haven, CT: Yale University Press, 2005).

35. OSCE/ODIHR, "Final Report, Ukraine Parliamentary Elections," 18.

36. Ibid., 9.

37. Ibid., 19.

38. *Ukraine Today*, April 17, 2000.

39. OSCE/ODIHR, "Final Report," 8.

40. See Yulia Tishchenko, *Vybory-99: Yak i koho my obyraly* (Kyiv: UNDTsP, 2000), especially ch. 9, 10, and 16.

41. See Steven Wagner and Elehie Skoczylas, "The 1999 Ukrainian Presidential Vote: A QEV Analytics Exit Poll Report," Figures 1 and 2, http://qev.com/reports.international.ukraine99exitpollgraphs.htm., accessed June 20, 2000.

42. See Wilson, *Ukraine's Orange Revolution.* Fraud and misconduct in 2004 were catalogued in "Ukraine Presidential Election: 31 October, 21 October and 26 December 2004 OSCE/ODIHR Election Observation Mission Final Report," May 11, 2005. For a series of reports of these various tactics, see the press releases of the Committee of Voters of Ukraine, www.cvu.org.ua/?menu=pres&po=election&topic_el=pres&lang=eng&date_end=&date_beg=&id=478, accessed March 20, 2005.

43. "Table of Some Provisions of the Law of Ukraine 'About the Judicial Organization,'" www.judges.org.ua/eng/sud-ukr.htm, accessed September 10, 2005.

44. U.S. State Department, "Country Reports on Human Rights Practices, Ukraine," 8.

45. Ibid., 9.

46. Human Rights Watch, "Negotiating the News," 7–8.

47. U.S. State Department, "Country Reports on Human Rights Practices, Ukraine," 8.

48. This section is adapted from a lengthier analysis in Paul D'Anieri, "The Last Hurrah."

49. On the role of youth organizations in the Orange Revolution, see Taras Kuzio, "Civil Society, Youth and Societal Mobilization in Democratic Revolutions: Serbia, Georgia, and Ukraine." *Communist and Post-Communist Studies* 39, 3 (Forthcoming 2006).

50. The role of elites in the Orange Revolution is explored in more detail in Paul D'Anieri, "Explaining the Success and Failure of Post-Communist Revolutions," paper presented at the annual convention of the Association for the Study of Nationalities, Columbia University, New York, March 23, 2006. In the popular media, the role of elites was stressed by C.J. Chivers, "How Top Spies in Ukraine Changed the Nation's Path," *New York Times*, January 17, 2005, 1. Chivers's view is critiqued by Taras Kuzio, "Did Ukraine's Security Services Really Prevent Bloodshed during the Orange Revolution?" *Eurasia Daily Monitor*, January 24, 2005, at http://www.taraskuzio.net/elections2004/revolution_sbu.pdf, accessed July 10, 2006.

51. Interfax, November 29, 2004; BBC Monitoring International Reports, November 29, 2004.

52. *Financial Times*, November 30, 2004, 6.

53. See Andrew Wilson, *Virtual Politics: Faking Democracy in the Post-Soviet World* (New Haven, CT: Yale University Press, 2005).

54. Sergei Karaganov, "Lessons of the Ukrainian Crisis," *RIA Novosti*, November 25, 2004. http://en.rian.ru/analysis/20041125/39774197.html, accessed January 10, 2005.

55. *Ukrayinska Pravda*, July 19, 2005. http://www2.pravda.com.ua/archive_day/20050719, accessed July 26, 2005.

56. This statement is based on interviews with Ukrainian government employees in Lawrence, Kansas, and in Kyiv in September and October 2005.

10. Ukraine in Comparative Perspective: Electoral Authoritarianism in the Former Soviet Union and Beyond

1. The literature on "electoral authoritarianism," labeled in various ways, was reviewed in Chapter Two. Among the most important works are: Thomas Carothers, "The End of the Transition Paradigm," *Journal of Democracy* 13, no. 1 (January 2002): 5–21; Larry Diamond, "Thinking about Hybrid Regimes," *Journal of Democracy* 13 (April 2002): 21–35; Charles King, "Potemkin Democracy," *National Interest* 64 (Summer 2001): 93–104; Steven Levitsky and Lucan Way, "The Rise of Competitive Authoritarianism," *Journal of Democracy* 13 (April 2002): 51–63; Guillermo O'Donnell, "Delegative Democracy," *Journal of Democracy* 5, no. 1 (January 1994): 57–59; Philip G. Roeder, "Varieties of Post-Soviet Authoritarian Regimes," *Post-Soviet Affairs* 10 (1994): 61–101; Fareed Zakaria, "The Rise of Illiberal Democracy," *Foreign Affairs* 6, no. 6 (November–December 1997): 22–43.

2. One can certainly debate where the line should be drawn between the middle group and the authoritarian states (perhaps Kazakhstan, Tajikistan, and Azerbaijan belong with the latter), but the question is unimportant for two reasons. First, the numbers themselves must be regarded as highly imprecise estimates; they are simply quantifications of very qualitative judgments. They are useful summary indicators, but it would be a mistake to take them too seriously. Second, since the categories are not held to have any crucial implications, the analysis in no way changes if countries are viewed as belonging in one group or another.

3. Timothy Frye, "A Politics of Institutional Choice: Post-Communist Presidencies," *Comparative Political Studies* 30, no. 5 (October 1997), 544.

4. M. Steven Fish, "The Executive Deception: Superpresidentialism and the Degradation of Russian Politics," in *Building the Russian State: Institutional Crisis and the Quest for Democratic Governance*, ed. Valerie Sperling (Boulder, CO: Westview Press, 2000), 177–92.

5. Frye, "A Politics of Institutional Choice," 545–46.

6. For a detailed analysis of the structure and functioning of the Russian parliament, see Steven S. Smith and Thomas F. Remington, *The Politics of Institutional Choice: The Formation of the Russian State Duma* (Princeton, NJ: Princeton University Press, 2001).

7. Joel Ostrow, *Comparing Post-Soviet Legislatures: A Theory of Institutional Design and Political Conflict* (Columbus: Ohio State University Press, 2000), 93.

8. On the weakness of parties in Russia, see Henry Hale, *Why Not Parties in Russia: Democracy, Federalism, and the State* (Cambridge: Cambridge University Press, 2006).

9. Pamela Jordon, "Russian Courts: Enforcing the Rule of Law," in *Building the*

Russia State: Institutional Crisis and the Quest for Democratic Governance, ed. Valerie Sperling (Boulder, CO: Westview Press, 2000), 193–212.

10. See Peter H. Solomon Jr. and Todd S. Foglesong, *Courts and Transition in Russia: The Challenge of Judicial Reform* (Boulder, CO: Westview Press, 2000).

11. Peter H. Solomon Jr., "Threats of Judicial Counterreform in Putin's Russia," *Democratizatsiya* 13, no. 3 (Summer 2005): 325–45. Solomon points out that these efforts run against the grain of efforts by Putin and by Yeltsin before him to improve the performance of the Russian courts.

12. *Economist*, June 28, 2003, 54.

13. Ibid.

14. Emil Danielyan, "Armenia," in *Nations in Transit 2002*, ed. Adrian Karatnycky, Alexander Motyl, and Amanda Schnetzer (New Brunswick, NJ: Transaction, 2002), 65.

15. Danielyan, "Armenia," 66.

16. State Department Human Rights Report, Armenia, 1998, at http://www.state.gov/g/drl/rls/hrrpt/1998/, accessed August 5, 2000.

17. Radio Free Europe/Radio Liberty (RFE/RL), "Caucasus Report," March 9, 2000.

18. ITAR-TASS, January 19, 2003.

19. Human Rights Watch Report, "Armenia," 1995, at http://www.hrw.org/reports/1995/WR95/HELSINKI-01.htm, accessed January 10, 2006.

20. Ibid.

21. Committee to Protect Journalists, "Armenia 2000: Country Report," www.cpj.org/attacks00/europe00/Armenia.html, accessed June 18, 2001.

22. Eurasianet.org, July 2, 2002.

23. Human Rights Watch, "Armenia: Mass Arrests before Runoff," Human Rights News, February 28, 2003, http://hrw.org/press/2003/02/armenia0228.htm, accessed March 25, 2003.

24. RFE/RL, "Armenia Report," March 22, 2003.

25. Organization for Security and Co-operation in Europe/Office for Democratic Institutions and Human Rights (OSCE/ODIHR), "Republic of Armenia Presidential Election 19 February and 5 March 2003: Final Report," April 28, 2003, www.osce.org/documents/odihr/2003/04/1203_en.pdf, accessed March 25, 2003.

26. Freedom House, *Freedom in the World 2005*, Country Reports: Armenia, www.freedomhouse.org/template.cfm?page=22&year=2005&country=6686, accessed January 15, 2006.

27. The U.S. Department of State asserts: "The court system's independence is compromised by legislative, administrative and constitutional arrangements that in practice subjugate the judiciary to the executive branch of government." Moreover, the president has the authority to dismiss judges, except members of the Supreme Court or chairmen of judicial collegia." See U.S. Department of State, *Country Reports on Human Rights Practices 2001*, Kazakhstan, www.state.gov/g/drl/rls/hrrpt/2001/eur/8275pf.htm, accessed March 22, 2002.

28. Ibid.

29. Human Rights Watch, "Background: Kazakhstan's Post-Soviet Political Process, 1992–1997," Kazakhstan, 1999, www.hrw.org/reports/1999/kazakhstan/Kaz1099b-02.htm, accessed March 24, 2000.

30. "Democracy Is a Goal We Must Attain," *Trud* (Moscow), cited in Human Rights Watch, "Background: Kazakhstan's Post-Soviet Political Process, 1992–1997."

31. Nurbulat Masanov, "Political Elite of Kazakhstan: The Changes of Kazakhstani Political Elite during the Period of Sovereignty," International Eurasian Institute for Economic and Political Research, http://iicas.org/english/publ_22_11_00.htm, accessed June 15, 2005. See also IREX Media Sustainability Index, "Kazakhstan," www.irex.org/msi, accessed July 19, 2005.

32. Aldar Kusainov, "Human Rights, Kazakhstan's Critical Choice," Eurasianet.org, January 13, 2003, 3–5.

33. Ibid., 4.

34. Human Rights Watch, "Violations of the Right to Freedom of Expression," Kazakhstan 1999, www.hrw.org/reports/1999/kazakhstan/Kaz1099b-04.htm. This section of the Human Rights Watch report contains considerable additional detail on the tactics used by Nazarbayev's government to squelch the press and on the effects of these tactics.

35. U.S. Department of State, *Country Reports on Human Rights Practices 2001*, Kazakhstan.

36. Ibid.

37. Human Rights Watch, "State Violations of the Rights to Assemble, to Form Organizations, and to Participate in Political Life," Kazakhstan 1999, www.hrw.org/reports/1999/kazakhstan/Kaz1099b-05.htm, accessed August 8, 2004.

38. Ibid.

39. Human Rights Watch, "Background: Kazakhstan's Post-Soviet Political Process, 1992–1997," Kazakhstan 1999, www.hrw.org/reports/1999/kazakhstan/Kaz1099b-02.htm, accessed March 24, 2000.

40. Freedom House: *Freedom in the World 2005*, "Country Reports: Kazakhstan," www.freedomhouse.org/template.cfm?page=22&year=2005&country=6764, accessed November 15, 2005.

41. Kyrgyz constitution, at http://www.coe.int/T/E/Legal_Affairs/Legal_co-operation/Foreigners_and_citizens/Nationality/Documents/National_legislation/Kyrgyzstan%20Constitution%20of%20the%20Kyrghyz%20Republic.asp, accessed January 20, 2006.

42. International Helsinki Federation for Human Rights, "2001 Annual Report," at http://www.ihf-hr.org/documents/doc_summary.php?sec_id=3&d_id=1783, accessed May 10, 2003.

43. Ibid. Similarly, in its 1999 Annual report, the Helsinki Federation stated that "the judiciary appeared to be both corrupt and dependent upon the executive branch."

44. Freedom House, *Freedom in the World 2005*, Country Report: Kyrgyzstan.

45. European Commission, "Kyrgyzstan: Political Situation," http://europa.eu.int/comm/external_relations/kyrghyzstan/intro/, accessed July 21, 2005.

46. U.S. Department of State, Country Reports on Human Rights Practices; 2001; World Press Freedom Review, Kyrgyzstan, www.freemedia.at/wpfr/kyrgyzstan.htm, accessed July 15, 2005.

47. Ibid.

48. IREX Media Sustainability Index, Kyrgyzstan, 132.

49. Eurasianet.org, "Promoting Media Freedom in Kyrgyzstan Proving More Difficult Than Originally Anticipated," November 9, 2005, www.eurasianet.org/departments/insight/articles/eav110905.shtml, accessed December 10, 2005.

50. OSCE/ODIHR, "Final Report, Kyrgyz Republic 29 October 2000 Presidential Elections," 9.

51. *Nezavisimaya gazeta*, May 6, 2000, 5, translated in *Current Digest of the Post-Soviet Press*, June 7, 2000.

52. "Eurasia Insight: Referendum Ratchets up Rancor in Kyrgyzstan—Political Analysts," Eurasianet.org, February 5, 2003, www.eurasianet .org/departments/insight/articles/eav020503_pr.shtml. Accessed March 10, 2003.

53. OSCE/ODIHR, "Final Report, Kyrgyz Republic 29 October 2000 Presidential Elections," 8, 12, 14.

54. RFE/RL, "Kyrgyzstan: Banned Parties Work to Compete in Elections," January 19, 2000, www.rferl.org/features/2000/01/f.ru.000119135522.asp, accessed April 14, 2000.

55. OSCE/ODIHR, "Final Report, Kyrgyz Republic 29 October 2000 Presidential Elections."

56. The events of the Tulip Revolution are summarized in Radio Free Europe/Radio Liberty, "Revolution in Kyrgyzstan: A Timeline," March 25, 2005, www.rferl.org/featuresarticle/2005/03/cbc9c4c2-c8ff-40c7-aec4-3f4d96427da5.html, accessed May 10, 2005. They are analyzed in Martha Brill Olcott, "Kyrgyzstan's 'Tulip Revolution,'" Carnegie Endowment for International Peace, March 28, 2005, www.carnegieendowment.org/publications/index.cfm?fa=view&id=16710&prog=zru, accessed May 10, 2005.

57. "Opponents to Kyrgyz President: Tackle Crime and Corruption or Resign," *Eurasia Insight*, April 18, 2006, www.eurasianet.org/departments/insight/articles/eav041806.shtml, accessed June 5, 2006.

58. Malaysia was formed in 1963 through the merger of Malaya with Sabah, Sarawak, and Singapore, the last of which separated in 1965. The dominance of the UMNO in Malaya predated the formation of Malaysia.

59. "Malaysia," in Freedom House, *Freedom in the World 2001–2002* (New York: Freedom House, 2002), 387–88.

60. U.S. State Department, "2001 Report on Malaysia's Human Rights," cited in Freedom House, *Freedom in the World 2001–2002*, 388.

61. Freedom House, *Freedom in the World 2001–2002*, 389–90.

62. Freedom House, *Freedom in the World 2005*, "Country Report: Malaysia," www.freedomhouse.org/template.cfm?page=22&year=2005&country=6783, accessed November 10, 2005.

63. Ibid.

64. Freedom House, *Freedom in the World 2005*, "Country Report: Venezuela," www.freedomhouse.org/template.cfm?page=22&year=2005&country=6862, accessed November 10, 2005.

65. Michael Coppedge, "Venezuela: Popular Sovereignty versus Liberal Democracy," Kellogg Institute Working Paper, no. 294, April 2004.

66. Alma Guillermoprieto, "Don't Cry for Me, Venezuela," *New York Review of Books*, October 6, 2005. The plan recalls a similar one by Franklin Roosevelt in the United States.

67. Freedom House, *Freedom in World 2005*, "Country Report: Venezuela."

68. Guillermoprieto, "Don't Cry for Me, Venezuela."

69. See Alma Guillermoprieto, "The Gambler," *New York Review of Books*, October 20, 2005.

70. For an effort to draw comparisons across these cases, see Michael McFaul, "Transitions from Postcommunism," *Journal of Democracy* 16, no. 3 (July 2005): 5–19.

71. See Edward Schatz, *Modern Clan Politics: The Power of "Blood" in Kazakhstan and Beyond* (Seattle: University of Washington Press, 2004).
72. Freedom House press release, December 20, 2004.
73. *Economist*, June 28, 2003, 28.

11. Beyond the Orange Revolution: An Agenda for Further Reform

1. Steven Levitsky and Lucan A. Way, "The Rise of Competitive Authoritarianism: Elections without Democracy," *Journal of Democracy* (April 2002): 51–63.
2. Guillermo O'Donnell, "Delegative Democracy," *Journal of Democracy* 5, no. 1 (1994): 58. The concept is applied to Ukraine by Paul Kubicek, "The Limits of Electoral Democracy in Ukraine," *Democratization* 8, no. 2 (Summer 2001): 117–39.
3. Paul D'Anieri, "The Last Hurrah: The 2004 Ukrainian Presidential Elections and the Limits of Machine Politics," *Communist and Post-Communist Studies* 38 (2005): 231–49.
4. Larry Diamond, "Thinking about Hybrid Regimes," *Journal of Democracy* 13 (April 2002): 21–35.
5. See Chapter Four for an overview of the events known as the Orange Revolution.
6. For an analyses of Ukraine's cleavages after the Orange Revolution, see Alfred Stepan, "Ukraine: Improbable Democratic 'Nation-State' But Possible Democratic 'State-Nation'," *Post-Soviet Studies* 24, no. 4 (December 2005): 279–308; Dominique Arel and Valeri Khmelko, "Regional Divisions in the 2004 Presidential Elections in Ukraine: The Role of Language and Ethnicity," paper presented at the first annual Danyliw Research Seminar, University of Ottawa, September 29–October 1, 2005; and Lowell Barrington, "Are 'Interaction Effects' More Important than the 'Regional Effect'?: Reexamining Region, Ethnicity, and Language in Ukraine," paper presented at the annual convention of the Association for the Study of Nationalities, March 23–25, 2006, Columbia University, New York.
7. *Ukrayinska Pravda,* July 25, 2005.
8. There were three major differences between Bill 4150, which Kuchma's supporters put forth in the spring of 2004, and Bill 4180, which was adopted on December 8. In Kuchma's bill, the president would have been elected by the parliament, while in the bill adopted in December, the president continues to be elected in a general election. In Kuchma's bill, the parliament elected in 2002 would have its term extended by a year, a measure removed from the later version. In Kuchma's bill, judges would be appointed for ten-year terms, rather than for life.
9. In negotiations over a coalition in 2006 among the Tymoshenko Bloc, Our Ukraine, and the Socialist Party, the assumption was that *all* the portfolios would be distributed among the coalition partners; those reporting to the president would not be reserved to him. This is one important way in which the functioning of the government could be vastly improved when the president and the majority in parliament can collaborate. The negotiations are described in Yulia Mostova, "Ti, shcho znovu pidpysalysia," *Dzerkalo Tyzhnia* April 15–21, 2006, www.zn.kiev.ua/ie/show/593/53174/, accessed April 20, 2006.
10. See also Andrew Wilson, "Ukraine: Two Presidents and Their Powers," in *Postcommunist Presidents,* ed. Ray Taras (Cambridge: Cambridge University Press, 1997), 67–105.
11. Matthew Soberg Shugart and John M. Carey, *Presidents and Assemblies: Con-*

stitutional Design and Electoral Dynamics (New York: Cambridge University Press, 1992), 56.

12. Legislationline, August 28, 2005, www.legislationline.org/news.php?tid=67&jid=53, accessed April 20, 2006.

13. Ihor Koliushko and Viktor Tymoshyk, "A vy chytali proyekt 4180? Krytychna otsinka 'politychnoi reformy,' *Ukrayinska Pravda,* December 15, 2004.

14. Yulia Mostova, "Ti, shcho znovu pidpysalysia."

15. Serhiy Leshchenko, "Orbity Yulii Tymoshenko," *Ukrayinska Pravda*, March 20, 2006, http://pravda.com.ua/news/2006/3/20/39944.htm, accessed April 20, 2006.

16. A broader agenda for reform in Ukraine was elaborated by the Blue Ribbon Commission for Ukraine, "Proposals for the President: A New Wave of Reform," 2005, www.carnegieendowment.org/files/BRCReport121204Eng2.pdf, accessed April 16, 2006.

17. Blue Ribbon Commission for Ukraine, "Proposals for the President," 84–92.

18. See, for example, Freedom House, *Freedom in the World—2005* (Lanham, MD: Rowman and Littlefield, 2005), 519–24; and Carnegie Endowment for International Peace, "An Update on Russian Domestic Politics," October 1, 2004, www.carnegieendowment.org/events/index.cfm?fa=eventDetail&id=746&&prog=zru, accessed April 16, 2006.

19. See, for example, Vyacheslav Nikonov, "Chtoby po-nastoiashchemu borot'sia s korruptsiei, nado vypolnit' dovol'no mnogo uslovii vekami proverrenykh," *Izvestia,* October 21, 2004, 4; and "Russian Analysts Evaluate Putin's Comments on Political Reform," BBC Monitoring International Reports, November 19, 2004.

20. See Anticorruption Network for Transition Economies, "Ukraine: Summary of Assessment and Recommendations," January 21, 2004.

21. Blue Ribbon Commission for Ukraine, "Proposals for the President," 24–25.

22. Interviews in Kyiv, October 2005.

23. "Barriers to Investment in Ukraine" (Kyiv: European Business Association, 2004), 9.

24. The flaws in the tax code, and proposed remedies, are presented in detail in Blue Ribbon Commission for Ukraine, "Proposals for the President," ch. 4.

25. Bohdan A. Futey, "Nikhto ne poyazhatyme suddiy, poky vony ne poyazhatymut' sebe," *Dzerkalo Tizhya,* July 1, 2006 at www.zn.kiev.ua/nn/show/604/53834/ accessed July 10, 2006.

26. This view was expressed by U.S. Supreme Court Justice Sandra Day O'Connor, in a speech at the University of Florida Law School, September 9, 2005.

27. Winston Churchill, Speech to the House of Commons, November 11, 1947, cited in *The Oxford Dictionary of Quotations* 3d. ed. (Oxford: Oxford University Press, 1979), 150.

Index

F

Paul D'Anieri is associate professor of political science and associate dean for humanities in the College of Liberal Arts and Sciences at the University of Kansas. He has held a Fulbright Grant in Ukraine, and has written several articles and books on Ukrainian politics and foreign policy, including *Economic Interdependence in Ukrainian-Russian Relations* (SUNY, 1999). He received his BA in International Relations from Michigan State University and his MA and Ph.D. in Government from Cornell University.